D1124381

*f*P

SEASTEADING

HOW FLOATING NATIONS WILL RESTORE THE ENVIRONMENT, ENRICH THE POOR, CURE THE SICK, AND LIBERATE HUMANITY FROM POLITICIANS

JOE QUIRK

WITH PATRI FRIEDMAN

FREE PRESS

NEW YORK   LONDON   TORONTO   SYDNEY   NEW DELHI

Free Press
An Imprint of Simon & Schuster, Inc.
1230 Avenue of the Americas
New York, NY 10020

First Free Press hardcover edition March 2017

FREE PRESS and colophon are trademarks of Simon & Schuster, Inc.

For information about special discounts for bulk purchases,
please contact Simon & Schuster Special Sales at
1-866-506-1949 or business@simonandschuster.com.

The Simon & Schuster Speakers Bureau can bring authors to your live event. For
more information or to book an event, contact the Simon & Schuster Speakers
Bureau at 1-866-248-3049 or visit our website at www.simonspeakers.com.

Interior design by Kyoko Watanabe

Manufactured in the United States of America

1 3 5 7 9 10 8 6 4 2

Library of Congress Cataloging-in-Publication Data

Names: Quirk, Joe, author. | Friedman, Patri, 1976– author.
Title: Seasteading : how floating nations will restore the environment,
enrich the poor, cure the sick, and liberate humanity from politicians /
by Joe Quirk with Patri Friedman.
Description: New York : Simon & Schuster, [2016] |
Includes bibliographical references and index.
Identifiers: LCCN 2016022049 | ISBN 9781451699265 (alk. paper) |
ISBN 1451699263 (alk. paper)
Subjects: LCSH: Artificial islands—Economic aspects. | City-states—
Economic aspects. | Marine resources. | Urbanization.
Classification: LCC GB471 .Q57 2016 | DDC 307.760914/2—dc23
LC record available at https://lccn.loc.gov/2016022049

ISBN 978-1-4516-9926-5
ISBN 978-1-4516-9928-9 (ebook)

To the Aquatic Generation

It is from the ocean that will be born the destiny of civilizations to come.

—Jacques Rougerie, marine architect

What if . . .

The way to decrease ocean pollution is
to increase ocean populations?

The way to decrease the number of wars is
to increase the number of countries?

The way to discover political solutions is to
empower your political enemies?

We won't need to fight when we can float?

It's easier to float than fly?

We built civilization in the wrong place?

You could create your own microcountry at sea?

CONTENTS

Prologue   xv

I. SEAVILIZATION NOW

1. HOME: This Isn't Planet Earth   3

2. HOUSES: Cities That Clean the Seas   39

II. ENVIRONMENT

3. FOOD: Feed the World with Greenhouse Gas   63

4. FISH: Farms That Swim with Fish   101

5. FUEL: The Ocean Is a Solar Panel   141

III. ECONOMY

6. WEALTH: The Miracle of Start-up Societies   183

7. HEALTH: Faster, Cheaper, Better, Fluid Care   219

CONTENTS

IV. FREEDOM

8. FEAR: War, Waves, Pirates, Pollution, Price! 255

9. HISTORY: Rights Flow from Frontiers 277

10. FLOW STATES: How to Double Global Wealth 293

Appendix 303

Notes 305

Thank You 347

Index 349

SEASTEADING

PROLOGUE

This book is divided into four parts.

The first part, "Seavilization Now," shows the strides to seasteading that have occurred already, and asks us to overcome the mental barriers that prevent us from seeing them.

The second part, "Environment," introduces environmentally restorative technologies currently serving humanity that are advancing rapidly and can be fully realized only on the ocean.

The third part, "Economy," describes the prosperity that is often unleashed once new nations are established, and asks us to confront the fact that these blessings cannot be rapidly realized within the jurisdictions of existing governments.

The last and fourth part, "Freedom," explains why floating societies will likely be more peaceful than continental governments, simply because fluid mobility will revolutionize the incentives by which individuals interact. In addition, it considers the possibility that the oceans will introduce us to a social technology that may solve one of the oldest and most intractable challenges in civilization.

SEAVILIZATION NOW

Chapter I

HOME

This Isn't Planet Earth

You Are Called

If you sit alone at night by the sea, your heart will adjust to the rhythm of the surf. Give it a minute. Allow the chatter in your mind to cease. Listen to your breath follow the cadence of the waves. In the silence, you'll get in touch with the best of yourself, your core values, and you'll know the job we have to do. If 9 billion of us are to survive in 2050, we are charged with six moral imperatives as ancient as they are urgent:

> feed the hungry,
> enrich the poor,
> cure the sick,
> restore the environment,
> power civilization sustainably, and
> live in peace.

In this book, you are going to meet six aquapreneurs who plan to fulfill these moral imperatives by working to build floating nations on the sea. They are launching their ambitions from four continents, and they are radically misunderstood by landlubbers. Several of them have independently cited 2050 as a deadly deadline: an approaching pinch point in the supply of several key commodities that humanity needs to survive.

Water. According to Growing Blue, a gigantic consolidation of data from industry analysts, scientists, academia, and environmental professionals, 52 percent of the world population will be exposed to severe water scarcity by 2050, and continuing our current course will put at risk roughly $63 trillion US, or the equivalent to 1.5 times the size of today's entire global economy.

Food. Even assuming a 50 percent increase in agricultural efficiency, by 2050 we will need to increase the land space devoted to farmland 22 million square kilometers, or 8.5 million square miles, an area nearly equivalent in size to North America.

Oil. Searching for consensus about "peak oil," the point in time when the maximum global rate of crude oil extraction is reached became a fool's errand when the hydrofracking revolution only further polarized the debate due to deep uncertainty about the actual size of undiscovered world oil reserves. Many of the most popular doomsdates refer to current economically available oil and not total physically existing oil, as if extraction technologies will never improve and prices never adjust. So let's just say that the most pessimistic analysts say "peak oil" has already occurred, while the most optimistic analysts say 2050.

Fish. In 2006 the journal *Science* published a four-year study written by an international group of ecologists from Canada, Panama, Sweden, Britain, and the United States, which predicted that, at prevailing trends, the world will run out of wild-caught seafood in 2048—though the assumptions behind these claims have been widely disputed.

Fertilizer. The soil is running out of phosphate, a crucial ingredient in fertilizer required for farming. The most optimistic estimate for "peak phosphorus," the point at which we reach the world's maximum rate of phosphorus production, is 2050.

Land. Eighty percent of the world's expanding megacities are sinking on a coast or river plain while sea levels rise. More than 1 million people move to cities each week, and by 2050, about half of the human population will live within 100 kilometers of a coast.

Humanity is poised to plunge in 2050. We can drown or we can float.

We don't know enough about each subject to judge whether the 2050 deadline predicted in multiple domains is realistic, or a convenient focal point around which forecasters simplify their perception of trends. For instance, as recently as 2012, scientist and policy analyst Vaclav Smil, who researches food production, technical innovation, and risk assessment, argues that the famous 2009 *Scientific American* article on this subject of peak phosphorus is balderdash. All we know is that through the ages, every Armageddon predicted by experts fails to occur, because humanity solves the problem. The bottomless source of solutions, as author Julian Simon argues in his classic book *The Ultimate Resource*, is human creativity.

What would you do with political freedom, almost limitless energy, and nearly half the Earth's surface?

See the Sea

The globally emerging Blue Revolution became conscious of itself when Google engineer Patri Friedman realized that the economic theories elucidated by his grandfather, Milton Friedman, and developed by his father, David Friedman, would soon be put to the test by a rapidly approaching technology. Milton and David each asserted that political conflict was caused by political power, and that the solution to political conflict lay not in further consolidating power in the most virtuous government officials, but by the radical decentralization of power among millions of individuals with freedom and choice. How could such an organic bottom-up system work? In 1973 David published *The Machinery of Freedom*, describing the practical details, and Milton and his wife, Rose, later wrote *Free to Choose*, explaining the moral principles. Millions were swayed by the ideas, which have been vigorously discussed and debated ever since, but a practical, full application of them was impossible. The Friedmans proposed that humanity rethink society from the ground up. Unfortunately, all ground was claimed by existing governments.

A third-generation Friedman realized that the assumption contained in the phrase "from the ground up" was the problem. Our terrestrially trained minds are blind to the terrifying potential for tyranny in the power to claim land—fixed, immobile, where people have no choice but to live. At least since the agricultural revolution, humanity's wealth and status had come from the power to control land and those who cultivate it. But that was about to change. A machinery of freedom was developing that would soon render citizens free to choose among governments and to disempower governments to claim monopoly control over land. To put Friedman theory into practice, all we had to do was imagine if civilization was founded not on "a solid foundation." We do not, after all, live on Planet Earth. Over two-thirds of our home's surface is Planet Ocean.

Our problem is not politics. *Homo politicus*, after all, is not going to stop politicking. The problem is one level deeper. It's the medium in which humans compete to thrive. On static Planet Earth, the struggle must be to enforce power over our political opponents. On fluid Planet Ocean, however, solutions would emerge from granting power to our political opponents. Much of civilization's capital is stuck to land and easily monopolized by dominant states, but "seavilization" could be disassembled and reassembled fluidly according to the choices of those who own the units. Imagine a thousand floating Venices with waterways for roads, except the components are modular. When individuals possessed the technology to settle the seas, they'd discover an aquatic world more than twice the size of Planet Earth, where citizens would engage in such fluidity of movement that tyrants would have a very hard time getting a foothold, and political power would be radically decentralized and shared. Floating cities that best pleased their inhabitants would expand, while others which failed to do so would decline and disappear. Democracy, a system by which majorities outvote minorities, would be upgraded to a system whereby the smallest minorities, including the individual, could vote with their houses.

David Friedman described a machinery of freedom. Milton Friedman advocated the freedom of choose. Patri identified a machinery of freedom to choose. In his now defunct personal blog, he proposed an idea that became contagious: imagine ten thousand homesteads on the sea—"seasteads"—where ocean pioneers will be free to experiment with new societies. Aquatic citizens could live in modular pods that can detach at any time and sail to join another floating city, compelling ocean governments to compete for mobile citizens like companies compete for customers. A market of competing governments, a Silicon Valley of the sea, would allow the best ideas for governance to emerge peacefully, unleashing unimaginable progress in the rate at which we generate solutions to the oldest social problem: How do we get along? By such means, an economic and moral argument could become a technological experiment. On a blog called *Let a Thousand Nations Bloom*, Patri predicted in the essay "Dynamic Geography" that a process of trial and error on a fluid frontier will generate solutions we can't even imagine today.

As if to confirm this prediction, pieces of a global puzzle coalesced around Patri's proposal, as marine biologists, nautical engineers, maritime attorneys, and aquaculture farmers, many of whom thought they were laboring alone, approached him to propose astonishing solutions to global problems he never would have imagined.

A dozen mega-industries awoke from their collective slumber to discover that the colonization of the oceans was already under way. Japan inaugurated the Aquatic Age in the year 2000 when large aircraft landed on a floating airport in Tokyo Bay more than a thousand yards long. In Singapore, the world's largest floating football field, the Float at Marina Bay, hosted the 2010 Summer Youth Olympics. Three solar-powered floating islands, each shaped like a flower, were inaugurated on the Han River in Seoul, South Korea, in 2011. India began installing a massive solar power plant on a 1.27-million-square-meter floating platform in 2014, the same year that Japan built a floating solar array of the same size, equivalent to twenty-seven Japanese baseball stadiums. The Dutch architectural firm Waterstudio has designed a floating stadium that it proposes could travel the world hosting the Olympic Games. Most extraordinary of all, Shimizu Corporation, a Japanese construction company that makes $14 billion US a year, is holding fast to its deadline to have self-sufficient, carbon-negative botanical skyscrapers floating in Tokyo Bay by 2025.

A global movement of seasteaders believe the Aquatic Age is upon us, and if humanity is to solve our most pressing problems, we must build a blue and green civilization on blue-green algae. As we write, a team of volunteer seasteading lawyers is negotiating with officials in several countries who want to host the first seasteads in their territorial waters and grant residents some measure of political autonomy. If all goes according to plan (and it never does), the first small floating city may take to the water around 2020.

All Hands On Deck

Seasteaders are a diverse global team of marine biologists, nautical engineers, aquaculture farmers, maritime attorneys, medical researchers, security personnel, investors, environmentalists, and artists. We plan to build seasteads to host profitable aquaculture farms, floating health care facilities, medical research islands, and sustainable energy powerhouses. Our goal is to maximize entrepreneurial freedom to create blue jobs to welcome anyone to the Next New World.

The Seasteading Institute serves as a nonprofit think tank that takes a pragmatic and incremental approach to empowering others to build permanent settlements on the ocean. We envision a vibrant start-up government sector, with many small groups experimenting with innovative ideas as they compete to serve their citizens' needs better. The most successful can then inspire change in governments around the world. We're creating this future because our governments profoundly affect every aspect of our lives, and improving them would unlock enormous human potential. Currently, it is very difficult to experiment with alternative social systems on a small scale: countries are so enormous that it is hard for an individual to make much difference. The world needs a Silicon Valley of the Sea, where those who wish to experiment with building new societies can go to demonstrate their ideas in practice. At the Seasteading Institute, we believe that experiments are the source of all progress: to find something better, you have to try something new.

As a nonprofit, we've produced hundreds of pages of research in the key areas of engineering, law, and business development freely available at http://www.seasteading.org/overview/. Our primary engineering focus is on structure design. Seasteads should be safe, affordable, comfortable, and modular. Our law and policy program seeks to foster diplomatic relations with existing nations and industries. The institute investigates viable business models that can take advantage of seasteads' unique political and environmental features. Our current strategy centers around the Floating City Project, through which we are crafting practical plans for the world's first seastead, designed to satisfy the specifications of potential residents, and located within a "host" nation's protected, territorial waters. As soon as we secure legislation for substantial political autonomy from a friendly host nation, we will invite businesses and residents.

Our efforts are entirely supported by at least a thousand people who have donated to the Seasteading Institute and hundreds who have volunteered their expertise and labor. We've been joined by more than a hundred volunteer ambassadors from 23 countries who speak and educate about seasteading all over the world. About 3,000 potential residents have filled out our Floating City Project survey, telling us what they want to see in their floating city.

Science Fiction Is Science Fact

Floating cities? The idea strikes most people as fantastical. But thousands of structures the size of skyscrapers already ply the seas. Some cruise ships are two-thirds the size of the Empire State Building. Most cruise ships provide thousands of "residents" with food, power, water, service staff, safety, doctors, trash removal—most with more amenities than your average town. On these floating minicities, residents enjoy rock concerts, ice skating, opera, bumper cars, ballet, a ten-story waterslide, planetariums, Disney excursions, simulated skydiving, ice sculptures, robot bartenders, and more extravagances, all included in the price of the ticket.

If you step off an American or European coastal city and step onto a cruise ship, your standard of living may rise, and your cost of living may drop. During the off-season, Celebrity Eclipse offers a ten-day transatlantic crossing from Florida to England, stopping at several Caribbean islands such as the Bahamas, Puerto Rico, and Saint Martin—at a cost of $31 per night, not counting tips. Want an ocean view? That's $38 per night. We expect the price to drop rapidly as seasteading scales.

And scale it will. The global cruise ship industry is caught in a virtuous spiral of ascending profits, with markets doubling in size every decade. The enormous size of ships helps reduces the price each passenger pays, which compels more people to board them, which drives more revenue, which incentivizes the construction of ever bigger ships. In the 1990s cruise ships rarely exceeded two thousand passengers. By 2010, ships were carrying six thousand passengers. If the cruise ship industry were a country, it would be ranked as one of the fastest in economic growth. Since 1980 the gross oceanic product of the cruise ship industry has grown at more than twice the average annual rate of the gross domestic product (GDP) of the United States. This de facto self-governing ocean economy has remained immune to economic cycles of bubble and recession. For instance, during the global financial crisis of 2008–9, the growth of the global cruise market *accelerated*. In effect, people vacationed from mismanaged governments by choosing privately governed floating cities. In 2016 at least 22 million people, a population nearly equivalent to the island nation of Taiwan, will temporarily take to the sea.

The transition from temporary to permanent "resident-sea" is almost complete. In 2014 Shell, the oil and gas company, anchored off the coast of Australia the world's largest floating offshore structure, which will remain at sea for up to twenty-five years. A hundred fifty feet longer than the Empire State Building is high, the Prelude floating liquefied natural gas facility is built to withstand Category 5 typhoons. The Prelude serves as a demonstration that technical challenges can be solved rapidly once a compelling business model is in place.

The Prelude is but a prelude of seasteads to come. It will be stationed 125 miles offshore. Park a dozen such floating skyscrapers next to one another, and we'd have a floating city with waterways for roads. If such a city were to float more than 200 nautical miles from shore—the outer limit at which a land-based government could assert any kind of jurisdiction—then its inhabitants would be free to start afresh with a new government. Beyond 200 nautical miles is the high seas, where ocean industries in cooperation with international governing bodies have developed a polycentric system of rules managing 45 percent of the planet's surface that is unclaimed by countries.

The United Nations Convention on the Law of the Sea (UNCLOS) is an international agreement signed by 167 countries—excluding the United States, which generally takes the position that most of the substantive portions of UNCLOS reflect long-standing customary international law. UNCLOS defines the limits of a nation's jurisdiction at sea in three zones of decreasing sovereignty. The first 12 nautical miles are a nation's "territorial waters," where land-based governments have the same power they have on land. The area 12 to 24 nautical miles from the coast is a sort of buffer called the "contiguous zone," where a state may pursue vessels that break certain laws or pose a threat to the coastal nation. Beyond that each nation is entitled to an Exclusive Economic Zone (EEZ) that extends 200 nautical miles, or the length of its continental shelf, whichever is longer, where nations reserve the right to exploit natural resources such as oil and minerals below the surface of the sea, though the surface waters remain international waters. This means that states won't regulate vessels within the EEZ, but they reserve the right to regulate "artificial islands, installations and structures."

It gets complicated. Vessels traverse international waters under the jurisdiction of the country whose flag they purchase permission to fly. That means little islands of sovereignty from one nation sail through the 200-mile EEZs claimed by two other nations. As on all frontiers, legal jurisdictions on the sea overlap and are contested.

This can be a good thing. The law of the land isn't as fluid as the law of the seas. The cruise ship industry flourishes in this flexible system of floating rules. Cruise ships dock in one nation, incorporate in another, and hire from anywhere. They pick and choose the national laws best suited to their industry, and through a sophisticated practice of "jurisdictional arbitrage," flourish as semi-independent pioneer entities, while maintaining friendly alliances with all nations. Passengers sign a contract for onboard security and medical services with these free-wheeling ocean skyscrapers that bring their own hospitals and security along with them.

So what nation do people belong to when they take a cruise? Don't expect clarity if you ask the experts. Some legal scholars uphold the "floating territory doctrine," which states that a vessel's flag determines the jurisdiction of everyone on it. Opposing legal scholars reject this in favor of the "nationality principle," by which nations retain jurisdiction over their citizens no matter where they travel. In many cases citizens are subject to several jurisdictions at once. Millions of people with conflicting legal statuses and contracts signed in different jurisdictions mingle on ships. It all works. In fact, it works so well that the average passenger on a cruise ship understands as little about his legal status as he understands about the ship's engine—as is true with all mechanisms that work.

Cruise ships rarely stay in ports overnight. They drop off passengers, pick up supplies and more passengers, and go back to sea. This is an inconvenient way to run a minicity. If seasteads remain permanently at sea, it's easier to ferry goods and people to the floating city rather than move the entire seastead to land every few weeks to pick up people and supplies. The vacationer's dream, *I wish my cruise would never end*, becomes true if the ship doesn't dock. If it doesn't dock, it could remain in international waters. If it profits, it could expand without foreseeable limit. If it succeeds, others could proliferate. If people move there, they would be homesteaders on the high seas.

A crazy idea became common sense in 2012 when Royal Caribbean International, which controls a 17 percent share of the world cruise market, initiated a bold advertising campaign:

Royal Caribbean Asks "Why Not?"
Starts Own Floating Nation at Sea

In an unprecedented move, Royal Caribbean International has offi-cially seceded from land, and established itself as the Nation of Why Not, a place where innovation and imagination rule supreme. The na-tion will sail the world's oceans in its 21 states (previously called ships), governed by the principles of "Why Not," according to representatives from Royal Caribbean.

The Nation's President & CEO [Adam Goldstein] is also quick to point out that the founding of the Nation of Why Not is not a revolution, but an evolution of what Royal Caribbean has always done . . . "Somewhere along the way, our ships became not just a way to travel, but a destination in themselves," Goldstein says. "With so many things to do here, it's like its own country, so we figured why not start our own nation?"

Harri Kulovaara, Exec. VP, Maritime, summed it up for the group by saying, "We asked ourselves one simple question—'Why Not?' Instead of just loading up with amazing experiences, why not create distinct neighborhoods? Why not create a Central Park at sea with lush tropical grounds? Or a boardwalk with the world's first floating carousel? Why not offer multi-level lofts with floor-to-ceiling windows and breathtaking views? Why not design dual climbing walls surrounding a state-of-the-art Aqua Theater? Simply stated, why not build 'incredible'?"

Their tongue-in-cheek tone can be interpreted as the way you laugh nervously after an audacious proposal to retain plausible deniability. The technology is no joke, their legal status is provocative, and the business case is unstoppable. Royal Caribbean Cruises is richer than many countries, and no other nation on Earth announced a goal to double earnings between 2014 and 2017. The Nation of "Why Not?" is incorporated in Liberia, an impoverished country that has no capacity to enforce governance over the more than 3,500 ships that fly its flag. Cruise ships are in large part self-governing, and last year more than 20 million people volunteered to pay for private governance on floating cities without switching allegiances or ideologies, demonstrating that you don't need to argue if you provide superior choices.

In fact, an eighty-eight-year-old widow has been living permanently on the ocean for a decade.

Ocean Princess

Since 2007, Lee Wachtstetter has lived on the ocean. Her home, the *Crystal Serenity*, is a mobile city that grants her access to cities all over the world. She has visited a hundred countries. Mrs. Wachtstetter rarely deboards but says she enjoys the bazaars in Istanbul, Turkey. She claims she's so spoiled she can never return to land. "Here I am living a stress-free, fairy-tale life," she told the British newspaper the *Daily Mail*.

Lee Wachtstetter pays a hefty price of $164,000 US per year for her fabulous life, a deal that includes pampering, dining, dancing, entertainment, movies, lectures, and cocktail parties with the captain. But higher prices are paid by blue bloods who enjoy similar amenities in New York City, and they don't have strolling access to the bazaars in Istanbul. Sultans of centuries past could not have imagined the international polyglot of dancers, musicians, comedians, scholars, acrobats, scientists, and authors who flow through the aquatic city offering complimentary services to the middle-class vacationers who flow through the cabins that neighbor Mrs. Wachtstetter's. They don't vote or argue about their leaders, but so far the *Crystal Serenity* has not descended into a *Lord of the Flies* society—though several countries have. In fact, floating cities are safer than many land cities.

Many don't pay to be on the boat, but instead *are paid* to be on the boat. Mrs. Wachtstetter's retirement income provided by her deceased husband (whose dying wish was that she enjoy the cruise life) is spreading the wealth among hundreds and even thousands of people from the developing world who accept the jobs voluntarily because the cruise ship industry offers them better options, including lodging, food, and medical care.

Though the press and other investigators have periodically accused some cruise lines of overworking and underpaying crewmembers, Cruise Lines International Association (CLIA) claims crewmember retention rates as high as 80 percent for cruise lines. What drives improved treatment of workers aboard cruise ships is not the promises of politicians but the power of the worker to jump ship and choose a better offer. What if such jobs were not seasonal but permanent?

Since no nation floats on the high seas, Mrs. Watchstetter remains a citizen of the United States. When seasteads prosper and establish permanent populations, they may be recognized as nations. When the first baby is born on a seastead, our team of maritime lawyers plans to petition the United Nations, which is unambiguously on the side of self-determination.

Though the UN's effort to ensure peace has been mixed, its success at negotiating national self-determination is the great unsung triumph of the institution. When the United Nations was established in 1945, almost a third of the human race lived in colonized territories. Today fewer than 2 million people live in colonized territories. We see no reason why this trend toward recognizing sovereignty should end, when self-determination becomes self-creation. Seasteaders believe the United Nations is behind us, serving as our tailwind.

Let the Sea Set You Free

Tomorrow's civilization may not be on the ocean, but next week's is. Much of what you will consume next week is currently on the sea. More than a hundred thousand ships are crossing the ocean right now. It's easier to move a cargo ship the size of a skyscraper across the ocean than it is to move your house to the next town. The amount of energy needed to move massive structures is a tiny proportion of what you would need on land, and the energy per ton required gets smaller as the structure gets larger. Ninety percent of all international trade occurs not on trains and trucks among bordering neighbors, but across vast distances on ships. The ocean isn't the middle of nowhere, but a superhighway to everywhere. Someday seastead residents will ask inland people, "How do you truck in all those goods every day? You don't even have barges!"

National economies would collapse without the ocean economy nourishing them, yet the entirety of this global flow must be squeezed though the bottlenecks of narrow ports. This situation cannot hold. William Reidy, executive director of the nonprofit Maritime Alliance, which "promotes blue tech and blue jobs," addressed at the third seasteading conference the economic imperative of seasteading.

"The world's population is going to continue to grow. Trade will continue to grow . . . forty percent of all United States imports come in through the ports of Los Angeles and Long Beach . . . It's not uncommon for some tankers to sit out in the Pacific Ocean offshore Los Angeles for up to a month waiting to get to a berth. That obviously costs the companies money. It hurts the economy. So the idea of building larger floating harbors offshore expands the capabilities of the ports we already have."

"The port business is all about real estate," said Dr. Neal A. Brown, vice president of technology for Float Incorporated, which patents technologies to "allow man to live on, play on, and form the oceans." "In some cases, containers are moved several times inside a port before they are loaded onto trains or trucks. None have enough real estate."

Enter the massive Portunus Project, a plan to build six floating megaports surrounding the United States, each four hundred acres in size and located twenty to forty miles offshore—outside the twelve-mile territorial limit of the United States—assembled from modules self-powered by wind turbines and wave energy converters. Named after Portunus, the Roman god of keys and doors, the megaport project is meant to open the floodgates of ocean trade to the continent. The plan for floating megaports was confirmed as an economic necessity by three of America's top ten business schools. Workers may soon be commuting to blue jobs on self-sustaining floating megaports. Will apartments be built? Will residents require services such as haircuts, food marts, dog parks?

People might not live their lives on floating cities yet, but some live half their lives there. Deep-sea oil rig workers typically live on floating facilities two weeks out of every four, often more than a two-hour helicopter ride from rescue, and they frequently describe their six-story living quarters—entirely separate from their working facilities—as "a floating city." Kathi Gilbreath, who works on the gargantuan Tahiti Field, a Chevron Corporation oil production platform about 190 miles south of New Orleans, describes her life spent half at sea:

"I've seen flying fish, I've seen whales, whale sharks, pods of dolphin that are just massive . . . It's hard to feel stuck when you go up beneath the heliport, and you can see three hundred sixty degrees around, and it's open sky and water. You see the most magnificent sunsets, sunrises, and even storms coming."

But isn't it lonely?

"Tahiti is very family oriented, believe it or not. You have your family offshore, and you have your family on the beach . . . We've been comfortable with it for thirty-eight years, so I think I'll stick with it for a while."

Would she recommend ocean living for her children?

"I taught my kids to be fearless. If you want to try it, do it. Never regret something you did. Regret something you did not do."

Hundreds of thousands of people like Kathi live on thousands of oil and gas platforms built to withstand hurricanes, which, unfortunately, is more than we can say for coastal cities. Modular floating cities could potentially move out of the path of advancing storms with a few days' warning, while coastal cities are sitting ducks. Tsunamis are harmless on the deep seas; destructive only when they reach land. When the 2004 tsunami struck Thailand, deep-sea scuba divers reported a change in visibility and an undulation in the water, while a quarter mile away, the hotel where they'd eaten breakfast was destroyed. In the future, we expect citizens of floating cities to ask land-based people, "How do you handle earthquakes, tornadoes, and tsunamis? Isn't it dangerous to be fixed to one spot?"

Everything about seasteading is counterintuitive, but solutions to the most difficult problems are always counterintuitive; otherwise we would have thought of them by now. Albert Einstein said, "The world as we have created it is a process of our thinking. It cannot be changed without changing our thinking."

To see the wealth of solutions offered by the sea, we must think outside our land-based box. We must come to understand that living on the ocean is safer than you think, and living on land is so dangerous it may be suicidal.

Megaquapolis

Imagine a futuristic floating mobile island. Let's call it the Isle of Maersk. Those who own this man-made island bring in a yearly revenue nearly equivalent to that of Microsoft. The island's unbeatable economic strategy is to disassemble into six hundred mobile units, some larger than the Chrysler Building in New York City, or the Burj Al Arab in Dubai, the third tallest hotel in the world; others no bigger than the Roman Colosseum. These spread swiftly over the world's oceans while remaining under one command. While land-based nations are stuck in place like plants, the distributed Isle of Maersk functions like a hive of honeybees trading economic nectar among the immobile nations, enriching the globe incalculably. These six hundred autonomous units are themselves composed of thousands of yet smaller detachable subunits, each the size of small to medium-sized apartments. The largest can be disassembled into up to fifteen thousand subunits. If all Isle of Maersk subunits were placed in a line, they would stretch 11,806 miles, almost halfway around the Earth.

This isn't the future. It's the present. We just described a few facts about one shipping company, Maersk Lines, the largest company among hundreds. If all the floating skyscrapers in the world were gathered together in one spot, we'd have a hundred thousand city blocks of a megaquapolis. More than 17 million shipping containers cross the world—some the size of large living rooms, others the size of small houses. On land, architects have already transformed shipping containers into stylish multistory apartment houses. In Amsterdam, Holland, a thousand stacked shipping containers serve as college dorm rooms. Outside Mexico City, a colorful shipping container community features businesses, restaurants, bars, and art galleries. Most sensational of all, the company Kasista has outfitted shipping containers with all the amenities of an apartment and designed them to slide into larger apartment house skeletons in cities. When the resident wants to move, she taps an app, whereupon a truck picks up her apartment and moves it to her chosen location. By providing mobility and fluid choice among locations in ten cities, Kasista plans to halve the rent market for studios.

Why are people living in mobile shipping containers only on land? The largest assembly lines in the world serve cargo ships, which are built in a modular fashion to accommodate the bewildering array of goods they must transport. Each cargo ship must be assembled like a three-dimensional puzzle piece before it is launched. The infrastructure to endlessly reconfigure the interior space of cargo ships can be adapted to provide for modular living quarters. If we could combine cruise ship luxury with cargo ship modularity, we'd have plug-and-play apartments.

Civilization is presently spilling into the seas. In Amsterdam it takes only four months to build a floating house in a coastal factory called ABC Arkenbouw and slide it into the water, where it can be towed to where it is needed. In that waterlogged land, floating mobile houses are cheaper to build than land-based static houses. They don't require driving piles thirty-field feet into the soft swampy ground, like the raised houses in New Orleans, and owners don't have to correct for slowly sloping floors as houses settle unevenly after a decade or two. The economics of sustainability have driven the Dutch to create a coastal assembly line to produce floating houses.

"It is much more a gateway to freedom than it is just a place to live," Koen Olthuis, Dutch founder of Waterstudio, told the *New York Times*. "These people living here are pioneers; they are willing to take a risk, they are willing to try stuff out. They all have a very strong feeling of freedom."

Let Freedom Float

It's not just capital spilling into the seas. Hundreds of thousands of desperate people are piling into makeshift boats to escape abusive countries. In 2015 more than a million arrived in Europe by sea. Not all poor people can swim to prosperous lands, but Koen Olthuis plans to float prosperous lands to poor people. To demonstrate that the rich infrastructure of Holland can be floated to the poorest people in coastal slums, he is working to transform shipping containers into "city apps": floating kitchens, Internet cafés, health centers, garbage collectors, water purification units, and schools. These apps can be upgraded in a flexible system of plug-and-play philanthropy.

"Just as you can download apps on your smartphone according to your changing needs," said Koen in his interview with the blog Inhabitat, "you can adjust functionality in a slum by adding functions with city apps. These are floating developments based on standard sea-freight containers, and because of their flexibility and small size, they are suitable for installing and upgrading sanitation, housing, and communication."

Koen has already transformed a standard shipping container into a sleek school classroom fitted with twenty computer screens and two large TV screens featuring a teacher. Painted on the side of the floating school is "City App," the first demonstration of what Koen hopes will be a humanitarian delivery system. As we write, Dutch children enjoy it where it sits next to Koen's office, which means it will probably pass muster among curious slum children. The first city app will be installed in the Korail wet slum in Dhaka, Bangladesh. Once it reaches its destination, a floating platform will be constructed from thousands of plastic bottles to be collected by slum residents. When floods come to slums, Koen says his floating school will be the safest places to be.

"We're working on a set of guidelines; a toolbox that will ultimately get us to the floating city you imagine," Olthuis told the magazine *Next City*, which featured his design for a floating multistory natural habitat called the Sea Tree. "Our cities today are too static. We make static cities for dynamic societies. We should make cities that can adapt to new demands . . . If someone isn't happy with their house anymore, they can ship it to someone who needs it in the Philippines."

Profit will drive this philanthropy. After an initial free trial, municipalities can lease the city apps for a monthly fee. Apps that profit coastal communities will be leased. Those that don't, won't. The apps can be installed, removed, and interchanged at any time, eliminating the risk and expense of building permanent infrastructure in unstable coastal regions. The fees will yield a return for the Dutch companies, which have already invested in Koen's technology and are reassured that their investments can be moved elsewhere at any time. Video cameras installed inside the city apps will allow investors to show off the results of their profitable philanthropy to clients and family.

Once the slums of the world are installed with floating mobile city apps, Koen proposes that the second wave of ocean philanthropy include floating agriculture, floating solar arrays, and floating electricity units—each lovingly designed and illustrated by his company. This he believes will jump-start the incremental steps toward what he calls "thalassophilanthropy," a play on the term *thalassotherapy*, which refers to the power of seawater to heal.

The Floating City That Almost Was

Oceanographers often remark that we know more about the surface of Mars than we know about the seafloor. In our race to space, why have we skipped the sea? We can blame the Great Depression of the 1930s.

In 1915 engineer and inventor Edward Robert Armstrong designed "seadromes," floating airports anchored to the ocean floor that would allow planes to refuel for transatlantic flights. After more than a decade of tests, Armstrong built a working scale model close to shore in 1926. When Charles Lindbergh completed the first transatlantic flight a year later, flying from Long Island to Paris in the *Spirit of St. Louis*, newspapers featured Armstrong's vision, and investors backed his plan. The Depression postponed Armstrong's ambitions until World War II, when aircraft carriers rendered his concept obsolete. But civilization still owes a great debt to Edward Robert Armstrong, whose design was applied to the development of floating oil rigs, which pump lifeblood into our global economy. If the Depression had occurred in the 1959 instead of 1929, we might have colonized the seas in 1969 and laughed at the futuristic notion of walking on the moon. In a world where space stations have been floating in the sky for almost a half century, we shouldn't be incredulous that sea stations can float on water.

Seasteading should have started soon after 1967, when designer and architect Buckminster Fuller revealed his detailed vision of Triton City, a floating city for five thousand residents designed to encourage people to share resources and conserve energy. Triton City is engineered in a tetrahedronal shape to resist tsunamis. Declaring "Three-quarters of our planet Earth is covered with water, most of which may float organic cities," Fuller published his book *Critical Path* in 1981 to describe his ongoing aqua project, revealing that the fundamental design proposed by our seasteading engineers had long been in place.

There are three types of floating cities: there is one for protected harbor waters, one for semiprotected waters, and one for unprotected deep-sea installations. The deep-sea type is supported by submarine pontoons positioned under the turbulence, with their centers of buoyancy 100 feet below the ocean's surface. Structural columns rise from the submarine pontoons outwardly through the water to support the floating city high above the crests of the greatest waves, which thus pass innocuously below the city's lowest flooring, as rivers flow under great bridges. The deap-sea, deeply pontooned floating cities will be as motionless in respect to our planet as are islanded or land-based cities.

Buckminster specified plans to desalinate ocean water and survive on such low operational costs that citizens would enjoy a higher standard of living than in land-based cities. "Floating cities pay no rent to landlords," he wrote. A wealthy Japanese patron commissioned Fuller to complete the design in the early 1960s but died before the architect finished.

Utopian? The United States Department of Housing and Urban Development (HUD) was so impressed by the technologically and economically coherent vision that it commissioned Fuller to complete his analysis. He wrote that Triton City's costs and feasibility were verified by an independent analysis by the US Navy's Bureau of Ships and again later by the navy's Bureau of Yards and Docks. Their cost estimates came to within 10 percent of Fuller's estimates. Fuller wrote, "President

[Lyndon B.] Johnson took the model with him and installed it in his LBJ Texas library . . . The city of Toronto, Ontario, Canada, and other cities of the U.S.A. are interested in the possibility of acquiring such floating cities. Chances of one being inaugurated are now improving."

Heartbreakingly, municipal and federal regulators stalled the project, which languished until Buckminster Fuller died in 1983. A great idea from one of humanity's greatest geniuses was never tested because old rules prevented the innovation.

No matter. Sea level rise is driving ocean colonization.

Sink or Swim

The Maldives, a nation of 1,300 or so islands, may soon be submerged. But as island paradises sink, floating cities will rise.

It's not a dream. It's a business. Koen Olthuis has partnered with hotel and restaurant entrepreneur Paul van de Camp. Their company, Dutch Docklands, is currently selling space on the emerging floating nation. A joint venture between the Maldivian government and Koen's team has led to an ambitious master plan to build several floating megaprojects, including a floating golf course complete with undersea transparent tunnels between eighteen holes offering aquarium views of wild tropical fish and manta rays, and Greenstar, a floating grass-terraced hotel in the shape of a starfish, where each arm of the starfish is removable and replaceable, like a cruise ship. These projects will total 80 million square feet of floating space. Currently for presale are 185 floating villas to be arranged in the shape of a flower. According to Waterstudio:

"This master plan for the Maldives is a solution in response to the urgency caused by rising sea levels, but these new developments will also be beneficial in encouraging social and economic advancement. All over the world, people have started to see the potential of floating developments. This has resulted in projects in several countries like China, UAE, and European countries."

For what Koen Olthuis calls "architects of the climate change generation," Dutch Docklands is building floating projects not just in the tropics but also above the Arctic Circle. He and van de Camp are currently working on a five-star hotel that will float in the fjords near Tromso⁻ in northern Norway. Built in the shape of a snowflake and designed to sparkle like ice, the Krystall will feature eighty-six rooms with glass roofs so that residents can view the Aurora Borealis.

Our future will not look like our past. Without any politician planning it, without most people even knowing about it, humanity has burst headlong onto the Blue Frontier, where a teenager named Max Lock plans to put the power of more than a hundred thousand ships in the palm of your hand. Ask yourself: Can a high school kid overthrow the global shipping industry?

Generation Flow

TechCrunch Disrupt is a yearly conference where entrepreneurs compete onstage in front of seven venture capital investors who interrogate them before media cameras, a live audience of thousands, and an online audience of millions. In 2014, a few weeks after he graduated from high school, Max Lock took the stage in front of this intimidating audience and told his story.

When he was fourteen, he didn't like the taste of ice cream in the store where he worked. He went home and invented his own ice cream, which he presented to his store and eventually sold to Whole Foods and KeHE, the latter a nationwide distributor of organic foods. Max's ice cream business grew so large that he decided ordering Dixie cups was too expensive, so he began importing ice cream cups directly from manufacturers in China. Max quickly became fed up with freight brokers, the middlemen who control the shipping market by keeping the process opaque, unreliable, and time consuming, while charging large markups.

"This is incredibly frustrating," eighteen-year-old Max told his audience at TechCrunch Disrupt. "Any industry that delivers poor service for a high price deserves to be disrupted, and that's why I created

Shipstr." Though still a teen, Max founded an online supply chain logistics service that gives the customer access to the same information the shipping broker sees. "Today what takes days, Shipstr does in minutes."

Under the tagline "Get Ship Done," Max put a dispute resolution team in place to monitor his supply chain company, which has since been renamed Fleet. You can download the app right now. If Max has his way, the cost of moving capital and consumer goods by cargo ship will get cheaper, faster, and easier, accelerating the flow of wealth to every person in the world.

"Think of everything around you," Max went on. "The seats that you're sitting on, the shirts on your back, the devices you're typing on. They all made their way here thanks to ocean shipping. With over eighteen million containers making over two hundred million trips annually, it's not hard to imagine that Shipstr will scale globally."

An eighteen-year-old announced his plan to go toe to toe with the freight brokers who facilitate the global shipping industry. Then he calmly answered rapid-fire interrogations in front of seven venture capitalists and entrepreneurs onstage, who declared him "awesome" to applause.

Max was a Disrupt Cup finalist, but he didn't win. Awards were granted to company founders a little older and a little less audacious. After all, who did this kid think he was?

A few months later, Max was awarded a prize as provocative as his proposal. In 2015 Max Lock became one of twenty kids awarded $100,000 to "stop out" of college and develop companies under the care of mentors. This wasn't an investment. It was a scholarship fund that pays seventeen- to twenty-year-olds *not* to go to college. The Thiel Fellowship offers to pay young people "to build new things instead of sitting in a classroom." In 2013 former Harvard University president Larry Summers called the Thiel Fellowship "the single most misdirected bit of philanthropy in this decade."

Two years later, by the summer of 2015, companies started by Thiel Fellows had an aggregate value exceeding $1 billion.

The founder of this fellowship, Peter Thiel, never made a dime from any of this.

Peter Thiel's Wager

Here in Silicon Valley, it's getting harder to be cool. Founding a company, changing the world, and getting rich is not enough to make you an alpha nerd. Such people are a dime a dozen in our neighborhood, which is infected with an acute sense of the luck involved in success and failure. But founding a company that changes the world, getting rich, and then risking your winnings on a *second* company that changes the world again? *That* makes you an alpha nerd. The difference between luck and genius emerges when lightning strikes the same nerd twice.

Peter Thiel is one of those guys, cubed. The former lawyer co-founded PayPal in 1998, declaring a year later, "Of course, what we're calling 'convenient' for American users will be revolutionary for the developing world." PayPal increased the speed and efficiency with which businesses transact all over the world. Coauthor Joe Quirk's wife pays vendors through PayPal for her business every week, and coauthor Patri Friedman collects rent through it every month. While the 2000 dot-com bubble crashed around him, Peter led the company until it was acquired in 2002 by eBay, from which almost a half million people today earn incomes. Peter went on to cofound Palantir Technologies in 2004, which provides advanced data visualization to "solve the world's biggest data problems," racking up successes in each of its stated goals: to "save lives, solve crimes, protect civil liberties, prevent disease, and curb fraud." The company has doubled in size every year since. In December 2013 Palantir had an estimated value of about $9 billion. In mid-2015 it was $20 billion.

The streak never stopped. Peter was most famously the first outside investor in Facebook, but he was also an early investor in companies that have since become household names, such as LinkedIn, Friendster, Causes, Zynga, Yammer, and Yelp, as well as the health care start-ups Practice Fusion and Zocdoc, and hard-science start-ups including Space X. The "Midas touch investor" has also earned a reputation as kingmaker. *Fortune* magazine reported:

"Among students of business, PayPal may be known less for its own success than for the subsequent achievements of the people Thiel helped attract to build it. Those [thirteen] individuals, now known as the PayPal mafia, went on to launch a raft of companies that have become household names, including at least seven now valued at more than $1 billion."

Those seven would be Tesla Motors, SpaceX, Palantir, LinkedIn, Yammer, YouTube, and Yelp.

Peter is perpetually preoccupied with how humanity is going to solve global challenges. He started the Thiel Foundation, which supports the Human Rights Foundation, the Committee to Protect Journalists, the Machine Intelligence Research Institute (MIRI), and the SENS Research Foundation charity for extending healthy life spans, as well as Breakout Labs, which funds ambitious science and technology research still in its nascent stages and unlikely to find traditional sources of funding.

In 2007 Jeff Lonsdale, vice president at Peter's hedge fund Clarium Capital Management, read Patri's blog about seasteading and arranged a meeting. Peter is a US-rated chess master; Patri has competed in the World Series of Poker. The two strategic thinkers hit it off. After years of contemplating the laws for governance while writing code as an employee at Google, Patri was able to describe to Peter why law is code and why government is in principle an information technology—which means that governance can progress to serve humanity with unimaginable Silicon Valley speed if only subjected to fluid market competition among anyone empowered to innovate. Peter was sold.

With Peter's help, on April 15, 2008, income tax day, Patri founded the Seasteading Institute with Wayne Gramlich, his early collaborator and former Sun Microsystems engineer, who coined the term *seasteading* in his seminal 1998 article "SeaSteading—Homesteading on the High Seas," where he outlined the technical feasibility for such an ambition. Peter has since donated more than $2 million US to researching the engineering, legal, and business challenges involved with creating politically independent floating cities. We have hosted three conferences that brought together aquapreneurs from four continents. Peter Thiel gave the keynote speech in 2009, saying:

"Decades from now, those looking back at the start of the century will understand that seasteading was an obvious step toward encouraging the development of more efficient, practical public sector models around the world. We're at a fascinating juncture. The nature of government is about to change at a very fundamental level."

Whatever Floats Your Boat

Seasteading is less an ideology than a technology. Among the dozen or so full-time people who have worked on our staff at the Seasteading Institute since 2008 are folks who have identified themselves as conservative, progressive, libertarian, and confused. All of us worked side by side straight through two national US elections and barely mentioned them. We share a conviction that humanity needs more experiments in governance, and start-ups are the way to discover solutions. That's why we work wearing T-shirts that say, "Stop arguing. Start seasteading."

Libertarians are particularly attracted to seasteading in part because libertarianism is founded on the nonaggression principle, and most libertarians define all state political action as the initiation of aggression against people who haven't harmed anyone. As a seastead supporter wrote on one of our discussion forums, a key difference between the founders of nations and the creators of seasteads is that "seasteading aggresses against *no one*. That humans may settle new territory consistent with the principle of nonaggression is a remarkable development in the human experience."

Environmentalists have also joined the seasteading movement in part because the primary energy technologies for ocean cities aggress against no ecosystem. Author Marshall T. Savage, in his book *The Millennial Project: Colonizing the Galaxy in Eight Easy Steps*," explained this unique quality of floating cities way back in 1992: "Marine colonies, will, like space colonies, make use of space which is now ecologically barren. The open oceans are largely lifeless due to lack of nutrients. The marine colonies will therefore displace no existing ecosystems."

The realization that ocean cities can "green the seas" instead of depleting the Earth has galvanized a new breed of ocean environmentalists. If we take to heart Michelangelo's counsel, "Criticize by creating," we transform from conservationists to aquaculturalists.

Interrogators often expect that we must have strong opinions about how to design a new society. We do not. We think this question is so deeply difficult that it can be solved only by settling the oceans and trying a diversity of experiments, evolving through trial and error over decades. We have no specific, coherent vision of a better future to entice people with or to inflict on them. Seasteading is not a political movement or a political party. It is a voluntary movement to empower all activists, all political parties, and all people to create new societies based on their unique ideals.

What We Believe

Think of seasteads as the hardware, and rule sets as the software for creating new societies. The Seasteading Institute does not prescribe laws. We plan to provide the physical modular platforms for microcountries that can assemble and disassemble according to the choices of citizens. *Abuses of power arise from the concentration of power, and the technology of seasteading is designed to prevent concentrations of power.* Decentralized markets serve us better than centralized monopolies, and complex social problems can often be made more complex and problematic by calling for further centralization of power. Seasteaders reject violence and embrace voluntaryism. We don't trust people with power. We trust people with freedom.

In the seasteading worldview, any set of rules is okay, *as long as the residents consent to it voluntarily and can leave whenever they choose.* We believe that citizens must opt in to a society with informed consent to an explicit social contract, and they must have the freedom to exit if they no longer believe that society is serving them. As long as those conditions hold, the details of that contract are not our concern. Additionally, we believe that people must be free to start new, voluntary societies, with whatever social contracts they wish.

A proliferation of choices leads to a profusion of solutions. Allowing the unique dynamics of the sea to reduce the incentive for political conflict was an idea Patri tossed like a pebble into a sea of information, never imagining it would stir a tsunami of volunteers from every continent to organize the seasteading movement in just three years. Like all aquatic solutions, it's a counterintuitive application of a very simple, very human idea.

Choice Beats Voice

On a fluid frontier, governments could form only if people chose to attach to one another. A single vote rarely sways an election, whereas withdrawing your house has a measurable effect on the government's size and scope. Ocean governments would dissolve if people removed their consent, and expand if people chose them. On a fluid medium, citizens wouldn't struggle to survive governments' choices; governments would struggle to survive citizens' choices.

On the ocean, the parameters of progress would be in place. In this primal soup of societies, we'd have variation by governments and selection by citizens—variation and selection—the same magic recipe that drives rapid progress in ecologies, technologies, markets, and science. Market competition among seasteads could bring about what Patri called "a Cambrian explosion of governments," a phrase that became a clarion call among seasteaders. The progress we've made from smoke signals to smartphones could occur in governance only if we provide the fluid forum for experimentation. Beyond the dominion of eighteenth-century governments, we have nearly half the Earth's surface to experiment with twenty-first-century governance.

Evolution is one of those phenomena that happens only once in a while—actually, almost never. The evolution of life comes to mind. Yet in recent millennia, and increasingly in recent centuries, ever-scrambling humans have tapped into the secret power of evolution and become the beneficiaries of it. It happened in technology: bone scrapers became skyscrapers in a few million years. It happened in cultures: bands of 150 became nations of 150 million in a few thousand years. It happened in markets: peasants who supported kings became consumers living better than kings in a few centuries. It happened in information technology: computers the size of your local post office became computers the size of a postage stamp in a few decades. Each of these spectacular accelerations of progress occurred suddenly relative to the barren ages that came before it. In every case, evolution emerged from a medium of fluidity: freedom to create, trade, and choose. Could the same rapid progress occur in governance?

When viewed as an industry, governance is the largest in the world, representing approximately 30 percent of global GDP, a showcase of all the classic inefficiencies of monopolies. The largest firm in the governance industry lost $1.3 trillion US in 2010, while some of the poorest performers kill their own customers. Any social entrepreneur can outcompete this. We can't wait any longer for politicians to reach consensus, or for bureaucrats to initiate revolutionary innovations. Brilliant people like Max Lock are generating exciting modern ideas for how to solve old governance problems—at a profit. Are these systems brilliant or bonkers? Nobody will ever know until we try them out somewhere. Most likely they will serve as core ideas from which better ones will evolve—if only we can release these experiments in a fluid market where they will survive by consumer choice, not political force.

It's a nice theory, but will it work in practice? Patri, who had already founded two intentional communities, set out to test his idea the year after the Seasteading Institute was founded.

Four years later, the principles of seasteading emerged in microcosm.

Like a Fish to Water

In the summer of 2009, the Seasteading Institute hosted the first annual floating festival of self-governance on the Sacramento Delta and called it Ephemerisle, which has since come to be known as "Burning Man on the water." Every year, a few hundred people create a makeshift island by connecting a variety of boats, platforms, inner tubes, and floating art projects. Want to attend? Bring your own land.

The annual event has since blossomed without our help and with no central organizer. This kick-start method is the essence of our nonprofit role. The vision was that Ephemerisle could grow in size, duration, and frequency until a man-made island was floating year-round, and as ocean folk learned the tricks of ocean living, eventually Ephemerisle would move to international waters. Upon this dream a small blue-topia was born.

Given that people are people, conflicts emerged. The people who wanted to dance and party clashed with the people who wanted peace and quiet. The people who set up a floating disc jockey clashed with the people who organized a lecture series. The people who brought children clashed with the adults who acted like children. Three years of peace and harmony culminated in the Great Shouting Match of 2011. After exchanging threats of excommunication, partiers, parents, pranksters, and lecturers stared down one another, eyeball to eyeball. Nobody could agree on what the "real Ephemerisle" was all about! What should we do? Hold a vote? Let the majority enforce its will on the minority? Which group should we kick off the island? We had a reality TV show in the making.

Incredibly, the principles of seasteading emerged without anyone commanding it or even remarking upon it until this writing, as far as we know.

In 2012 Ephemerisle split off into three islands. People who wanted peace and quiet formed Titan, an orderly avenue of houseboats requiring life jackets, safety whistles, and a strict buddy system. The party people renamed it Uptightan. The loud twentysomethings who wanted their rave parties built a floating dance floor made of wood and nails. Titan residents named it Tetanus. A group of environmentalist artists known as Los Angelopes, an LA bicycle gang, improvised Blanket Fort Island, constructed mostly from recycled materials such as barrels, pallets, canoes, and anything else that could be lashed together to float. As it tilted and partially sank, it was christened the SS *Shit Show*. Anyone who glanced at *Shit Show* risked being mooned by a butt with the words "sell out" painted on it. Perhaps in response, a medical nurse crowd-funded Meditation Platform, a shaded "quiet space in which to recharge without any social pressures."

Once partiers, scholars, artists, and introverts formed their separate jurisdictions, do you think they each sat, sulked, and refused to interact? Not a chance. Separation made all hearts grow fonder. A taxi system of motorboats was organized among the islands. The "seatizens" of Tetanus allowed a freewheeling approach of boats to dock and launch at will, leading to some laugh-inducing fender benders. Horrified, the seatizens of Uptightan instituted an immigration policy, enforcing an ordered approach of motorboats, especially those filled with suspect party people. Unfortunately, this policy involved bullhorns, leading to a policing innovation known as "the roving DoucheCam," where people who lost their tempers were videoed and publicly humiliated on YouTube. What if no taxi was available? A flotilla of pool rafts was anchored to a spot between the three islands, serving as both a remote getaway and a rest stop for swimmers between the islands.

No boss planned any of it, and everybody participated in it. The emergence of these arrangements only increased the fluid rate at which people migrated and visited neighbors as the mood struck them. Want to be among children? Head to the family-friendly island. Want to stay up all night dancing with the under-thirty crowd? Go hang out with those people, if that's your bag. Want to enjoy peace and quiet with the fortysomethings who hold formal lectures about economics and political theory? Head to that island and maybe crash there amid the quiet. Sick and tired of all these rules, man? Blanket Fort, the recycler's paradise, tilts defiantly a short swim away. Patri has two kids, loves to dance, loves to lecture and attend lectures, and volunteers to drive motorboats between all three main islands. Joe is a proud seatizen of Uptightan, where kids need to respect their elders' need for naps.

So far, conflicts are rare, but when they occur, they are policed by mockery, painful nicknames, and subversive performance art. Want to spite the libertarian consensus that prevails during the lecture series? Name your subisland Revenge of Cuba, which is the most recent act of "seacession." Imagine a political science scholar carefully parsing the nuances of Federal Reserve policy, while just offshore, residents of Cuba make a big show of offering free first aid services to anyone who may one day be injured on Tetanus.

Sure, seasteading is supposed to be about breaking away, but what about merging? Stop reading for a moment and guess which islands are the least likely to join forces. How long do you think it took for enemy islands to marry?

By 2014, the rave dancers and Titan residents had become one. The party people admitted they needed the Titan residents to help them organize, and the Titaniers admitted they needed the party people to help them have fun. The orderly avenue of Titan houseboats formed a neighborhood block, with front doors facing inward and docks facing outward, so boats could approach from any side, meaning they could nix the bullhorns. What do you think was built at the center? A magnificent dance floor free from nails, with a posted schedule for quiet times during lectures. Splitting in a huff in 2012, the Uptightans and Tetanusitians formed one island paradise by 2014. Hugs all around.

Is bluetopia finally at hand? Not exactly. The Cubans continue to give the public middle finger to every island that doesn't offer free health care to all Ephemerislians, flying their flag of socialist spite and spending most of their time on Titan's dance floor and mooching from Titan's alphabetically arranged snack tray, which offers vegan, paleo, vegetarian, gluten-free, and dairy-free vittles organized by spreadsheet.

On water, human nature does not change. What changes is the technology by which humans establish rules. Ephemerisle started as an experiment in getting along, and already several new start-up experiments have broken away and learned lessons. We'd venture to guess that every single year, every single Ephemerislian visits every single island, proving that good waters make good neighbors.

The success of the Ephemerisle community so far is evidenced by its rejection by a reality TV production company. In 2015 a seasoned TV production team contacted the Seasteading Institute curious to create a TV documentary. Once scouting Ephemerisle, they became discouraged by how readily conflicts were quelled on a fluid medium. How to add drama? Get rid of mobility and choice. They went back to the United Kingdom and elected to set up their own reality TV show on several fixed offshore military forts, to set up the traditional dynamics for land-based conflict. If you want people to fight, condemn them to a crowded space where they can't take their land and go elsewhere.

Ephemerisle began as a do-it-yourself seasteading start-up, and it has evolved in ways no one could have planned. Even the distributed Ephemerisle community is smarter than any centralized governor. The social mechanics of seasteading have emerged already.

Youtopia

Every person in Western society is living in a blend of utopian experiments that largely succeeded. The sailors who took ships to the New World were utopians. They were also fed up. The new continent was a giant life raft where they could try out their utopian ideas. Nothing worked out exactly the way anybody predicted, but the cauldron of competing ideas produced a unique social experiment in freedom and democracy that became a model for the world. If there had never been a New World, the revolutionary firestorm of representative democracies might never have been sparked, and monarchy might be, as Winston Churchill would later quip about democracy, "the worst form of government except for all the others that have been tried."

The most unrealistic utopian fantasy is that we will vote our way to solutions to world hunger and poverty: that we will provide affordable health care, restore our oceans, and clean our atmosphere by electing the smartest, most saintly politicians, based on their promises.

Since 1990, at least thirty-four countries have been created. Yet since 2008, the supply of new nations has all but stopped. In the face of the pent-up worldwide demand for start-up innovation in governance, Peter Thiel expressed why he cofounded The Seasteading Institute with Patri.

"I think seasteading is not just possible, or desirable, but necessary," he said in his keynote address to the second Seasteading Conference held 2009. "Seasteading is one of the few technological frontiers that has the promise to create a new space for human freedom."

Defining politics as "interfering with other people's lives without their consent," Peter wrote that "we are in a deadly race between politics and technology . . . The fate of our world may depend on the effort of a single person who builds or propagates the machinery of freedom that makes the world safe for capitalism.

"For this reason, all of us must wish Patri Friedman the very best in his extraordinary experiment."

The time from Orville Wright's first twelve-second airplane flight in 1903 to Neil Armstrong's happy dance on the moon in 1969 was 66 years. If a military empire can put a man on the moon in 1969, free people can put a nation on the ocean in in the twenty-first century.

Let's meet our first aquanauts. They are currently preparing their launch from a nation sinking beneath the sea.

Chapter 2

HOUSES

Cities That Clean the Seas

The Amphibious Nation

The Dutch are famous for the legend of the little Dutch boy who plugged a dike with his finger and saved his country. Well, things have since gotten a lot more dire for the Dutch. The Dutch live in the Netherlands, and you can't live there without contemplating the ocean. On the one side, the Earth's largest sea gate, the $4 billion US Oosterschelde Barrier, 5.6 miles long, holds back the North Sea. On the other, snowmelt from the Alps disgorges into waterlogged lands through the artery of the Rhine River. The Dutch people prepare for sea level rise like others prepare for retirement. The Flood is coming, and many citizens are building their ark. Even in the central Netherlands, along the Meuse River, you can count fifty "amphibious houses," thirty-six of which ride up and down steel poles when flooding occurs, and fourteen of which float permanently. These are built on a foundation of buoyant foam, the same substance of which egg cartons are made. Residents in these houses can fall asleep on solid earth and wake up afloat, and then step outside to tend their gardens planted atop their foam yards.

The Netherlands holds Aquaterra Conferences, celebrates International Water Week, and throws around words such as *aquainnovation* and *aquaindustry*. They're basically aqua-people living in an aqua-nation. They build kindergartens next to dikes several feet below rising sea level.

"I was trained as a civil engineer," says Rutger de Graaf. "A big part of my training was about flood control, building dikes. Most Dutch civil engineers already do that. I specialized in another field. I thought, *You cannot keep on raising the dikes forever. Half of our country is already below sea level.* We need to work in a more adaptive way."

Rutger graduated cum laude at the Delft University of Technology studying civil engineering. That's where he met Karina Czapiewska, a multidisciplinary specialist studying architecture with a minor in sustainable development.

"I love to be my own boss and not have to listen to other people telling me what to do," smiles Karina. "I'm a vegetarian because I think we should live with nature and not against it. Rutger and I both applied for a competition to solve flood challenges in delta areas and discovered we shared the vision of the floating city. So we started selling real estate here in the Netherlands."

Real estate? Sure. Rutger de Graaf says that in his country, any landowner who digs a hole hits water. Anyone with a houseboat who sticks a rod down a few feet hits land. The Dutch have a unique perspective that land and water are not that different. Maybe this is why instead of selling plots of land, the city of Delft has started selling plots of water.

Karina and Rutger cofounded the aquatic architecture firm Delta-Sync, announcing a mission to "design and develop the first self-sufficient floating city in the world."

If you want to find a country that isn't dragging its feet with regard to seasteading, go to a nation that's sinking. The city of Rotterdam announced its goal to be "climate proof" by 2025, which includes halving its greenhouse gas emissions. DeltaSync was charged with the task of researching and finding the solution. In his PhD talk at Delft University, Rutger presented his solution to the people of Rotterdam.

"I think that the first steps in living on the ocean will be coastal expansion of existing cities," he announced to his audience. "The most logical way is that we first see urban densification in all port areas, like we're seeing now in Rotterdam. Then the next step would be probably coastal expansions on the water. Then the step after that will be perhaps first floating cities in territorial waters and then floating city-nations."

What's wrong with the Dutch crowd? Why aren't people making the "This guy is crazy!" face? Joe and Patri see this expression every time we address an audience. We were confused until Rutger cited a recent survey that says that 30 percent of the Dutch population said they consider living on water a reasonable option.

Design Your Own Neighborhood

Rutger de Graaf explains that seastead technologies don't need to be built. We just need to snap together the modules that are already in use. The struggle against people's incredulity lies not in their disbelief about what is possible but in their disbelief as to what already exists.

"We already know how to build floating platforms," he says. "We know how to make floating buildings. It's not science fiction, as you can see from [sixty thousand] floating houseboats in Amsterdam. Floating biofuel production is not some crazy idea. Organizations like NASA are already working on it. Floating crop production is already done in combination with breeding fish, both in freshwater and saltwater systems. Wave protection? We're very good at that in the Netherlands. We can use artificial reefs to create habitats for wildlife, which also protect cities from waves. This is proven technology, already used by the Incas. Floating wetlands? American companies have already created it to treat wastewater and protect cities from waves. All the building blocks are already there. I am working with my colleagues on floating wastewater treatment plants integrated into the floating roads. Rotterdam intends to build twelve hundred sustainable floating homes over the next twenty to forty years."

These components can be designed as snap-on modules that can be rearranged like Legos. Karina Czapiewska stresses that the subcomponents of a floating city are endlessly rearrangeable. "You can easily take an old part out and switch it with a new arrangement as needed by the growing population," she explains. "If you want to move to a new job, you can take your house with you."

"In a floating city, there will be no need for demolition," Rutger explains. "You can detach components and rearrange them into new neighborhoods, creating dynamic urban development. Such water-based districts can adjust to new needs at a fluid rate unimaginable in land-based cities."

"This is reality in the Netherlands," says Remko van Buren, the

Dutch pioneer in sustainable architecture at Waterstudio, as he displays a photo of a ten-story floating building being towed on a barge. "This office building was empty. The people who ran it went bankrupt. So it was transported from Rotterdam to another location. So it's not theory. This is happening already."

Remko asks us to contemplate the astounding waste involved in constructing cities on land. Buildings that should last more than a century are treated as disposable. "To demolish a perfectly good building after ten or twenty years is not very sustainable."

Every time people create a new city, they utilize new knowledge that was not available to an old city. Karina emphasizes that fluidly changing cities will be forever new, thus permanently empowered to integrate future ideas.

"Water cities are not designed according to a rigid blueprint but as an organic ecology of freely moving components that can grow, and it's all natural."

A Living City

Karina describes a floating city as if it is a living being. When challenged about this—what kind of civil engineer talks like an evolutionary biologist?—she says, "I think it *should* be alive. It's very crucial to view the man-made environment as a living thing and not as a static structure that should be set in place forever. The best way to anticipate future needs is to be flexible."

Rutger's favorite word is *logical*. Karina's favorite word is *alive*. They both perk up when anyone says "challenge." You can see why they founded a company together. Imagine if both hemispheres of the human brain could talk independently. That's Rutger and Karina.

To demonstrate the fun and feasibility of aquatic architecture, DeltaSync, together with the sustainable urban design company Public-Domain Architects, designed and constructed the solar-powered Floating Pavilion, a floating exhibition and conference center on the Rhine Harbor (the Rijnhaven, one of the old ports close to the city center of

Rotterdam). Developed by Dura Vermeer, a construction company specializing in infrastructure and environmental engineering, it has a floor space the size of four tennis courts, accommodates 500 visitors, and includes an auditorium that seats 150 guests. It was built directly on the water in six months. "The Floating Pavilion in Rotterdam is the first step toward floating districts," says Rutger.

"Technically everything needed for floating cities is easy," says Karina. "The most challenging part is the regulations."

Local Dutch governments have implicitly acknowledged the obsolescence of their old regulations and provided for a free zone where aquapreneurs can experiment. DeltaSync organized a consortium to research and create a pilot project of a small-scale floating ecosystem. Named AquaDock, it will serve as a free research zone where floating urbanization can be tested, improved, and scaled up with fewer legislation and permit constraints. Rutger calls AquaDock an "innovation niche, protected from mainstream market and legislation selection mechanisms that so often inhibit innovation."

Karina says that by starting close to shore and slowly expanding and moving out to sea, land folk will view the transition to floating cities as a natural evolution. In the Netherlands, she can already see the chasm to mainstream acceptance being crossed. "People buying floating houses are often families with children," she says.

You know you have a good idea when you stir up competition. Waterstudio, the architectural city planning company in Rotterdam, plans to build Citadel, the world's first floating apartment building, with sixty luxury apartments. The Citadel will be entirely off the grid. But how will floating neighborhoods get electricity?

"Water is a very good solar collector," Rutger explained in an interview with the European Environment Agency, which is mandated to help the European Union integrate the goal of sustainability into economic policies. "In summer, you can also use water to cool houses. It's much more energy efficient, and you no longer need fossil fuels . . . we calculated that compared to conventional heating of buildings, it's a CO_2 reduction of sixty percent."

DeltaSync and Waterstudio codesigned the floating foundations for cities: buoyant foam slabs encased in solid concrete. The larger the platform, the more stable it is in waves, which provides a natural incentive to make ocean cities big. Architect Koen Olthuis, founder of Waterstudio and coauthor of the book *Float! Building on Water to Combat Urban Congestion and Climate Change*, told the Discovery Channel, "All the things you do on land, you can also do on floating foundations, and by using concrete, which is very, very strong—that gives you a life span for more than a hundred years, and that's exactly the same life span you [have] on land."

The Dutch are done with dikes. In fact, when an engineer from Rotterdam uses the English verb *FLOAT* as a noun, he or she is likely to be referring to Olthuis's anagram: flexible land on aquatic territory. In cooperation with the Inholland University of Applied Sciences, DeltaSync has drawn up plans for the Rijnhavenpark, a floating park in Rotterdam that will include a hotel, underwater restaurant, theater, sports facilities, a swimming pool, a floating market, and flexible office space. DeltaSync intends to create a portfolio of floating snap-on modules. Rutger sees DeltaSync's current projects merely as test beds for acquiring knowledge to generate jobs, stimulate aqua-business ideas, and encourage students from the local universities to create research topics.

"If you find this inspiring," Rutger announced to his Dutch audience, "come talk to me about it. It doesn't matter what your background is; I can always find a link to a floating city."

Karina's and Rutger's primary ambition is to set an example for the world as to how vibrant floating neighborhoods and businesses can be environmentally sustainable and enviable places to live and work. Once established in the mainstream consciousness, this will be the first step in what we might call DeltaSync's master plan to rescue Planet Earth.

Because, according to Rutger, as goes Rotterdam, so goes the world.

Poised to Plunge

Today 30 percent of all people live within 100 kilometers (62 miles) of a coast. By 2050, it will be half the human population. At least fifteen of the world's twenty megacities grow on a coast or river plain. Human enterprise flourishes closest to the fluid medium, where goods flow speedily and cheaply per pound. As great coastal cities gear up the frenzy of international trade, the human race is racing toward many areas that will soon be flooded. Not only will coastal cities soon run out of livable space, but also the resources produced by inland agriculture will eventually not be able to support them.

Karina says the Netherlands is a harbinger for what is quickly becoming a global flood problem. Not only are sea levels rising, most delta cities in the world are sinking due to intense groundwater extraction. Many Asian cities are becoming Rotterdams, and many land areas much larger than the Netherlands will soon be flooded. Those countries don't possess an infrastructure of flood protection built on a thousand years of Dutch farmers windmilling water from their fields. Old land cities, tragically, can't adapt. Coastal cities are built to be permanent despite the dynamic nature of sea levels and rely on inland agriculture as if it were an infinite resource.

"The metabolism of current cities resembles the behavior of parasites," says Rutger.

Karina agrees. "They extract water, nutrients, and fertile soil from the environment, but they don't give anything back."

The DeltaSync team crunched data to create some compelling graphs to demonstrate that humanity has no choice but to move agriculture out to sea. Even if you assume a 50 percent increase in the efficiency of agricultural production, in 2050 the world will lack 22 million square kilometers of arable land. That's an area twice the size of China.

Isn't there something else we can do? Rutger and his team ran all the sunniest scenarios. What if we increase agricultural efficiency by 75 percent? What if we all eat 24 percent less meat? What if we reduce our carbon consumption by 85 percent? Even if we combine all the best-case scenarios, we still lack 12 million square kilometers, which would reduce the number of extra Chinas we need from two to one.

"Humanity now uses one and a half times the resources than the globe can provide in a sustainable way," Rutger explains. "This means that the natural resources are being depleted faster than they are replenished. It is estimated that in 2050, the equivalent of three planets will be required to supply the world population with their needs."

According to DeltaSync's figures, humanity has a choice: either build two extra Earths, or cultivate 0.8 percent of the ocean.

"Only 0.8 percent of the global sea surface is needed to accommodate 5 billion people in floating cities at the same average urban density as current land-based cities."

How is that even possible? The trick, says Rutger, is to get cities to stop functioning as parasites and to start functioning as symbionts.

If Cities Were Gardens

Karina and Rutger ask us to rethink all the assumptions we bring to the word *city*.

Right now cities use up land. What if cities *created* land?

Right now coastal cities create flood risks. What if coastal cities *protected* from flood risks?

Today cities consume vast amounts of energy and food from land-based farms. What if cities *produced* energy and food *for* land-based farms?

Today cities produce waste. What if cities *cleaned up* waste?

Today cities degrade ecosystems. What if cities *created* ecological habitats?

"My favorite quote is by Richard Buckminster Fuller," Rutger says, referring to the systems designer who envisioned floating cities. "You never change things by fighting the existing reality. To change something, build a new model that makes the existing model obsolete."

Rutger doesn't know it, but he is about to propose an idea that has been independently generated by several of the aquapreneurs you are about to meet in this book.

"I propose a cyclical metabolism," Rutger told his Dutch audience, "where a floating city will capture the nutrients and wastewater to create food, fuel, and to supply that back to the city," claiming further that,

"Any coastal city can environmentally and economically pay for itself with an offshore floating city."

According to DeltaSync's plan, artificial reefs and wetlands will protect the coastal cities from waves. These will absorb the wastewater to grow algae and fish, which will then produce organic fertilizer for land farms.

"Symbiosis allows you to close the circle," says Karina, "so you capture the nutrients and wastewater, and you just reuse it in a land city. It's not one solution but an interlacing of all solutions that reinforce each other and create synergy."

"Both freshwater fish and marine fish can be produced in floating tanks," says Rutger. "This is much more efficient than cattle farming on land to fulfill the world's rising protein demand. Extracting CO_2 will also lower the acidity of the sea water, which is a major threat to coral reefs worldwide and has a negative impact on marine ecosystems."

Clean the Ocean with Your City

Joe caught up with the DeltaSync duo and confronted Rutger with one of the many extraordinary claims he wrote in his booklet *Adaptive Urban Development: A Symbiosis Between Cities on Land and Water in the 21st Century*, wherein he stated: "It is possible to make the combined development of cities, food production, and biofuel on the sea 50 times more efficient than average land productivity by closing the loop and the application of best practices."

How does he figure *fifty times* more efficient?

"It's actually quite a simple back-of-the-envelope calculation," he explains. "The efficiencies of biofuels and aquaculture are all very well documented by the Food and Agricultural Organization of the United Nations. The efficiency of algae as biofuel production compared with sugar cane is already twenty times as efficient per hectare. If you compare intensive aquaculture to cattle farming, protein production can be two hundred or three hundred times as efficient. Combine food and biofuel, and it should be possible to make a floating city that's fifty times as efficient. I think that's a very logical solution."

"When specialists think about problems, they put everything in its own box," says Karina. "This is the box of food, and this is the box of water, and this is box of energy production. We have to show how these boxes are interlinked in one big system."

What if we use *all* the nutrients and waste of *all* coastal cities?

"We could potentially provide forty-four percent of the world's food demand by using all the waste nutrients and CO_2 from current cities." Rutger claims that if humans cultivate less than two-tenths of 1 percent of the ocean, we would free up one-third of all land used for agriculture.

"We need a total global floating area the size of Madagascar," says Rutger, which is 226,657 square miles, or a little larger than France. "And how many people would be needed also to work in those biofuel production and aquaculture? In the optimal ratio, thirteen percent of the world population would live in floating cities. In the end, it's fairly astonishing to see that result, but, actually, if you think about it, it's quite logical. In 2050 we'll have about nine billion people. So thirteen percent of that would be about one billion people living on the water."

Rutger repeats the survey that says that 30 percent of the Dutch population consider living on water a serious option. Granted, that's the Dutch, who don't enjoy the luxury of denial as the sea comes to claim their homes, but more and more coastal cities will experience the same imperative to hustle, and Rutger and Karina want Rotterdam to be an example for how to rethink the relationship between civilization and nature.

We Are the 13 Percent

"I'm not proposing that we're going to abandon land-based agriculture," says Rutger. "As soon as you make a floating city that turns waste into resources, you're no longer talking about efficiency. It's more about synergy. In nature, everything has a positive and productive impact on the environment. Biomimicry is quite inspirational in this respect."

"Biomimicry is learning lessons from nature," says Karina. "As we close the metabolism loop, cities will become like ecosystems, where everything serves a lot of purposes until it becomes so integrated, it disappears and has no burden to nature and its environment."

"Nature already knows how to do this," says Rutger. "All we have to do is build cities to imitate what nature already figured out. We should build a city modelled after some biological system. A water lily, for instance, uses seawater, sunlight, carbon, and nutrients, just like a city."

The most valuable land in the world is coastal land. With floating cities, Rutger plans to expand the amount of coasts in the world. He calls it "the land-water interface, where most of the wildlife and the coral reefs are concentrated." Today we think of coastal cities as destroying coastal ecosystems. But Rutger says, "Floating urbanization on artificial reefs will increase the number of habitats for marine and bird life."

Yes, constructing a city on land may destroy wildlife, but constructing a floating city will increase local wildlife. Many misunderstand oil rigs as symbols of environmental blight, but environmental scientist Steve Kolian, founder of the nonprofit EcoRigs, with a mission to save retired platforms to be redeployed to help the environment, says that when old rigs are torn down, lovers of the marine environment should despair even more than when a coral reef the same size is destroyed. Oil rigs are more environmentally benign than natural coral reefs by an order of magnitude in several dimensions. He writes in a report "The Benefits of Leaving Oil and Gas Rigs Intact to Serve as Artificial Reefs":

"When rigs are left standing, the fish biomass is ten times greater, per unit area, than the fish biomass at the Flower Gardens Fish Sanctuary. The Gulf of Mexico is home to 4,000 artificial reefs that are ten times bigger, ten times stronger, and ten times more prolific than average artificial reefs. They create one of the most prolific ecosystems on the planet. . . . The platforms are currently used extensively by fisherman and divers; they generate $324 US million annually and create 5,560 full-time jobs in the marine sport fishing and diving industries."

Rutger says that cyclicity is the best solution to the peak phosphate problem. Humanity is rapidly using up the amount of phosphate available on land to fertilize crops. A century of industrial agriculture has resulted in most of the available land's phosphate running into the seas. Phosphorous is one of the three macronutrients that crops require to grow. Phosphate and sugar make up the spiraling backbone in DNA. No phosphate, no food.

"Floating cities could use algae to recover phosphate from the wastewater of land-based cities to produce biofuel and food and fertilizer for land crops. The main problem is that our intensive agriculture on the land depletes soil faster than the natural soil production process can replace it. That actually means that we need to start looking at ways to produce food without using soil."

The solution is so well understood that in 2010 the US Army Corps of Engineers built floating islands on lakes in Pennsylvania to improve water quality and protect habitats from surges in nutrient pollution, particularly phosphorus.

"A rainforest, if it is in a fully developed state, is in equilibrium," says Rutger. "So it doesn't store that much CO_2, whereas developing algae farms will store a lot of CO_2. We have this *really crazy idea* at our company and we don't . . . well . . ."

Rutger pauses. Here it comes. The "really crazy idea" every seasteader has to screw up his courage to say.

"I didn't say this in my lecture, but actually the sustainable way to get the CO_2 levels down is to start doing what nature has done for millions of years, which is to start capturing CO_2 with algae, and then produce biofuel, and then store that biofuel in empty oil fields, so that future generations can use it."

Before we can tell him that several seasteaders prefaced similar ideas with the fear that it sounded "really crazy," Rutger rushes to reassure us he's not crazy.

"That's what nature did for the last hundred million years, and we've burned it in a hundred years. Every year, we burn the equivalent of one million years of fossil fuels."

Algae could allow us to put it back. Once a symbiotic "ecocity" is established in the Netherlands, Rutger says that floating cities could sell themselves to coastal cities all over the world. The residents of floating ecocities should theoretically be able to replace mankind's money-based economy with nature's symbiotic economy.

But how? Cities are broke, and countries are bankrupt. Cities won't splurge on the extravagance of a floating city.

There's only one way: make them an offer they can't refuse.

Floating City, at Your Service, for Free

Floating cities could offer their services to coastal cities all over the world. They wouldn't be paid in money, says Rutger. All floating cities ask for is the coastal city's pollution. In essence, pioneers interested in founding floating cities could approach any coastal city and say, "You give us your pollution, we'll give you food, fuel, and flood protection."

Expounding in his booklet, *Adaptive Urban Development*: "Such a non-monetary, symbiotic economic model could prove to be of great value as a possible alternative to the current growth-dependent global financial system that is not properly functioning and unsustainable in the long term." Once this nonmonetary relationship is established, the blue economy will be under way. "Floating cities could be created near international shipping routes, giving companies connectivity advantages over land-based companies. The extensive aquaculture around floating cities would also generate jobs and create opportunities for high-tech companies to develop and implement new technologies. Ultimately, decentralized sustainable technologies will be better able to compete with the land-based outdated infrastructures that are dependent on fossil fuel input and were invented during the industrial revolution."

"We call it Blue Revolution," says Karina, as Joe does a double take, "and we see it as the next human step. What we want is to make a new ecosystem that closes the loop of an existing city. If you can just plug a little floating ecosystem into a land city, you can create a healthier environment for it. Our mission is to convince people it will work."

Rutger expands on the idea, "In floating cities that are near the deep ocean, ocean thermal energy conversion, OTEC, can be applied as an additional energy source."

This time Joe does a triple-take. Karina mistook Joe's shock for disbelief. She describes OTEC in engineering terms, referring us to another company, Bluerise, that works in same building with DeltaSync and has already built a room-sized OTEC plant to demonstrate that it can work. In fact, Bluerise was planning an OTEC plant off the Caribbean island of Curaçao, but it isn't installed yet—

Hang on! Hang on! Has Rutger or Karina ever heard of OTEC enthusiast Patrick Takahashi?

"No, I haven't," says Rutger.

How did you come up with the name *Blue Revolution*?

"We were in a brainstorm session with our team, and we just thought it was a great idea to come up with Blue Revolution."

Now here's where it really got surreal.

"With floating cities, you can choose the government you have," says Rutger. "Today you don't have so much choice. You can vote, maybe, but that's quite disappointing, because you always get the same thing with a little bit of change. In the future, you might leave with a part of your city to another nation-state on the ocean. Then you would have competition. You would really need to provide good governance."

Where did Rutger get this idea?

He sighs. "Technologically we can do many things, but most obstacles are related to governance legislation. The bulk of my work was spent on solving these governance issues, which is quite difficult for an engineer to do. I ended up writing half of my PhD thesis about urban water governance, institutional frameworks, and these kinds of things. That is the main obstacle to floating urbanization."

Karina agrees. "Sometimes we feel like crusaders trying to break this enormous governmental maze. In the Netherlands, you can have two kinds of real estate: mobile or immobile. If you're immobile, you have a house or an office. If you're mobile, you're a house on wheels, or a boat."

Wait a second. Where did they get *this* idea?

"These two categories are a very big issue right now," says Karina, "because if your building is immobile, you have to look at what regulations, what building code, you need to use for it, so it becomes a very, very large discussion among different layers of government. Because of that, a lot of projects take a lot of time. It's a maze of different regulations that are not very clear. Look at the idea of seasteading: that would be a very nice way to bypass this regulation zone."

Seasteading? Joe asked Karina if she's ever heard of Patri Friedman.

"Friedman? The last name does ring a bell a little bit, but I don't associate it with anything right now." Yet she expounds thusly: "The idea of seasteading is to detach from the political structures and have your own political structure, and actually, I think it's quite a good idea. The current political structures are very old-fashioned, and they don't work. It should be something that works for the people instead of the people working for it."

"It's really disappointing how much influence we have as citizens," says Rutger. "Basically, all we can do is vote every four years, and we can go shopping. We are passive voters and passive consumers, whereas what I experience in this project is that people can do much more. They can design their own living environment, their own house, their own water management and energy. This potential in society is not yet fully realized. People are better educated than ever before, we have more knowledge than ever before, and we can do much more than ever before. And we face so many problems with the government performing all its tasks. I definitely think in the future we are becoming more like nomads again. We will move with our house to a new city."

If you check Rutger's booklet *Adaptive Urban Development*, you can find him expanding on this idea.

"How could a floating city be governed? Over the last decades, there has been a shift from top down hierarchical steering (government) towards more network driven decentralized forms of policy making with multiple actors (governance). Floating cities offer an opportunity to take this development a step further."

Has Rutger heard of Patri Friedman?

Rutger strains to remember. "I read about Patri Friedman in the *Economist* Science Technology section. Was it published this year?"

Joe had to finally break down and tell them about all the aquapreneurs who are already making progress on all these fronts. Ricardo Radulovich wants to use seaweed to create food; Lissa Morgenthaler-Jones wants to use microalgae to create fuel; Neil Sims talks about using algae to decrease the acidity of the ocean; Patrick Takahashi pitches ocean thermal energy conversion as an energy source and calls his effort the Blue Revolution; and Patri Friedman talks about how rearrangeability of floating buildings will create a peaceful market of competitive governance. By the way, the word they use, *seasteading*, is a portmanteau minted by Patri's partner, Wayne Gramlich.

"That's fascinating," says Rutger. "It's like a global consciousness, maybe."

The name Takahashi rings a bell for Karina. "One of my colleagues was Googling the Blue Revolution, and then she came across this Hawaiian initiative. Right? We were like, 'Oh my God, we're not the only ones!'"

"I think it would be a great idea to create a global network," enthuses Rutger. "We want to collaborate with people who work on the same things and then start a global movement with this Blue Revolution idea."

"If we could join forces, we could add more aquatic businesses," says Karina. She laughs. "At first, we were the *only* crazy guys, and now we find out we're just *one* of the crazy guys."

There Must Be Something in the Water

Karina had to dash off to attend to her fussy baby. Joe didn't want to ask Rutger the "Are you crazy?" question every seasteader must answer, because Rutger seems so visibly sane. Rutger from Rotterdam states possibilities plainly and without fanfare in the voice of a civil engineer who's tasked with a municipal assignment. The Dutch people listened to his presentation as if it was the most reasonable proposition in the world. On his turf, nobody asks him if he's crazy, because his turf is sinking. So rather than ask him if he's crazy, Joe asked if the whole idea is crazy.

"In order for floating urbanization to be a feasible solution," Rutger replied, "we need to move fast. We cannot make a hundred floating houses here and another thousand there. It will be only a drop in the ocean, literally. Can we roll it out fast enough all over the globe to really solve the problem? On paper, I think in my presentation we more or less solved the problem, but can we implement it quickly enough to actually make it happen? Because getting one billion people on the oceans in the next eighty years"—he laughs—"it's big. Big challenges require big solutions. Global food security is a big challenge."

Every time the word *challenge* is used, Rutger perks up.

"I think, in the end, whether we at DeltaSync do something or not, people will live in city-states on the oceans for sure. I'm quite convinced of that. But there are many steps between floating pavilions and the city-states on the ocean. I do think we can be making floating airports tomorrow, and I think we can make a small floating city within the next five years, or we should be able to make a large floating city in the next ten years for sure. Then the idea is, how do you distribute the knowledge, and how do you get people all over the world doing the same thing?"

We decided to find out.

If We Build It, Will You Come?

We asked DeltaSync how much it would cost to design the first seaworthy city. Rutger and Karina said they'd create an in-depth feasibility study for $40,000. Hmmm, we thought, stroking our chins. How do you ask people to donate money to such an unusual project? The Thiel Foundation pledged to match every dollar donated, not fund our projects wholesale. Peter doesn't want seasteading to be his project. He offered to support people who choose to support seasteading. Would people around the world really put skin in the game?

We took a leap of faith, trusting that anonymous folks would to step up to our ambitious $20,000 goal. We pitched the Floating City Project at a crowdfunding website called Indiegogo. We asked people to participate in a survey to let us know what living accommodations they would like to see on a seastead, and, if they were so inclined, to donate to help us pay DeltaSync to engineer a novel seastead design.

The results exceeded our expectations. Donors contributed $27,083. We were amazed by the sheer number of people who gave at all levels, from $10 to more than $1,000. More than $20,000 was raised by people contributing less than $500 US each. Almost half of all donors earned less than $50K a year. More than three thousand people from well over sixty countries filled out our survey to let us know what they wanted from a seastead, and they specified security, comfort, personal freedom, community space, greenery, and, of course, reliable, high-speed Internet. All expressed a willingness to pay realistic prices for modestly sized units on the world's first floating city. And all we did was post a plan on a website.

That year, 2013, we raised more than $215,000 of the $250,000 maximum that can be matched by the Thiel Foundation. These aren't investments. These are donations. People have spoken—through our survey, their pocketbooks, and the hundreds of volunteers who have donated their time. The groundswell of international support allowed us to commission the best aquatic architects in the world to design a novel and aesthetically pleasing seastead.

Karina Czapiewska led the team at DeltaSync to complete the now widely discussed *Seasteading Implementation Plan.* In their vision, the floating city is composed of eleven square or pentagonal platforms with fifty-meter sides, each supporting three-story buildings and walkable open green space. The platforms will be constructed of reinforced concrete and will last more than a century. The eleven modules would be interconnected to form a small village, intended for a population of 225 to 300 residents. Their design includes apartments, terraced housing, office space, and hotels. They calculated that the cost would be roughly $393 per square foot of gross space, but since 20 percent of each platform is reserved for open gardens, parks, and walking paths, the report projects issuable space to cost $504 per square foot ($5,425 per square meter), about what it costs to live in London.

Can you afford it? For comparison, Manhattan real estate prices averaged $1,363 per square foot in 2014, ranging from $430 per square foot in Inwood to more than $3,393 on Central Park South. How do hot-dog sellers and shoe-shine entrepreneurs live in Manhattan? How do college students and sculptors? Where there is wealth, services are required. Where services are required, people are hired. Many business owners who filled out our detailed survey expressed an eagerness to hire, especially from a stock of pioneers willing to take the plunge into ocean living.

Following our strategy of "strategic incrementalism," we knew we couldn't start out with a mighty seastead weathering the high seas. We needed to ask a coastal nation to host the first seastead in shallow territorial waters, as close to an active port as possible, to reduce the cost of transporting people and goods to and from the seastead. If the host country would grant residents and business owners substantial political autonomy, the floating city-state would provide it with economic benefits such as hiring its citizens for work and offering unconventional entrepreneurs a forum to fail or succeed on their own terms. What better way to signal that a country is focused on twenty-first-century innovation than by bringing the world's first floating laboratory for governance to its coastline?

It was a tall order, and geopolitical scholars Paul Aljets and Paul Weinger volunteered their time and expertise to help us identify twenty countries we believe could be amenable to hosting a seastead in their territorial waters. We've got the ear of several important politicians in various nations. As of 2016, we are finishing phase 2 of the Floating City Project, which includes testing DeltaSync's novel seasteading designs in wave tanks, acquiring more detailed financial calculations, deepening our diplomatic negotiations with potential host nations, collecting potential resident feedback, prospecting investors, and identifying businesses that would like to be located on the first floating city. By 2020, we plan to float the first small seastead and model of future governance.

Humanity is poised to fulfill Buckminster Fuller's dream of a floating city. To solve humanity's most pressing problems, we need millions to climb aboard. To explain the reasons why, we need this story to go deeper and wider.

DeltaSync gives us a glimpse of the marine engineering required, but cities require more than buildings, parks, and public utilities. Cities require immense amounts of biodiversity to feed their populations. How will ocean farms work? How wide could they be? How deep could they go? What kind of food will they produce? Where will we get the resources to grow so much food?

To answer these questions, we must jump from Holland to Costa Rica, where a scientist from the developing world plans to feed 9 billion people by 2050 with a food most people don't even know they eat every day, yet have never tasted.

PART II

———

ENVIRONMENT

Chapter 3

FOOD

Feed the World with
Greenhouse Gas

We Have Problems

You know the litany. We're destroying the environment. We're running out of fresh water. We're fighting over dwindling fossil fuels. We can't figure out how we're going to feed growing populations. We've eroded most of the topsoil, chopped down much of the forests, and devoured 90 percent of the large fish stock since 1950. The profit motive overpowers the stewardship motive. Everybody blames the oil companies, but we really enjoy our cars, bottled drinks, and computers, which require oil to produce, so we might as well point the finger at everybody except the Amish and Jain monks.

The human race is faced with eight of what futurist Peter Diamandis, founder of the XPRIZE Foundation and Singularity University, calls "humanity's grand challenges." The problems list is actually larger and scarier than the list he proposed, so we've updated it:

Sea level rise, fish extinction, poisonous coastal "dead zones," food shortages, peak oil, water crisis, resource wars, and poverty.

Given the amount of time we have—5.3 billion scheduled to experience water shortages by 2025, and 8.1 billion set to fight over it—we don't have time to find eight stately solutions to each of the eight grand challenges. We need to look at how all eight grand challenges interlock. In other words, we need to solve all eight grand challenges with a single solution.

Four aquapreneurs say they know what the solution is. A fisheries biologist, a marine agronomist, a biochemical engineer, and the discoverer of the *Titanic* wreckage each independently contacted the Seasteading Institute and presented us with the same solution. Climate change, world hunger, peak oil, freshwater depletion, ocean acidification, and resource wars are not separate problems, each to be solved one at a time. They are all symptoms of a bigger problem. When you think through this bigger problem and see the simple solution, all other solutions flow from it: the climate stabilizes, nine billion are fed, fossil fuels are not vital, water is virtually infinite, oceans are purified, and no more blood for oil.

To understand, all we have to do is solve this riddle:

What do fossil fuels, food, and pollution have in common?

Think Different

Ricardo Radulovich says the lightbulb went off over his head thirty years ago.

"I was *so well trained* as an agricultural water scientist; specially trained in how you get limited water to distant crops." He lists the names of agricultural water scientists legendary only to agricultural water scientists. "I worked with the best of the best, trying to find a solution to our water problem. Then I made my own field obsolete."

Ricardo Radulovich is a professor of water science at the University of Costa Rica, with a PhD in soil-plant-water relations from the University of California. Everything about Ricardo's professional expertise suggests a land-and-soil man. Yet he's always wet. He sports a deep tan and wiry muscles from constant swimming, diving, and hauling in the Pacific Ocean and the Caribbean Sea, which he calls his "fieldwork." He splits his time teaching crop-water relation at the University of Costa Rica and sleeping alone on floating sea farms he constructed himself.

Ricardo Radulovich calls himself "a third worlder." Raised in Chile, he grew up acutely aware of the plight of the underfed, spurring a career-spanning preoccupation with how to increase global food yields to match growing populations, and how to empower the poor to enrich themselves by growing this food.

"It bothers me every day that people are starving, and we leave such a miserable situation. It is unbearable. People tell me I am antisocial, because I am always working alone on the sea. But I think I am more social than most. I worry about the starving, the wars, the ignorance, while the ocean contains vast resources that we can use. That's what moves me. That's what motivates me."

It's one thing to imagine how the desperately poor coastal people could grow enough crops to prosper by selling to global markets. It's another to head out on the water by yourself and work to demonstrate it. This is even more difficult than it sounds. Ricardo has returned to his makeshift sea farm to find that roving low-tech pirates have stolen everything he has: floating drums, fishing lines, crops, tools. He's lost a dinghy and two outboard motors.

"They are wild people, man," he says. Ricardo admits people have been murdered for less than he brings to his floating farms. He could finish his career as a tenured tie-wearing professor. What is a specialist in the use of land irrigation doing shirtless on floating farms amid the most desperate sea people?

"I was lucky enough to see it, and now I have to push for it. It took me a long time to learn about the sea. I don't have much time left, and neither does humanity."

See what?

"The solution."

Yikes

The United Nations has declared that the world is facing a "water bankruptcy." More than a billion people do not have access to safe drinking water. The twenty-five poorest countries spend 20 percent of their GDP on water. Next time you eat an omelet, consider that it takes 120 gallons of water to produce one egg.

"A rule of thumb," Ricardo said, "is that a dietary calorie takes a liter of water to be produced, meaning we each consume about 3,000 liters of 'virtual' water per day just in our food alone."

The lack of clean water kills far more people than warfare. The Blue Planet Network, a charity dedicated to organizing globally to bring safe drinking water to people around the world, lists some sobering facts. Six thousand children die every day for lack of clean water to drink. Diarrhea has killed more children in the last decade than all humans killed in armed conflict since World War II. Eighty percent of diseases in the developing world are caused by contaminated water, and half of all hospital beds are filled with people suffering from water-related illnesses. African and Asian women walk an average of six kilometers each day to provide water for their families.

Now for the bad news: Peter Gleick, a scientist who cofounded the nonprofit Pacific Institute to solve global water challenges, calculates that by 2020, 135 million people will die for lack of safe drinking water. By 2025, two-thirds of the world's population—the equivalent of all humans alive in 1990, which was 5.3 billion people—will suffer from water shortages.

Worldwide, 70 percent of all available freshwater is used to irrigate agriculture. Roughly a third of all land is used for agriculture. As a result of freshwater consumption from the mid-1990s to 2000, the United Nations estimated that an average of 1,374 square miles of land turned to desert each year—an area about the size of Rhode Island.

"Imagine if this freshwater were freed up for other uses," Ricardo says.

From the Green Revolution to the Blue Revelation

Norman Borlaug, a plant geneticist from Iowa, is credited by admirers with saving more than a billion lives. Detractors say he really "only" saved several hundred million. Whatever. He and his team spent twenty years applying novel advances in molecular genetics, painstakingly trying thousands of breeding experiments until they cloned a mutant wheat strain that was high yield, resistant to pests and diseases, and required few pesticides. In 1965 Borlaug and his colleague Monkombu Sambasivan Swaminathan initiated a campaign to ship the "miracle wheat" to starving nations such as India and Pakistan. In 1968 the US Agency for International Development dubbed Norman Borlaug's achievement "the Green Revolution." In 1970 he won the Nobel Peace Prize.

During the second half of the twentieth century, global food production doubled, and in developing countries it tripled. Between 1980 and 2000, global food prices halved. In southern India, the Green Revolution was estimated by the World Bank's *World Development Report 2000/2001: Attacking Poverty* to have increased farmers' earnings by 90 percent and those of landless peasants by 125 percent over twenty years.

In 2018 more than half a century will have passed since this stupendous humanitarian achievement, by which time human population will have about doubled. Now humanity faces a new problem, and it's not too many humans. All 7 billion of us, standing shoulder to shoulder, would fit inside the city of Los Angeles. People aren't taking up too much space; their food is. The overpopulation problem is an agricultural problem. By transforming much of the wild continents into vast tracts of industrial farms, humanity has created several dire dilemmas.

Carbon Pollution. Roughly one-third of greenhouse gas emissions produced by humans come from agriculture, according to a 2012 sum-up of the literature in the journal *Nature*, and 86 percent of it is carbon dioxide. Humanitarians and environmentalists are in conflict because feeding the world and saving the planet are at odds.

Coastal Pollution. Vast ocean dead zones—areas that cannot support life—are increasing along the world's coastlines due to agricultural runoff, which floods the seas with excessive amounts of nitrogen and phosphorus. These nutrient densities form a cloud over the afflicted ocean ecosystem, triggering weed algal blooms that eat up all available oxygen, killing all life below it. This ultimately causes the suffering and death of sea lions, seals, sea otters, porpoises, and blue whales.

Food Limits. When debates over potential food shortages due to climate change become hopelessly politicized, who ya gonna call for clarity? Companies that make billions selling food. In 2015 American food giant General Mills announced a plan to invest more than $100 million to reduce its greenhouse gas emissions 28 percent by 2025. Why is General Mills acting like the Dutch? CEO Ken Powell told the Associated Press, "We think that human-caused greenhouse gas causes climate change and climate volatility, and that's going to stress the agricultural supply chain, which is very important to us. Obviously, we depend on that for our business, and we all depend on that for the food we eat." Unilever, Mars, and Nestlé have set similar targets. Maybe it's politics. Maybe it's business. Probably it's both.

Poverty. The World Bank reports that 923 million were undernourished before the 2008 food crisis. Since then, wild swings in food prices have become a way of life for the poorest billion. One more large swing could have devastating consequences. Worldwide food riots in 2008 should give us a hint that humans do not starve without a fight.

Health Crisis. Michael Pollan reported in his book *The Omnivore's Dilemma: A Natural History of Four Meals*: "While the surgeon general is raising alarms over the epidemic of obesity, the president is signing farm bills designed to keep the river of cheap corn flowing, guaranteeing that the cheapest calories in the supermarket will continue to be the unhealthiest."

Environmental Degradation. Growing crops in soil requires us to use up its nutrient wealth. Protecting crops from pests requires a never-ending arms race between pests and pesticides, as fast-breeding pests develop resistance to past pesticides. This problem is the primary motivator to develop genetically modified foods, which don't threaten human health as much as the political backlash against their use, which threatens the poor most of all. Less topsoil, newer pesticides, and more misinformation is an unholy trinity for food prices.

Running Out of Room. In 2015 the United Nations Food and Agriculture Organization completed a landmark study estimating that 25 percent of the world's land is now "highly degraded," yet the world's farmers must produce 70 percent more food by 2050 to feed the 9 billion mouths that will be crying out for calories.

The solution to these problems has got to be as big—in fact, bigger than the Green Revolution.

Ricardo's Oceanic Epiphany

Ricardo's oceanic epiphany occurred a third of a century ago, when he was a horticulturalist conducting an experiment growing tomatoes on a tiny floating farm at sea. Much of agricultural technology can be viewed as a ten-thousand-year battle against pests. On Ricardo's floating farm on the Pacific coast of Costa Rica, pests were nonexistent. Infesting insects didn't fly over the ocean. No birds arrived to eat the tomatoes. Vermin couldn't swim, and weeds didn't grow. Not even pathogens blighted his crop. Once the tomatoes ripened, Ricardo abandoned them on the vine for three months. When he returned, he claims they were still ripe in the sun, utterly without blemishes. He photographed himself biting into them and says they were sweet.

Dr. Radulovich felt he was on the edge of a breakthrough to feed the world with organic horticultural crops on the ocean. It would be cheap and initiated by the world's poor, who could grow and sell the crops on floating farms that could expand to any size. If he could prove it worked in microcosm, he could prove to investors it would work on a global scale.

If only he could get the water distillation process right.

It wasn't working the way he designed it. Alone on his tiny floating farm, stooped, sun baked, coated with salt, Ricardo struggled to jury-rig his water distillation contraption. Frustrated, he stood up in the sun, took a deep breath, and looked at the vast sea that surrounded him.

"Here I was, floating on a little farm, looking around at this great un-used resource. Suddenly I realized we had everything we wanted at sea. I was thinking like a land-based agriculturalist. What I was doing was so small and insignificant compared to what the sea was already doing."

The ocean holds 97.5 percent of the world's water, with another 2 percent bound up in polar ice caps. Most of the remaining 0.5 percent is mixed in the soil or lies deep underground in inaccessible aquifers. That leaves roughly .007 percent of the world's water available for human use. Why are seven billion people fighting over .007 percent of the world's water?

"The story I like to tell is," Ricardo recalls, "I was searching the coast, wondering how we are going to find enough water to feed all the crops of the world, and a wave hit me and rolled me over, and I said, '*Eureka!*'" He smiles. "There is no water shortage. We have all the water we want."

Ricardo always chuckles at how people furrow their brows at this part of the story. *Waaaait* a second. It's salt water! You can't grow anything in that . . .

. . . except the most common plant on Earth.

"I believe I am a specialist now, because I have made all the mistakes that could be made. I also claim the status of a scientist, because I've made mistakes nobody has made before."

Only after basking in ocean and sun for twelve years, struggling to grow land crops at sea, did Ricardo realize that the solution to mankind's most colossal problems lies in how sun and ocean have worked together since the dawn of life. Now the scientist who spends his working days lashing together fifty-gallon drums is publishing scientific papers announcing plans "to use the sea to double the world's food production capacity and thus achieve worldwide food security."

Ricardo worked out the details of a proposal that would attract a grant from the World Bank, which allowed him to found the Sea Gardens Project. After preliminary success, Ricardo would then attract funding from the Bill & Melinda Gates Foundation, allowing him to found and direct the more ambitious Cultivated Seaweeds for Food Project. But none of this happened until after Ricardo fought a hard, uphill twenty-year battle to be heard.

Water, water, everywhere, nor any drop to drink.
—Samuel Taylor Coleridge, *The Rime of the Ancient Mariner*

Astronomer Carl Sagan stunned the world when he instructed the *Voyager 1* spacecraft to turn around and take a snapshot of the Earth after it finished its loving photo shoot of Saturn, taking one last look back before it headed into interstellar space, never to return. For a brief moment in 1990, hundreds of millions of earthlings were awed and inspired to see past our petty disagreements before we got back to bickering. You couldn't see borders. You couldn't even see continents. "The pale blue dot" had only one characteristic to distinguish it from all the other insignificant motes. It was blue. If an alien race glanced at our little corner of space, the first thing they would notice is that they were looking at an aqueous planet, covered almost entirely by liquid water.

The oldest photosynthesizers are blue-green algae, otherwise known as cyanobacteria, the evolutionary bridge between bacteria and green plants. These ancient creatures have been photosynthesizing for 3.6 billion years, which is where we get our oxygen to waste arguing. Alga are the foundation of all life and fossil fuel, they're crucial to the Earth's self-regulating system, and they represent two-thirds of the world's biomass.

In 1630 Flemish physician Jean-Baptiste van Helmont planted a 5-pound willow branch in 200 pounds of soil. Five years later, he had a willow tree weighing 165 pounds, yet the soil had lost only 2 ounces. Where did the 164 pounds and 14 ounces of tree come from? Now we know the answer: water and carbon atoms in the air, two things of which the ocean has plenty. Photosynthesis is the most common chemical process on the planet, alga is its greatest engine, and growing algae requires megatons of carbon.

Algae and phytoplankton absorb nutrients from the water and manufacture their own food by using energy from the sun. Except for a few rare organisms near heat vents in the ocean floor, all life relies on the magic of photosynthesis, using sunlight to weld two carbon atoms together, giving off oxygen as a by-product. Phytoplankton, the microscopic plants of the sea, produce more than half of the world's oxygen—and by some estimates, 85 percent.

"Food is the product of recent photosynthesis," says Ricardo, "and fossil fuels are the product of ancient photosynthesis. We depend on photosynthesis, yet nobody knows how to do it. Nobody has invented a machine that can take CO_2 from the air and, with added water and energy, churn out sugar. Not with any amount of energy."

Human knowledge of photosynthesis has not yet reached the intelligence of kelp, a brown seaweed chock-full of nutrients, which performs this trick effortlessly.

"Photosynthesis has been mastered only by plants and bacteria," says Ricardo. "All food and fuel energy is created by photosynthesis. Why not use the best and most plentiful photosynthesizers to power everything: food, energy, you name it?"

Exactly 97.5 percent of the free liquid water is in the sea, which is filled with seaweed, the most nutritious plant in the world, a healthy protein source, and the greatest carbon collector on the planet. All seaweed needs to grow are water and sunlight, two of the most common resources on the planet, both plentiful at sea.

A growing chorus of aquapreneurs argues that all eight of humanity's grand challenges can be solved with algae.

Eat Greenhouse Gas

Insert seaweed, otherwise known as macroalgae, into the middle of our eight global problems, and the entire snafu transforms into a global circle of life. Consider how each of the grand challenges can be solved by the common weed of the sea:

Reduce Carbon Pollution. Seaweed builds itself with the CO_2 in the ocean, which reduces the acidity of the ocean, which pulls CO_2 out of the atmosphere.

Clean the Dead Zones. To build itself with CO_2, seaweed eats nutrients such as nitrogen, found most abundantly in ocean dead zones poisoned by farmland runoff. Our sewage is seaweed food, and seaweed is sashimi food, and sashimi is people food.

Feed the World. All food, for all life, is based on photosynthesis, performed most spectacularly by powerhouses like seaweed.

Power Civilization. Fossil fuel is the product of ancient photosynthesis, which was performed by ancient algae like seaweed.

End Poverty in Coastal Nations. Seaweed is farmed most commonly by poor people tying it to strands of rope and letting it grow. Infrastructure required: ropes and rowboats. What if we increased the demand by a thousand times?

Get Healthy. Doctors tell us to eat more omega-3 fatty acids, found most abundantly in fish. Fish don't synthesize their own omega-3s; they get it by eating seaweed. Doctors also tell us to eat low-calorie, low-fat, high-quality fat, high-fiber, nutrient-rich, high-amino-acid protein. Where on earth are we supposed to find this perfect food? Oh, yeah. Seaweed.

Save the Environment. Conservationists tell us we've depleted the topsoil, wasted the water, poisoned the pests, and destroyed ecosystems with our endless eating and consuming. Where are we supposed to find an abundant food that needs no soil, fresh water, or pesticides? We could try seaweed. Okay, but where can we establish farms that need no farmland and can be expanded to virtually any size; farms that suffer no droughts and don't know the meaning of floods? We could try the sea.

Fine, but how are we supposed to fuel it? The best possible nano-technology would be self-assembling solar panels that are also edible. Hey, wait a minute. Seaweed again!

Ricardo Radulovich had his revelation thirty years ago, but the seaweed solution was not greeted with open minds.

"The first few years," he recalls, "I kept arranging meetings with very important colleagues, and when I explained everything to them, they said, 'Oh, yes, very interesting, Ricardo,' and when I left, I had this clear feeling that they said, 'Well, I guess we've lost Ricardo.' He laughs. "But now people are listening, because the crisis is deepening, and there's more talk about alternatives."

It's the Bioeconomy, Stupid

All life relies on carbon, the magic atom with four bonding sites that stick easily to oxygen, hydrogen, nitrogen, and more carbon atoms, allowing nature to experiment with long Tinkertoy molecules perfectly suited to create complex life.

Animals inhale oxygen and exhale CO_2 (though they also exhale a little oxygen). Plants take in CO_2 and release oxygen (though they release CO_2 at night). When this "carbon cycle" is in balance, the total carbon dioxide animals are emitting and plants are absorbing is roughly equal. Since the industrial revolution in the late seventeen hundreds, humans threw this cycle out of whack by burning ancient sources of carbon such as oil, coal, and gas. Mass deforestation has cut back the amount of plants removing CO_2 from the air. As a result, global atmospheric concentrations of CO_2 are roughly 35 percent higher than they were before the industrial revolution. Roughly a quarter of the CO_2 in the atmosphere is absorbed by the oceans when it rains. There it forms carbonic acid, like you would find in a carbonated beverage, which deprives sea life of the carbonates they need to calcify bones and shells. This even threatens some species of plankton, the foundation of the ocean's food chain. Since the industrial revolution, ocean acidity has increased 30 percent after holding steady for about 21 million years.

Okay, that's not reassuring. But wait a second. CO_2 isn't pollution; it's the molecule of life. Plants crave it so they can make oxygen and food for animals. Seaweed is willing to do this on a mass scale without requiring much from land. As Ricardo says, "The ocean is a bioeconomy that takes nothing from land. It's self-sustaining."

"Each square kilometer of seaweed cultivated will sequester two thousand metric tons of carbon dioxide per year," says Ricardo. That means 0.4 square miles will sequester 4,409,245 pounds. As a rule of thumb, remember that a seaweed farm covering one square mile will capture well over 10 million pounds of CO_2.

Algae are among of the fastest-growing organisms in the world. "Algae can double their mass in anywhere from twenty-four to forty-eight hours," reports Phil Lane, program manager at Touchstone Research Laboratory, an algae farm in West Virginia. Talk about exponential change. Corn can't grow that fast, and it harvests seasonally. Seaweed, if farmed profitably, could scale up to large enough proportions at sea to reverse CO_2 trends. Algae consume *almost twice their weight* in carbon dioxide.

While industrial agriculture requires the eradication of biodiversity—an American corn field requires that polyculture be clear-cut and turned into a monocrop—seaweed aquaculture increases biodiversity.

"They provide safe a harbor for lots of biodiversity," says Ricardo, describing his prototype farms. "You see around seaweeds little creatures that hide, so they promote sea life. Thus we are decreasing the need for fishing."

In the early twentieth century, when mankind became impatient with the natural nitrogen cycle, a German chemist named Fritz Haber created a process to transform nitrogen in the atmosphere into fertilizer. Borlaug's high-yield crops would not have been as productive without the technology to harvest nitrogen straight from the air. If intensive burning of fossil fuels allows mankind to harvest nitrogen from the air, the cultivation of algae can allow mankind to harvest nitrogen from the sea.

"The next Green Revolution should be blue," says Ricardo. "The productivity of giant kelp has been compared with that of the most highly productive land crops, like sugar cane. Macroalga cultivation, attached to ropes or even free floating, is possibly the easiest form of sea farming, and it requires the least financial investment. Thus it is more implementable in poorer countries. The sea has all the needed water and space and generally sufficient nutrients for macroalgae to grow. Fertilizing them is already a common practice in Asia in areas of intensive production.

"Instead of getting more water to the farms," Ricardo continues, "we must simply move the farms to the water. Such sea farming is already a reality in some places. I have been doing it for over fifteen years. Many thousands of hectares of marine areas can be farmed right now, with millions of tons of new food added to the stream. Each ton of seaweed harvested frees one million liters of freshwater from agriculture. It will be soon possible to produce billions of tons."

Every hectare of agriculture that becomes aquaculture means less land devoted to farming, less CO_2 released into the atmosphere, more CO_2 absorbed from the atmosphere, less water used to produce food, fewer pesticides, cleaner oceans, less need for depleting wild populations of fish, and more incentives for increasing populations of farmed fish.

According to Ricardo, algae will allow us to feed the world with the CO_2 that's already in our atmosphere and the nutrients that are already in the sea. You don't have to choose between saving the environment and feeding the world. You feed the world *by* saving the environment.

In 1999 economist Peter Drucker predicted, "Aquaculture, not the Internet, represents the most promising investment opportunity of the twenty-first century." The green economy aspires to protect the environment, but the blue economy aspires to restore the environment. The bridge from green to blue is blue-green algae. Algae, the basis of life, must become the keystone of the blue economy.

How to Feed 9 Billion

Wheat, corn, and soybeans are only types of land plants. Alga is the entire category of plants that grow in water, and the varieties are almost endless. Approximately 10,500 species of seaweed have been counted. For centuries, only about 500 have been used for food or medicine, and only about 220 are cultivated worldwide.

"Seaweeds are quite edible and rich in protein, considered similar to soybean," says Ricardo. "Algae are high fiber, low in calories, and rich with minerals like thirty percent iron and calcium, as well as vitamins like B_{12}. This could be an option for vegans. No agrochemicals are used, and the produce can be certified organic."

Vegans and health food enthusiasts know spirulina as a type of blue-green algae that is chock full of key nutrients, including B complex vitamins, beta-carotene, vitamin E, manganese, zinc, copper, iron, selenium, and gamma linolenic acid (an essential fatty acid). Compare that with corn chips and white bread, two of the top most consumed foods in the United States.

Heck, compare spirulina with land vegetables. Most vegetable proteins are deficient in at least one of the amino acids. Wheat, corn, and rice are low in lysine. Soy is high in lysine but low in methionine. Vegetarians who do not research a scientific approach to diet can discover that Mom's counsel to "eat your vegetables" can leave young children with rickets. B_{12} is scarce in land vegetables, since it is synthesized by primitive orders of life such as mold, bacteria, and algae. Spirulina contains the most concentrated form of B_{12} known to man.

Spirulina is more than 60 percent protein, more than triple the amount in beef, with more than triple the amount of vitamin B_{12} found in animal liver, with five times more beta-carotene than carrots, and high volumes of gamma-linolenic acid (which can reduce cholesterol and prevent heart disease). Spirulina contains phycocyanin, which can be found only in spirulina.

Vegetables grown in soil are not the perfect food. Spirulina is the perfect food. Don't take our word for it. Ask NASA, which cultivates it for astronaut food in space. The National Aeronautics and Space Administration plans to grow and harvest space spirulina, and Joe Quirk was invited to speak in 2014 at the Planetary Sustainability Collaboratory at the NASA Ames Space Portal about the potential in algae. Is seasteading the best way to train for spacesteading? NASA already trains astronauts underwater to prepare for zero-gravity space missions. If it wants astronauts to farm algae sustainably on space stations, perhaps the best way to practice is submerged in sea stations. The brainstorming continues, and we remain optimistic about collaboration.

Ew!

Show the average Westerner a cup of algae, and he squinches up his nose and says, *"Ew! I don't want to eat that!"* But then show the average person a stiff stalk of wheat grass, and she'll say, *"Yuck! I really don't want to eat that!"* How do you eat a tiny row of stiff husks spiking at the top of an inedible grass? Only through intensive industrial processing. Algae are much easier to process into healthy food than soy or wheat is. Microalgae, as single-celled organisms, do not waste any of their energy growing stems, leaves roots, thorns, or flowers. For instance, spirulina is easily digested because it contains no inedible cellulose. Every part of microalgae is edible, none is wasted, and each cell is a seed that can split into two more seeds and grow exponentially as long as more nutrients, water, and sunlight are available. Algae are the most efficient life-sustaining products humans can produce and develop.

If human populations starve en masse, it will be because of the collapse of one of our key foods; possibly because of water shortages. Corn, wheat, and soy are subject to blight. Mankind is only as hardy as its food source, so mankind should base its food source on the hardiest, most robust plant—and the most digestible. Blue-green alga is the oldest, simplest, and most prolific plant on the planet, growing in almost every damp habitat in the world where nutrients are available—even the interstices of Antarctic ice.

To alleviate malnutrition, Ricardo coordinated the Cultivated Seaweeds for Food Project. "When you add seaweed to flour, substituting, say, twenty percent," he explains, "you don't increase cost, but you add a substantial amount of protein, fiber, minerals, and vitamins that you don't have normally in wheat flour. You might even lower costs. Moreover, if poor coastal communities are able to grow their own seaweed or harvest it from nature, and they are able to add it to their recipes here and there, we're improving the protein content of meals.

"My team at the University of Costa Rica has identified and is cultivating the best native species for alleviating food shortages. We are constantly innovating methods of producing biomass for human, animal, and industrial applications. Most important, our systems are replicable on nearly any near-shore waters in the world. At this point, the major challenge is not the cultivation of seaweeds but their use. A leading objective of our research efforts is to characterize and learn to use the most cultivable local species for food in a manner that entices the population to eat them."

Ricardo lists the rich arsenal of commercially viable uses, many of them already on the market for their medicinal and pharmaceutical importance, including antioxidant, antitumor, antiobesity, and antiviral activities. Most of us don't realize we eat seaweed every day.

"Seaweed products are used everywhere," Ricardo says. "Alginate, agar, and carrageenan are used in toothpaste, ice cream, sausages." Also in orange juice, peanut butter, beer, salad dressings, muffins, medicine, fertilizer, cosmetics, paints, adhesives, dyes, and many other products integral to our lives. Seaweed is like electricity; it infuses everything.

"We're talking only about *wild* seaweed," emphasizes Ricardo. "We haven't even *started* the artificial selection process that land-based agriculturalists have enjoyed for thousands of years." The original wild corn, a grass called teosinte, was an inch-long cob before it was bred into the large sweet corn we know today. Wild tomatoes look like purplish grapes, very different from the fat red tomatoes we buy in stores. "Imagine the tremendous potential that will unfold when genetic manipulation techniques are applied to more than ten thousand species of seaweeds, even if only with conventional breeding techniques. We could have seaweeds that taste like tomatoes. Who knows? Seaweed flour, in its wild state, is already more nutritious than wheat flour, even though wheat has benefited from thousands of years of selective breeding to make it palatable, and still many of us are gluten resistant."

Ricardo says the starting assumptions from which experts talk about food and fertilizer shortages are wrong. One is "maximum planetary capacity." We're approaching a globe-sized problem while thinking inside our land-based box.

"People have placed the planetary carrying capacity of humans at ten billion. It's a bunch of baloney. We're not even considering the sea! That's 70 percent of the planetary surface, which has 98.5 percent of all the liquid water, and most of the solar radiation, and most of the nutrients. It's not even considering the equation. It's silly."

In 1975, ten years after Norman Borlaug initiated his Green Revolution in starving nations, India blithely declined all foreign aid because it was too busy selling surplus food to the rest of the world. This would confirm our contention that solutions do not come from the available options presented to us by experts. They come from out of the blue.

Our Dirty Secret

David Pimentel is a professor of ecology and agricultural science at the College of Agriculture and Life Sciences at Cornell University, and he will scare the dirt out of you. Susan S. Lang, senior science writer at Cornell, felicitously summed up Pimentel's 2006 paper "Soil Erosion: A Food and Environmental Threat" published in the journal *Environment, Development and Sustainability*.

> *Around the world, soil is being swept and washed away 10 to 40 times faster than it is being replenished, destroying cropland the size of Indiana every year, reports a new Cornell University study . . .*
>
> *The United States is losing soil 10 times faster—and China and India are losing soil 30 to 40 times faster—than the natural replenishment rate.*
>
> *The economic impact of soil erosion in the United States costs the nation about $37.6 billion each year in productivity losses. Damage from soil erosion worldwide is estimated to be $400 billion per year.*
>
> *As a result of erosion over the past 40 years, 30 percent of the world's arable land has become unproductive.*

Topsoil forms at an agonizingly slow rate of about five centimeters every thousand years. Figure a half centimeter per century. That means centuries of nature's work can be washed away in a season or two. Any conservationist will tell you humans have depleted the world's topsoil of nutrients and bled megatons into the sea. This polluting effluent is compounded by acid rain, which is produced by the burning of fossil fuels. These hyperpolluted coastal areas have long been given up for dead, and Ricardo and others plan to make them pristine again.

Breathe Life into the Dead Zones

"We throw tremendous amounts of organic waste directly into the sea through the effluence from city sewage and runoff from agriculture," says Ricardo. "Instead of costly treatment plants that have very limited capabilities, we could position bioengineered seaweed to absorb these nutrients. With photosynthesis, we can create tremendous amounts of biomass that we can use for biofuel. All this nitrogen we're releasing into the water eventually becomes a greenhouse gas. So we're not only cleaning the water, we're reducing the greenhouse effect."

Many people, when they think about agricultural runoff, think of algae blooms that devastate local wildlife. But the difference between algae blooms and algae farms is the difference between weeds and crops. Weeds grow out of control, but crops are cultivated. Crops are edible; weeds choke out edible crops.

David Pimentel himself hints at a solution in the opening sentence of his 2013 paper "Soil Erosion Threatens Food Production," coauthored with Michael Burgess: "Since humans worldwide obtain more than 99.7% of their food (calories) from the land and less than 0.3% from the oceans and aquatic ecosystems, preserving cropland and maintaining soil fertility should be of the highest importance to human welfare."

What if we reversed this ratio and farmed the seas? Marine dead zones full of excess nutrients cover nearly a hundred thousand square miles. That's a total area larger than Oregon. If seaweed can clean the tiniest proportion of these zones, producing food or fuel at a profit, it can be scaled up to colossal proportions. What works in microcosm can work better in macrocosm. That's the magic of profits. It's how one oil well becomes a million oil wells, one lightbulb becomes a trillion lightbulbs, and one voice carried along a wire to the next room becomes a planet crisscrossed with telegraph lines and undersea cables.

Ricardo cites an oft-repeated fact in his academic paper: "Up to 90 per cent of wastewater flows untreated into densely populated coastal zones contributing to growing marine dead zones." But he offers a unique solution: "[I]t is logical . . . to take advantage of these nutrient-rich water sources for production, as well as cleaning them through 'bioremediation.'"

Bioremediation is sciencespeak for the process of culturing microorganisms to metabolize the resources that humans consider pollution. Buckminster Fuller said, "Pollution is nothing but the resources we are not harvesting. We allow them to disperse because we've been ignorant of their value." Bioengineering projects are under way to create microbes that eat plastic. Usually, when scientists think of bioremediation, they think of micro-organisms. But Ricardo says that if we want to quickly remove and store massive amounts of CO_2 and nutrients to feed the world, we need to use one of the fastest-growing macro-organisms in the world: seaweed. Ricardo says this could begin immediately.

Thierry Chopin, a Canadian marine biologist, is already acting on this solution in New Brunswick, Canada. After eight years contemplating how to deal with the waste from salmon farms, Chopin found his solution in seaweed, which thrives in fish poop and food waste. By positioning seaweed farms downstream from the salmon pens, he spares the surrounding ocean. The pollution-eating seaweed becomes a home for various creatures that can be sold on the global market. Mussels in particular are positioned near the pens so they can eat the scraps. The seaweed and mussels each grow up to 50 percent faster when they're awash in salmon waste than when feeding naturally. Sea cucumbers and urchins are positioned beneath the salmon pens to feed off the meatier scraps, and they produce delicacies such as roe, one version of which landlubbers know as caviar.

On the website SciDev.Net, Ricardo reports, "This idea has been tested successfully using human wastewater in experiments at US institutions, including the Woods Hole Oceanographic Institution and the Harbor Branch Oceanographic Institute."

About half the weight of seaweed is oil. Will biofuel ever become cheaper than fossil fuel? The trajectory looks good. Over the last two decades, the cost of producing biodiesel from algae has dropped from hundreds of dollars per gallon to tens. If biofuel technology had no future, fossil fuel giants would not be investing so heavily.

Investment from capitalists can pay for capital and research. But Ricardo thinks the world's coastal poor are excellently positioned to get the jump on them. Right now sea farming is being driven not by millions of investment dollars but by millions of micropreneurs.

How the Poor Will End Poverty

"While an investor can only get in business if a profit is involved," Ricardo explains, "a subsistence farmer or fisherman will get into business if there is adequate coverage of their labor—even if there is no profit whatsoever. Literally, no profit is required."

Modest seaweed farms initiated by the poor could expand among millions without any real profit for quite a while. We might even say the poor will jump-start the blue economy.

"Neither developed countries nor large corporations need to get into seaweed farming to promote the practice in the most critical regions," says Ricardo. The Global Hunger Index, a statistical tool developed by the German nonprofit organization Welthungerhilfe (World Hunger Aid), counts twenty-six countries with "alarming" or "extremely alarming" hunger problems. Ricardo notes that eighteen have coasts.

Ricardo has shown that his most basic sea farm costs only $200.00 US to construct, covers only a half hectare in size, and supports five people with year-round harvests of diverse crops. These self-sufficient floating farms can attach and expand to any size. Many of Ricardo's farms are already floating in Pacific Costa Rica, Caribbean Panama, the Gulf of Thailand, and off the coasts of Tanzania and the island of Zanzibar. Ricardo calls this "a franchise of floating microfarms" that will allow poor coastal fisherman to initiate their own enterprises. The knowledge to build them is teachable, and you need only five people to get started and at least break even. Each sea farm serves as a science laboratory as well. Ricardo plans to train the third world aquapreneurs to collect data for future improvements to sea farm technology, as well as measure socioeconomic impacts on the local populations. If they work in microcosm, they can scale to any size. This is a ratchet that could colonize the shallow seas.

Will poor sea farmers seize this opportunity? Norman Borlaug, reminiscing about the Green Revolution, was adamant on this point:

"Everybody says the peasant farmer in these countries is resistant to change. That's not true. If he sees, demonstrated on his own land, that that package of technology can double, triple, quadruple [yields], like happened in India, Pakistan, and later in China or in Argentina," he will embrace any practice that improves his life.

It's not like poor coastal populations lack for entrepreneurial initiative. Do you use lotion for silky skin, shampoo for luxurious hair? A key ingredient is carrageenan, a thickener derived from seaweed, which might have been cultivated by a poor coastal villager who constructed her own seaweed farm in shallow oceans to sell her product to the world market. For instance, in Nusa Lembongan, an island off the southeast coast of Bali, Indonesia, subsistence fishermen and fisherwomen have developed a micro-industry of aquaculture that has commandeered every microniche of available seaweed. Locals sell low-quality seaweed for 600 rupiah per kilo (5 cents), high-quality seaweed for 3,500 rupiah per kilo (30 cents), and every available seaweed in between. Each type of local seaweed is cultivated by its specialist. And we're talking about only one island.

Few prosperous Westerners know that alga is the economic lifeblood of their civilization. It's in everything from fertilizer that grows our food, to the dyes that color our products, to the oils that transport them to our homes. Consider that a growing proportion of the people cultivating alga and selling it on the world market are the ultrapoor.

In the Gulf of Nicoya off Costa Rica, Ricardo demonstrated that shrimp farming could provide coastal populations with alternative sources of income while simultaneously reducing pressure on natural resources. Merely with a few prototype shrimp farms, Ricardo produced what he calls a "shocking density" of shrimp. He and his team counted five hundred adult shrimp *per cubic meter.* When the local fishermen heard that, Ricardo says they were looking around their ocean calculating how many cubic meters were in their view. The potential for ramping up production of cheap, healthy protein for poor coastal people is incalculable, and Ricardo describes it as "a very low-input activity."

Ricardo's technical breakthrough are accelerating. In order to see his latest, you have to board a motorboat.

The Sea Trellis

Suppose you could hang an upside-down forest from a trellis? How tall would that trellis have to be? Suppose that trellis is as tall as the ocean is deep?

Approaching on a boat, you can't even see Ricardo's "sea fields" until you get within fifty meters, whereupon you find yourself squinting at what looks like an optical illusion. The ocean surface is parceled into large hexagons so that the sea surface looks like a giant kitchen floor. Once parked at the side of a hexagon, an observer sees only a few hundred baseball-sized buoys, connected by ropes inside PVC tubing, which form perfect hexagonal shapes. How do the floating hexagons maintain their shape in the swift currents? It seems eerie, magical, until a worker notes that a great weight of seaweed forest hangs below.

Ricardo explains. "You can hang from this structure just about any sea farming option. My low-cost floating device is moored at the center only, and it can be free floating, with currents moving up to one meter per second. If this holds, a lot of things can be done, implementable in ever-larger areas. For example, flexible cages can be placed within each hexagon, while ropes can provide room for suspended bivalve and seaweed culture, and more. Next steps are to make it bigger, like a spider web in concentric rings. This is the basis for a soft-tech form of seasteading. Imagine giant flexible farms of seaweeds floating freely over any ocean area. I envision large versions of this sea trellis floating free in the dead marine zones, mopping up excess nutrients, revitalizing the oceans, and at the same time providing a harvestable yield.

"This unmanned sea trellis could serve as a big vacuum cleaner, circling on a gyre, with a GPS tracking its location. Invite scientists to measure the water coming in and going out; measure the difference in carbon and nutrients. We'll create sea prairies. The diversity we see on the bottom of the ocean will be drawn up and expanded all the way to the surface. We'll attract fish, create hubs and hot spots for biodiversity, grow corals, harbor seashells. We could transform the seascape with this biodiversity enrichment. The only way to win over the conservationists is to introduce them to a better idea."

Ricardo believes that conservationists and aquaculturalists could work together if they only called themselves restorationists. When asked how he keeps producing sea farming innovations on the cheap, he says, "Keep experimenting, and the sea tells me what to do.

"Humanity went from a hunting/gathering lifestyle to agriculture," Ricardo says. "Now it's time to go from only fishing the sea to farming it as well. This time has come now, thousands of years after we made the move to agriculture."

Professor Ronald Osinga at Wageningen University in the Netherlands calculated that a farm of sea vegetables totaling 180,000 square kilometers—roughly the size of Missouri or Cambodia—could provide enough protein for the entire world population, and Osinga claims it would be enough to compensate for the rise in acidity that started with the industrial revolution.

This can happen only if the ocean remains a frontier to be settled, not a colony of land governments to be exploited. Right now the oceans are treated as a vast hunting ground by people who don't even live there. But the time is now to choose whether we do this working with the carbon cycle, or against it. All we have to do is turn the entire global carbon wheel in the opposite direction.

Here's the way the natural carbon cycle stays in balance: each year, about 200 billion metric tonnes of CO_2 are belched into the sky by rotting, respiration, digestion, and volcanoes, and about 200 billion metric tonnes of CO_2 are absorbed from the atmosphere by plants, especially algae. Here's how we screw it up: humans add an extra 10 billion to the belching. That's only 5 percent extra. How much algae would we need to grow to lower this to 4 percent? How much to balance it out? How much to *reverse* it? We don't know, but the point is that each small step is a decrease in CO_2 and a gain for algae biomass we can use for food, feed, or fuel.

In a scholarly book published in 2015 called *Seaweed Sustainability: Food and Non-Food Applications*, Ricardo led a multidisciplinary team of six experts on four continents to write chapter three, "Farming of Seaweeds," where they calculated that if 1.4 percent of the world's ocean area were farmed, roughly the total present amount of carbon emissions from fossil fuel would be captured: "This type of massive biomass production scheme could sustainably alleviate the world's food gap and provide a source of bioenergy." Explaining that land-based jurisdictions are simply not up to the task of governing the complexity of interests involved, they write, "Seaweed farming in both national and international waters requires a new legal framework that protects the interests of all stakeholders, including farming entrepreneurs."

"Sea farms should be self-sufficient, because the sea is self-sufficient," says Ricardo. "Aquatic life does not depend on biomass coming from land at all. They generate the whole cycle. It shouldn't be impossible to emulate that."

World population is expected to level off to somewhere between 9 billion and 11 billion by 2050, give or take, as populations enter the developed world and have fewer children, a universal phenomenon observed among developing societies.

"Quality of life is improving," says Ricardo. "What do people want to eat? Fish and meat. All these demands are putting more pressure on production. I think we have to farm the ocean, and we can do it sustainably. I don't think it's even questionable."

For Ricardo, the tide is changing and carrying him across the world to work directly with people from Haiti and Zanzibar.

Ricardo laughs about the growing popularity of his idea. "At the beginning, they say, 'You're crazy.' Then at the end, they say, 'Of course. We've known it all along.'"

So what's the next step?

"We need to make a big splash. I need to implement this on a big scale. It has to come out on the cover of the *Economist* and the front page of the *New York Times*. I want an aerial photo of a free-floating ten-hectare farm on the Caribbean which is being used for food production, carbon cycling, nutrient removal, biodiversity enrichment, fisheries enhancement—all of it. Then people will say, 'Oh, wow, we can influence the world with this.' I want people to think about the poor coastal fishermen who have no food. Sea farm projects for coastal people will be easier to make after the big splash. I want to see a hundred tons produced as a demonstration of what is possible. The seas trellis could be the generator of new wealth. There's so much to be done. Most of the seaweed production worldwide is in seven Asian countries, including China, Japan, North Korea, and South Korea, which are temperate. Tropical seaweed production is in Philippines, mostly, as well as Thailand and Indonesia. Tropical seaweed for food has barely been tapped! Seaweed production is growing exponentially in the Philippines, Thailand, and Indonesia. Imagine what that means. Exponential curves start slow and speed up. So this is already happening, and it's going to keep happening. Moving to the sea is a necessity for mankind."

Abundance

We live not in a world of scarcity but a world of abundance. The carbon cycle ensures this. So why are we growing our civilization by working against the carbon cycle? Why don't we get the carbon cycle working for us? In our debates about planetary pillage, we keep talking about nutrient "runoff" and water "depletion" and carbon "pollution" and food "waste." But nothing in nature goes away. It's merely moved. Phosphorus that once nourished the topsoil of farmland has been drained off and poisons the oceans. Carbon that was once contained in underground reservoirs is now belched into the sky. Over the past century, we've increased our wealth by attacking the global carbon cycle at every turn, which has moved all the required ingredients for life to all the wrong places. Only one force is powerful enough to move all this carbon and nutrient pollution back to where it is healthiest for humanity, and that's algae, which sits firmly at the base of the planetary food chain.

Dr. Fred Lubnow, director of aquatic programs for Princeton Hydro, which builds floating islands in Pennsylvania lakes, says, "A two-hundred-fifty-square-foot island can remove about ten pounds of phosphorus. It may not seem like a lot, but every one pound of phosphorus has the potential to create eleven hundred pounds of algae goo," by which he means wet algae biomass.

Here's the crazy part: seaweed and pond scum already volunteer to do this job. Humans just have to cooperate with these two branches of algae, and they will provide a boon of food, feed, fuel, fertilizer, and water, freeing up vast tracts of farmland for the songbirds. Want to restore the oceans, lower greenhouse gases, increase oxygen, feed the world, empower the poor, and fuel civilization cheaply? Algae is already on it. We just need to cooperate with it instead of ignoring it. We can feed the world with our waste if only we let algae convert waste into food. Humans can't overpopulate the Earth faster than algae can be grown. Algae can beat humans and their farm animals in a race to grow living tissue any day of the week.

Ricardo laughs. "It sounds too good to be true, I know. Anyone who works at sea knows nothing is easy at this point. But when we were colonizing the Amazon or the Wild West, it wasn't easy at all. Beginnings are hard."

By putting seaweed at the center of our global cycle of life, we can clean the oceans, reduce greenhouse gases, feed the world, fuel civilization, save fresh water, empower poor coastal people to support themselves, and make an enormous amount of money. So why don't we just do it?

"So many interests," sighs Ricardo. "Soybean cartel, energy cartels, fresh water cartels—they have a business-as-usual approach; a status quo to preserve. And I agree with them! The establishment is good in many ways. It keeps things going, but they are slow to change. We have to present them with the right information, so they will allow themselves to take advantage of this. When the establishment catches on, and puts their efforts into this, the new wealth that will be created will be immense."

The big players in the industry can influence government to write regulations to prevent innovators like Ricardo from threatening their lockdown. This is a classic case of what economists call "regulatory capture." It's a race against time to get technologies up and running before entrenched interests can stop them through their influence on governments.

Asked if he worries about this, Ricardo says, "All the time. I fear regulators more than pirates, more than sharks. We may need seasteads to move into international waters, where there are fewer regulations. We have to run to get ahead of regulatory burdens stopping us. Nobody knows about this solution. They don't understand that this is best option possible."

Ricardo stresses this option will make everybody happy: environmentalists, investors, the poor, fish connoisseurs, and humanitarians like him, yet land-based governments take too long to adjust to game-changing discoveries. Consider that the Green Revolution, which was funded almost entirely by developing countries and private charities, was nearly crushed in its infancy by government regulations.

Bureaucracy Versus Borlaug

In the fifties, Norman Borlaug bred a strain of wheat that produced three times as much food per acre as conventional wheat. Why did it take until the sixties to feed the starving people in India? Government monopolies. India's centrally controlled state grain monopolies mobilized to prevent the new strains from entering the country, claiming they wanted to foster local farming and fertilizer industries. The Wheat Revolution had already swept Mexico, where wheat production had sextupled since Borlaug showed up, increasing dramatically the incomes of millions of Mexican farmers. Borlaug travelled to India to lobby, pointing to progress in neighboring Pakistan, and was told his miracle wheat would have to wait. While citizens starved, bureaucrats chose more bureaucracy, just to be safe. The Green Revolution that would save hundreds of millions was a hair's breadth from not happening because Borlaug's new technology threatened entrenched interests. As he wrote,

"One of the greatest threats to mankind today is that the world may be choked by an explosively pervading but well-camouflaged bureaucracy."

Could similar impediments threaten the Blue Revolution? The US government already subsidizes industrial corn farmers, who provide cheap corn syrup, which has a hand in causing American deaths through many obesity-related diseases. Corn and cow farms produce unhealthy food and pollute the oceans. Algae and fish farms produce healthy food and purify the oceans. If the corn industry can hijack the political structure of the most powerful nation in the world to ensure its monopoly, it can lobby government officials to throw bureaucratic barriers in the way of developing algae farms.

"We have to move fast," repeats Ricardo.

Sea Farming: A Starter's Guide

The Seasteading Institute hosted our third Seasteading Conference in 2012 at San Francisco's luxurious Le Méridien Hotel. The goal was to create an atmosphere of collaboration for investors, naval engineers, ocean law experts, maritime professionals, and other ocean enthusiasts to catalyze new enterprises. Ricardo arrived eager to submit his proposal to expert scrutiny. With minimal upfront investment, Ricardo plans to create a microcosm of the planetary ecosystem. If he can make the carbon equation work on a small scale, he will show investors they can make billions by feeding billions. His team has selected a spot off Costa Rica and Panama, where the poor live right now.

Before an audience of seastead investors, he drew out a blueprint for a self-sustaining floating seaweed farm with living facilities that, once established, would require no input whatsoever from land, while adding diversity and health to the local oceans. Local seaweed will be cultivated from carbon dioxide, nutrients, and sunlight. Filter feeding mollusks, such as oysters and mussels, can be grown on the seaweed. As demonstrated by Ricardo's prototypes, diverse life-forms congregate among the seaweed, gobbling up the carbon and forming a dense ecosystem. He lists a dozen species of local fish that can be fed exclusively on local seaweeds. Ricardo wants to demonstrate that his system will sustain and pay for itself for one year, including maintenance and salaries for the farmers living on the farm. He proposes growing and selling lobster to provide profits that will eventually propel the operation into developing algal biofuel.

Ricardo emphasizes that fish can be grown without feeding them, relying on grazing and secondary growth within cages. "We have kept shrimp and sardines within cages for months without providing them any feed—just allowing sardines to filter-feed from passing waters and shrimp to graze from microalgae fouling, actually cleaning the oyster bags." (These are mesh bags used to cultivate oysters.)

Ricardo displays two oyster bags, one filthy bag kept in a cage without shrimp, and one pristine bag kept in a cage with shrimp. Why clean your instruments when shrimp will do it for you? The increasing population of shrimp can then be harvested and sold. As long as this shrimp is built ultimately from carbon dioxide pulled from the environment, you're not degrading wild stocks of the oceans.

The humans living on the farm will also be sustained by the cycle. This is the tropics, after all. "Freshwater will be obtained by harvesting rainwater from roofs and other surfaces and storing it in semisubmerged large plastic bags." Where Ricardo is working, it rains between 1.5 and 4 meters per year, which is more than enough to sustain people and plants on a 6-meter-by-6-meter farm, and that's not even including distillation processes.

Energy for light and communications will be secured through the use of solar panels. Land cities must ultimately dump their waste into the ocean. On Ricardo's farm, a biogenerator, run on solar power, will convert all human and fish waste into electricity and gas for cooking. Excess waste will be used to feed seaweed to grow biomass for fuel. Though initially the prototype may need a battery-powered generator, Ricardo says he can supplement the farm's electricity needs with windmills only four feet in diameter, which need no mooring. At sea, wind is plentiful.

Ricardo even proposes security through seaweed, an idea surprising to landlubbers but already common sense among farmers interested in seaweed cultivation. The first land-based cities protected themselves with a moat of water. Ocean-based farms will protect themselves with a ring of seaweed. Seaweed fields are grown in a dense tangle moored to crisscrossing underwater ropes. The simplest of nets can disable an outboard propeller. Ricardo proposes that seaweed farmers could create a labyrinthine entry path through their dense farms. If approaching boats must zigzag slowly through a maze of seaweed farms, visitors can be easily policed and inspected with a handful of security personnel stationed along the path.

Show Me the Money

This is all well and good, but aquaculture investors want to see a profit. Low-cost high-quality fish can feed the poor, but initial costs prohibit investors from seeing profit until high-quality fish are produced at the end of the experiment. If we want scale up to a size where we can farm mass quantities of fish, we're talking about the infrastructure of fish cages and the costs of their constant upkeep and repair, which will drain off significant profits. The deep sea is brutal on fish cages.

The world already gets half its seafood from fish farms that pollute a little and profit a lot. Why rock the boat that's already bringing in money? Between 1970 and 2009, aquaculture production grew at an annual average rate of 8.4 percent and remains among the fastest-growing food production sectors in the world. How does Ricardo's Sea Gardens Project propose to overtake that?

This is another moment that makes Ricardo grin. Aquaculture investors always start from the assumption that the current cost of fish farming is fixed. The problem, he says, is that they don't have experience thinking like "third worlders," who, if they excel at anything, it's getting stuff done on the cheap.

Suppose, Ricardo says, he can cut the costs of producing fish cages 95 percent?

Relishing the long moment of silence that always follows this proposal, Ricardo displays his photos and charts. Right now, estimates for constructing fish cages come to $100 per meter. Ricardo has already designed fishing nets custom-made in Mexico and Peru for his farms. Cost? Just $2 to $5 dollars per cubic meter. These low-tech nets are not only cheaper but also work better than high-tech cages. Rigid expensive cages break easily in rough seas and are expensive to repair. Flexible nets rip rarely in rough seas and are cheap to repair.

"So we can have larger nets, and the larger, the cheaper, because the perimeter goes down in relation to the volume," he explains. As the fish farms get bigger, the cost per meter gets cheaper. While we're on the subject of too-good-to-be-true, Ricardo says the system of nets he's been implementing on the small scale "could be sustainable with almost no maintenance."

Boom. Ricardo just dropped initial costs of fish farming infrastructure to less than 5 percent of common projections, and these will drop to infinitesimal as the project scales up.

Anybody bring a checkbook?

Let's Get It Done

Ricardo, concluding his talk at the Seasteading Conference, confronted his audience. "We are ready to do this. Okay? *We are ready to do this.* We are not talking about things that *could* be done. This is what I humbly offer. I am not offering a high-tech thing. I am offering a cheap thing that has already been tested. This is doable, right now."

But testing each element separately just doesn't cut it anymore. The whole system needs to be run on the spot. "Particularly important," says Ricardo. "The *right combination* of production options must be explored in order to optimize food production both technically and financially in low-income countries for minimum seasteading facilities with a small permanent crew."

Ricardo emphasizes again and again that resources must not be brought in from land—whether soil, water, food, or fertilizers.

"The ocean is self-sustainable. That means we can be self-sustainable too. To the extent that we are successful, this effort will become a paradigm which will allow replication and the expansion of sustainable food production operations at sea."

It's not just the farms and profits that will scale up, but the learning. If Ricardo can demonstrate that his environmentally sustainable farm is also financially sustainable, he thinks he can get money to make one ten times bigger, incorporating all the lessons learned from the first prototype. The knowledge and efficiency will increase with the size and profits. Give him the tools, and Ricardo aims to achieve financial sustainability in twelve to eighteen months. If he can make it work on a farm the size of a football field, it can work on a farm the size of a nation.

What do you want? asks Ricardo. Feed the world? Restore the oceans? Reduce global warming? Make a profit? Fuel civilization? The only way to do any of these is to do all at once, implementing Ricardo's carbon equation. All we need is carbon, nutrients, and photosynthesis, and we can turn around the world. Fortunately for humanity, we have plenty of carbon and nutrient pollution to feed the hungry, and oceans of water to feed and fuel human flourishing.

After hearing Ricardo's message, a "Big Ag" businessman, who happened to be a passionate scuba diver and boater, contacted the Seasteading Institute and volunteered to serve on our advisory board.

"I'm in with both feet," he said.

John Guido is a business engineer who has spent twenty years working with some of the largest food and agricultural companies in the world. When he heard about Ricardo's seaweed solution, he said it changed his life.

"The big *aha* moment happened during the summer of 2014 while listening to a video presentation called 'The Eight Great Moral Imperatives of Seasteading,'" he explains. John found himself consuming research about which particular aspects of seaweed can be broken down and used in particular ingredient markets he already knew. "I wanted to show my colleagues in the food industry how this effort can make them feel valued by a world looking for sustainable solutions. I quickly became an evangelist for restorative blue-green living."

In fact, John conceived a company called BlueGreen Living Inc. As the Seasteading Institute facilitated conversations between John Guido and Ricardo and other hardscrabble seaweed farmers, we were shocked to learn that John had already quit his previous ventures and devoted himself full-time to this effort.

"I had the conversation with my wife," he said.

John admits he has a hard row to hoe selling this to Big Ag industries. Even though Americans consume algae products in their food staples all day, most non-Asians think raw seaweed is weird and slimy. How to transform algae from a secret ingredient into a requested delicacy? The answer came within months of John Guido's signing up to be our seasteading business advisor.

The Bacon of the Sea

In 2014 America discovered it is completely surrounded by an environmentally friendly ocean vegetable that tastes like bacon, has twice the nutritional content of kale, and is 16 percent protein by dry weight. The fast-growing bacon of the sea grows along both the Pacific and Atlantic Coasts and is also common in Ireland, Iceland, and the Atlantic side of Canada.

Scientists with Oregon State University in collaboration with Portland's Food Innovation Center were searching for ways to prepare and market an ultrahealthy algae species called dulse that looks like translucent red lettuce. When they tried smoking it as if it were meat they were astonished to find it tasted like a beloved breakfast staple. Journalist Barb Randall was invited to participate in the taste test with the Food Innovation Center and reported, "The result? Absolutely delicious—meaty and very satisfying," going on to note that "[t]hrough research at Hatfield Marine Center, it is apparent that dulse can be grown anywhere in the world, meaning it can help end world hunger."

Iron Chef America 2011 champ Vitaly Paley began serving the seaweed at all three of his restaurants, proclaiming on Portland television, "My job is to make [my customers] understand that it's not just good for them, but something that they really want to eat. So at first they didn't know they didn't need it, and now they can't live without it."

"We think it's the most productive protein source on Earth," said Chuck Tombs, an instructor in Oregon State University's College of Business, "and that has implications not only for a commercial product, but it can also go as far as helping to feed the world."

When we followed up with Ricardo about this development, he didn't pause to celebrate. "I have more proposals, all of them aquatic. I want to get people from Mexico, Panama, Malawi, Tanzania, and India to join efforts with me. So busy busy busy. But, hey, nobody said that Nobel Prize winning was easy!"

An ailing economy looking for green solutions is already leaning on algae, the powerhouse plant. The small steps to seasteading are becoming strides, and we've barely begun to meet our list of aquapreneurs. Next we'll meet a man who believes he has created "Seasteading 1.0," and his quest to repopulate the oceans with fish has carried him from Australia, to the Cook Islands, to Hawaii, to Mexico.

Chapter 4

FISH

Farms That Swim with Fish

"The Blue Prairies Await!"

Neil Anthony Sims is an Australian marine biologist and serial entrepreneur who specializes in the management of fisheries.

"I used to have this guiding principle that a day wasn't complete unless you'd been in the ocean or on the ocean in some way: swimming, diving, or spear fishing."

Spear fishing?

"Yeah, and surfing. Kona [Hawaii] is a wonderful place to live." Neil's business clothes are flippers and snorkel, and his commute is a step off the side of his boat. "I just have to grit my teeth and bear it as best I can."

Neil talks about fish with a passion that seems unseemly. Of the parrot fish: "The males get big, blue, beautifully painted faces and big trailing fin filaments. The biologist in me gets *goose bumps* when I think about that."

We don't know whether the sea attracts storytellers, or storytellers are attracted to the sea, but we can confirm one stereotype of seamen: they are raconteurs. Neil Sims is what journalists call "a gold mine," effusing a wealth of adventure stories, witticisms, rants, and scientific digressions.

"I trust you've read *Four Fish*?" he asks people with no interest in fish. Not until you check the source do you understand the bemused twinkle in his eye. It turns out we're not the first to discover the inimitable Neil Anthony Sims. He and his previous fish-rearing company, Kona Blue Water Farms, which is based in Kona, Hawaii, and in La Paz, Mexico, are featured in Paul Greenberg's bestseller *Four Fish: The Future of the Last Wild Food*, which, it turns out, is Neil's favorite book to cite.

Sims and Greenberg share the same heartbreak. In his book, Greenberg reports that the worldwide catch of wild fish is "equivalent in weight to the entire human population of China." In one memorable phrase, he says that fish hunters think of wild fish as "a crop, harvested from the sea, that magically grew itself back every year." As a result of this superstition, at least 90 percent of large fish such as marlin, tuna, and swordfish have vanished from the seas in the last half century.

"In the US, ninety-one percent of seafood is imported," says Sims. "We have no idea of how it's grown or where it's caught. We are exporting the ecological footprint of our seafood to other countries."

But what about *managed* fisheries? Aren't those doing better? It turns out top-down management isn't saving us. In 2009 the UN's Third Global Biodiversity Outlook reported that 80 percent of fisheries are exploited or overexploited. Three years later, the Food and Agriculture Organization measured again in 2012 and reported the estimate had risen to 87 percent. There's no time to lose.

If you want to see joy in Neil's face, say *fish*. If you want to see agony, say *overfishing*. The pain in Neil's voice when he talks about overfishing is palpable.

"If you knew what the catches were like a hundred years ago, you would be just aghast at the depredations that we have visited on the oceans. I've seen this up front, and it's horrid. Up to now, a lot of the depredations have just been reckless, wanton disuse of the sea no matter what the cost and pollution—just treating the ocean like a toilet. We have to do something else to feed the world, but we've also got to stop these massive impacts that we're having on the ecosystems out there. It's both a subsistence development imperative and an economic incentive, but it's also an environmental imperative that we start to move toward aquaculture. I wanted to find a way to marry a commercial venture with an environmental imperative, and I wanted to do it right."

Neil got his start as a twenty-three-year-old environmentalist volunteering for the Australian version of the Peace Corps. His ambition? Help build sustainable fisheries in the developing world. After studying marine biology and zoology at James Cook University, Neil travelled to the Cook Islands.

"I walked into their Ministry of Marine Resources office, and somehow I got an audience with the minister himself, and said, essentially,

"I've got a fisheries biology degree, and I speak a smattering of the local language, and I will work for food and scuba fills.' And he said, 'Great! You can be the fisheries research division. Go away and write yourself a job description and get started.' So here I was, twenty-three years old, with fifteen tiny islands covering two million square kilometers, and I was essentially the researcher in charge."

Two million square kilometers is a space the size of India. In a world full of young scientists searching for a research niche, Neil was granted a research continent. Have you guessed that the young Neil bit off more than he could chew? The instinct to think globally that would grant him success in his forties started as a fiasco in his twenties.

Go Fish, Go

As a budding biologist and fish lover, Sims had immersed himself in historical descriptions of fish populations in the early- to mid-twentieth century. His actual visits to these classic ecosystems is a story of Armageddon. Campers have ghost stories. Seamen have extinction stories.

Neil swallows before addressing the issue of his beloved parrot fish. He sailed for two days to reach the remote Palmerston Atoll. "By the time we got there, the stocks were pretty much gone. We talked to an old man who said that so many parrot fresh used to be grazing with their heads down in the reef, you could look out over the lagoon and see the tails of the parrot fish waving. The fishery had collapsed in less than a year. It was over."

Sims's early career became a tragic story of racing from locale to locale to see if he could help save a stock, only to find that it had already disappeared. Neil learned the hard way that when you're managing a public resource, you can't pass rules and ask everybody to agree. The temptation to take one more fish from the common pool is too great for fishermen who rely on it for survival, which compels every competitor to scramble to cheat before everybody else does.

"To go and try and manage commercial fisheries under that sort of pressure where people have no other real source of income, then all of a sudden you've opened the lagoon to, say, a trochus [a sea snail] fishery. So you set an island-wide quota, and you set up size limits, and you set aside a reserve area, and it's all ignored. You open up the lagoon, and it's just mayhem. People will go and plunder as much as they can. It's a natural human reaction to the common property resource. As soon as you put a dollar value on a shared resource, all of a sudden all hell breaks loose, and Garrett Hardin's "The Tragedy of the Commons" comes charging to the fore."

He asks if we've read the classic 1968 essay by the famous ecologist elucidating the economic reasons why people care for their private property but ravage public property. "Everybody should read it!" he says. For those who don't get the economic principle, Neil tells a story that, in retrospect, represents for him his breaking point.

Feeding Frenzy

"It was a day or two after the end of the trochus season had been closed, it was toward sunset, and I'm bumbling along the beach in the remote area of an island. I had the local fisheries officer with me in tow, and we came upon this old man with his canoe pulled up on the beach, and inside his canoe there was a bunch of live trochus. I got livid at him, because all the frustration that had built up, and I started to berate him. 'We're going to have to confiscate these trochus! You knew that the season was closed two days ago!' We started putting these trochus into a bag to take them back to the reef. He starts crying like a child. He was like eighty years old, with about three teeth left in his mouth. 'That's my Christmas money!' And that got me even more riled up, because he's appealing to emotion rather than reason. I said, 'It doesn't matter! You should have gone out when the season was open! Why can't you just stick by the rules? You've got to have rules to for the benefit of everybody!' And then he starts in on me with this really accusatory tone. 'Why you close the season? Why you stop it?' He points out at the reef and shouts, 'There's still some left!'"

Sims hangs his head in despair at the memory. "The fact that that old man there, at his age, when he'd seen over how many years the cycle of boom and bust for this trochus fishery, and he understood far better than I ever could the limitations of living on a small island, and *he* didn't get it? He *still* didn't get it? The fact that if you left some trochus out there, there'd be something for next year? What hope is there? And so that, combined with a number of other experiences, led me to the growing recognition." His blue eyes seize upon whoever will listen. "We have to start moving from hunting and gathering in the ocean toward fish farming, because that's the only way we're going to be able to feed the world sustainably."

The way of hunter-gatherers was to hunt for wild animals and gather wild plants. They could extract from the environment only what the wilderness made available to them. As a result, vast tracts of land could support only a small number of people. It was not until agriculture was developed that food yields increased ten-thousand-fold, and children stopped dying as fast as they were born. Only with agriculture could civilization begin, and wealth beyond mere subsistence could be imagined.

With regard to the oceans, we are still hunters and gatherers. The wild ocean is treated as a giant commons, where each fisher-gatherer is incentivized to get as much out as he can. What abundance could be unleashed if fisher-farmers developed floating fish farms? The economic incentive to cultivate and care for the surrounding ocean would be overpowering. The profit motive and the stewardship motive would align.

Neil says that people have to stop romanticizing the practice of fish hunting. The story of human migration is a story of extermination. "We can't rely on hunting wild stocks anymore. We proved that with mastodons. We proved it with bison. We proved it with deer and ducks. There was commercial hunting of ducks on the Chesapeake Bay up until the 1920s, and now if you went out and you suggested that you wanted to go commercial duck hunting? You'd be tarred and feathered. Commercial deer hunting? No. And yet people used to be professional hunters. It was a noble employment. That's what they did for a living. We can't keep doing that in ocean any more than we can keep doing it on land."

To young Neil Sims, humanity was hell-bent on exterminating the fish populations to which Neil had devoted his life, and that island people needed to live. The economic imperative and the environmental imperative were at odds, destroying both. Young Sims realized that humanity had to change the entire incentive structure of fishing.

But even if we stopped the extermination of all fish tomorrow, it would be too late. The seas aren't just empty. They are sick. Human activity is turning our oceans to acid.

"The ocean acidification is being driven by the added CO_2 in the atmosphere," Neil explains, "which is trying to find equilibrium with the CO_2 in the oceans. If we increase a little CO_2 in the atmosphere, that pushes CO_2 into the ocean surface water. And that then increases its acidity."

This trend has increased drastically in the twenty-first century. A 2016 study funded by the National Science Foundation showed that the absorption of man-made CO_2 in the North Atlantic doubled in the last decade. To Neil, increasing acidity is the greatest threat to ocean populations, and thus the greatest threat to world food supplies.

"If you're going to mess with the pH of the ocean, we're going to make it impossible for shellfish to deposit calcium shells." Corals and mollusks require a certain pH level in the surrounding water to build their calcium carbonate-based shells and exoskeletons. "How does an oyster grow when it can't build a calcium shell? How does a lobster or a crab grow? What about all the microscopic life in the oceans that use calcareous shells as a structure? Messing with the ocean's pH is far more immediate a crisis than global warming. It's incontrovertible. And its impacts are going to be immense. It's the three Is . . ."

"Immediate, Incontrovertible, and Immense"

Neil loves acronyms. He says the only way to confront the three Is while simultaneously creating the four Fs—"food, feed, fuel, and fertilizer"— is to move beyond the four types of fish that are commonly cultured, which Sims calls the four Ms: "mahimahi, milkfish, mullet, and moi."

But these fish have been shown to be the most profitable! Why do we have to stop farming them?

"We need to bring together the environmental motive, the humanitarian motive, and the profit motive, so they are not at odds with each other, but aligned with each other," says Neil. "It's an economic incentive plus an ecological imperative." Only by culturing a very unlikely fish can you feed the world while reducing the amount of carbonic acid in the ocean.

Wait, *increasing* our fish consumption while *reducing* carbonic acid in the ocean? How?

Neil echoes Ricardo Radulovich: "So the only way to sustainably take carbon out of the ocean that I can conceive of—and that anybody else can conceive of—is photosynthesis. That's going to bind up that CO_2 into glucose and into more complex carbohydrates. The *only clear path* that I can see going forward that's going to mitigate the impacts of ocean acidification is we have to culture more plants in the ocean."

Sims says this the morning before he meets Ricardo Radulovich for the first time at a Seasteading Conference. That so many environmentalist fish farmers are insisting on algae cultivation on a mass scale hints something is burgeoning in the zeitgeist and is moving people toward solutions. Patri and Joe were privileged to be solicited by many of these people who felt they were laboring alone just before they learned they were part of a seasteading community made up of folks who all had the same insight.

"We're going to have to scale up macroalgae culture in a huge way if we're going to have a significant mitigating effect on ocean acidification," says Neil. "What's the alternative? The alternative is mass extinction throughout the oceans, and massive economic disruption as ecosystems are crushed, and real challenges to our food security."

Aquaculture refers to all aquatic farming in both seawater and freshwater. Mariculture is a specialized wing of aquaculture that refers specifically to farming in seawater.

Neil Sims became the founding president of the Ocean Stewards Institute, a mariculture trade association that advocates for building food business on the high seas by *restoring* marine resources and habitats. That's right, "sustainability" is not ambitious enough for Neil. Who wants to "sustain" the depleted and acidic oceans we have now? The imperative is to feed the world by restoring the oceans to the rich abundance that existed in 1900.

"If it's not profitable, it's not sustainable."

Thus began Neil's mission to repopulate the oceans with fish.

"This Is Wrong"

It began, as so many marine biologist epiphanies do, with poop.

"Back in the early eighties, my partner Dr. Dale Sarver had been working for a salmon farm in Ireland. Dale is a superb naturalist, a great fisheries biologist, but he is also a very passionate naturalist. He's been a card-carrying member of the Sierra Club for years. He tells this story of how he dove near a salmon farm that was just nailed together two-by-fours. Yet it was tucked right up against the shoreline in a protected bay. He swam underneath it, and he said the muck underneath was so deep, he could stick his arm down into it, and he couldn't touch the bottom. And he came up to the surface, and he said, 'This is wrong. We can't keep doing this.'"

Soon after Dale dove to confront the problem, Neil dove and saw the solution. He wanted to see if oysters placed outside a fish pen could clean the particulates being released and be used to grow pearls. This test was similar to what Ricardo was doing 4,955 miles away in Costa Rica with his shrimp nets, and similar to what aquaculture scientist Thierry Chopin was doing 5,222 miles away in New Brunswick, Canada, with seaweed, though none of them knew about one another yet.

Off the coast of Honolulu, Neil descended into the deep and nearly gasped in his entire scuba tank when he beheld a UFO-shaped contraption made of galvanized steel and Kevlar nets. Perfectly still, it served as a permeable fish tank that was impervious to the passionate sea. It remained eerily placid in the most powerful waves. Somebody unzipped the opening, and Neil was allowed to enter and be engulfed in a thick, darting school of fish.

"It was like swimming inside a cathedral," he says. It was called a SeaStation, and it is designed specially for aquaculture, not on the coasts but on the open ocean.

"I came back to Kona that night and got on the phone to my partner and said, 'Dale, I've seen the future of aquaculture, and we've got to be part of this. This is huge.'"

Poop! Pollution! Parasites! Pesticides! PCBs! Oh My!

Often a predator fish sits at the top of a long, inefficient food chain that goes like this: CO_2 and nutrients are eaten by algae, which are eaten by krill, which are eaten by a filter-feeding fish like a sardine, which is eaten by a bigger fish, and then a bigger fish (you've seen the cartoons), and then eventually an adult top predator fish like albacore tuna. Each of these devourings is called a "trophic step." At each trophic step, 90 percent of the nutritive value is lost. Even worse, toxins become more concentrated. This is why nutritionists instruct pregnant women to eat fish low in trophic levels such as sardines and anchovies and to stay away from high-trophic-level fish like albacore tuna, king mackerel, and swordfish. From both health and environmental perspectives, the closer your fish is to algae on the trophic ladder, the better.

The only problem is, top predator fish such as yellowtail taste really good, sardines are less thrilling, and anchovies are even less popular. Hundreds of millions of people around the world pay a premium for sashimi, and the demand won't go away. In 1980 10 percent of the world's seafood came from fish farms. Today it's more than half, and the rate of growth is increasing.

To supply this growing demand, we run old-style coastal fish farms the way we run industrial agriculture on land: by releasing more animal waste into the local environment than it can absorb, much of which ends up draining to the seas. The environmental community has responded with a massive backlash. The story it tells the public goes something like this: Polluting the oceans is bad. Salmon farmers are doing much of the polluting. Ergo, all fish farming is bad.

What Neil Sims has accomplished requires us to abandon all previous beliefs about fish farming and see the world anew.

The Redemption of a Rejected Fish

Over decades of trial and error, fish farmers have whittled down the number of species to those that prosper in traditional coastal fish farms, which Sims calls the four Ms: milkfish, mullet, moi, and mahimahi. Over decades of research, scientists have warned us against eating unhealthy wild fish at the top of the food chain. Sims realized that if he wanted to pioneer open-ocean mariculture and compete with traditional fish farms, he had to rethink all traditional assumptions about what makes the best fish. No fish would be off the table, so to speak.

"We cultured seven or eight different species in the hatchery," he recalls. "Some of them were species that have never been cultured in captivity in the past. Kampachi was just hands down the species. It was one that sort of stood up in the tank and waved. 'Culture me! Culture me! Look at me! I'll spawn regularly. I'm relatively easy to rear in the hatchery. There's no cannibalism here. We maintain a good feed-conversion ratio, and we taste great.'" He switches to the voice of a salivating fish connoisseur. "They really do. I mean, it's a sashimi-grade fish."

Farming wild kampachi (called kahala) is a provocative move. Most fisherman who catch wild kahala throw it back. Wild-caught fish typically have internal parasites, and many carry ciguatera, a natural toxin produced from a weed species of algae that grows on the reef. Kahala is a top predator fish. Once considered a delicacy, it's now considered poison.

But with the method that Sims and his team have pioneered, these former pariah fish eat directly from pellets of fish meal made from anchovies. Neil Sims calls it a "one-step trophic transfer." Algae are eaten by anchovies, which are in turn are eaten by kahala.

The improvements to the nutritive value of the stocks were dramatic. Kahala have a body fat percentage of 4 percent. Random samples taken of Sims's yellowtail kampachi revealed a fat content of 33 percent, high in heart-healthy omega-3s.

"Kona kampachi has no internal parasites, zero chance of ciguatera, and no detectable mercury."

Sims calls his fish kampachi, but it's genetically the same species as kahala, which is native to the waters of Hawaii. New names have taken hold because farmed kahala looks, behaves, and tastes so radically different from wild kahala. By finding a way to feed a top-predator fish directly from the bottom of the food chain, Sims has produced a toxin-free, parasite-free, happy, profitable fish that satisfies the demand for premium quality.

But what about when the Kampachi become adult? Every conservationist knows that raising carnivorous fish requires them to be fed a wasteful amount of wild fish.

"Carnivorous shmarnivorous," says Sims. "It's not that it's carnivorous that's important. It's the fact that it's carbohydrate-intolerant."

Vegetarian Predator Fish

In the Pixar animated movie *Finding Nemo*, ocean predators struggling to overcome their addiction to killing recite the "Fish-Friendly Shark Pledge." It goes like this:

"I am a nice shark. Not a mindless killing machine. If I want to change this image, I must first change myself. Fish are friends. Not food."

When Bruce the Shark (who has the same accent as Sims) rediscovers his taste for blood, his friends stage an intervention.

Neil has staged this intervention for literally millions of killing fish.

"For most marine fish, their dietary system is set up to digest protein and oils, but not carbohydrates," says Sims. "As long as you give them a diet that's high in proteins and oils, they're fine. It just so happens that the cheapest source of proteins and oils, *in the past*, has been fish meal and fish oil. As there is increasing competition for these resources, the price has gone up, so now one of the challenges that Kampachi Farms is trying to address with aquaculture is to make the transition where we can be using agricultural proteins and oils for these high-end species."

The result? Vegetarian carnivorous fish.

"For the past six years, we've been working very closely with the US soybean industry and gradually whittling away at dietary improvements, using soy oils and soy proteins. So far they've gotten down to just twelve percent fish meal in the diet, with forty percent soy protein concentrate—just tofu. They are very keen on seeing an expansion of aquaculture globally because they see that as a future market for their soybeans. And they've been funding a lot of this work.

"I can't say enough good things about the soybean industry. They're just the true visionaries. They 'get' all of this. Some of these farmers from the Midwest have probably hardly ever seen the ocean, but they understand that we're trying to *farm*. They also understand the problems that we encounter; the political public policy issues. They're tremendous partners in this quest."

Sims says the time to start restorative fish farms is now. The global demand for seafood is growing unstoppably.

"People want to eat animal protein," says Sims, "and you can't mandate vegetarianism, so, with a planet of nine billion by 2050, either we're going to find alternative sources of sustainable animal protein or we are going to start increasing pressure on the wild stocks of the ocean. If we want to grow agriculture in the most efficient way possible, we can't do it on the backs of Peruvian anchovies and sardines. We have to find alternative *scalable* sources of proteins and oils. The best source of agricultural protein out there that I know of is soy because nothing else comes close to it in terms of the percentage of protein in the bean. It's why soy is fed to pigs, chickens, and cows that land-animal eaters continue to eat. Instead of feeding that soy to pigs or chickens or cows, we should feed it to fish. It has far lower environmental impact than any land-based protein production system."

Sarah Simpson, reporting about Neil Sims's company for *Scientific American* in 2011, wrote: "Aquaculture is the fastest-growing food production sector in the world, expanding at 7.5 percent a year since 1994. At that pace, fish meal and fish oil resources could be exhausted by

2040. An overarching goal, therefore, is to eliminate wild fish products from feed altogether, within a decade or so, asserts marine ecologist Carlos M. Duarte, who directs the International Laboratory for Global Change at the Spanish Council for Scientific Research, in Majorca."

Sims set out to achieve this goal, too.

The Golden Ratio, the Holy Grail

Nature, it turns out, is far less efficient at producing a predator fish than the least efficient farms are. Sims estimates that in a wild ecosystem, it takes 60 pounds of wild baitfish to produce one pound of wild-caught salmon at the top of the food chain. When Patri first heard about Neil's work in 2008, Sims was being celebrated by conservationists for lowering the ratio of feed-to-farmed fish by two-thirds. It seemed amazing that it took only three pounds of anchovy to produce each pound of kampachi. By 2010, the *New York Times* was reporting that it typically took just 1.6 to 2 pounds of fish to produce a pound of kampachi.

We were especially intrigued by Sims's bold claim that he was determined to bring this ratio down to 1:1. This is the "golden ratio" that even the most optimistic environmentalists declared unattainable: to actually produce high-quality fish protein with the same amount of low-quality fish protein. Sims put his reputation on the line by announcing this impossibility was feasible in the near future.

By the time we got to Sims, he had already surpassed the ratio. This shocked us. Neil's Velella Mariculture Research Project was *increasing* the amount of fish mass in the ocean.

"Kampachi are net marine protein producers," he told us. "If you put in a pound of Peruvian anchovies, you get *more* than a pound of kampachi out the other end. Before, achieving the one-to-one ratio was the Holy Grail. Now we've done that. And we can do that at an industrial scale." We thought it was time to break out the champagne, but Sims didn't even break his stride before he was once again declaring the impossible: "Now the goal for research is to create a fish diet that contains *no* fish meal or fish oil."

We scoffed. Soybeans are deficient in methionine and cystine, two essential amino acids that, out on ocean farms, you must get from fish meal.

Two years later, the breakthrough came. A company called TwoXSea determined the forty nutrients fish need to stay healthy, partnered with fish nutritionist Rick Barrows at the US Department of Agriculture (USDA), and invented an entirely plant-based fish pellet composed of algae, soy, pistachio meal, flax meal, corn, yeast, and other ingredients. Now eight species of carnivorous fish have been proven to get enough nutrients from plants. This is why we define *expert* as anybody who can explain in technical detail why something is impossible six months before it works. Next challenge? The TwoXSea vegetarian fish food is still twice the price of anchovy-based fish meal. Meanwhile, the cost of soy and corn has been decreasing. When vegetarian fish meal becomes cost competitive, all bets are off.

Fish to Feed the Multitudes

Sims declares himself pescetarian, a person who does not eat flesh unless it is fish, but he is really a fish connoisseur. The only subject that can distract him from talking about fish as biology is talking about fish as cuisine. He boldly put his claims of quality to the test. Oregon State University performed an extensive taste test on the formerly pariah fish newly renamed Kona kampachi, setting up a food quality lab with a trained tasting panel.

"These people get paid to eat sushi!" Sims salivates jealously. "It's their job! And they couldn't tell the difference between the soy-fed kampachi and the fish-meal-fed kampachi."

The first to swear by the creamy texture and health benefits of Kona kampachi was famous Hawaiian sushi guru Alan Wong. The wild fish that was once considered too toxic to eat is now a farm-raised delicacy among sushi chefs, as long as you get the kampachi from the farm started by Neil Sims and Dale Sarver, which has since been bought by Blue Ocean Mariculture.

Neil had his fish. Now he needed a sustainable deep-sea infrastructure to farm them. For that he would need a breakthrough.

Neil spent many years staring at the oceans off West Hawaii, stroking his beard while puzzling on how to grow sustainable fish. Parasites are a negligible problem with wild fish because they keep moving but are a huge problem with farmed fish because they hold still. Protecting farmed fish from infestation requires spraying chemicals. Keeping them caged in one spot causes poop to pile up. Fish, to be healthy, gotta swim. But to be farmed, they have to be contained. Somehow Sims had to arrange for moving fish farms. But he didn't want to use any gas or oil with his system. Fish may be healthy for us, but fishing is often not healthy for the planet. Diesel is the greatest source of greenhouse gases for the fishing industry and its single largest expense.

"If the goal is to pull CO_2 out of the oceans, you can't add more CO_2 to the atmosphere by burning fossil fuels, especially if the idea is to scale up to colossal levels," he points out. "So everything scaled up has to be positive, economically, environmentally, and a net gain on the protein the ocean produces."

How do you farm fish that swim for miles without using motors? Staring into the eddies off the Hawaiian islands, Neil had his revelation.

"I've worked right there at Keahole Point, the western tip of the Big Island, for twenty years, and have watched the currents there, and the patterns. As the ocean currents flow from east to west, past the Big Island, it's like a rock in a stream, and you get little whirlpools at the back of the rock as the water goes rushing past it."

Imagine a leaf swirling in circles in an eddy behind a rock. Downstream of the Big Island of Hawaii, the eddies remain fairly consistent within a sixty- to ninety-mile diameter.

"If you could have an unanchored pen entrained in those eddies, you wouldn't have to go and chase it all over the ocean. You would stay in the eddy and go around in a circle. If you need to use sail power to jump out of one eddy into another when you need to, that's great—the wind is free. I was thinking about this possibility, and I said to our research team, 'Okay, we have to start work on a drifter cage concept.'"

Turns out research teams like to gossip. Neil's contagious idea spread faster than he could imagine.

Swords into Sea Farms

"And about a week later, I got this phone call from this guy." Neil calls forth his talent for voice mimicry. "'I'm Jason, and I work for Lockheed Martin, and we're really interested in the idea of drifter cages.' I'm like, 'Yeah, yeah, who put you up to this?' 'Ahem. I'm sorry, my name is Jason, I work for Lockheed Martin. We'd like to talk to you about the potential for ocean and drifter cages.' I'm like, 'Come on! Come on! It's a joke.' I figured somebody was pulling my leg! Lockheed Martin called me up! Please! And he's like, 'Sir, this is a genuine inquiry. We have satellite technology and remote-command control technology that we think would be useful to your venture, and it would be exciting to test the true benefits of these technologies. We're looking for partners.'"

But why would a globe-spanning aerospace and defense contractor volunteer to fund his research into floating fish farms?

"Lockheed Martin sees it as turning swords into ploughshares," Neil says, smiling. "They're out there looking for where the next big industry's going to be. They've identified open-ocean aquaculture. They understand that as this industry grows offshore, it's going to rely on remote command-and-control technologies that are satellite mediated. It's using US military technology to help feed the world! And so, in partnership with Lockheed Martin, we got some funding from the National Science Foundation, and we went and sent some drogue buoys out there in the back of the Big Island, and they go round and round the eddies like a horse around the race track." (A drogue buoy has a trailing net to provide stability in waves.)

Sims named the project after an enchanting blue creature called the Velella, a hydrozoan that looks like a small jellyfish but skims over the sea's surface by means of a sail. The curious organism is actually a colony of polymorphous individuals cooperating to form a sailboat the size of a quarter. The implication of sails, floating, diversity, and cooperation made the name irresistible, even if land folk didn't know what it is and can't spell it. With the Velella Research Project, Sims had the infrastructure and circular eddies to run his free-swimming farmed fish. Fish farms that were once dirty cages bolted to coasts had become a constellation of floating SeaStations orbiting among circular eddies.

Better Than Wild

Sims and his Velella Mariculture Research Project team commissioned Ocean Farm Technologies to build 132-cubic-meter AquaPods: futuristic underwater fish pens with a geodesic design that would make Buckminster Fuller proud. These spherical screen cages float just below the surface and allow a constant inflow of fresh ocean water without flushing out the fish. Occasionally towed by a schooner, the fish school through the ocean while contained within a moving bubble that suggests a transparent soccer ball. Neil, in his diving gear, can open the cage door, swim inside, and be mobbed by fish in what he described to Paul Greenberg as "the rock star effect." After inspecting his fish, Sims can exit the pen, closing the screen door behind him with the fish safe inside. When it's time to harvest the fish, the pen is raised to a boat and fish sucked up through the top. The AquaPod can then be stocked with new fingerlings, released, and allowed to drift freely in a circular eddy, tracked by a GPS so that it can be located later. In this manner, the fish school in an environment as similar as you can get to the wild, but with first-class dining. Free-floating Velella pens drifted in the currents of the ocean three to seventy-five miles offshore, in waters up to two miles deep. The AquaPods are simple to assemble and scalable for different sizes. The smaller AquaPods can be assembled by two people and rolled by hand in and out of the ocean. No antibiotics, hormones, or pesticides are used on the yellowtail kampachi, and the parasites are controlled.

The standard mortality rate for a fish farm usually hovers around 15 percent, and it's a lot worse in the wild. With the Velella beta test, it was less than 2 percent.

"The biological performance of this fish in the Velella beta test was phenomenal," Sims told us. "Something magical happened out there. The growth rate was about twice as fast as we expected. The feed conversion rate—how quickly it converted that feed to sashimi—was great. And the survival of the fish was ninety-eight percent. And we're also able to control the skin flukes, an ectoparasite that gets on this fish a little like fleas on a dog. But we were able to control them without any use of therapeutants [a type of medicine] in the Velella project. The potential that portends for open-ocean aquaculture is tremendously exciting."

Okay, that's an elegant solution to several problems with traditional industrial fish farms. What about all the poop?

No problem at all. Waste concentrated on the coasts can be destructive. Waste distributed in the deep is healthy. In fact, fish poop to the deep ocean is like bird poop in the desert. Famous deep-sea explorer Robert Ballard, discoverer of the *Titanic* wreckage, is a Sims evangelist.

"Sims farms his fish in twelve thousand feet of water, so they're way out to sea, so you don't even see them, and when they poop, it's like a godsend." Ballard spends so much time on the sea floor, he tends to speak from the perspective of fish, like an underwater Lorax. "The deep sea is so nutrient deficient, anything that comes down there is greatly appreciated. Plus, it's carbon sequestration. What they don't turn into fish protein, they send to the bottom of the ocean, so the carbon is out of the ecosystem."

Intrigued, the National Oceanic and Atmospheric Administration (NOAA) conducted an environmental assessment (EA) of the Velella Project. The environmental impact on the ocean was predicted to be zero. The water quality upstream and downstream of the pens was identical on the moored fish pens closer to shore. In a show of confidence and commitment to complete transparency, Neil posted third-party water quality updates on his company website.

Sims knew the Velella Research Project would pass the NOAA test with flying colors, recalling his earlier success with stationary cages with his former company, Kona Blue. "Directly inshore from our cages, there's a pristine reef area that is frequented by tourist divers, and there's a garden eel cove, a dolphin resting site there, and a manta ray diving site. If there was going to be any impact on the coral reef from the fish farm, you would hear about it in a heartbeat. And there's not a peep! Most of the visitors loved to come and dive on the farm side." He makes direct eye contact, to make sure we get it. "There was *no measurable impact* from *a million pounds a year* of that farm site. The Kampachi Farms North of Keahole Point has been in production now for almost ten years."

His claim checks out. In 2008 Kona Blue Water Farms, featured in Paul Greenberg's book *Four Fish*, produced over five hundred tons of sashimi-grade kampachi from the submersible pens. That's over a million pounds, worth about $6 million US a year. Blue Ocean Mariculture has since taken over that facility, which was initiated in 2005, and still no ecological impact has been measured.

"I mean, really, from a humanitarian, empathetic perspective, I want to eat fish that have actually swum in the ocean, that have tasted raw salt water, rather than something that's just kept in a feedlot on a land-based system. We're trying to create an open range where the fish participate in the natural ecosystem out there."

Name your aquaculture complaint: poop, pollution, parasites, pesticides, toxins. "What the Velella Project did was take every one of those objections and knock them back," said Robert Ballard. "It was just beautiful."

The Velella Mariculture Project was named one of *Time* magazine's "25 Best Inventions of 2012."

Neil announced to the website SeafoodSource.com: "The success of the Velella Research Project demonstrates that we can grow fish in the open ocean with no negative impact on pristine ocean ecosystems. We must now apply ourselves to responsibly scale up this industry, to meet the growing global demand for high-quality seafood."

"Fish Without Footprint"

When challenged about the sheer scale of his ambition, Sims launches into a disquisition straight out of the Radulovich handbook.

"If you can grow seaweed on the deep ocean that sucks carbon dioxide out of the water through photosynthesis, and you can use that macroalgae for food, you can use macroalgae to feed herbivorous fish or land animals." He winces. "If you *have* to eat land animals. I don't know why you'd want to eat *land animals.*"

Every time Neil says "land animals," he either shudders, winces, or pretends to spit with disgust.

"Or you can use that macroalgae for fuel. Part of the challenge is breaking down macroalgae so we can reduce it to the methane and the carbon dioxide, but that's just a biotech challenge. We're getting pretty good at biotech stuff. They're just complex organic molecules. Nature finds ways to break these things down. It's just a matter for us to find the right molecular pathways to do this efficiently and get the products we want."

Craig Venter, the first private entrepreneur to sequence the human genome and creator of the first synthetic organism, has already sailed across the planet collecting thousands of new species of algae. According to Venter, his team discovered a staggering 2 million new genes and thousands of new protein families. Venter plans to genetically customize organisms that will produce plastic, metal, food, and fuel from nothing but seawater, sunlight, CO_2, and pollution.

The mind boggles at the potential. Blue-green alga is such an ancient life-form, it doesn't have a nucleus. Its genetic material simply floats freely in its body. Algas with no nuclei are easily genetically engineered. As biology becomes information technology, humans can reprogram any of thousands of species to produce new strains that can produce virtually any biological compound, in any quantity desired.

Sims's excitement intensifies as he counts off on his fingers: "If you can grow algae in oceans, sucking CO_2 out of the oceans, getting food feed and fuels out of it, and the by-products are nutrients that flow back into the algae system . . ."

Sims pauses for an instant when the scale of the possibilities leaves him at a rare loss for words. Every ocean enthusiast who discovered this solution and contacted the Seasteading Institute has invented a different name for it. DeltaSync calls it "cyclicity." Biochemical engineer Patrick Takahashi calls it "closing the growth cycle." Baoguang Zhai and

Charlie Deist, who ran Project OASIS (Ocean Aquaculture for Seastead Integrated Solutions), call it a "closed-loop system." They mean a global bonanza of food, feed, and fuel built from carbon and nutrient pollution already extant in the oceans and atmosphere.

Don't worry, Neil hasn't run out of acronyms: there's IMAGEn— Integrated Marine Agronomy and Geo-Engineering—his plan to reduce ocean acidification, mitigate global warming, and meet humanity's energy and food requirements, all at a profit, by establishing a symbiotic relationship with algae.

"If we have new data, we need a new acronym," he says with a grin. According to Sims, the global demand for sashimi will drive ocean pollution, or ocean purification.

Pollute or Purify?

The Keeling Curve is a famous graph that has measured the increasing concentrations of CO_2 in the atmosphere for over fifty years. Noting that every spring and summer plant growth in the Northern Hemisphere causes a dip in the Keeling Curve, Sims hopes that "by stimulating macroalgal growth in tropical oceans, this inflection could be extrapolated continuously downward, season after season, year after year."

Sims helped create the Blue-on-Blue Initiative, a plan to reverse ocean acidification and global warming. Writing in his 2011 paper "The Blue-on-Blue Initiative":

The conventional wisdom that the open ocean is a virtual desert is indeed correct, and in the Blue-on-Blue Initiative, we will be "greening the blue desert." The primary changes in the ecosystem will be increasing biomass, productivity, and biodiversity . . . Of these values, the latter two are considered by "Deep Ecology" adherents to be the critical criteria for evaluating human impacts on ecosystems: if productivity and biodiversity increase, then deep ecologists would generally accept the changes as beneficial.

Many have suggested that excess carbon dioxide can be absorbed from the atmosphere by planting trees. Romantic as this notion is, it's mistaken. Land plants die and decay, releasing their carbon back into the atmosphere. The amount of carbon you can draw out of the environment with algae, however, is virtually unlimited.

"Anything you don't use for food, feed, or fuel can be dropped to the deep-ocean floor," says Sims. "Just take it out of the biosphere." To take trees out of the carbon cycle, you have to bury them deep beneath the Earth's crust. On the ocean, you just have to drop organic matter to the ocean floor. "I like quoting Gandalf when he's fighting the Balrog: 'Get back into the darkness from whence ye came!'"

A read through the *Lord of the Rings* trilogy reveals that Gandalf didn't say this, but when Sims cops his Gandalf pose, you know he *should* have said it.

"The *abyssal plain* is a technical term that we like to use for the abyss. Where's that James Cameron [director of *Titanic* and *The Abyss*] when you need him? He should be helping us in this work. He designed a machine so he could dive to the bottom of the Marianas Trench [the deepest known recess of the ocean]. That's *playing* in the ocean! Stop *playing* in the ocean! We have *work* to do! This is a *scalable* system that, as we like to say, would be fish without footprints. So this is the question I challenge you with:

"Is This Seasteading 1.0?"

Every seasteader is eventually confronted with this question: "Are you crazy?" In fact, they're asked this most often by their fellow seasteaders. To demonstrate he's not crazy, Neil Sims performs a spontaneous play.

"Go back ten thousand years to the Fertile Crescent, where some bloke drags a wild gazelle into the middle of the village on a rope, and he says, 'Hey, hey, hey! Come here! I caught this thing! And I've got an idea. Instead of killing it, why don't we keep it? We can get the milk from it, and maybe it will have baby gazelles, and then we'll be able to grow them. I'm tired of chasing these bloody things all over the hills. It takes a lot of work. Sometimes they're nowhere to be found. Let's grow them here!'

"You can imagine the *furor* that ensued! 'You're out of your mind! What do you mean grow them? We've always been hunters! We're going to have to look at that thing in the middle of the village! What are you going to feed it? And oh, the poo! Think of the stench! And the noise, it's going to be horrendous.' And he would have just been *roundly* castigated and shunned.

"At some stage, one of those guys persevered. And I hope it wasn't with gazelles, because there's got to be this winnowing process of figuring out what species to grow, and gazelles obviously weren't going to be it. Another guy went and got a goat, and said, 'Maybe I'll try it with this.' Another guy went and got sheep. Another guy got a cow. And gradually we figured it out. Jared Diamond does a great job in *Guns, Germs, and Steel: The Fates of Human Societies* talking about the winnowing process that we went through on land to identify the nine mammals and four birds that we've domesticated from all the available land animals in the wild. The same winnowing process has to go on in the ocean. We've got to figure this out. We've got to find the right fish and algae to feed nine billion while restoring the oceans.

"And gazelles weren't going to be it, because they jump over fences, and they've got spiky horns, and they tend to stampede, and there's not a very good meat yield. Sheep and goats are it. And out in the ocean, mahimahi probably aren't going to be it, because they are like the gazelles of the ocean, jumping over the fence, constantly trying to jump out of the tank. But kampachi are like the placid sheep of the ocean, because they were perfectly happy in a school. They wouldn't beat on each other. They would just swim at a moderate pace. They are quite happy to sit in the tank and hold their position against the current. So they are a fish *designed* for domestication. This is the winnowing process that we've got to go through trying to find which fish, which seaweeds, which shellfish are most appropriate, and then start selectively breeding them.

"What really drove the westward expansion in America wasn't people's desire for freedom. It was people's desire to farm. The towns grew up on the prairies to service the farms. The open-ocean mariculture equation is incontrovertible, and it contains incentives that will only grow with time as we get the technology to support it. And it will scale, and scale, and scale." He describes Kampachi Farms as "an incremental advancement, but if we're wanting to really make some great leaps forward here, then we need people with the vision of the Seasteading Institute."

When asked what his fondest wish is, Neil doesn't even pause to consider.

"I want people to come to the realization that responsible cultured seafood is *far and away* an environmentally preferable way to go, and it's probably the best source of animal protein on the planet." Neil stares off into the sky, and his voice become dreamy: "So when they sit down at a restaurant, and they see salmon on the menu, and they ask the waiter, 'Is this salmon farmed or wild?' the waiter says proudly, 'It's farmed, sir.' And the customer is overjoyed."

Neil sighs beatifically. After a moment relishing his fantasy, he comes back to earth with the sneer he reserves for domesticated land animals.

"You go to a restaurant, and you order *beef*," he spits, "you don't ask *them* if it's farmed or wild."

A Tsunami Has Started

Neil's tide has turned too. In 2014 *National Geographic* featured a marvelous photo-essay about sea farming, announcing, "Aquaculture has expanded about 14-fold since 1980 . . . exceeding beef production clearly for the first time . . . with no soil or fresh water and no fertilizer except runoff from the land. Oceans cover 71 percent of Earth yet provide less than 2 percent of our food—for now."

National Geographic refered to this global phenomenon with a phrase familiar to many seasteaders: "the blue revolution."

Something is happening in the zeitgeist. Ricardo Radulovich with his Sea Gardens Project, Patrick Takahashi with his OTEC initiatives, and DeltaSync with its floating ecofarms, each independently coined the term *blue revolution* years ago. We know, because we talked to each of them before any of them had heard of one another.

Significant stakeholders believe that Sims's plan will work, including NOAA, the National Science Foundation, Lockheed-Martin, the International Copper Association, Ocean Farm Technologies, the Illinois Soybean Association, and the Mexican government, the latter of which recognizes that the future of food is in aquaculture, and it wants to grab market share and secure jobs for Mexican citizens. The commercial production arm of Sims's company Kampachi Farms has relocated to Bahia de La Paz in the Sea of Cortez, a spot seemingly designed by Neptune to test the Velella method on a larger scale. The partially enclosed bay features a giant circular oscillating current.

"In the US, the regulatory framework is highly restrictive to the point of being dysfunctional," Neil told writer Neil Ramsden of the Undercurrent News, a seafood business news site. "You cannot get an aquaculture permit for commercial aquaculture in US federal waters. They do not yet have the regulatory framework for this, and they have been working on it for four years! I would encourage governments around the world to look to Mexico as a model they might emulate."

An exasperated Miranda Pryor, executive director of the Newfoundland Aquaculture Industry Association (NAIA), asserted that old regulatory structures in Canada also need to be scrapped and new ones developed.

"Aquaculture is a modern industry that requires a modern legislative framework to be at least competitive," said Pryor. "On the federal side, the industry is managed by an antiquated piece of legislation called the Fisheries Act. It makes no mention of aquaculture, and is designed to protect wild fish only. Numerous sections of the act are invoked to regulate aquaculture activities and are simply not used in a fish farming context."

Leading environmental advocates such as Conservation International and the World Wildlife Fund have undergone a complete about-face with regard to aquaculture, adding to their ranks of supporters the International Union for the Conservation of Nature, the Nature Conservancy, and the Environmental Defense Fund.

"World Bank is leading a new initiative," says Neil, "called the Global Partnership for the Oceans. There has been an increasing recognition among the rational environmental NGO community that aquaculture *has* to be part of the solution to that which ails the oceans. And *that's huge.* Even Ocean Conservancy—watchdog of all things oceanic, who have always been suspicious of caged fish—*even they* have realized this is a sustainable model to replace the methods that abuse the ocean."

Conservation International, a nonprofit environmental organization, reported on a landmark global assessment of environmental impacts of aquaculture. It showed that farmed seafood is less damaging ecologically than meats such as beef and pork, with great potential for improved efficiency. After almost two years of data gathering, scientists were able to compare and contrast seventy-five different types of species-production systems to determine their environmental impacts on ocean acidification, climate change, energy demand, land-use demand, and other ecological factors.

"They looked at aquaculture in the context of all the other animal protein on the planet, including land animals," Neil explains, "and they looked at it from the complete life cycle analysis of all of the various energy and water and food impacts, and the downstream impacts of these production systems, and said, hands down, far and away, aquaculture is the environmentally preferable way to produce animal protein."

Neil has stopped referring to Greenberg's famous book and started citing this landmark study everywhere he goes. How many times, and in how many ways, must he exonerate his work before the world will listen, and investors bank on the future of floating food?

"It's a fairly dark and lonely work, chipping away at the blue horizon," he admits. "And I've been really excited to find in the Seasteading Institute the sort of visionaries that the next generation for aquaculture really needs. And so to find a fellowship of folk who are saying, 'Let's not think in a five- or ten-year time frame; let's think of a fifteen- or fifty-year time frame. Where do we want to be in a hundred years' time?'—that is the real game changer. That's what this community represents."

Neil says this raising a glass as a toast to a restaurant full of seasteaders. When he finishes, he clinks glasses with a woman from a military family who worked on Wall Street and then launched a campaign to amend the US Constitution to allow former California governor Arnold Schwarzenegger to run for president. Even though seasteaders want to build their own floating countries, not all seasteaders are rebels. Some are patriots. Let's meet a woman who believes the best way to end US wars abroad is to build floating cities on the ocean powered by algae.

Living Fuel

"Our goal is to free the US from energy dependence on *any* other country," says Lissa Morgenthaler-Jones. She and her husband, Dave Jones, founded LiveFuels, which they call "a mini–Manhattan Project" to turn algae into biofuel. Lissa and Dave have already invested their personal fortunes in their project to replace fossil fuels with biofuels, and they've convinced investors it can work, raising north of $12 million US so far.

"This is the greatest nation on earth," Lissa says. "I don't give a damn what Bill Maher says. The idea that it is not going to remain so, because we were too stupid to get ourselves out of hock to OPEC, really sticks in my craw. [My father is a] retired major from World War II, in his nineties. My grandfathers both fought in World War I. Dave's father was in Korea. I'm sorry, we don't go down without a fight."

Lissa is the daughter of David Turner Morgenthaler, founder of the prestigious Morgenthaler Ventures, one of the oldest venture capital firms in the United States. Lissa graduated from Princeton University with a degree in economics and didn't waste any time proving she wasn't a trust fund baby. After swimming among sharks on Wall Street and flourishing, Lissa managed a futuristic mutual fund specializing in biotechnology investing since 1990. By 1998, she had become portfolio manager of the Murphy New World Biotechnology Fund. Two years later, in 2000, out of eleven thousand funds, hers was ranked number one. Today she leads strategic planning and corporate development for LiveFuels.

Dave Jones has an MBA from Stanford University. He developed business and ran financials for Bayhill Therapeutics, Cell Genesys, Virage, Perception, and Apple Computer. Today he's chief operating officer at LiveFuels, overseeing research, taking care of all administrative functions, and planning scale-up activities.

Together they form a perfect team of contrasting personalities. Dave is the behind-the-scenes guy, a certified scuba diver, a man of few words who dispenses with pleasantries, laser focused on technical details. Lissa is outgoing and articulate, the perfect public face of the company. She served on Governor Schwarzenegger's finance committee, which is where she must have cultivated the charm that takes the edge off her contrarianism.

"We're interested in the *practical realities* of seasteading," says Lissa. "Can you technologically do it? Of course you can. The petroleum industry has been building seasteads since the sixties. Among the engineering firms we retained is one in Louisiana that built the biggest oil platform to date, a mile in length."

Whoa. We're a long way from Ricardo's floating rafts for the poor.

"I look at seasteading and say, *Meh!* With courtesy, the physical challenges are not that great. I do worry about rogue waves. I worry about security. But the rest of the challenges, if you're willing to throw enough money at it—it ain't no challenge."

Lissa says seasteaders should stop worrying about naval engineering and worry about bioengineering. Engineering a gigantic floating metropolis at a profit is easy. But engineering a microscopic algae cell that makes biofuel cheaper than oil? That's where seasteading is going to face its biggest engineering challenge, and nobody has spent more time on this than Lissa.

Ever try to squeeze oil out of an algae cell? It's even harder than it sounds. Even at the level of basic research, biofuel scientists work not with test tubes but with pools the size of football fields. To industrialize biofuel would require farms the size of states—at least until extraction can be made more efficient. How much land space would be required for biofuel to compete with fossil fuels beneath ground? How much water would need to be pumped in? On the sea, the limiting factors— water, nutrients, and space—are virtually limitless. Some think the frontier for biofuels is in the vast oceans, where it would be environmentally sustainable.

In 2011 Fatih Birol, the chief economist of the International Energy Agency (IEA), which represents twenty-eight nations, tossed out a terrifying factoid on Australian radio. He said that after a comprehensive study of eight hundred oil fields around the world, his department concluded that "in the next twenty-five years, we have to find and develop four new Saudi Arabias."

Would any of this finding and developing involve conquering and cozying up to tyrants? In 2012 Lissa and Dave weren't waiting to find out. In an effort to forestall future resource wars, they began partnering with researchers around the world with the goal to "reduce the cost of algal biocrude to one dollar per gallon."

World Peace Through Pond Scum

Dave and Lissa pride themselves on relentless realism. "We didn't get to be successful by being unrealistic," says Lissa. "My father funded Apple. My brother was director of Siri."

What sounds like bragging to most is modesty to a Morgenthaler. Members of her family and their investment firms also funded the Hospitalist Company, Microchip, Nextel, Ribozyme Pharmaceuticals, Synopsys, VeriFone, Evernote, NexTag, Practice Fusion, PeopleMatter, Transcend Biomedical, Lending Club, and at least three hundred other companies. This family makes Silicon Valley investors look like neophytes.

"We're accustomed to taking risks," says Lissa. "We try to manage those risks. One of the fastest ways to nose-dive is to be unrealistic . . . Nothing focuses the mind like investing your own money."

Why are Lissa and Dave so driven to do this? Both became very successful managing money and running companies. Either could have retired on a couch made of cash. Dave, a devoted seaman, could spend the rest of his days sailing and scuba diving. Why bank everything on biofuel?

"I got mad as hell in 2003 and 2004 as I looked at this country [the USA]," Lissa says. "I had retired from the money management firm, done some pro bono work, liked doing it, but I needed real work again. DOE was MIA."

She means the Department of Energy and missing in action. Lissa uses military acronyms.

"Here we were seventy percent dependent on OPEC at that time. Dave watched what I was doing and said, 'This is the right thing to do.'"

In June 2005 they began their quest to find the fuel that would wean the world off fossil fuels, go along way toward ending US involvement in wars in Middle East, and render the United States energy independent.

"We looked at ethanol, biodiesel, butanol, propanol. Dave looked at a thorium reactor on the thirty-foot skiff. We looked at lithium-ion batteries. Most of these are old ideas that have come back 'round again."

Over years of research, they became experts in the scientific realities and economic possibilities of most known sources of potential energy and dispensed with each. Now they specialize in seeing through other specialists' claims and spotting the flaw. Once an entrepreneur knows more than the experts he hires, he knows he's in trouble. Millions of dollars in, they began to get frustrated.

Then in 2005 Lissa attended the United Nations World Environment Day in San Francisco.

"That's when I first really grokked the idea that algae might work."

When Algae Becomes Oilgae

"Nature does it, and she does it well and easily," Lissa says. "When nature degrades biomass, she turns trees into coal and algae into oil. Trees don't have fat in them, so they become coal. Algae typically has a lot of fat in it, so it becomes oil." Fish oil can be turned into biodiesel, which is a fatty acid. "Nature proves it works, so let's see if we can."

Humans don't know how to extract enough oil from algae to replace all the fossil fuel in the world. But fish do. Dave and Lissa's plan, in a nutshell: feed algae to fish, let their digestive process extract the oil and store it in their bodies as fat, and then squeeze the oil out of the fish. Squeezing dead fish until oil oozes out sounds gross until you realize the same method produces the omega-3 fatty acid dietary supplements so many health enthusiasts take every day. The rest of the fish can be used as fish meal. Each year, fully a third of the world's total fisheries' catch is ground up into fish meal to be fed to pigs, chickens, and farmed fish.

The real challenge isn't just extracting oil from a microscopic algae cell; it's harvesting trillions of microscopic algae cells from large volumes of water at reasonable cost and effort. Humans can't even come close to trawling for algae. But filter-feeding fish can. By allowing grazing fish to perform the work of bioreactors, Lissa drives down considerably the cost of making oil.

"What if we allowed all that CO_2 to mix with nutrients to become algae, which become fish? We pull all that carbon out in the form of fish. If we are correct, this is a way to reduce ocean acidification, feed the world, and potentially prevent future wars over food."

Pond scum know how to turn CO_2 into pond scum. Fish know how to turn pond scum into oil. With the LiveFuels process, you put carbon pollution in one end and get biofuel out the other. That's how we get carbon out of the environment and back into our gas tanks.

"A fish is eleven percent carbon by weight," she continues. "So every time you haul a fish out of the ocean, you have just hauled eleven percent of that fish's weight out in carbon. You don't have to argue with anyone about, 'Oh, how much carbon did you pull out?' You say, 'Here! Here's how much fish we pulled out. It's eleven percent carbon by weight. *That's* how much carbon we pulled out!'"

Imagine if all the biofuel we burned were carbon neutral. Imagine if the process of harvesting this biofuel were carbon *negative*. As many have suggested, fish parts not turned into oil can be ground up and dropped to the ocean floor, where the remains will be out of the carbon cycle for tens of millions of years. Can we monitor carbon in the oceans and atmosphere by growing fish for oil?

Like Sims, Lissa wants to eliminate all the trophic steps involved in building a big oil-rich predator fish. Who wants all that mercury in their gas tank? Lissa wants to find filter-feeding herbiferous fish that graze on algae directly from the bottom of the food chain.

One Fish, Two Fish, Red Fish, Blue Fish

Right now LiveFuels is experimenting with green-gobbling fish such as carp, tilapia, and sardines. They want a fish that just chills out and eats; an aquatic bovine that puts most of its energy into producing body mass and doesn't waste energy swimming around. When they figure out which one is what Lissa calls "the couch potato of fish," they plan to ship the fish to the mouth of the Mississippi River, where runoff from agricultural waste created a gigantic "dead zone." After its size dropped to an encouraging 2,889 square miles in 2012—which is about the size of Delaware—it nearly doubled to 5,840 square miles in 2013, which is about the size of Connecticut. Then it reached 6,474 square miles in 2015, which is Connecticut plus Rhode Island. Shouldn't entrepreneurs find a way to make money reversing this ever-expanding zone of death? Lisa wants to park a few algae-eating fish farms amid those algal blooms, which feed on nutrient pollution, and see how much oil we can get out of it.

Dave sums up why algae are the optimum solution: "Most people believe that algae will give you more biomass per area in time than anything else, including sugarcane or switchgrass or *miscanthus.*" Miscanthus *giganteus* is a giant grass classified as a cellulosic ethanol crop due to its high yield potential, but Dave says the humble algae have even got that beat. Best of all, says Dave, algae will not compete with food crops. Nobody will be stealing corn or soy from the mouths of the hungry to create fuel. Also, algae multiply so quickly, store so much carbon, and produce so much oxygen that they could very well reverse what Dave, with his flair for understatement, calls "the carbon dioxide problem."

Once "oilgae" becomes cheaper than oil, Lissa has no doubts about how rapidly it can be scaled up. As they say on their website, "Under the right conditions, algal growth occurs at an exponential rate, where one cell turns to billions, even trillions, in a matter of weeks."

Instead of pleading with the world to cooperate, Lissa and Dave want to forge the technology to align everyone's incentives to pursue the same goal, whether you're an environmentalist who wants to reduce CO_2 in the water and atmosphere, or a humanitarian who wants to feed the world, or an investor who wants to profit selling biofuels. With algae, all these imperatives will lock together in a positive feedback loop, such that algae will be the keystone to the new economy.

Lissa stresses: "It's really driven by the need to feed the world. At first, I was furious that we're so deep into nations that hate us, just because we're addicted to oil, but as we and our team pursued this, I was even more horrified to find out we're going to starve on our way to finding out we're not going to have enough energy to drive."

In October 2014 *National Geographic* reported that 99 percent of biofuels produced and consumed worldwide in 2011 were made from food crops. This situation obviously can't hold. LiveFuels started as Lissa's answer to the chant "No blood for oil" and became "No hunger for gas."

That year, the turning point came. Unilever, the British consumer products megacorporation, announced an ambition to double the size of its business while reducing its overall environmental footprint. How will they pull this off? They've pledged to buy roughly 3 million gallons of algal oil in one year from Solazyme, a San Francisco–based biofuel company. Unilever sells personal care products that include brands such as Dove soap, Brylcreem, and Noxzema, and food brands such as Hellmann's, Lipton, and Breyers and Ben & Jerry's ice cream, not to mention home care products such as laundry soaps and cleaning products, and they have begun to incorporate algae oils into their products. The two companies plan to build an algae oil plant in Brazil with Bunge, a leading agribusiness company. There they plan to increase algal oil production by ten times, producing roughly 30 million gallons of algae-based oil a year. By 2016 Solazyme had renamed itself TerraVia and signed a supply agreement with Unilever for $200 million for high-performance algae oils.

Even politicians are recognizing their kinship with pond scum. The White House pointed out in a fact sheet that algae for biofuels can feed off the CO_2 and wastewater emissions from power plants, as if it were its idea. Throw a few pools around these power plants, and we're ready to go. President Barack Obama shocked the world in a speech on energy policy when he said, "We could replace up to seventeen percent of the oil we import for transportation with this fuel that we can grow right here in the United States."

"It is not just about natural security. It also strengthens national security." Rear Admiral Philip Cullom, director of the Chief of Naval Operations Energy and Environmental Readiness Division, appears to share Lissa's motives. "By having reliable and abundant alternate sources of energy, we will no longer be held hostage by any one source of energy, such as petroleum . . . Energy conservation extends tactical range of our forces while also preserving precious resources. Our goal, as a navy, is to be an 'early adopter' of new technologies that enhance national security in an environmentally sustainable way."

CNN Tech reported in 2014: "Researchers at the U.S. Naval Research Laboratory, Materials Science and Technology Division, said this week they have demonstrated proof-of-concept on the ability to draw carbon dioxide and hydrogen from seawater and turn it into forms of gasoline. Heather Willauer, a Naval Research Laboratory chemist, called the technology 'game changing.'"

The US Department of Energy (DOE) claims in its fact sheet that microalgae—pond scum—can potentially produce up to a hundred times more oil than the same amount of soybeans. Is this true? John Williams, a spokesman for the Algal Biomass Organization, says that right now an acre of soybeans can produce only sixty to a hundred gallons of biofuel, while an acre of algae can provide two thousand to five thousand gallons.

Got waste? One of the thousands of species of algae will probably eat it. Toronto-based Pond Biofuels cooperates with forms of algae that flourish in southern Ontario, Canada. This alga's favorite food is gas emissions from the production of raw cement, which the Pond Biofuels people refer to as "feedstock." This alga gobbles up the raw smokestack emissions, producing a waste known as oxygen and growing a large amount of biomass that Pond Biofuels says it is eager to sell for "oil production, bioplastics, gasification, coal replacement, biodiesel." One metric ton (or tonne) of algae yields about a hundred liters of diesel. The emissions from this diesel can again be used as feedstock for the Pond Biofuels process, which is called a closed-loop continuous harvest system. Everybody feeling his or her way toward the blue economy keeps minting the same names. They system is now under way. Pond Biofuels has set up shop at two places in Ontario: St Marys Cement and US Steel.

Though many seasteaders fret that governments will stop them from farming the seas, governments can be friends of this research. Look at Canada. The National Research Council of Canada, in partnership with oil giant Canadian Natural Resources, have funded about 90 percent of the aggressive project proposed by Pond Biofuels. Gary Goodyear, minister of state for science and technology, announced excitedly that this was "not just to reduce emissions of carbon dioxide but to recycle their emissions and use them as a nutrient to grow algae—I'm not kidding—and then turn that algae into value-added products."

A spokesman for Pond Biofuels said, "The challenge is that oil from algae costs twice as much as oil from soybeans. To halve the current costs of algal biofuel, research and development has to be coordinated among a broad range of technical fields. But imagine the profits and benefits once this milestone is achieved. Microalgae—common pond scum—can be grown in pools in the desert."

Pools in the desert are not big enough for Dave and Lissa. They know they are taking a big risk, but doing nothing is a bigger risk. Lissa puts her hope in what she affectionately calls "ocean nuts," adding that her husband is one.

Lissa has her own hypothesis about ocean acidification. Carbonic acid in the water seems to be increasing much faster than CO_2 in the atmosphere. Lissa doesn't think the increasing CO_2 input from the atmosphere is the only cause. She thinks the rate at which CO_2 has sunk out of the surface water has decreased in the last century.

"Most of the CO_2 is in the surface three hundred feet. It's not diffusing down fast enough. It may be that ocean acidification is not due to fossil fuel use only. This idea was first proposed by Charles Darwin's grandson. When you look at those charts with [atmospheric] CO_2 building up—yes, it coincides with the industrial revolution, but it also coincides with massive motorized fishing of the ocean."

The surface ocean moves horizontally according to winds, tides, and currents. But what scoops into the deep-ocean floor and mixes it with the surface ocean?

"The fish. They are the vertical mixers. They pull nutrients up from the deep to the surface where CO_2 and sunlight are, which we algae folk care about." Large mammals such as elephant seals and bottlenose whales dive deep, with sperm whales getting close to two miles. "Is it possible that the reason we are seeing such fast ocean acidification in the surface water is because we have fished out the vertical mixers? The people who said 'Save the whales!' were dead right, probably for reasons they never suspected."

Like so many aquapreneurs, Lissa appears first to channel Neil Sims, and then Ricardo Radulovich, without any indication that they have proposed similar solutions. Each aquapreneur we met started this journey trying to solve a specific problem and learned that his or her solution intersected with many global problems. Lissa, trying to find an alternative fuel to prevent war; Neil, trying to reduce ocean acidification to save fish; and Ricardo, trying to find food to feed billions, were all led inexorably to the planetary carbon cycle rooted in the oceans. They tapped into different tributaries to the ocean solution and found themselves face-to-face at a Seasteading Institute conference in 2012.

Monopoly Is Weakness, Diversity Is Strength, Ignorance Is Reality

Lissa calls herself a registered Republican. Neil Sims calls himself a passionate environmentalist. Ricardo Radulovich calls himself a third worlder. When they meet at the conference, they fail to discuss politics. Instead, they debate how to solve technical problems they all agree will solve numerous problems at once. They won't stop expressing mutual admiration for one another behind their backs. (Lissa especially professes admiration for Neil Sims's encyclopedic knowledge every time Neil's back is turned.) Their different personalities and backgrounds reflect their differences in emphasis. Lissa wants to wean her country off Middle East oil, and clean the oceans and feed the world in the process. Neil wants to restore the health and diversity of the oceans, and feed and fuel the world in the process. Ricardo wants to feed the poor, and restore the oceans and produce biofuel in the process. They all support one another's priorities, and they all agree the carbon cycle is the magic equation that can incorporate all concerns. They just don't agree on the fastest, most efficient, most effective method, and that 2050 deadline they each mentioned really fires the sense of urgency. Their key disagreement seems to be over which disaster will arrive first.

Neil says the overriding emergency is the total collapse of the ocean ecosystem, and our only salvation is rapidly scaling up aquaculture to global proportions, which won't happen until you demonstrate profit, at which point trillions of investment dollars will pour into the Blue Revolution, driving everything else. Ricardo says cleaning the ocean and making profits is all well and good, but it's secondary. The first goal is empowering the poor to feed themselves directly with artificially selected seaweed, and developing strains that will be healthier, cheaper, and tastier than wheat, corn, and soy. The oilgae and bioremediation of the coasts will follow. Lissa says we don't have time for artificial selection. She and husband Dave have bred many interesting species of pond scum, but how do you fellows plan to fuel all this? We need to use the microalgae that are *already* in the dead zones, feed them to filter-eating fish, and use the fish oil to power the fuel and food. Ricardo says he agrees, but we don't have time for all these extra steps; we need to work on macroalgae directly to prevent starvation. Neil says you can't feed the world with a dead ocean, so we have to reverse the acidification immediately. Lissa says the world is going to hell in a handbasket over wars over dwindling oil, and if we don't find an alternative energy source soon, we can forget about feeding the poor and saving the oceans.

And so it goes. All three are competing to make their solutions work, and all three are trading information and learning from one another. We hope the governments of the world allow experiments at sea to flourish, so a hundred start-ups like Kampachi Farms, LiveFuels, and the Sea Gardens Project can seek to provide an abundance of food, fuel, feed, fertilizer, and fish populations restored. Will their success provide the infrastructure of floating econations?

A curious fact: Lissa and Neil both refer to the same expert to support their points. "Patrick Takahashi says . . ." "Well, as Patrick Takahashi observed . . ."

Who is this guy? Sims points to a senior Asian man smiling like Buddha in the corner of a room full of arguing seasteaders and calls him "the Grand Old Man of the Blue Revolution."

Chapter 5

FUEL

The Ocean Is a Solar Panel

"The Grand Old Man of the Blue Revolution"

Just as science fiction fans admire Robert Heinlein for writing about technologies decades before they became real, ocean enthusiasts talk about Patrick Takahashi, who was explaining the science and economics of floating cities in the 1970s. He was planning the Blue Revolution before the public had heard much about the Green Revolution.

Patrick Kenji Takahashi is a Hawaiian biochemical engineer and popular science writer who has published more than a hundred scientific papers and several books. Did he coin the phrase "Blue Revolution"?

"I'm sure I didn't," he says. The "Father of the Blue Revolution" is not interested in living up to his mystique. He's still interested in thinking light-years ahead of everybody else. "One of the big things I have been trying to push, which is like five steps beyond Neil Sims, is to close the growth cycle in the open ocean."

Close the growth cycle? Does he mean the carbon cycle of the planet? Yes. Get the whole thing working on one giant seastead. Patrick Takahashi, biochemical engineer and cofounder of the Pacific International Center for High Technology Research, plans to integrate Ricardo, Neil, and Lissa's plans all in one giant megaquapolis.

Impressed? Ho-hum, says Takahashi. We're still not thinking big enough. These are old ideas he was explaining to Congress during the Jimmy Carter administration. Making sustainable ocean cities is small potatoes. His goal is to sustain the total energy and food needs of all the nations of the world with ocean cities that, once up and running, will require virtually nothing from the continents of the world except its poor immigrants to come get wealthy amid the ocean bonanza.

Takahashi talks about futuristic ideas as if they already should have happened. In 1975 he was deep into a campaign to explain the technological, environmental, and economic feasibility of floating ocean cities. He was way ahead of his time. In 2012 he was talking about floating cities replacing fossil fuels, land crops, and hiring the bottom billion for blue jobs. As a side benefit, hurricanes will be stopped before they start, and rare earth minerals will become abundant earth minerals. Oh, and people will eat fishes the size of buses.

Fasten your seatbelts and don your lifejackets. You're about to have a conversation with Patrick Takahashi.

The Fountain of Life

Look to the bottom of the ocean, says Takahashi. That's where humanity's hope lies. The ocean floor is so dark and under such intense pressure, it's very hard to sustain life, yet the ocean floor contains all the nutrients in the exact proportions necessary to do so. That pileup of dirt is the sunken treasure to sustain seavilization.

A blue marlin tears a lobster limb from limb. A nematode tears an amoeba pseudopod from pseudopod. Where do the scraps go? The marlin and nematode both poop. Where does the poop go? Waste sinks. This has been going on for billions of years.

"Microorganisms grow in the eutrophic zone, the upper layer of the ocean where there is sunlight," says Takahashi. "When they die, they drop to lower depths and decompose into the compounds that made them. The ratio of the resultant elements, carbon: nitrogen: phosphorus, in both the organism and the upwelled fluid, happens to be 106:16:1, the Redfield ratio."

The Redfield ratio was first measured by oceanographer Alfred C. Redfield, showing that the atomic ratio of carbon, phosphorus, and nitrogen is consistent in all marine organic matter across all oceans, whether you measure plankton, fish, algae, or dead organic matter. While the most intelligent species worries about the lack of phosphorus, nitrogen, and general topsoil on land, megatons of this life-making matter is piled up the ocean floor, just sitting there.

A modular wavebreaker shelters Artisanopolis in shallow coastal waters.
Aquaponics greenhouse domes will provide locally grown food.

Courtesy of Gabriel Scheare, Luke Crowley, Lourdes Crowley, and Patrick White, Chile.

2020

2030

A Dutch aquatic engineering firm, DeltaSync, designed the *Seasteading Implementation Plan*. It lays out incremental steps to the sea, starting with environmental restoration, that eventually lead to political independence.

DeltaSync/Blue21, Holland.

2040

2050

The first permanent businesses on the high seas could be
sovereign floating hospitals that provide cutting-edge care
to patients who choose them.

Design concept by Edward McIntosh, 2014, Ecuador.

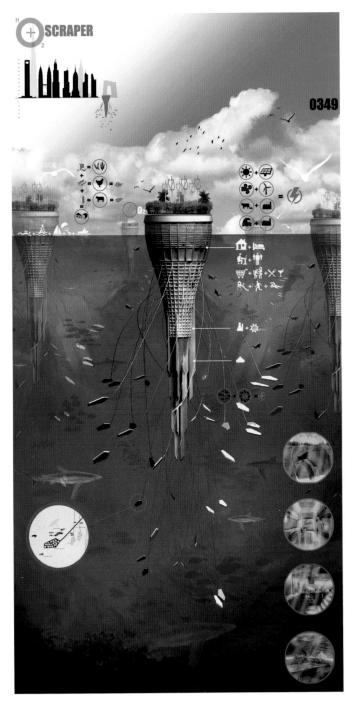

This is Water-Scraper. The deeper and heavier the hull, the more stable in waves.

Courtesy of Sarly Adre Sarkum, Nik Syazwan Nik Ab. Wahab, Amy Roshida Othman, Ahmad Azri Idrus, Muhamad Zharif Amir Sharifudin, Malaysia.

A beach is a most effective wave break. A buoyant tube upholds a flexible hammock to support sand that protects vertical farms.

Courtesy of Tyler Kreshover, USA.

Metropolis 2055: Modular neighborhoods can detach and move to other seasteads or form new seasteads. These are the fluid mechanics of voluntary societies.

Courtesy of Tyler Kreshover, USA.

Seasteads 3D-printed on the ocean will not resemble skyscrapers rooted in bedrock. The City of Meriens follows the form and function of a manta ray.

© *Jacques Rougerie Architecte, France.*

And the wealth starts only five hundred meters below the surface. "The nutrients themselves are not at the bottom of the ocean," Takahashi explains. "At five-hundred-meter depths, there is very little sunlight, so almost no growth." Photosynthesis can't work without sunlight, so algae can't gobble up the nutrients. "Thus the concentration of minerals only slowly increases with continued depth, yet it maintains the Redfield ratio at every level." The deep ocean is a reservoir of nutrients. "Phosphate is particularly of interest because, like peak oil, farming is beginning to experience peak phosphate. In other words, terrestrial farming could well be compromised in the not-too-distant future, whereas ocean farming will continue to have phosphates forever."

The oceans are mostly a barren desert overlying a superabundance of fertilizer that the sunlight never reaches. Most sea life flourishes near land, where the ocean strikes the continental shelf and upwells. When this superabundance of nutrients reaches the sunlight, algae start their photosynthetic engines, becoming the foundation of rich marine ecosystems of life. Incredibly, nearly half of all wild seafood is harvested from one-tenth of 1 percent of the ocean. Unfortunately, these lavish ecosystems have been drastically overfished. Now that humans have plundered the 0.1 percent of the sea where so much sea life congregates, humans are at a loss as to what to do.

Takahashi asks, why are billions of hungry humans relying on natural upwellings covering 0.1 percent of the ocean? Why not create man-made upwellings, each supporting an ocean city? All the carbon, phosphorus, and nitrogen in the deep ocean can be transformed into life. All it has to do is reach sunlight.

Patrick Takahashi writes in his paper "The Blue Revolution: Oceans as Ultimate Sustainable Resource," coauthored with Leighton K. Chong, "If large volumes of this rich deep-ocean water can be brought to the surface, ocean ranches can be supported . . . the bacteria-free, nutrient-rich cold waters are ideal for stimulating growth of marine biomass that may be used for sustainable feed. The ultimate goal would be a self-supporting sustainable marine ecosystem."

"This upwelled fluid is like free fertilizer for marine biogrowth," Takahashi explains to us. "Add the fact that this deep-ocean fluid is essentially pathogen free. That means you eliminate yet another problem faced by land aquaculture. Even more attractive is the fact you also have free irrigation and free space. And that's not all, folks! Under controlled conditions—we might need to add some iron—some of us think we can suck up carbon dioxide from the atmosphere to remediate global warming."

It's even more exciting than it sounds. A test conducted in 2004 indicated that each atom of iron added to the water would foster enough plankton growth to draw between ten thousand and a hundred thousand atoms of carbon out of the atmosphere. The authors suggest that adding iron to the Southern Ocean circling Antarctica alone could reduce carbon dioxide levels by 15 percent.

Author Marshall T. Savage explained this potential for floating cities in his 1992 book, *The Millennial Project*.

"When the nutrient-rich water from the depths reaches the sunlit waters of the surface, it has much the same effect on the barren ecology of the open ocean, as the Nile itself has on the sterile sands of the Sahara. Just as the Nile created an oasis which nurtured one of mankind's oldest and most splendid civilizations, the new river of life will nourish mankind's newest and most dynamic civilization."

It gets better. Pipes drawing up seabed minerals from the ocean floor have the potential to create not only unlimited food, but also unlimited power. Any land-based battery scientist will tell you that the storage of energy is a critical challenge. But nature already stores it for us.

"The ocean is the largest solar collector in the world," says Bob Nicholson, former president and director of global market development of OTEC International. Four-fifths of all solar energy that reaches the Earth is stored thermally in the oceans. "We have three hundred times the amount of energy in the tropical ocean than the world currently consumes, and it's replaced every day," Nicholson claimed at the Seasteading Conference in 2012. Incredibly, the ocean's stored energy can be tapped by OTEC, or ocean thermal energy conversion. "Our challenge is to design a system that can harvest or convert that solar energy into electricity."

The ever hardheaded Lockheed Martin scientists are much more conservative in their estimates, claiming that each day the tropical oceans absorb the energy equivalent of 250 million barrels of oil. That's only triple the world's current daily consumption rate. But even if Bob Nicholson's estimates are off by two orders of magnitude, the potential of this technology is enough to put dollar signs in the eyes of the pragmatists at Lockheed Martin. Count the number of countries that may be clients for such a technology.

"The ocean thermal conditions needed for OTEC are favorable in more than eighty countries in tropical areas of the world," the company reports "including the southeastern United States, Central America, much of South America, southeast Asia, China, Australia, and many Pacific and Caribbean islands."

Say we produce a superabundance of energy from the solar panel of the sea. How do we get it to shore? There are two ways, each with benefits and drawbacks. One method is submerged power cables, which have the potential to fuel an entire coastal city. The downside is that some energy will be lost during the transmission, which will reduce the efficiency of the OTEC plant. Plus, ocean floor cables are expensive to maintain, since they soak in corrosive saltwater and require deepwater upkeep.

The second method is to use OTEC's considerable electricity generation to produce fuels at sea that are then shipped to land. Fuels such as hydrogen could be shipped anywhere in the world, so that even landlocked countries could utilize OTEC power. However, electricity is weightless, but hydrogen fuels are heavy. Transporting the finished fuels will add costs, and a portion of OTEC power would be used in the process of manufacturing fuels at sea.

Shell took the second option, hiring six hundred engineers from across the world to construct the Prelude, the world's first floating liquefied natural gas project, which will be moored around 125 miles off the coast of Australia. It's not OTEC, but in 2017 it will be pumping up fuel from under the seabed and turning it into a liquid that they plan to cool in part by tapping the cold ocean depths. You could line up four soccer fields on the Prelude, and it will remain at sea for up to a quarter century, acting as a filling station for ships to bring natural gas to an economically ascending Asia. Could this mega-engineering project serve as a prelude to OTEC?

OTEC produces no greenhouse gases, blights no land, is not visible from shore, requires minimal maintenance, and runs twenty-four hours a day, 365 days a year. So what's the problem? Why hasn't humanity built a thousand OTEC plants over the last few decades?

Once up and running, OTEC can be maintained with relatively low running costs. It's the up-and-running part that's expensive. In order to profit from that long-term flow of cheap blue-green energy in OTEC, you need a gigantic up-front investment. The start-up costs to build a pilot plant generating 10 megawatts, and then scale up to 100 megawatts, and so on, has always made the immediate profits of oil easier. Put simply, a global infrastructure for fossil fuel extraction and transport is already in place. The infrastructure of OTEC is just getting started.

But Lockheed Martin reports that the cost of OTEC construction is getting cheaper every year. "Improvements in composite materials, fabrication, and modeling, along with related technology advances in the offshore oil industry, are facilitating OTEC's development." So far, Lockheed Martin has invested $15 million in developing the first prototype OTEC plant. "As the OTEC technology matures and more plants are built, costs for the energy they generate will decrease. Labor efficiencies, improved technology, quantity and capacity, size and incentives would reduce the cost of future plants."

So they're building their first commercial plant. Lockheed Martin has partnered with the Hong Kong–based Reignwood Group to build an OTEC plant off the coast of China that is expected to support all the power needs of a green resort.

This has stimulated something of a race. The Ocean Thermal Energy Corporation is slated to construct two OTEC plants in the Bahamas, and Takahashi thinks they may get the first commercial OTEC plant in operation before Lockheed Martin. Jeremy Feakins, chief executive of Ocean Thermal Energy Corporation, explains that the company's vision is that OTEC plants in the Bahamas would support mariculture and aquaculture and other aspects of a blue economy. The islands of

Tahiti, Martinique, and Réunion are now courting OTEC companies, creating the first glimmerings of a market that will drive costs down. Bluerise, a Dutch OTEC company founded in 2009 that works in the same building as DeltaSync, is commissioned to build another OTEC plant off the coast off the island of Curaçao. Lockheed Martin claims on its website that "each commercial OTEC plant would create 3,500 to 4,000 direct jobs. With the potential for thousands of OTEC plants, the economic impact would be enormous." When companies like Lockheed Martin are funding the Velella Project and OTEC research, you know the blue-green economy is on its way to becoming profitable.

As if the cornucopia of clean energy and renewable seafood is not enough, OTEC plants create fresh water as a by-product. Producing energy by evaporating seawater and condensing the resulting vapor means that you are left with clean, drinkable freshwater. Sea farms won't need water from land; sea farms supported by OTEC will produce water *for* land. "This additional capability would prove invaluable in areas of the world where fresh water is a dwindling resource," Lockheed reports.

Energy, food, water. If we see outside our land-based blinders and take a planet-sized view, we can see renewable solar energy stored in the ocean, a thick layer of nutrient wealth covering the ocean floor, and clean water as a by-product from harvesting this abundance.

"So the question is how many megawatts can you generate ultimately?" asks Takahashi. "The answer is, we don't know. One of the engineers from the University of Hawaii, whom I hired a long time ago, came up with a figure of twenty-five terawatts [25 million watts] that you can sustainably draw from the ocean. That's much higher than all the energy humans use today. So, for seasteading, this is your technology."

The Gold Rush Ain't Got Nothing on the Blue Rush

Takahashi calls it the ultimate ocean ranch. Such a system would not compete for resources with land communities, because it needs no water or food. It would generate plants and fish entirely from nutrients brought up from the deep through water it uses for energy generation. No existing fish would need to be killed. No existing plants would need to be harvested. All this life would be *created* simply by bringing the elements of life up out of the deep and into the sunlight, where algae will work their magic.

As he proposed in this 2011 paper, *"Blue Revolution: Oceans as Ultimate Sustainable Resource,"* coauthored with Leighton K. Chong:

> OTEC power generation in deep-ocean waters can support integrated plantations or plantships to produce a wide variety of marine bioproducts, including seafood, biopharmaceuticals, bioresource materials, biofuels, etc. In the very long term, there is reason to believe that integrated OTEC-powered plantships could become floating cities, and, of course, countries . . .
>
> Someday, perhaps, a thousand OTEC-powered Blue Revolution nations could well be plying our oceans, providing clean and sustainable resources for humanity in harmony with the ocean environment. Picture a United Nations with 1,192 members . . . by then we can hope to have overcome peak oil and global warming.

To understand the titanic power of nutrient upwellings to sustain life, consider the most desolate example. Antarctica is, on average, the coldest, driest, windiest, and highest-elevated continent. Set in permanent deep freeze, plunged in six-month nights, it's very difficult to sustain birds, insects, plants, herbivores, and predators on this frigid wasteland at the bottom of the Earth.

So what's up with all the penguins? We can thank the Great Antarctic Convergence, where the cold Antarctic waters meet the warmer waters of the sub-Antarctic, pushing up a rich broth of upwelling nutrients that explodes with phytoplankton. Perpetually sprayed with fertilizer from below, the unique ecosystem supports a wealth of blue whales, orcas, colossal squids, fur seals, and albatrosses. If ocean upwellings can support a riot of life in a desert of ice, they can support floating cities at the warm equator.

Could we see perpetual fountains of renewable food, fuel, and fresh water on the oceans? The technology is not as futuristic as it might sound. In fact, a working OTEC plant was introduced the same year as the Sony Walkman. In 1979 Takahashi spearheaded the passing of the original OTEC research and development bill while working as special assistant for Senator Spark Matsunaga of Hawaii. That same year, Lockheed Martin led a consortium to put into effect off the Hawaiian coast the world's first floating "Mini-OTEC," which produced 50 kilowatts of clean, emission-free electricity. With excitement for OTEC building, Hawaii's other senator, Daniel Inouye, sponsored the first OTEC commerce bill around 1980. As chairman of the Defense Appropriations Subcommittee, he had wide powers concerning what would be spent by the military. Everything was in place to make the newly elected president, Ronald Reagan, the most environmentally progressive administration in history.

Soon after Patrick Takahashi addressed Congress on the potential of OTEC, fossil fuel prices dropped, and interest in OTEC dropped with it. After extensive consultation with energy industry lobbyists, OTEC was put on the backburner and forgotten.

More than three decades later, Takahashi sighs. "The United States government is broken. We all know that. The lobbyists control almost everything in Congress. Our economy is weak. The cash you can use is actually declining in value. However, we remain the only supreme power in the world. Can you imagine how great we could really be if we got our act together? It boggles my mind."

Patrick Takahashi says he admires that the Seasteading Institute wants every incremental step in the process to turn a profit. That's all fine and dandy, but humanity can't afford to start small and scale up. Too many entrenched interests are in place to employ government lobbyists to pass new laws or enforce obsolete laws that quash threats to their profits. Takahashi's Blue Revolution Hawaii group a partnership of leading OTEC experts and marine pioneers, wants to overleap the small, risky start-ups and jump straight to a giant ocean metropolis. All he needs is a $1 billion. Okay, maybe $1.5 billion.

It's time to ask the seasteading question, because there's just no way around it: Are you crazy?

Takahashi leans forward on his knees and seizes upon the same analogy that Ricardo employs: "The International Space Station cost 150 billion dollars, okay? Our group, Blue Revolution Hawaii, have proposed the Pacific International Ocean Station to be the ocean counterpart of the International Space Station, except we can do it for one percent of the 150 billion. It's only 1.5 billion, and we can have the platform from which different companies and different nations can cooperate to develop what these blue technologies may be. We perform the developmental research to get it to the stage where it can commercialize. The Pacific International Ocean Station can serve as the platform from which can come sustainable fuels, ultimate ocean ranches, marine biomass plantations, Disney at Sea, and, someday, floating cities."

How does he expect to pay for this?

"We don't want to get a buck of government money. We don't plan to get a buck of industry money. The only way we could conceive of this being built—and this is why I love seasteading—is to get some of my computer friends involved."

By "computer friends," he means Silicon Valley angel investors—you know, the type of people with a billion or so to throw around.

"It's going to take a billionaire—if only that person has the guts to do something like this. We haven't found our billionaire yet."

Wink, wink, nudge, nudge.

In the absence of man-made islands, Bob Nicholson's former company OTEC International has gone to real islands. Bob's company was selected by the state of Hawaii, Takahashi's home, to build a 1-megawatt demonstration plant on the island of Niihau. After intriguing initial promise, officials in Oahu contacted Bob's company and requested that it build a 100-megawatt plant four hundred miles off the coast. The plant would float upright like a wine bottle as tall as the Washington Monument. It needs three thousand feet of depth to reach down to the nutrient-dense water. Bob says they've gotten the projected cost down to nineteen cents a kilowatt-hour. But that's still roughly twice the cost of coal or natural gas. "That's just the first plant, which are always more expensive. When you get economies of scale, I'm convinced we can get it under ten cents," Bob says.

OTEC International aspires to sell power to the rest of the world at competitive prices. It plans to produce a hundred thousand gallons of jet fuel *per day* with nothing but sea water and solar energy.

"I think the two concepts of OTEC and seasteading are just the perfect combination," says Bob. "All floating cities are going to need freshwater, and they're going to need electricity. And if you put this in the equatorial zone, you have both. That can really lower the cost and make seasteading extremely attractive. The starting point for seasteading, in addition to Pat Takahashi's effort on algae, is creating the means to produce jet fuel from seawater. We're developing the means to capture carbon dioxide from the ocean. Scientists have designed a Fischer-Tropsch reactor [a technology that normally converts carbon monoxide into fuel] that can combine carbon dioxide with hydrogen in a 100-megawatt power plant and produce a hundred thousand gallons of jet fuel *per day* using seawater as the feedstock and solar energy as the energizer. So it's a cleaner-burning jet fuel. It's lower cost. If you have several hundred of these power plants floating in the equatorial zone producing jet fuel, then you could have floating cities that would house workers and professionals that would be operating on these vessels. So I think it's important for seasteaders to become OTEC enthusiasts, and I think if we could team up with Pat's organization, we could really expedite success very quickly."

When Nicholson announced this to an audience of seasteaders, he provoked a lot of questions.

So will OTEC work only in equatorial zones? Not at all, says Bob.

"In the case of the Persian Gulf, we could dedicate the hundred-megawatt plant to produce nothing but freshwater at the rate of 130 million gallons per day."

Could we have air-conditioning?

"Oh yes. You have everything if you combine OTEC with seasteading."

Imagine ecofriendly Saudi Arabias at sea, running OTEC plants that will harvest CO_2 from the surface water, produce millions of gallons of freshwater, and provide all the energy for an ocean city to operate—plus extra to sell to the world. Any carbon harvested from the ocean water that is not used for fuel will be dropped to the ocean floor. Imagine Tokyo running on giant batteries sent from an OTEC seastead.

The idea has already caught on. Nine countries besides the state of Hawaii are negotiating with OTEC International to get the jump on the next generation of clean energy, food, and water production. Investors have committed billions to Bob's project because OTEC International plans to pull in profits from what he calls the Big Four: fresh water, deep-sea fish harvests, surface fish farming, and clean energy. Besides undercutting the old fossil fuel systems on price and efficiency, OTEC International plans to win the publicity battle on environmental issues alone. Imagine when the public gets a whiff of the news that titanic amounts of energy and food can be derived entirely from floating cities. Consider the fact that more nutrients and carbon exist on the ocean floor than all the nutrients and carbon that support land life.

Imagine if oil fields were the size of an ocean, and instead of drilling through rock for stored oil, we dipped long pipes into water for stored sunlight.

"Water Will Be the Next Oil"

"Water will be the next oil," said Dr. Ted Johnson. Under his leadership, the Oceans Systems Group at Lockheed Martin created the world's first floating OTEC plant, "Mini-OTEC," in 1979. Claiming "Clean energy and clean water equals peace," Ted Johnson has pushed the advancement of the nonpolluting carbon-free OTEC technology with lifelong single-mindedness. In an interview with colleague Mike Straub he said:

"Logically, OTEC is the ultimate answer. It's clean because you're not burning anything. The world is still stuck in an age of fire, but when you burn, you release carbon. OTEC simply uses the ocean's temperature difference—nothing is burned."

After being neglected for thirty years, the OTEC vision is coming back into favor and Ted Johnson is finally being recognized. In 2009 the Ocean Energy Council, a nonprofit organization advocating the development of sustainable ocean energy sources, honored him with the Ocean Energy Pioneer Award for his work with OTEC. In 2011, he was tapped as vice president of the Ocean Thermal Energy Corporation.

"When we flip the switch on a ten-megawatt OTEC plant, the world is really going to change," Dr. Johnson continued. "Fifty-four percent of the world's population live within the OTEC belt, and 98 countries are a fit for OTEC systems . . . OTEC uses no fuel—so once you pay off the capital cost of building a plant, you're producing electricity far cheaper than nuclear and fossil fuels, it's much cleaner, and it runs forever."

The age of OTEC began two years later, in 2013, when an OTEC plant was installed on Japan's Kume Island to demonstrate its validity to the public. That same year, a fully operational OTEC was open for free tours on the island of Okinawa. Two years after that, Ted's prediction came true. In 2015 the governor of Hawaii flipped the switch to activate operation on the first true closed-system OTEC connected to a U.S. power grid. Plans are in the works for the mainland United States and the United Kingdom as well, but the communities most interested in OTEC are islands.

Ted Johnson's company has projects planned in the Cayman Islands, the Virgin Islands, Puerto Rico, and the African island of Zanzibar. In 2011 the Bahamas Electricity Corporation signed an agreement with Ocean Thermal Energy Corporation to construct *two* OTEC plants.

"In general, in the markets we are in, the cost of OTEC energy is comparable to fossil fuel," said Ted in a follow-up interview with colleague Jess Philips. "But OTEC can beat fossil fuels on guaranteed price stability. With OTEC the cost of fuel is free because the 'fuel' in this case is ocean water. So the price doesn't increase or decrease over time . . . The price of fossil fuel is continuously increasing and decreasing so it is difficult to compare the costs. You have all these wild gyrations, which create instability. No one is going to guarantee a price for thirty years." But Ted's company is offering thirty-year purchase power agreements.

What about poor countries?

"A lot of these countries that we work with don't have the money to buy an OTEC plant," he continued, "so we provide the financing so that the country doesn't have to pay anything to build a power plant. We will have a power purchase agreement (PPA) and they pay a certain amount of cost per kilowatt-hour. We retain ownership of the plant and maintain it and a portion of the revenue that's generated."

According to Ted Johnson, OTEC is simply a microcosm of the planet's temperature gradient system. "If you look at the whole system that controls the earth: water gets heated up by the sun, it gets evaporated, turns into a gas, rises, then cools, then turns back into water. That's the same way OTEC works . . . The good news is, a lot of OTEC plants could help reverse the heating of the ocean in a small way, which would help slow down climate change."

Like cruise ships, OTEC plants have the incentive to get bigger. "What's really interesting about OTEC is that as the plant size gets larger, the relative cost of electricity decreases. In other words, a one hundred-megawatt plant produces a lot more electricity per one-dollar capital cost than a five- or ten-megawatt plant. That's really important to remember. We can build very large OTEC plants."

For Ted Johnson, this is just the beginning. "I dream of thousands of floating OTEC ships roaming the seas of the world providing an inexhaustible supply of clean energy, fuel, and water, for all people of the world."

Imagine millions of blue jobs causing a mass emigration comparable to the California Gold Rush.

Patrick Takahashi believes it's a no-brainer. Hopefully, seasteading enthusiasts will become OTEC enthusiasts, as we OTEC enthusiasts become seasteading enthusiasts. I think bringing us all together, we can really be successful, in the rather short term . . . Let's see if we can work together and really go off in a much faster pace."

But Takahashi doesn't give you time to call him crazy before he's moving on to more proposals. Wait until you hear his idea for the animal that's going to support the planet's protein needs on the cheap.

"[Consider that] when you bring this deep-ocean fluid up into the sun, it's high in phosphorus, nitrogen, etcetera. The Redfield ratio is perfect for what it takes for plankton to flourish. You don't want to grow fish to feed another fish, to feed another fish, that will feed the world, as we do with swordfish and albacore tuna. You lose ninety percent of the nutrients with each trophic step. You want to have some species that consumes plankton directly, a filter feeder. That way, if you skip four trophic steps, you can grow a thousand times more of this species than you could with, say, tuna or marlin."

Okay, we'll bite. What kind of fish would you need to grow a thousand times more fish meat on the same amount of plankton?

Such a farm animal would optimally need to have certain properties, Takahashi explains. It would have to be big, make lots of babies, and be as docile as a domestic land bovine. We don't need to breed such a creature. It already exists.

The Biggest Fish Story Is True

"It's called a whale shark," says Takahashi, "which is not a whale. It's a shark. Okay? You can see it in the Georgia aquarium and the Osaka aquarium." The largest fish in the world, these bus-sized gentle giants average thirty feet, nine tons, and live seventy years. This filter feeding shark eats plankton and tiny fish. "The whale shark has babies instead of eggs, and they give birth to a hundred to three hundred babies at a time. Compare that to a cow, which only has one baby, and rarely twins."

Wild whale sharks are so naturally tame, divers frequently grab a fin and catch rides. These sharks give sharks a good name. "Compare a land ranch full of cows with this potential ocean ranch of whale sharks." One trophic step from plankton to shark means you can support a thousand times more of the shark meat than salmon meat, and each shark can produce hundreds of offspring. That's what we call an efficient use of resources. But there may be a catch.

"Have I had whale shark? No. Will it taste good? I don't know."

The Taiwanese have tasted them. In Taiwan, their taste and texture had earned them the name "tofu shark." Okay, so it's not kampachi. But, hey, humans eat tofu. By domesticating and farming large plankton-eating sea bovines, such as the whale shark, we can feed the world at miniscule expense compared with land bovines. If human ingenuity can turn wild fowl into chickens and seaweed into bacon, it can make whale shark into sashimi.

Environmentalists concerned about greenhouse gas emission place most of their emphasis on mitigating the impact of cars, trains, and planes. But the Food and Agriculture Organization of the United Nations concluded that livestock production is responsible for more greenhouse gas emissions than the entire global transportation sector. As algae farms scale up, they will reduce greenhouse gas pollution through two OTEC-powered methods: removing what's extant and reducing what's contributed.

"That's where, over the next hundred years, investment should be placed," says Pat Takahashi. "Create new industries, new jobs, new products, and at the same time improve the environment. We can close the growth cycle of the planet just with OTEC, and we have the ultimate ocean ranch."

Done. Global hunger and energy problems solved. But Takahashi is already on to the next problem.

"Did you know that hurricanes don't cross the equator?" he asks.

Stop Hurricanes Before They Start

"You cool temperatures one or two degrees on the ocean surface, hurricanes won't form. It's as simple as that."

Hurricanes form at the rare moments when the sun heats the surface ocean to a temperature warmer than the air above it. The warm ocean water evaporates and rises and then hits colder air and condenses into precipitation, which cools the air even more. When the ocean water hits about 80 degrees Fahrenheit, this loop becomes self-sustaining, and we get a hurricane. Bill Gates and a team of inventors filed several patents for techniques that would prevent hurricanes over the Gulf of Mexico by mixing deep cold water with surface warm water.

"But it makes no economic sense," says Takahashi, "because all he was trying to do was cool the ocean using some contraption that didn't have any sellable product. You cannot succeed today by just trying to save the environment. You have to save the environment and make a profit at the same time. For that, you need giant ocean platforms."

Hurricanes spin clockwise in the Southern Hemisphere and counterclockwise in the Northern Hemisphere. A hurricane has never been documented to switch sides because the equator spins faster than the poles. This effect which drives hurricanes is called the Coriolis force, and it becomes negligible near the equator. The OTEC-powered ocean cities Takahashi proposes will lie in the equatorial zone, where winds are light, temperatures tame, and waves small. It's also the natural habitat of the whale shark.

Floating cities may be expensive, but platforms in equatorial waters are cheap. "You can put some of these platforms in the path of potential hurricanes. They won't be able to gather enough energy to get started." OTEC draws cold water up, cooling the surface water near the seastead. This will significantly stabilize the coastal economies, which won't be wracked with hurricanes. In Takahashi's view, hurricanes are not a threat to seasteads; seasteads are a threat to hurricanes.

"Between hurricanes and global warming, what else is there?"

We couldn't think of anything, but Takahashi could.

"We might have to at least take a look at the potential of harvesting rare earth minerals from ocean platforms."

Rare earth minerals are required for smartphones, televisions, hybrid cars, rechargeable batteries, fluorescent lamps, wind turbines, satellites, medical imaging, jet engines, natural gas drilling—basically, every technology in modern civilization. These precious minerals are not actually rare, just so infernally difficult to sift from the earth without destroying the environment and poisoning your workers that the minerals are known in the mining industry as "unobtainiums."

"One of the bills that I submitted in 1979 was the Hard Minerals Act."

A checkout of this claim reveals it's true. Takahashi served as staff director for the Hard Minerals Act in the U.S. Senate in 1979. Back when he was still trying to convince governments to see beyond the next election, he proposed a plan to harvest "strategic minerals and marine methane hydrates from the seabed." Bottom line: it's easier to dig through water than rock. You just have to go a lot deeper.

Or send robots into outer space. In recent years, companies such as Deep Space Industries, Planetary Resources, and Kepler Energy & Space Engineering announced hopes to land rockets on asteroids and build "space infrastructure" to exploit them for rare earth minerals, prompting criticism that the quality of ore is speculative and the cost is even more astronomical than the ambition. We have to ask ourselves why billionaire aerospace entrepreneurs are talking about mining asteroids when we should be mining the sea. According to a 2011 paper published in the British journal *Nature Geoscience*, the bonanza of rare earth minerals that might reside on asteroids is available in at least seventy-eight places on our seabed. "Just one square kilometre (0.4 square mile) of deposits will be able to provide one-fifth of the current global annual consumption," reports Yasuhiro Kato, an associate professor of earth science at the University of Tokyo, who led the team that discovered the rich deposits. The race to the ocean floor has already beaten the race to asteroids. Nautilus Minerals is the first company to commercially explore the ocean floor for minerals.

"The ocean is our next frontier for promise," Takahashi says. "Let's not screw it up. We have screwed up the lands and the air. Now let's do it right this time. Not only can we do it right, but with these ocean systems, we can improve the land and air we screwed up. What seasteading is doing is very appealing to us. This could be the future of humanity over the next hundred years."

After forty years of shouting into silence, Patrick Takahashi has stopped worrying that this won't happen. If OTEC International succeeds only in the roughly fourteen countries that are already interested, the economy of the world could change.

"It's amazing how things happen in ways you don't expect," Takahashi says.

"The Covered Wagon of the Sea"

What do you expect happens when the world's most famous astronaut meets the world's most famous aquanaut on the *National Geographic* channel? Do they make common cause, clasp hands, and agree to propel humanity into the future? Well, no, actually. What actually happens is they get into a big fight.

Robert Ballard is a superstar oceanographer best known for discovering the *Titanic* and the sunken German battleship the *Bismarck*, and for being among the first team of humans to witness alien life in the deep-sea hydrothermal vents; the first creatures ever discovered that did not rely on energy from the sun but from the Earth itself. But his career of proving science textbooks wrong goes back to the very beginning of his career. When many scientists considered rogue waves—sudden waves more than twice the size of surrounding waves—to be folklore akin to mermaids and sea monsters, Bob Ballard, at age seventeen, faced down one from the bridge of a ship. As he told the story in the National Geographic documentary *Alien Deep with Bob Ballard*:

"It destroys the bridge, all the windows were knocked out, it blew out the portholes, took away the mast, and we almost sank. I was hooked for life."

As a graduate student in the 1960s, he was among the rebellious researchers who established the existence of plate tectonics. As a high-risk deep-sea explorer in the 1970s, he discovered "black smokers": hellish vents in the ocean floor that spew out boiling water, which experts thought were impossible. Today he is just as much a contrarian swimming against the tide.

"We're not gonna live in outer space," he told Joe and Patri. "That's a complete bunch of baloney. We're running out of land. We have no other option but to move out onto the ocean."

Bob has had a long and storied career of transforming visionary ideas from science fiction into mundane aspects of science fact, and he says the final task of his life is to colonize the ocean. Here is how he concluded a TED Talk he gave that was seen by more than a million people:

"And my final question: Why are we not looking at moving out on to the sea? Why do we have programs to build habitation on Mars, and we have programs to look at colonizing the moon, but we do *not* have a program looking at how we colonize our own planet? The technology is at hand!"

When we spoke to Bob to strategize with him about seasteading, he said, "NASA has spent millions growing peas in artificial Martian soil on a space station, but our same government hasn't said, '*But what about living on the ocean?*' We haven't done *any* research. Zip! NASA's budget is one thousand times more than NOAA's ocean exploration budget. Why is everybody ignoring the vast resource of the seas in favor of the emptiness of space?"

Why does space exploration get all the funding?

"God is up, and the Devil is down," says Ballard. "We look to the heavens for salvation. The last thing we want to do is go down to the underworld. Although the Hawaiian culture loves down. A lot of cultures think the underworld is a good place. Unfortunately, the Western culture dominates, and we think it's bad down there. We equate good with up."

If you became fascinated with the ocean as a child, Bob might have been your teacher. Bob Ballard pioneered "distance learning" with the JASON Project, an educational juggernaut that educates more than a million students every year, earning him the nickname "Carl Sagan with gills." Right now you can go online and watch live as Bob's remotely operated vessel the *E/V Nautilus* explores the deep ocean.

Great teachers are great storytellers, and Bob is a natural star for *National Geographic*, so they featured him in a five-part series called *Alien Deep*. One of the episodes was called "Inner Space vs. Outer Space." The producers invited Buzz Aldrin, the second man to walk on the moon, to discuss the relative merits of sea and space exploration on their family program.

"I really took off the gloves and told the astronauts that populating Mars was a crock of shit," Bob told us. "And Buzz Aldrin yelled and screamed . . . He's off on this evangelistic concept of taking people to Mars, and I say, Well, who gets to go? So I've been shooting my mouth off a lot, but then as part of that show, I met Neil Sims, and I learned about the Velella Research Project, which fascinated me, because he really knows his stuff, and he was taking on all the criticisms by the environmental community and he created answers for every one."

According to Ballard, Buzz Aldrin did not have the answers for humanity, but Neil Sims did. He made enemies with Buzz and became an evangelist for Neil.

"First, he took a predator, a kampachi, and he converted it into a herbivore. So he *flipped it*, so it's now eating sunlight, basically soybeans, so he moved it right down the trophic level to this base level so he can capture energy from the sun and turn it into protein. And then he puts the cages underwater, so you don't see them. And he puts them in the middle of nowhere where it's twelve thousand feet deep, so what soybeans the fish don't turn into protein, they poop, so they're performing carbon sequestration on the deep sea. Absolutely a perfect solution. He's not using hormones. He's not using dumbed-down DNA manipulation. He's using the wild stocks! He took on every one of those objections, and he nailed it. Now Neil is getting to a point where he's ready to go commercial. So I sat down and ran the numbers as compared to a pig farm. How many pigs? What does it cost? When do you bring them to market? How does that compare to fish? I ran all the numbers, and it all works. The damn thing works!"

Bob says we're economically ready to start colonizing of the seas now. "I've spent fifty-five years of my life at sea and been involved with every aspect of the ocean you can imagine. When I first came in contact with you seasteaders, I said, 'You've got the equation backward! Before you had a town in Oklahoma, you had farmers. The town follows the farmer.' We've done our Lewis and Clark expedition. Now we need to start the Oklahoma land rush. So we need to get the covered wagons of the sea out there, so the farming families can make a viable income. And then the cities will follow. So I've been focusing on the basic building block for farmers and herders. What is the tech base for this to happen?"

Robert Ballard announced that the answer has existed for over a half century. It's not a boat. It has no motor, sail, propeller, or any ability to move on its own at all. It's not a barge, either. It's shaped like a wine bottle, and it's about the length of a football field. The first model was carved from a Louisville Slugger baseball bat. It's called a floating instrument platform (FLIP), and Ballard insisted that members of the Seasteading Institute come see it. He gave us a tour.

The FLIP, with no propulsion power, must be tugged like a log to its desired position. Once in place, the log is flipped to the vertical position by flooding ballast tanks, whereupon it floats like a wine bottle, with only one-seventh of it above water. In this position, the FLIP becomes as steady as an iceberg, even during severe storms with eighty-foot waves. As a result, the FLIP is described as "almost as stable as a fencepost."

Most who experience the FLIP express awe for "modern technology," but the FLIP was launched in 1962 by designers Phillip Rudnick, Fred Fisher, and Fred Spiess, who led the Marine Physical Laboratory at the University of California Scripps Institution of Oceanography. It's used mostly by scientists who need to stay at sea a long time. Otherwise it flies under the radar of popular perception. Most ocean enthusiasts want to sail, not sit.

"The FLIP is a single-family ocean ranch house," says Ballard. "A few floors down where it's still sunlit, I have a giant aquarium in my living room. The wave action only occurs on the upper part of the ocean. At the bottom of the FLIP, three hundred feet beneath sea, there's no movement. You don't get seasick. It's quite pleasant. I feel sorry for people on a sailboat!"

But how are families going to afford a FLIP? we asked. It looks a lot more expensive than a townhouse.

It's not a technology for a townhouse, says Ballard. It's a technology for a town.

"You set up four FLIPs, throw a platform over the top of them, and you have a stable platform with which to build your town." As Buckminster Fuller envisioned, the platform could be held high above the waves. "Oil companies already demonstrated the basic concept. You'd have a helicopter pad. You'd have your experimental platform with which to conduct research and prove that it would have limited impact on the environment. You have plenty of room for solar panels to run it. You could grow mollusk crops on the sides of FLIP. Since a FLIP is three hundred fifty feet long, you have a geothermal gradient to provide air conditioning at low cost." Ballard has been on the water for over a half century, from the depths to the surface, in every kind of vessel, testing all kinds of technology, and he says, "The FLIP is just a ship that doesn't move. It's clearly the first kind of home or ranch that you can use as a test base to prove your point."

Four FLIPS, one platform, and you have something as stable as a table. Then these tables can be latched together like leaves added to a Thanksgiving table as more companies arrive for the banquet. Make it the size of Manhattan. Why not? The wider, the stabler. Ballard claims a megaplatform secured by FLIPs has all the qualities a seastead needs to provide the basic infrastructure for Radulovich's seaweed farms, Sims's fish crops—even Takahashi's ocean thermal energy conversion.

"I don't see *any* engineering challenges," he continues. "All you need is a successful reason to go out there and make a buck. The first one will be expensive, but then you start to scale it."

So how do we fund the first one? Bob offers his celebrity power and narration skills. "I want to capture the imagination of the public by featuring a family living at sea." Bob proposes we could financially support the venture with a reality TV show starring a family on a FLIP defending a marine sanctuary. Bob suggests a California sea lion as a companion animal. In Bob's vision, it would be like *Flipper*, the popular movie series and TV show from the 1960s featuring a dolphin, but a reality TV show featuring a family of scientists.

FLIPper

"I picked Catalina Island, so we'll be right off Los Angeles, where you'll draw a lot of attention. You want to get out of California State water, because you run into an amazing amount of crap in California State waters. I want to be careful to bring in as partners the responsible environmentalists, not radical environmentalists. We don't want people who say, 'We want all humans to go away, except me, because I want to appreciate Mother Nature, but I don't want to share it with any other human being.' That's the radical end of environmentalist, who want to get rid of all humans except the environmentalists. We want the *responsible* environmentalists who are ready to realize that there are ways to save the seas and *not* turn the entire ocean into a national park.

"Now look, I've worked hard to be a founder of the National Marine Sanctuary Foundation. I believe in the Yellowstone Parks and the Yosemites of the underwater world. But you don't take the whole damn seventy-two percent of the planet and make it a damn park. See, what the public doesn't understand is that we are going to *increase* the productivity of the ocean."

But are farming families ready to move out onto the sea?

"They're *already* living out there. I can show you families in Asia where the kids have never touched land. They have rafts tied up, and they have their own communities making a living harvesting mariculture in wetlands and marshes and bays. When Hurricane Katrina hit the Gulf of Mexico, twenty-five thousand people came ashore. In Hong Kong and Vietnam, they have entire cities rafted up."

What are we waiting for? Bob asks. The social dynamics of sea life have been demonstrated among poor aquaculture communities. The most successful seasteaders are the nomadic Bajau Laut who lived entirely on their boats for centuries off Southeast Asia until the 1950s, when floating families would form moorage communities of between five and fifty families. The organization of these communities was egalitarian, with no formal authority providing governance. The cost of exit from these communities was low. The Bajau Laut were mobile; there was little tying them to a particular mooring site. Since there was certain to be another lord a little farther up the coast willing to trade for goods produced or transported by the Bajau Laut, lords were forced to compete to provide protection for Bajau Laut communities. This ensured decent protection, reasonable trading terms, and no interference in the internal organization of Bajau Laut communities. Thus these floating communities were war free.

When Bob first contacted us, he wrote in an email: "Imagine a community of seasteaders drifting relatively close to one another. Such a community will require a central town to serve as their connection to shore to support their fish farming community. Imagine all the fish that need to be processed, including the hatcheries, soybean food supply, harvesting process, etc. The seasteaders could also be growing mussels, oysters, etc. on the hulls of their 350-foot-long vertical homes, and they'd need a town to support those activities. Imagine this operation on a much larger scale. Imagine that each seasteader is taking care of 10–20 large versions of these fish pods while living on a FLIP-like home."

The vintage FLIP from 1962 cost $600,000 US. That's nearly as expensive as a Silicon Valley shack. How do we drop the cost of a FLIP to something the average middle-class American family could afford? The only answer is to mass-produce twenty-first-century FLIPs for twenty-first-century families.

We let Bob know that the the Seasteading Institute served as incubator for a business plan developed by our former managing director, Chris Muglia, a seasoned entrepreneur with fifteen years of experience at sea as a professional mariner. Chris is developing business models to create a practical pathway to 3-D printed seasteads.

Is he crazy? Here was our chance to put Chris on the spot. Joe introduced him to the world's foremost oceanographer and turned on his audio recorder. If Bob wasn't afraid to tell Buzz Aldrin he's full of beans, he wouldn't hesitate to tell Chris Muglia.

3-D Seas

The world is full of visionaries. Suppose you could hand them a machine that could make anything they imagine? Innovators in many industries have already used 3-D printers to produce hearing aids, race cars, bikinis, perfect statues of their unborn child, and a wheelchair for a puppy. And it's not just inanimate objects. Medical researchers are printing human body parts out of human cells. Dr. Anthony Atala is director of the Wake Forest Institute for Regenerative Medicine. At TEDMED, an annual conference focusing on the future of medicine, Atala wowed an audience by showing a film of a partial kidney and a two-chambered heart being printed into existence using a normal desktop inkjet printer rigged to print one layer of cells at a time—the invention of Tao Ju from the Department of Computer Science and Engineering at Washington University in Saint. Louis. It takes forty minutes to print and four to six hours for the heart muscles to beat.

In China, a company called WinSun printed a five-story apartment building and a mansion, and then claimed to have printed ten houses in twenty-four hours. Instead of ink, a fast-rotating printer head extrudes a quick-drying paste. It performs like a robot baker layering icing on a cake, except that the batter is made from recycled construction and industrial waste. The inventor, Ma Yihe, hopes his printers can be used to build bridges and skyscrapers in the future. Will the industry scale up? WinSun plans to open a hundred manufacturing plants in the years ahead.

Every year, the cost of 3-D printing halves, while its speed and printing area double. No reason printed structures should remain house-sized.

"3-D printing will transform key components of physical construction into a digital technology and engage exponential trends," says Chris Muglia. "With each iteration, 3-D-printed seastead modules will get cheaper, more nuanced, stronger, and, very soon, self-repairing. Within a decade, 3-D printing will allow us to design and construct increasingly sea-capable floating structures in a matter of a few days rather than months, with comparable profit margins at least an order of magnitude higher than any shipyard or contractor." Chris dared to tell the world's most adventurous ocean explorer his vision was too small. "I think the FLIP is the Model T of getting out to sea, and it's time to build the Tesla of the sea."

That's when something unprecedented happened. Bob Ballard stopped telling stories. He just listened.

Joe pointed out the first challenge: functioning seasteads would have to be many miles out to sea. Ships may live at sea, but they are built on dry docks. For a large portion of his maritime career, Chris has worked in shipyards run by contractors who are not exactly open minded about his futuristic vision and have the industry pretty well locked down. How would seastead designs get out to sea, and then be shared among seasteads and improved?

In *Star Trek*, an engineer in an orbiting spaceship could use a transporter to "beam" anything to the planet. Humans can't teleport things, but we can scan things and transport the digital model to an orbiting spaceship where it can be printed from raw materials that consist of a pile of powder and some binding material. In 2014, NASA transmitted a design file to a 3-D printer on The International Space Station which printed tools for astronaut use.

Chris Muglia says that when key aspects of construction become an information technology, and every module design is tested at sea, improved on computer, and emailed to a floating 3-D printer, Peter Thiel's vision of "atoms" become "bits" will unleash exponential progress and rapidly drop the price of seasteads.

How cheap could this get? Space Exploration Technologies Corporation, better known as Space X, is an aerospace manufacturer that builds and launches space rockets, founded in 2002 by Peter Thiel's co-founder at PayPal, Elon Musk, who is also CEO of Tesla Motors. Elon's goal is to reduce space transportation costs to enable the colonization of Mars.

"SpaceX is already 3-D printing essential elements of its rockets rather than purchasing machined parts from a contractor," says Chris. "SpaceX launches cargo into space at a much lower launch cost than the incumbent players. How? Elon Musk reasons from first principles. Begin with what is known to be true and eliminate assumptions—especially those coming from long-established industries. Musk doesn't price rocket parts from Boeing. He asks for the commodity price of the raw materials that make up a rocket. All of the aluminum, titanium, copper, plastic, everything—including the rocket fuel—adds up to about two percent of the total cost."

Chris consulted with Dr. Russell Loveridge, managing director of the National Centre of Competence in Research (NCCR) Digital Fabrication, in Zurich, Switzerland. Russell's research team encompasses all the required technical elements: robotics, athletic algorithms, materials, and printhead design. Right now Dr. Loveridge's lab can reproduce shapes of structures down the level of the micron, which is thinner than the human hair, which means his technology is capable of fantastically complex architectural sculptures.

In New York City, architect Adam Kushner partnered with American architect James Wolff and Italian Enrico Dini, who has 3-D-printed artificial coral reefs, to construct a 3-D-printed house shaped like a Möbius strip. It includes an estate that features a 3-D-printed swimming pool and Jacuzzi. What happens when you can code the shape of large structures at even smaller levels of detail?

Author Marshall T. Savage foresaw the possibilities in 1992 when he imagined his floating city, which he named Aquarius, writing in his book *The Millennial Project*: "The organic nature of Aquarius will be apparent in its interior architecture. Natural free-flowing lines will be evocative of their shared heritage with sea shells, corals, and other crustaceans . . . The cybernetic growth process will free architecture to create designs tailored to the physical and psychological needs of human beings, unconstrained by the rigid structures of geometry."

"We need work modules, laboratories, and living modules fitting interchangeably," Chris told Bob. "We need docking modules that will allow any number of FLIPs to lock together above and below the waterline and allow safe passage between them while at sea. No one FLIP design will work for every job, so the new FLIPs should be infinitely configurable so they can do an insanely great job at whatever our markets require of them. All of these modules should be easily interchangeable without the use of a shipyard. Elon Musk will finally have a stable, multi-FLIP rocket recovery base. That's our Step One market. Our Step Two market will involve people finding value in other ways that we can't imagine yet."

Bob Ballard didn't tell Chris he was crazy. Bob thinks going to Mars is crazy, and mass-producing FLIPs is a necessity. Bob was already familiar with the leading 3-D printing researchers, and he invited Chris to come visit his Inner Space Science Center and agreed to partner. Chris's team now includes the managing director of the world's foremost 3-D-printing research center, the world's foremost nanoscale innovator, and the world's foremost oceanographer, all committed to building affordable seasteads soon.

Bob is seventy-three. "I've accomplished a lot, and I've got one more good run in me. This is my next challenge. I can definitely see seasteaders starting aquaculture ventures in the next few years in scaled-up versions of the Velella Project based on FLIP-like ships. We don't have a choice but to move out onto the ocean. Great ideas that don't survive in America will survive somewhere else and flourish. I spent most of my life doing things in spite of the system."

Suppose the trio produces hundreds and then thousands of 3-D-printed FLIPs from cheap recycled materials that get ever more nuanced and seaworthy? How big could FLIPs get?

Chris explained to Bob, "It's really easy to see how something that is designed digitally, that can be translated into the physical world—whether it's through concrete or steel or aluminum—becomes very inexpensive very quickly, and you can build them rapidly. Everything doubles every year: the agility of the robots, the resolution of the printer head, the speed. Soon the printer head is going to move so fast all you'll see is a blur. As that capability expands, we can create more ambitious projects, whether it's the FLIP or the seascraper."

What does Chris mean by "seascraper"? For that we have to head to Malaysia.

The Seascraper

Building structures for the ocean has disadvantages that are easily perceived. For instance, waves on the high seas make ships seesaw and passengers seasick. But building structures on land has disadvantages that are not so easily perceived. For instance, on land, gravity is an architect's enemy.

Why do land skyscrapers go high, but they don't go deep? It sure requires a tremendous load of cost, materials, and brain power to design a safe habitation that defies the most ubiquitous force in the universe for dozens of stories. Yet constructing ever upward is a lot cheaper and easier than digging ever deeper into the bedrock required to stabilize a skyscraper. Once you can stabilize your heavy skyscraper, it is always easier to go up.

Ocean architects allow the most ubiquitous force in the world to work for them. The deeper the hull, the lower the center of gravity and the more stable it is in waves. This already exists in microcosm. Koen Olthuis, founder of Waterstudio, designs two-story floating houses in Holland that are almost as deep as they are high. The first story sits entirely below the water, dramatically lowering the center of gravity and securing stability. On high-wave seas, builders have an incentive to allow gravity to drag their designs ever deeper. Olthuis applies this principle to his design for the Sea Tree, a proposed floating apartment house for wildlife, almost as deep as it is high, designed with multiple stories for birds, bees, and bats above the water, and several species of fish at different levels below the water.

Ocean living requires us to flip our land-based assumptions. On coastal cities, land space is a radically limiting factor, and gravity is a radically limiting factor. On the ocean, horizontal space is abundant, and gravity is your friend. Upside-down floating skyscrapers—seascrapers—could one day be more stable and safer in a typhoon than a land city is in an earthquake.

The first underwater skyscraper has been envisioned. The $^hO_2$-Scraper, designed by Malaysian architect Sarly Adre Bin Sarkum, utilizes a long list of blue-green technologies, including solar, wave, and wind power, and it is designed to produce its own food through farming, aquaculture, and hydroponics. The top exposed to sunlight will contain animals grazing on grasslands. The $^hO_2$ is kept upright using a system of ballast tanks—just like the FLIP, only gigantic. Sarkum's out-of-the-box vision earned an honorable mention in *eVolo* magazine's 2010 Skyscraper Competition which invites architects to design skyscrapers to solve technological or environmental problems, and it's attracted more attention than the winners.

Speaking of the oceans as "covering more than two-thirds of the Earth's surface" radically understates the available space in the oceans for colonization. Thirty feet below the surface, waves are not much of a factor. British designer Phil Pauley has developed Sub-Biosphere 2, composed of interconnected spherical modules that could submerge during storms and float at the surface in good weather. This underwater habitat is meant to sustain all life support systems for air, water, food, and electricity by controlling the variant atmospheric pressures that occur at depth.

How deep could ocean communities go? The deeper you go, the higher you can build. As Ballard suggested, deep-going seascrapers could support ocean skyscrapers. The physics of floating cities implies that aquatic engineers will have reason to build wider, deeper, and higher. Exactly how large could an ocean metropolis get? If we incorporated Ricardo's seaweed, Neil's fish, Lissa's biofuel, and Patrick's OTEC into one city, what would it look like?

A Japanese corporation with more than two centuries of experience has already laid out detailed blueprints for a floating restorative civilization.

Shimizu Corporation is recognized as one of the top five contractors in Japan and among the top twenty in the world. For two centuries, Shimizu has never stopped building impossible futures. When the company was founded by Kisuke Shimizu in 1804, it would have seemed outlandishly futuristic to propose that if only Japanese leaders allowed the port of Yokohama to open, Shimizu's employees would acquire foreign construction technology that would allow them to build the Tsukiji Hotel and the Dai-Ichi National Bank. In 1915, when the company transformed from private management to a corporation, it would seem unimaginable that after bombs with the power to incinerate cities were dropped on Japan, this construction company would help build a new Japan unimaginably taller and wealthier, with no emperor and no military. In 1997, as this company began construction of the Tokyo Bay Aqua-Line, one of the largest underwater tunnels in the world—which would feature an artificial island called Umihotaru (meaning "ocean firefly")—its plans for an ocean civilization in the twenty-first century seem, yet again, unfathomable.

Mega-Lily

"We can make a city like a single plant," claims Shimizu. It plans to take OTEC to the next logical step, with a megaproject it calls Green Float, a plan to have self-sufficient, carbon-negative botanical skyscrapers floating in Tokyo Bay by 2025.

Imagine looking out the window of your Tokyo high-rise to view a thousand-meter-high flower floating in Tokyo Bay. The flower is a skyscraper made of magnesium alloy floating on a giant lily pad platform. The petals of the flower are seven hundred to a thousand meters high, where fifty thousand citizens reside. The stamen rising in the middle of the ring of petals contains offices, hospitals, gymnasiums, and other services. The skyscraper-sized stem holding these residences aloft is a vertical garden of vegetables—what the designers call "a plant factory." The gigantic lily pad on which the structure floats contains forest, fields, waterways, reservoirs, and grasslands. The inner circle hosts land agriculture fed by algae biomass, as well as grasslands with grazing livestock. The outer rim adjoins marine forests, lagoons, and beach resorts.

Green Float is designed to be carbon neutral and self-sustaining, employing state-of-the-art environmental protection technologies and producing energy from the waves, wind, ocean thermals, and solar power generated from satellites. As the designers announced in the English version of their financial report: "Departing radically from traditional ideas of the city, this concept emerged from a consideration of an ideal living environment, one that would impose no burdens on and exist in perfect harmony with the environment, like a plant."

Shimizu Corporation proposes a cyclical metabolism akin to Delta-Sync's, except vertical. Masaki Takeuchi, project leader of Green Float, described his vision of an urban "arterial cycle" and "venous cycle" to DigInfo, which translated his Japanese:

"The carbon dioxide, wastewater, and garbage from the urban area become nutrients for the plant factory below. They also become nutrients for the arable and marine cultivation at the bottom. In other words, we want to achieve a natural cycle, where the city gets back fish from the shallows and cereals from the fields, and vegetables from the plant factory."

Once demonstrated on Tokyo Bay, Shimizu Corporation claims that future Green Floats will be situated at the equator, where residents will experience warm temperatures, low winds, and calm seas.

"At the equator, temperatures are constant, and typhoons aren't a problem. Everyone will have an ocean and a green view, and we've already had people reserve spots," Takeuchi explained to *Japan Times*. Then he joked, "The president of Shimizu bought the first one."

Shimizu asks us to imagine being residents of Green Float and stepping out of our high-rise apartments. "Summer beaches spread out before your eyes, and the lagoons are teeming with fish and shellfish. Living here raises the happiness index, not economic indexes. New business models are born here. Future businesses that fuse nature and technology will begin."

The project has provoked much skepticism, but it's hard to argue with the Shimizu Corporation, which makes about $15 billion US each year. When challenged about the 2025 deadline, the company confirms it is committed. Shimizu makes seasteaders look like we're floating on inflatable rubber inner tubes. What could inspire such a grand vision?

It has everything to do with the mother of invention, necessity, and its father, terror.

Living on Land: Are You Crazy?

The Japanese people are intimately aware that their expanding island population relies on plant and animal seafood. Japan is a group of densely populated islands that sit entirely inside the Pacific "Ring of Fire," where volcanic and tectonic activity give rise to unpredictable earthquakes and tsunamis. Japanese elders today remember both the atom bombs and the 2011 Fukushima disaster, and every tsunami and earthquake in between. As Americans worry about crime and terrorists, the Japanese worry about earthquakes and tsunamis, neither of which occur in the equatorial zone, where Shimizu Corporation plans to build their floating islands.

As Yoichi Miyamoto, president of Shimizu Corporation, wrote in the Shimizu 2012 *Social Responsibility Report*, "Not only did the Great East Japan Earthquake cause damage that surpassed all fears, its impact was enough to alter the nation's fundamental values," elaborating on "the resulting tsunami, nuclear power plant accidents, massive flooding in Thailand, and financial uncertainty in Europe that shook the world."

This peaceful, overpopulated island culture—subsisting on fish and seaweed, running out of options for energy, traumatized by repeat apocalyptic disasters—is perfectly suited to initiate ocean civilization, and Shimizu business leaders have already staked their honor on success.

Miyamoto's mission statement for Shimizu reads less like a company prospectus and more like a moral lecture. "We live remarkably convenient lives in cities that have developed along economic lines. But happiness should be measured separately from material wealth."

We managed to procure a rare interview with Green Float's elusive Masaki Takeuchi, leader of Green Float.

He believes the seismic shift in the values of the Japanese people reflects a change in global consciousness, and that Green Float "represents the unity of ethics and economics.

"Our Green Float project [will] put an entirely new paradigm in place, and then work to develop the technologies and business plans needed to bring this vision to life. Revolutions require completely new modes of thinking with regard to processes, technologies, and business models. I have taken to heart the words of Albert Einstein: 'We can't solve problems by using the same kind of thinking we used when we created them.'"

A novel translation of the same quote Rutger de Graaf repeats. So why is Green Float modelled after a floating flower?

"We're focusing on technologies that take their inspiration from nature," he replies. "We have much to learn from vegetation and plants that make their living on the surface of the water, including things like how to design a floating structure or how to design thriving growth systems."

We couldn't help but be struck by how this sounds like Karina.

"The design inspiration for a single module, consisting of multiple large and small circular floating structures, derives from the Mandelbrot set, a mathematical model of a complex system whose essence recalls the self-similar organization of plants."

Takeuchi is explicit that water lily cities should be sovereign nations.

"Like it or not, nations and peoples are tied to specific circumstances and limitations, both geopolitical and historical. Given a pervasive sense of helplessness in the face of current global problems, including economic, resource, environmental, and conflict-driven issues, we believe humanity may need to strive for a revolutionary kind of sustainability, something distinct from that achieved through incremental improvements based on international agreements or compromise. We therefore believe an international shared asset under United Nations rule may offer greater hope and potential than an island that already belongs to an existing state."

Shimizu's website describes a floating foundation similar in conception to DeltaSync's: "The honeycomb structure incorporates hexagonal cells. Widely used in construction and leading-edge aerospace fields, this structure is more than ninety-percent air, making it both strong and lightweight. We will construct an artificial offshore ground structure by linking these honeycombs."

The Green Float vision includes every technology that seasteaders are developing, and several more. For instance, the Green Float skyscraper will be over a thousand meters tall, considerably taller than today's tallest building in the world, Dubai's Burj Khalifa, which is 830 meters. Is this realistic?

"On land," says Takeuchi, "Shimizu can begin constructing a thousand-meter or two-thousand-meter building at any time, as the construction technologies required to build extremely high structures are already in place."

Ask yourself: Which is more difficult, building a thousand meters into the sky or a thousand meters into the earth? Japan is ready to complete construction of the Mizunami Underground Research Laboratory: *two* shafts that will reach an astonishing one thousand meters deep into the earth. If Japan can dig one of the deepest shafts in the world in its quest to develop nuclear power for its people, it can create a skyscraper of equal height that will relieve it from the need for nuclear power. A thousand meters below the earth, it is hot, stuffy, and dangerous. A thousand feet above the tropical oceans, it is cool, breezy, and hospitable.

The design calls for the towers to be built from magnesium harvested from seawater. "Sea water is composed of about 0.13 percent dissolved magnesium by weight, so one ton of magnesium can be extracted from seven hundred seventy tons of sea water. Because its specific gravity is a quarter that of steel, magnesium has a superior specific strength. In addition, it has gained attention as an environmentally friendly material. The remarkable magnesium alloys developed at Kumamoto University are the strongest in the world and are not likely to cause explosions due to fire. These materials are already in use in motor vehicles, and the university is sharing its related research with the Green Float project. While these alloys need to be made somewhat stronger to meet project requirements, the university is making progress with its research and development in this area."

As futuristic as it sounds, "seament" or "seacrete" is a technology as old as OTEC, and seashell cities are an old idea. German architect and inventor Wolf Hilbertz patented the process in 1979 but died before he could create his seacrete island, which he named the Autopia Ampere, in the Mediterranean Sea. He claimed it would house, feed, and employ fifty-thousand residents, the same population that Shimizu suggests.

Consider that on Planet Earth, man must dig into rock to extract minerals. On Planet Ocean, minerals float freely to cities. Minerals dispersed through rock present different challenges from minerals dissolved in seawater. With the Wolf Hilbertz technique, aquatic engineers simply immerse a metal grid in the ocean, apply a small electrical current, and minerals flowing through the mesh bond electrochemically to the charged metal. In this manner, the calcium carbonate and other mineral ions in the water accumulate on the meshwork. The accreting substance, as hard as cement, is the same substance from which sea-shells, limestone, and marble are made. Instead of lifting and pouring cement, the architect immerses the electrified rebar of a structure and simply waits for the seament to form. The structure grows as long as current flows. On earth, cities must be built. On the ocean, cities could be grown.

The process has been in operation for decades. Man-made coral reefs all over the world are built from the Wolf Hilbertz process. Biorock Inc. has grown biorock reefs worldwide to restore marine ecosystems, creating colorful coral nurseries of sea life. Reefs made of biorock strengthen as they age and are self-repairing, as Chris Muglia suggested. At the Seasteading Institute, barely a week goes by without some aquapreneur soliciting us to make seament breakwaters for seasteads. It's a long way from skeletal coral reefs to floating skyscrapers, but Takeuchi believes that biorock technology could be ready for the industrial growing of cities by 2025.

But what about Shimizu's plan for "space-based solar power"? Isn't that overambitious?

"The Japan Aerospace Exploration Agency [JAXA] plans to launch a satellite for a space-based solar power plant in 2030," replies Takeuchi. JAXA frequently works with NASA. "Development work is proceeding at a steady pace, and we're in the process of exchanging information with JAXA developers. Ultimately, we'd like to install a floating power-receiving base for Green Float, using laser waves or microwaves to receive electricity."

By 2040, JAXA plans to beam microwave energy from satellites to Tokyo. Two giant mirrors in orbit could reflect sunlight onto solar panels in space. These would collect power that could be beamed down to antennas in Tokyo Bay, which could convert microwave energy into DC electricity—about one gigawatt, equivalent to the average nuclear power plant. JAXA independently plans to build its own man-made island, three kilometers long, to receive this power.

Takeuchi believes all doubts will be dispelled when the first Green Float is constructed. Even if the project fails, it will serve as a means of inspiring and generating aquatic innovation that will inevitably serve ocean industries. If you were an aerospace engineer, and JAXA offered to pay you to help build giant space mirrors, would you take the job?

Measured by the technological innovations it inspires, the moon shot could be surpassed by the ocean launch.

Perhaps populations must be provoked to seize upon ambitions worthy of their challenges. In May 1961, when President John F. Kennedy announced that the United States "should commit itself to achieving the goal, before this decade is out, of landing a man on the Moon and returning him safely to Earth," there was no fuel in existence that could achieve this science fiction feat. Whole new subfields of chemistry had to be invented to create the fuel cell that would make the impossible possible. Eight years later, skeptics were silenced.

If the Cold War can put men in space, maybe man's war with the Earth can put cities on the ocean. Nothing motivates a people to work with nature like a natural disaster. The Dutch and Japanese, both traumatized by climate, are laboring to build floating econations on the seas. They believe the world has no choice but to follow them.

DeltaSync wants a billion people on the seas by 2050. Let's talk about the billion who may be the first to show up.

PART III

ECONOMY

Chapter 6

WEALTH

The Miracle of Start-up Societies

We Are the 1 Percent (And So Are You)

If you can afford to buy this book, you may be in the 1 percent. According to former World Bank lead economist Branko Milanovic, if you're single and make more than $34,000 US after taxes, you're a member of the global 1 percent. Take a moment to contemplate where you reside along this graph.

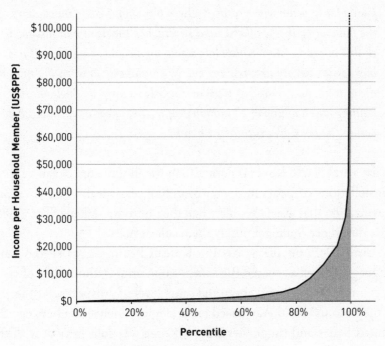

Based on a graph by Toby Ord.

This graph is evidence of inequality. It's also evidence of a humanitarian singularity. For most of history, the vast majority of people resided in the bottom part of the graph, and virtually nobody, not even kings and emperors, could imagine the upper part of this graph.

The reason you and I are among the wealthiest people in the world is because of breakaway experiments in governance.

If We Build It, They Will Come

The civilized world stared with astonishment at the NASA Earth Observatory satellite photo of the Korean Peninsula at night. Journalist Barbara Demick describes the photo in her book *Nothing to Envy: Ordinary Lives in North Korea*:

> *Next to this mysterious black hole, South Korea, Japan, and now China fairly gleam with prosperity. Even from hundreds of miles above, the billboards, the headlights and streetlights, the neon and fast-food chains appear as tiny white dots signifying people going about their business as twenty-first-century energy consumers. Then in the middle of it all, an expanse of blackness nearly as large as England. It is baffling how a nation of 23 million people can appear as vacant as the oceans. North Korea is simply a blank.*

Today rural North Korea is darker than the illuminated oceans. Dense constellations of boats in the surrounding seas speak of an emerging seavilization that wasn't visible when the photo was taken in the 1990s. This difference is almost purely the result of rules.

Until 1945, people across the Korean Peninsula spoke the same language, as well as shared the same ethnic origins, thousands of years of common history, and about the same level of prosperity. At the end of the Second World War, based on strategic maneuvering between the United States and the Soviet Union, Korea was split in two; with the North following the principles of Communism and the South capitalist democracy. This divergence did not happen due to any differences between Northerners and Southerners. In many cases, they came from the same families. The arbitrary nature of the division rendered the fate of those on the Korean Peninsula a natural experiment in the influence of formal rules.

Ralph Hassig and Kongdan Oh write in *The Hidden People of North Korea: Everyday Life in the Hermit Kingdom*, "Between 1946 and the beginning of the Korean War, an estimated 580,000 people came down from the North, and another 400,000 to 650,000 came south during the Korean War. After the war, the border between the two Koreas was tightly shut," and the flood of hundreds of thousands slowed to a trickle of hundreds.

In 1955, North and South Koreans earned about the same income on average. Today the average South Korean earns eighteen times as much as she did in 1955, and eighteen times more than the average North Korean today. The average South Korean also lives an average of ten years longer.

Satellite photos of Earth reveal the tragedy of mankind's hubris in governing others. Lights at night reveal stark differences in economic performance. Shining in full color by day are stark differences in environmental stewardship.

Haiti and the Dominican Republic share the island of Hispaniola. The border that cleaves the island between two states can be seen clearly from space. The Dominican Republic is lush with forests near the border, while Haiti is barren, brown, and eroded. Does a great river separate them, leaving one side to locusts? No, nothing separates the forestland from the wasteland except a line that humans made up. The differences in social well-being between Haiti and the Dominican Republic need not be described.

Examples of the power of borders to alter the rules of development abound. The stories of East Germany versus West Germany, Hong Kong versus mainland China, Singapore versus Malaysia, Zimbabwe versus Botswana, Brazil versus Bolivia, Greece versus Albania, and the United States versus Mexico all attest to the power of formal rules. Arnold Kling and Nick Schulz claim in their book *Invisible Wealth: The Hidden Story of How Markets Work* that crossing the border from Latin America into the United States "appears to make the productivity of a low-skilled worker ten to twenty times higher, based on the wage differential." Education entrepreneur and seastead humanitarian Michael Strong asks us to "[i]magine if you could walk across an invisible line and raise your income tenfold."

Dr. Francis Fukuyama writes in his magnum opus *The Origins of Political Order: From Prehuman Times to the French Revolution,* "Poor countries are poor not because they lack resources, but because they lack effective political institutions." Deranged rules are "one of the principal reasons why poor countries can't achieve higher rates of growth."

If North Korea were a modular seastead, it could dissolve. If residents could sail or tow their homes to South Korea, the physical size of the country would shrink along with its population until it disappeared or adapted to attract residents. If it adapted and produced innovative benefits that attracted South Koreans back to North Korea, then South Korea, if it required residents to choose to live there to survive, would step up its efforts to service residents. We'd have a market competition operating in the most powerful industry on earth: governance.

Wealth Rockets

The vision of man-made islands on the sea, each experimenting with new governance rules, didn't just come out of the blue. It was inspired in large part by the astonishing success of a dozen island nations, many of them created by historical accident. Some are peninsulas, some are merely legal islands, and some are actual islands. These small new polities, politically unleashed from larger nations, resulted in millions of people racing from poverty to prosperity in less than a generation. If anything should inspire us to experiment more with governance rules, it's these dozen or so new minipolities established in the second half of the twentieth century, each of them unique, that fostered sudden hyperaccelerations of wealth for the impoverished.

Start with a global view. The World Bank says that in 1981 half the developing world's population was impoverished, living on less than $1.25 a day. Three decades later, by 2012, less than a fifth were that poor.

Why is this happening? Focus in on a regional view. East Asia includes China, South Korea, and Taiwan. Dr. Mark J. Perry, professor of economics at the University of Michigan, calculated that in 1960 East Asia had the highest poverty rate in the world, at 58.8 percent. In the thirty-six-years between 1970 and 2006, the poverty rate in East Asia descended to 1.7 percent.

How did this happen?

Pre-steads

It started with Hong Kong. This tiny peninsula and group of islands on the southern coast of China was ping-ponged back and forth between various rulers; first as part of China; then a colony of the British Empire in 1842 after the First Opium War; then occupied by Japan during World War II; then reoccupied by the British, who would eventually cede control back to China in 1997. China, not sure how to reintegrate Hong Kong into its ancient nation, renamed it the Hong Kong Special Administrative Region (SAR), promising it some measure of legal and economic autonomy.

As a result of this unique historical trajectory, this very small piece of China was administered according to British common law, whereupon Hong Kong became an international melting pot, with Chinese traditions and British rules, earning it the nickname "East Meets West." Chinese and British pioneers seeking new opportunities beyond the reach of the laws and mores of their home countries arrived in the cordoned-off islands and peninsula of Hong Kong. Dodging Chinese border guards, hundreds of thousands of refugees swam or boated across shark-infested waters to Hong Kong. In 1960 Hong Kong's 3 million inhabitants were less than 0.5 percent of China's overall population of 667 million. The caprice of history had created a rare controlled experiment in economics. What was the result?

Let's set the perspective. Many consider the period between the American Civil War and the year 2000 to be the greatest growth of prosperity for the average American. And, indeed, it was unprecedented in world history. During the 130 years between 1870 and 2000, US GDP per person grew tenfold, as measured in 1996 dollars.

During the thirty-six years from 1961 through 1996, Hong Kong's GDP per person grew 87 times.

The Hong Kong Miracle

Patri's grandfather Milton Friedman marshaled popular attention to "the Hong Kong miracle":

In short, from 1960 to 1996, Hong Kong's per capita income rose from about one-quarter of Britain's to more than a third larger than Britain's. It's easy to state these figures. It is more difficult to realize their significance. Compare Britain—the birthplace of the Industrial Revolution, the nineteenth-century economic superpower on whose empire the sun never set—with Hong Kong, a spit of land, overcrowded, with no resources except for a great harbor. Yet within four decades, the residents of this spit of overcrowded land had achieved a level of income one-third higher than that enjoyed by the residents of its former mother country.

In China, disastrous economic policies from 1949 to 1976 had led to over 36 million dead. One of the most liberal market economies in the world nestled aside the most hard-line Communist nation. Next to the behemoth, Hong Kong seemed fragile as a butterfly. So why didn't the behemoth invade, squash the bug, and confiscate its wealth? Remember this answer the next time somebody predicts large nations will invade seasteads. China didn't attack. It learned and adapted.

Chinese leaders were so impressed by the Hong Kong experiment, leader Deng Xiaoping announced China's new "open door" policy in December 1978. In 1980 it designated four "special economic zones," or SEZs, which curled along the crescent of China coastline. The first was Shenzhen, established just across the river from Hong Kong, followed quickly by Zhuhai, Shantou, and Xiamen. Sudden growth in these SEZs was so startling, only four years later, former Communist strongmen designated fourteen coastal cities to be SEZs, triggering the construction of modern container ports, which would come in handy as China began to produce and export the goods that drove a cornucopia of consumer goods for the West. Only four years after that, Chinese rulers, flush with new tax revenue, realized they were on to a good thing. Why not allow a little capitalism in the economy, as long as the Communist Party remained in control of the government? They picked their first island experiment, designating the entire island province of Hainan an SEZ, prompting a new term: SEMZ, or special economic megazones. Thus began China's pattern of political absolutism and economic freedom.

China's conversion from authoritarian Communism to authoritarian capitalism did not primarily have humanitarian motives, but it had humanitarian effects. An exodus of poor farmers migrated from China's interior to these new "islands" of economic freedom where local entrepreneurs flourished and employed people. Between 1981 and 2004, an absolute minimum of a half billion Chinese were freed from extreme poverty. By 2010, World Bank data showed that the total amount of impoverished Chinese declined by at least 680 million people in three decades. With Hong Kong and later SEZs as startling examples of what was possible, the Chinese government liberalized its entire economy and decentralized economic power, ceding tremendous freedom to business. Import tariffs were sliced to less than one-fifth over twenty years, from 55 percent to 10 percent. The result was an economic miracle. Between 1978 and 2010, the Chinese economy grew by an average of 9.5 percent per year, one of the fastest periods of economic growth in world history, although the exact figures are often disputed. The Hong Kong–based author Robyn Meredith celebrated, "And 30 years after reforms began, China now exports in a single *day* more than it exported during the entire *year* of 1978."

China has never taxed Hong Kong. All it got from Hong Kong was knowledge. In 1990 China accepted Hong Kong's modest constitution and promised it free trade, free enterprise, and low taxes for at least fifty years. The Chinese government stopped controlling most markets, remaining Communist in name only. And it's all because the defenseless islands and peninsula of Hong Kong set a better example.

Thus do ideologies fall: not by violence but by examples showing a better way. The Soviet Union didn't collapse because a thermonuclear war proved who was right. The example of Western goods, and the fresh sound of exuberance arriving with Beatles music, drove a black economy that was more vibrant than the state-sanctioned economy, and it became obvious to everyone, even the leaders, that economic freedom worked better for everyone. Even an empire needs a robust economy to feed its military.

Asian hyperaccelerations of wealth sparked the beginnings of a movement around the world to establish special economic zones, usually designed to encourage foreign private investors through lower taxes and tariffs. The rush of small states to embarrass former empires was under way. The island of Ireland, one of Europe's poorest countries for more than two centuries, set a new economic policy favoring open markets in the 1990s, and by the end of the decade, "the Celtic Tiger" had surpassed the per capita wealth of the United Kingdom. Later, the Baltic states of Estonia, Latvia, and Lithuania adopted more market-friendly policies and transformed themselves into modern productive societies, easily surpassing their former Russian occupiers.

Tariffs do not exist in Hong Kong. No business licenses are required for any business. No restrictions of any kind are imposed on financial transactions in and out of Hong Kong. It's impossible to overestimate the role Hong Kong plays as a melting pot and mecca for poor people. Gordon Mathews, an anthropologist and author of the book *Ghetto at the Center of the World: Chungking Mansions*, estimates that 70 percent of global trade is conducted not by rich Westerners trading digital bits by computer, but by Africans, Asians, and Middle Easterners flying to places like Hong Kong to trade and sell goods.

Today Hong Kong has one of the highest GDPs per person of any nation in the world. It has one of the lowest infant mortality rates in the world, and one of the highest life expectancies in the world. It has one of the lowest murder rates in the world. Hong Kong has the most skyscrapers of any city in the world, and people who live in those skyscrapers remember when those same areas were squatter villages in the 1970s.

So who wins the humanitarian argument? Progressives or conservatives? They both do. Because of astronomical land values, Hong Kong is the most expensive place to own property in the world. So how do millions of modest means live there? The Hong Kong government generates massive revenue by extending the surface area of the land into the ocean and selling this new land to real estate developers who created, for instance, the airport and the Disneyland Resort. As a result, Hong Kong citizens pay no sales tax, no capital gains tax, no goods and services tax, no value-added tax, no annual net worth tax, no inheritance tax, and no estate tax. This sounds like an arrangement out of the American Right's most fevered fantasies. The government's Housing Authority provides homes for 30 percent of its population, about half of Hong Kongers live in some form of subsidized housing, and residents receive free emergency health care. By 2007, the bottom 60 percent of earners paid no income tax while the top 8 percent paid almost 60 percent of the total tax burden. This sounds like an arrangement out of the American Left's most glorious utopia.

While the West argued, the East experimented.

Singapore Spectacular

Singapore is another island nation that produced prodigious growth in sharp contrast with the large neighboring nations of Malaysia and Indonesia. In 1960 Singapore was almost as poor as many African countries. After race riots broke out in Singapore in 1964, the Malaysian parliament voted 126 to 0 to expel Singapore, thus becoming the only nation in history to gain independence against its will. When it was left to run itself in 1965, Singapore was a tiny British naval base and trading outpost with a per capita GDP of $516. In 2010 it was $43,867, an 85-fold increase in only forty-five years. Over that time, Singapore has grown at more than triple the rate of the nation from which it broke away. Today it boasts standards of living, when adjusted for purchasing power, higher than America's. The average citizen of Singapore is wealthier than the average citizen of Germany.

In 1965, 70 percent of Singaporean households lived in dangerously overcrowded conditions, half its population was illiterate, and a third of its people squatted in slums. Today the island nation leads the world in millionaires per capita. Seventeen percent of all Singaporean households possess at least $1 million US in *disposable* wealth, and that's excluding capital wealth invested in business and property in a place where property is one of the world's most expensive. Income tax is capped at 20 percent. Singaporeans get rich quick. According to a wealth report released by Barclays Bank in 2013, 51 percent of Singapore's wealthy people have taken less than ten years to become millionaires.

Western polemicists from the Left and the Right claim Singapore as their own. With no minimum wage, Singapore maintains an unemployment rate of a little more than 2 percent. Singapore's efficient government maintains large budget surpluses and universal health care. The orderly, litter-free society has been the publicly expressed envy of citizens in a few neighboring countries suffering rampant corruption. Today Singapore's primary social concern is coping with all the immigrants flocking to work there. Almost half their workforce is non-Singaporean, because so many workers choose to live there. Singapore is a parliamentary republic based on English common law with draconian laws for littering and no freedom of speech, yet the society flourishes. What causes societies to flourish? The evidence suggests . . . we just don't know, and never have. We haven't generated enough experiments to discover it.

Like Hong Kong, Singapore is devoid of any natural resources, except its large harbor. Hong Kong and Singapore are two of a few governments on earth that make a profit. The 2016 Index of Economic Freedom ranked Singapore as the second-freest economy in the world, with Hong Kong the first. The Global Competitiveness Report 2015–16 ranked Singapore as the second most competitive country in world, behind Switzerland but ahead of the United States and Germany.

Imagine if we didn't have to wait for the caprice of political history to create Hong Kongs and Singapores.

SEZsteads

Singapore is a seastead that can't move, prosperous in part because it is situated right smack in the path of the world's most vital shipping artery. Singaporeans are so grateful to the sea, a cruise ship is perched atop each of three Marina Bay Sands hotel towers that are fifty-five stories high. Imagine if islands didn't have to rely on the grace of geography to place them along the main veins of the global wealth flow. Seasteads could position themselves optimally where they would best serve cargo ships, and change locations as markets changed.

Trumpeted as the "Four Asian Tigers," the offshore islands and peninsulas of Hong Kong, Singapore, South Korea, and Taiwan all experienced breathtaking growth rates, rapidly creating wealth for the poor and shifting from inefficient traditional economies to the vanguard of the world economy within a generation.

How fast could prosperous seasteads be scaled up? Taiwan is an island nation more than seven times the size of Singapore. After the United States ceased economic aid in 1960, GDP per capita in Taiwan was $154. Today it boasts GDP per capita levels similar to Germany.

Real GDP per person is a blunt instrument to measure overall quality of life, because GDP lumps together all financial transactions. If you get beaten and mugged, the costs of your health care, having to replace your mobile phone, and the policing that fails to catch the criminals are included in GDP. The Good Samaritans who chase away the muggers, notify the neighbors, and offer to babysit your kids while you're in the hospital are not included in GDP. Also, the painkillers you purchase on the down low from your brother-in-law and the pet sitter you pay under the table are not included. If the unseen shadow economy represents less than 10 percent of the US economy and more than two-thirds of the nation of Georgia's economy, what does GDP even mean? Most confounding of all, GDP includes whatever governments confiscate and spend inefficiently, so whether they spend 10 cents or $10 on the same package of Post-it Notes is included in the GDP.

The primitive science of economics must use crude tools to compare countries. Nevertheless, "gross domestic product" is a grossly imperfect proxy for overall well-being, because GDP per capita correlates strongly with measures of life expectancy, happiness, and education. Though taking a one-year snapshot of any country's average GDP does not account for how the wealth is distributed, *growth* in real GDP per capita usually indicates growth in incomes of the poor. We can say with confidence that when the impoverished are unleashed from state restraints and allowed to start anew with their own countries, health, wealth, and happiness are produced that no graph or statistic can measure.

When we consider the many staggering accelerations of wealth and freedom that have occurred in modern history as a result of political accidents, we must ask: What would happen if small-stakes experimentation in rules were common? We would see many more ideas being tested against reality. Many would fail and be abandoned. A few would succeed and be imitated by old powers, just as the success of Hong Kong drove China's rulers to embrace a probusiness model for the whole country. Over time we would see a dramatic improvement in the quality of rules—perhaps even a governance revolution to complement the commercial and industrial revolutions of the past.

The magnificent success of these special economic zones, has sparked a movement among entrepreneurs—most prominently cofounder and CEO of Whole Foods Market, John Mackey, who said in an interview with the Internet forum Big Think:

> What is unprecedented is not poverty. What is unprecedented is wealth, wealth for not a few, but prosperity for literally billions of people. Every year now, we see hundreds of millions of people escape from poverty just in two countries, China and India. It is the greatest revolution in human prosperity in all of human history. It's all occurred in the last 20 years, and it's a fact that you almost never see reported in the media.
>
> The beauty of Conscious Capitalism is the realization that the pie

*can grow ... and it's a win, win, win, win, win game, and that turns me
on. I'm very fired up and excited about that because it means human
flourishing isn't trapped in some type of limited set of constraints.*

John Mackey teamed up with educational entrepreneur and seasteading
enthusiast Michael Strong to create the nonprofit FLOW movement,
standing for Freedom Lights Our World, an organization of "Conscious
Capitalists" who are "dedicated to liberating the entrepreneurial spirit
for good." They coauthored a book with several leading lights of free
enterprise called *Be the Solution: How Entrepreneurs and Conscious Capitalists Can Solve All the World's Problems.* Strong, founder of innovative
versions of Socratic, Montessori, and Paideia schools, has spearheaded
a campaign to organize entrepreneurs to unleash wealth creation where
wealth is needed most. He travels the world speaking publicly to world
leaders, business leaders, and those working for poverty alleviation.
With his background in education, Strong knows how to bypass the
facts and figures and tell by showing. He displays a photo of Shenzhen,
China, in 1980, near the outset of a special economic zone development. It looks like a crowded ghetto of squat tenements. Then he displays a photo of Shenzhen in 1995, showing the results of fifteen years
of SEZ growth: fabulous shining skyscrapers and a city that appears so
futuristic that viewers ask if it's been Photoshopped. It's real.

At the time of its designation as an SEZ, Shenzhen was a small
fishing village, lacking even a traffic light. In fifteen years, property values in Shenzhen soared 8,000 percent. In the same amount of time, it
attracted 4 million immigrants. When looked at over thirty years, land
values in Shenzhen increased 18,000 percent. That isn't a typo. In 1980
Shenzhen was not a bad place to be born poor. Millions of poor people
knew it. That's why they moved there. Thousands of foreign investors
knew it. That's why, one year after it was designated an SEZ, Shenzhen
accounted for 50.6 percent of all foreign direct investment in China.

Once opened to foreign investors, the rush of capital investment
was beyond imagination. Between 1979 and 1995, Shenzhen's industrial output increased 1,256-fold, creating job opportunities that drew
poor people from all over the world to work in factories that produced

electronics, pharmaceuticals, chemicals, textiles, building materials, and processed foods, which in turn stimulated growth in the surrounding agricultural area. When the SEZ was established, 30,000 people lived in Shenzhen. Twenty years later, the population had risen to 7 million. The population of temporary workers increased 1,640-fold. The accommodating building constructions set records for speed of construction and created economic opportunities for real estate development. Imagine your city population growing 30 percent per year for thirty years. Shenzhen rapidly followed Hong Kong into the ranks of the five most densely populated cities in the world.

Shenzhen's humanitarian singularity flourished in the shadow of a dogmatic nation that had recently executed or imprisoned millions of its own citizens for real or imagined disobedience. Shenzhen's territory had to expand against this ancient rigid jurisdiction. Imagine if Shenzhen were a self-assembled floating island on the ocean with no deadly empire to petition, "Please, leaders, may we annex more of your land so we may further demonstrate that your ideology is wrong?" It could expand or contract fluidly according to the choices of people who moved there, not the strategies of politicians.

How do land values rocket from worthless to priceless in a decade and a half? Humans have trouble thinking in terms of exponential increases in information technology, and governments are a form of information technology. Tweaks in initial rules end up having irreversible effects that were not predicted even by the tweakers. Every time we "hit restart" on a nation and start again from scratch, we see dazzling differences in human flourishing.

In chapter 9, "Eliminate Global Poverty," Michael Strong cowrites a subsection called "Women's Empowerment Zones," with Mark Frazier of OpenWorld, which helps free zones become self-funding. They eliminate rhetoric from their argument and allow the mind-expanding facts to speak for themselves.

Throughout the developing world, after a piece of land has been designated as a free zone with Singapore- or Hong Kong-class business climate improvements, the value of the land climbs by 500% to

3,000% or more ... In the San Isidro free zone in the Dominican Republic, land values rose 2,000% after the land was freed of taxes, customs duties, and telecommunications monopolies. In Dubai and Freeport Bahamas, property value increases have been on the order of 8,000% over the initial 12-year period following introduction of free zone incentives. ... Consider the implications of this process of near-instantaneous wealth creation.

If these facts don't shake you up, read them again. With new politico-economic experiments, we have a chance not only to fulfill every parent's dream of providing a life for their children that's better than their own, but also to allow them to live long enough to witness it. Strong writes, "We can expect steadily increasing global immigration flows in the coming decades as hundreds of millions of poor people escape their current political jurisdiction to move to one that provides greater opportunity."

Strong has put his back behind seasteading, writing in the *Huffington Post*: "This is the new frontier of poverty alleviation, one in which cutting-edge thinkers are exploring the possibility of creating new legal systems at sea ... The leading venue for exploring this world of entrepreneurial legal system creation is cleverly named 'Let a Thousand Nations Bloom,' the home to the most progressive movement on the planet."

A 2009 Gallup World Poll finds that if you look at the countries in the poorest quintile—the bottom 20 percent of nations in terms of wealth—you find that more than 40 percent of adults "would like to move permanently to another country" if they were offered the opportunity. The nine poorest countries in the world are all in Africa. Where can poor Africans go to create their own wealth?

The Mauritius Megastar

Off the coast of Eastern Africa is the big island of Madagascar. Off the coast of Madagascar is the Mascarenhas Archipelago. One tiny island in this archipelago is Mauritius.

Mauritius gained independence from England in 1968. Once again, we have another example of a newly independent nation with not much going for it and a whole lot working against it. Mauritius is teensy, remote, with few natural resources, and at the time, it contained a large amount of ethnic hostility. Think of it as a seastead subject to earthquakes that can't move out of the way of tsunamis.

James Meade, later a Nobel Prize recipient in economics, predicted in 1961 that Mauritius was doomed, what with repeated sudden weather catastrophes, power concentrated among a small ethnic elite, little arable land, rapid population growth, and an economy—reliant entirely on a monocrop of sugar—that couldn't employ most of its 680,750 inhabitants. Pack all that onto a tiny volcanic island, stir in a three-way racial inequality, and Mauritius looked like a powder keg.

Mauritius hosted three ethnic groups: Mauritian Creoles, Indo-Mauritians, and Franco-Mauritians. African Creoles were brought to the island as slaves to work sugar plantations. After slavery was abolished in 1835, Indo-Mauritians were brought to Mauritius as indentured laborers. Then came the French, who remained in Mauritius after the British took over in 1810. Promising to put aside their bad blood, these three mutually antagonistic groups planned Mauritius's legislative system based on a classic parliamentary Westminster system borrowed from Britain. This set up a battle between four major parties. Best of luck, guys. Another Nobel laureate showed up in 1972 and offered a second opinion. Author V. S. Naipaul declared Mauritius "an overcrowded barracoon, with problems that defy solution."

If you were a poor, recently laid-off plantation worker in Mauritius with five children the day James Meade made his prediction, the smartest thing you could have done was to have a baby. Between 1970 and 2009, the island nation's GDP per person grew tenfold. As of this writing, per capita income is one of the highest in all Africa. Mauritians managed this heady growth magisterially, diversifying their economy rapidly from sugar to textiles to tourism to banking, attracting more than nine thousand offshore companies to the island. Investment in the banking sector alone brought in a cool $1 billion. Looking at the World Bank graphs of percentage of GDP makes Meade's prognostication downright funny. Between 1976 and 2009, sugar dropped from 40 percent to about 5 percent of GDP, while "financial intermediation" commanded the largest percentage of GDP by 2009.

While ethnic diversity would go on to spur genocides in Rwanda and Burundi and civil wars in Nigeria and Guinea, the diverse population of Mauritians behaved like a smart start-up. Ever flexible in their structural reforms, committed to winning investors with sound and transparent legal systems, friendly to entrepreneurs local and foreign, they speedily integrated their island economy into the global marketplace.

Between 1970 and 2010, Mauritius's GDP averaged a growth rate almost five and a half times that of the rest of Africa. According to the World Bank, between 2002 and 2008, foreign direct investment inflows to Mauritius multiplied by over ten times. The inconsequential island has become an economy of consequence in three decades.

Those plantation workers sure got sophisticated fast. Today the remote African island is considered one of the developing world's most successful democracies. Rank among sub-Saharan African nations in the Rule of Law Index from the World Bank's World Governance Indicators? Number one. Rank in the Index of African Governance? Number one. Rank in the United Nations's Human Development Index among African nations? Number one. As of 2011, 87 percent of Mauritians owned their own homes. Beat that, America.

Is it just a coincidence that the highest-performing African nation is an island nation? After Mauritius, the next two African nations with the highest governance rankings are also small island nations: the Seychelles and Cape Verde.

We study Mauritius as a test pilot seastead. Mauritians decided to make their remoteness a strength, becoming consummate middlemen and deal brokers in a global network of trade. Policy makers in Mauritius studied the export processing zones (EPZs), a version of SEZs that encourage exports through exemptions from certain taxes and regulation, in East Asia. In 1970 Mauritius passed the Export Processing Zone Act, a mishmash of powerful incentives to attract foreign manufacturers, including a low flat corporate tax rate of 15 percent (foreign firms receive a subsidy of close to 10 percent, leading to an effective tax rate of 5 percent), favorable long-term loans, and cheap labor drawn from unemployed Mauritian workers, most of whom were women joining the labor force for the first time. In the early 1980s, the unemployment rate was 20 percent. By the late 1980s it was 3 percent. Almost all of this increase in employment (87 percent) and local entrepreneurship (90 percent) was created by an export processing zone that permitted the easy flow of ocean goods.

It goes without saying that EPZs will most benefit nations that have a lot of coasts in relation to their size. If you have a lot of coast, you can engage in a lot of ocean trade. If you are small, you can benefit maximally from this ocean trade. If you are remote, it's possible the global trade will require your services. If you are mobile, you can strategically place yourself in the path of the longest arteries of shipping routes.

Let's take a moment to savor these glorious numbers. In 1975 roughly 40 percent of Mauritian households were living in poverty as estimated by the country's Central Statistics Office. By 2010, absolute poverty was less than 2 percent. During this time, women joined the labor market in massive numbers. Out of 102 countries in the 2009 Social Institutions and Gender Index (SIGI), Mauritius was ranked number 11. You can measure a nation's deep-rooted success by the flourishing of its women and children. Infant mortality dropped to less than a quarter of what it was in less than forty years. Compare almost any measure of Mauritius's success with that of its nearest neighbors, and you'll find Mauritius is an exception in every measure. For instance, in Madagascar, 36 percent of children who start first grade reach grade five. In Mauritius, its 99 percent, and the average citizen is more than eight times richer.

Today the Mauritian mosquito is provoking the Indian elephant, offering tax laws incredibly favorable to mobile business compared with

Indian tax laws. Much to the chagrin of Indian regulators and tax collectors, "about 80% to 90% of foreign direct investment into India flows through Mauritius via private-equity, hedge funds, and mutual funds," as reported by macroeconomist Ali Zafar, author of the World Bank Group paper "Mauritius: An Economic Success Story." Mauritius is commandeering market share by offering better deals. At the moment, Indian policy makers are hustling to rewrite tax laws. This is how tiny islands alter the course of great nations.

Now imagine if Mauritius were mobile.

Raise All Boats

Let's defy another economic stereotype. Income inequality is measured by the Gini coefficient. If your Gini coefficient is 0, every resident owns the same amount. If your Gini coefficient is 1, one resident owns everything, and everybody else owns nothing. In many cases, extremely speedy growth in developing nations corresponds to extremely inequitable income distribution. It's such a consistent pattern, some economists consider it akin to an economic law. For instance, Hong Kong's Gini coefficient reached 0.50 in 2011, well above the 0.40 level used by analysts to measure the potential for social unrest—and, indeed, labor strikes in Hong Kong have been increasing. Mauritius utterly defies this pattern. At the same time that the nation experienced stellar growth, its income inequality, as measured by the Gini coefficient, *fell* from 45.7 in 1980 to 38.9 in 2006.

Richer *and* more equal? Mauritius is a new political experiment that educates nations on the other side of the Earth. Consider this 2010 report from Dr. Satish Chand, adjunct professor of economics at the Australian National University's College of Asia and the Pacific, who visited Mauritius to research lessons that could be applied to the island nation of Fiji:

The sugarcane fields, the mountains in the backdrop, the greenery, and the people look deceptively similar to Fiji . . . Mauritius is facing the loss of preferential access to its sugar into the European Union; the very same challenge faced by Fiji . . . Pacific islands policy makers could learn much from Mauritius. Mauritius has managed to ameliorate the handicaps of (small) size and isolation.

The nation has also managed to maintain a harmonious and vibrant multicultural community. Many of our island's leaders and policy makers could learn much from Mauritius.

Why not a field trip to this prosperous nation soon?

The lessons don't stop with Fiji. In 2011 Joseph E. Stiglitz, yet another Nobel laureate in economics, wrote an essay called "The Greatest Country on Earth: What the United States Can Learn from the Tiny Island Nation of Mauritius."

As we were writing this, the World Economic Forum—the internationally renowned Swiss nonprofit dedicated to public/private cooperation—released its annual *Global Competitiveness Report 2013–14*. Among African nations, Mauritius was ranked number one.

Considering the despair so many humanitarians have felt watching the motherland of humanity, the most culturally and genetically diverse continent of people on the planet, spiral backward into barbarism in numerous regions simultaneously, let's contemplate the tiny candle of hope that is Mauritius, an island experiment of new rules coughed up by an accident of history and geography.

Much debate has been stirred about the "Mauritius miracle." Like Hong Kong and Singapore, this island of experimentation had few natural resources and relied on economic freedom and local management. What Hong Kong caused in China on a large scale, and what Mauritius is causing in India on a small scale, is exactly why we want to see more small nations driving innovation and service in the large behemoths by competing with them. You can't be a megamonopoly with a Hong Kong or a Mauritius enriching itself right next door.

Would the world profit from a thousand Mauritiuses? Judging by our spell-checker, this word has never been pluralized before, but plural Mauritiuses, Hong Kongs, Shenzhens, and Singapores, each unique, is the exactly what the future wants to see. If there is any doubt left that islands of new rules can create stupendous and unpredictable improvements in the well-being of the world's poor, we point you to the formerly humble African nation of Mauritius, now a firmly established lynchpin in the global trade network.

Nordic Wonders

Perhaps by now you are detecting a bias. The examples we've described so far suggest that the smaller the role of government in people's networked freedom to choose, the better the results for the poor. Naturally, Patri would love to declare his grandfather the Nostradamus of economics. But not all analysts agree with our narrow assessment of spectacularism. Free market fans love to cite the Asian Tigers to prove their point. Those who support government welfare states love to cite Nordic successes. Every development economist must face the inevitable moment when reality turns his theory to bunk.

The four Scandinavian countries are Sweden, Denmark, Norway, and Iceland. The Nordic nations include these plus Finland. The five Nordic nations impose very high personal taxes while providing generous cradle-to-grave welfare services, yet they maintain low levels of unemployment, high levels of wealth and production, and a per capita standard of living ranked among the world's highest. For most of these countries, trade union membership is up above 65 percent of the workforce. Employees work fewer hours than in almost any other country in the world, yet Nordic nations top the international rankings of the most competitive regions globally.

These nations are often called "socialist," though their various arrangements resemble Russia about as well as they resemble America. As with all innovations, we must cast out our mind-limiting polarities to see them for what they are. FLOW entrepreneur Michael Strong says they're better described as "free market welfare states."

In broad outline, the Nordic nations' method goes like this: high taxes on individual income, but lower taxes for business, which keeps the international trade brisk. Despite some state-owned industries, they maintain low regulations on private businesses, which keeps business folk happy. Despite high taxes, they maintain low regulation of private life, which keeps citizens happy. The people in these regions report themselves as some of the happiest people in the world, with Denmark the happiest.

These small, culturally homogeneous nations with fewer than ten million people each have the lowest corruption and the highest civic mindedness. Most citizens consider themselves to be all sharing the same boat. Surveys reveal that, in large ethnically diverse nations, people tend to think social welfare benefits other groups who are free riding, whereas smaller monocultural nations think of social welfare as support for the tribe. The Nordic nations are bastions of humanism and enforced egalitarianism that have eliminated poverty for most of their citizens, and few seem resentful about it. The World Economic Forum released *The Global Gender Gap Report* in 2014, which ranks countries on their ability to close the gender gap in four key areas: economic participation, education level, health, and political empowerment. Out of 142 nations measured, Iceland, Finland, Norway, Sweden, and Denmark occupy the top five spots.

Those of us swooning over the scattered successes of free markets in uplifting the poor, and distrustful of centralized planning, are confounded by Nordic nations' demonstration that effective macroeconomic management is actually possible. Five nations of saintly politicians and benevolent bureaucrats! Who woulda thunk it? The radical right in Sweden got so rabid they almost voted to lower tax rates below 55 percent of GDP, but they were defeated by organized voting blocs that demanded they continue paying the second highest taxes in the world. As with Singapore's "authoritarian democracy," we must say, *"Who cares what we think? Most people who live there like it."*

Swedish author and scientist Nima Sanandaji, who is of Kurdish origin, argues that free markets catapulted Scandinavian countries from poverty to prosperity first; generous state-sponsored welfare supports came second. But the only important moral point is that, increment by increment, most Scandinavians chose their models. As heirs to a legacy that flows straight from Rose and Milton Friedman, coauthors of *Free to Choose*, we know this is the moral point to which they would hold us.

Run through the list of recent economic miracles in your mind: Hong Kong, Shenzhen, Ireland, Mauritius, Dubai, Iceland. We can't think of a way to use these examples to win a single argument, but each can be used to defeat every single argument. All they have in common is that they are seaside states. Is it possible that nobody knows what causes society to flourish? Note that *each is unique, unprecedented in world history, and, despite its faults, fabulously successful at promoting overall well-being.*

A Sea of Confusion

So which system works the best for overall human welfare? More government taxing and spending, or more freewheeling freedom to choose? Most of us experience a visceral reaction and then point to Scandinavian successes or Asian Tigers to justify what we already believe. Both groups of countries are extraordinary examples, but any generalization drawn from a dozen and a half Tigers or a half dozen Nordic utopias leaves 165 nations in the muddled middle, which won't show many decisive patterns. We have 193 in the United Nations to look at, and taking the data as a whole, we have to admit, we just don't know. All these countries have wildly different immigration rates, cultures, climates, cuisines, natural resources, legal systems, relationships with other nations, and are at different junctures in their sagas of economic development.

Suppose we didn't have 193 nations, but 187. Suppose Scandinavia was an ocean, and Finland a swamp having never been settled by humans. We would be confident asserting that low taxes and minimal bureaucratic management allow the poor to uplift themselves and foster the most overall well-being. All available evidence would attest to this. With only 187 experiments, this is all we would know of possibility. But possibility is all about the stuff we don't know.

Thomas Edison was supposed to have said, "I didn't fail ten thousand times. I successfully eliminated, ten thousand times, materials and combinations which wouldn't work." What if Edison had to stop after 193 experiments? He offered an answer: "Many of life's failures are people who did not realize how close they were to success when they gave up." The governance equivalents of lightbulbs and molecular biology are out there waiting to be discovered amid the mass of failures.

All We Are Saying Is Give SEZs a Chance

The United States of America was founded by people who at the time were considered radicals; who were seeking greater autonomy and freedom to fulfill of some wacky ideas, such as *the people shall rule themselves by voting for rulers to force the people to do what the people want*. There was so much doubt about their success that, in Europe, the country was commonly referred to as "the American Experiment." It worked so well that constitutionally limited representative democracy is now the "industry standard" form of government, copied by countries around the world.

What if there had never been a New World? Would democratic constitutional republics never have been demonstrated as feasible? Would the USSR and China have imposed their ideas on the rest of Asia and Europe? Would the world think that Communism was the best possible way, simply because no other experiments could be tried?

Here's what we'll put money on: whatever emerges in 2047 will prove everybody in 2017 wrong. History shows that success emerges not from our predictive powers but our passion; not from rationality but creativity; not from consensus but diversity. Enforcing predictions on people who disagree has always been the road to ruin.

The seasteading movement requires us to embrace humility as to our ability to know what's right for everyone, and gratitude for the manifest ability for humanity as a whole to discover what's right when freed from political enforces who claim to know what's right. The networked ecology of 7 billion human brains repeatedly presents us with astonishing solutions that we as individuals never expected. More are on the horizon, but we won't find them staying here and arguing. We'll find them by following the example of our former intern at the Seasteading Institute, Baoguang Zhai from China.

Zhai, to us, is the point man; the first pioneer in a future flow of immigrants who will embrace the seasteading lifestyle. The deepest human need is to belong, and Baoguang Zhai reminds us that the world is full of talented people who are not permitted to belong, even in the place they've lived their whole lives.

Fish out of Water

Zhai grew up in Gansu. Of the thirty-one provinces in China, Gansu, in terms of GDP per capita, is third from the bottom.

"Different places in China have very sheer differences in socio-economic performance," Zhai explains, "and my home town is an underdeveloped inland province. Education resources are so scarce. I'm prohibited from taking a college entrance exam in Beijing because I am from a different class, which is manifested on your record."

Zhai explains China's *hukou* system, a discriminatory practice instituted in Mao Tse-tung's Communist China in 1958 to stem the migration of rural Chinese to cities. People born in urban areas received state jobs, state services, and state education, which only increased the incentive of rural people to become city citizens. Mao is long dead, the Chinese economy has mostly abandoned its socialist ideals, and—pause here to gasp with shock—the government has failed to adjust. A half century later, the law still requires that anyone who wants to move from a poor village to a wealthy city has to petition the *hukou* authorities. This, of course, incentivizes a mass system of bribery, which few rural Chinese can afford. Most rural high school students are required to be educated in their local village unless they are exceptional performers. Chinese universities are also strongly biased against admitting students from the countryside, unless they are the most exceptional among the exceptional performers.

Zhai is so humble he refuses to talk about his accomplishments. "I'm not very good at math," he says.

We have his resume in hand. We know that all his SAT I and II and AP test scores were nearly perfect.

He shrugs. "I have Chinese training. We don't even study for that."

Well, if the *hukou* system designated him a peasant, how did he attend high school in Beijing?

"I was very fortunate," he replies.

We have to practically pin him against the wall to get him to admit that, yes, he scored very highly in his middle school exams, but he deftly diverts attention to his cousin, who set out to score in the top thirty of the entire province, which included close to a million students. She failed. She scored only around number three hundred. Thus she could not seek schooling in Beijing. "The whole educational system is based on hypercompetition," he says.

For reasons that will remain mysterious, Zhai was part of the rarefied few from Gansu who got to attend high school in the metropolis of Beijing.

"On the first day, one of my teachers told the students that they are lucky to be born in Beijing, so they should behave themselves, and not act like those backward people from inland provinces."

Zhai remained quiet, knowing the teacher was talking about people like him.

"My accent strongly identified me as a peasant who didn't know anything about the city. Popular music, popular clothes, popular television shows—I didn't know anything about those. The psychological position you are in is hard to rub out. I can practice my speech, I can watch American movies, but I can't change something very deep inside."

When the local students went to take college preparation classes, Zhai's teacher told him not to bother to attend. A boy from Gansu would never be allowed to go to college in Beijing.

"My teacher encouraged my dad to bribe some officials to get me a registration. They know only two options: bribe an official or go home. My dad didn't want to bribe."

After eight years of Beijing schooling, with no options for advancement, Zhai returned to Gansu, where he learned that his golden opportunity was actually a curse. The only thing worse than being born in Zhai's home town with no prospects was being the one in a thousand who got to go to a Beijing high school without becoming one of the one in a million who got to go to a Beijing college. Treated as a backward bumpkin in Beijing, Zhai was treated as an uppity failure when he returned to Gansu.

"They teased me. I was just some guy who had big ambitions who tried to make it big in big city and failed. Since I was not educated in my home town, I didn't fit in there anymore. It seemed completely hopeless. I was seventeen. It's a very sad thing, but I feel a sense of detachment from everywhere."

Zhai got back in touch with friends he had known in grade school. "Some of my old friends got involved with local gangsters because they couldn't get into college, so they don't know what to do. They'd sit around and drink. We had nothing in common to talk about anymore.

"My father showed me the gravestones of my great-grandfather. And one step away was the gravestone of my great-great grandfather. And one step away from that was the gravestone of my great-great-great grandfather. For hundreds of years, my family had been living there and never looked out from that little piece of land."

Zhai resolved to win a scholarship to an American college. The only springboard to the West was Hong Kong. He studied the English dictionary and saved money to fly in just for one day to take the American SAT. He returned to Hong Kong a second time to take the test in science. His scores were so strong that several schools in the United States accepted him, but he had no money to pay tuition. Zhai had spent his life savings on two flights to Hong Kong. Only Tufts University offered him financial aid, so "without hesitation," he said good-bye to his life and attended Tufts near Boston.

"Being a fish out of water became part of my identity," he reflects. "I don't see myself strongly attached to any existing places. It's like you're traveling on a train. You've been to this city, you've been in that city, and you know in ten more minutes, you're going to depart again."

Tufts proved to be a transformative experience. "We were very close to MIT and Harvard, which are exposed to many very innovative ideas and people. I probably spent half of my evenings at lectures at MIT or Harvard listening to people like Mark Zuckerberg—very enlightened people. By day, I did my homework, but at night, instead of staying in my dorm and partying with people, I went to these lectures. I probably learned more from these lectures than from my course work.

"Peter Thiel visited MIT one month after I arrived for college to give a speech in which he talked about seasteading. I still have the name tag I used in that event. This Peter Thiel lecture opened up a new door for me. He only briefly touched on the idea of seasteading, but that was enough for me to look into it. I felt he was talking about the ultimate new option."

Zhai consumed research on the potential for ocean cities.

"Everybody has a hometown, but if you ask me what my hometown is, I don't really have an answer. I think seasteading is for people like me. It's a place for people to belong who do not belong to other places. It's like the people in Europe in the nineteenth century who were persecuted because they were not welcome, so America became a new place where they could belong."

Purely on his own initiative, Zhai designed a detailed development plan for the ocean industry and created a video about his vision of an ocean-based algae energy cultivation system, which he posted on You-Tube. The Seastead Institute was unanimously impressed. We offered him a summer internship, whereupon he excelled instantly. It didn't take long before Zhai was coordinating Project OASIS (Ocean Algae for Seasteading Integrated Solutions), the world's first systematic cross-industry study of ocean-based algaculture.

Zhai's secret talents are revealed when he describes international banking as his "comfort zone," but he wants to defy the easy path available to hyperachievers from China who are schooled in the United States.

"I could go to work for a bank in the USA or China, working ten hours a day to make rich people richer. But during Peter Thiel's lecture, somebody asked him why entrepreneurship was so important. And his answer was very philosophical. He said we had to ask ourselves whether we wanted our careers to be interchangeable, or if we want to explore unique possibilities that could change the world for the better.

"Historically, the people involved in the great projects from the beginning are very lucky outsiders: the people who helped build the first Apple computer, the first airplane, or the people who helped found the United States. I regard seasteading as one of these great projects."

Zhai says his modest socioeconomic background and rootlessness give him unique psychological advantages with regard to seasteading. As a global nomad, he travels lightly and lives monastically.

"I have always moved from place to place, so I can't own many goods. That has enabled me to maintain a very high level of mobility. The people who live on the first seasteads should be people who are always ready to move, ready to explore, not settled, not looking for luxury, but willing to start something possibly under very difficult circumstances. The first people who homesteaded in the USA did not experience a very high comfort level, but they had a very high excitement level."

Zhai's journey took him halfway around the world, driven by a lack of options, a high tolerance for loneliness, and a temperament suited to the detachment required for large personal risks. He has slipped through crack after crack, through high test scores in Gansu, nearly perfect test scores in Hong Kong, a scholarship to Tufts, and then emerging as the second-place winner of a Tufts Energy Competition for innovation in ocean-based algae energy. Tens of millions of talented Chinese peasants were weeded out before Zhai found his way to ultimate rootlessness, loneliness, and freedom. All this propelled him to seek what he calls "the ultimate new solution."

"I read Malcolm Gladwell's *Outliers: The Story of Success*, a book that examines the exceptional circumstances that produce high achievers. If I didn't break rules, I'd still be in my hometown. I think I will break more and more rules."

Imagine the deep sense of meaning we felt at the Seasteading Institute when Baoguang Zhai arrived at our door all the way from Gansu with his backpack and simple smile, announcing: "I am committed to working on this idea for a lifetime."

"I know I am probably one of the youngest people to get involved in the seasteading movement," he says. "I know there are a lot of people like me in China, and I think I am very lucky. I somehow got this opportunity to go to one of the best schools in Beijing and the United States. I know there are a lot of others who didn't, who are stuck to their hometown without getting any information from the outside world. There are a lot of others who have suffered because of the discrimination against them, and I think seasteading could help them.

"Republican theory was conceived in Europe by people like Montesquieu," the eighteenth-century French philosopher, "but it was not initially realized in Europe. It was realized in America, but the aftereffect is that all countries in Europe went democratic after the founding of the United States. That's the essence of seasteading. You try experiments in new places, and people in the old world discover, 'Oh this is pretty good,' and they adopt it. Alexis de Tocqueville, another Frenchman who was highly influenced by Montesquieu, wrote *Democracy in America*, which inspired a lot of people in distant worlds. 'Look, they invented new systems! Why don't we adopt new policies?' Seasteading could inspire the Chinese government to adopt new practices."

Without being prompted, Zhai moves on to our favorite example, Hong Kong—but with a twist. When Zhai read Patri's explication of the principles of competitive governance, he immediately thought of Xiaogang Village, which he calls "the Chinese version of seasteading."

The Eighteen Farmers Who Moved a Billion

During Mao Tse-tung's enforced agricultural collectivization during the Great Leap Forward of 1958 to 1961, more than half of the Xiaogang Village population of 120 starved to death in two years, along with tens of millions of other Chinese. When food shortages threatened again, the villagers decided the inefficient Communist system had to go. Though private property was forbidden by law, eighteen heads of families met in December 1978 and agreed to divide their "People's Commune" into eighteen private plots, signing a document pledging that if any were caught and executed, the others would provide for their families. While turning over the required quotas of production to the commune and the state, the villagers specialized in their best skills, traded among themselves in a secret market, and kept the surplus that always results from specialization and trade. As the rest of the nation starved, Xiaogang Village produced more grain than it had in the previous five years combined, and per capita income rose twentyfold. The sudden wealth attracted attention, the plan was disclosed, and neighbors accused the Xiaogang villagers of "digging up the cornerstone of socialism." The heads of the eighteen families awaited their execution. By this time, however, Mao had died, in 1976, and the new leader, Deng Xiaoping, received the news of this curious experiment in outlawry.

"This is how the entire new Chinese economy started," explains Zhai. "They divided this property, which was supposed to belong to the state. But the party official who discovered this illegal activity did not arrest them. He wrote a secret report to Deng Xiaoping, who ordered that the village be observed. They spread this policy all around the country and changed the entire ecosystem for one billion farmers. This is a very good example of how a small experiment can lead to a great change in a larger country."

The decollectivization of agriculture sparked a wildfire of "capitalism in the countryside." The tiny village became a national model as other communes began dividing their collectivized land into privately owned plots, provoking the whole country to reform to a market-based economy. In the mideighties, village entrepreneurs expanded rural industry while China opened to international trade and experimented with coastal SEZs. A sudden flourishing of private enterprise catalyzed a natural evolution of property rights and an economic expansion that broke world records. In 1979, a year after Deng announced his plan to emancipate farmers, only 1 percent of households owned private agriculture. Five years later, in 1984, it was 99 percent. Today China's economy is the second largest in the world.

"I found this case so compelling to the implication of seasteading," says Zhai, "because, in a sense, the astonishing growth of China, with thirty years of over nine percent annual growth, could really be traced back to the small-scale experiment among those eighteen people. In this case, eighteen farmers risked their lives to try this experiment, whereas seasteading enables many more people to peacefully experiment without having to risk being executed. The impact of seasteading on established societies could be immeasurable, and Xiaogang Village is a vivid example."

Did we mention Zhai is twenty years old? He is not yet old enough to legally drink alcohol. Yet he has jumped ship yet again.

"I 'stopped out' of college after my sophomore year at Tufts to participate in Peter Thiel's '20 Under 20' community. After working at the Seasteading Institute, I joined Blueseed, a project to station a ship twelve nautical miles from the coast of San Francisco, in international waters. The location will allow start-up entrepreneurs from anywhere in the world to start or grow their company near Silicon Valley, without the need for a US work visa. As the first and only Chinese member on Blueseed's team, I work on marketing, business development, public relations, investor relations, and have helped raised angel investment from Xu Xiaoping of ZhenFund, the most active angel fund in China."

If seasteading happens, it will be because people like Zhai make it happen. He is already acting as a liaison between American entrepreneurs and Chinese investors who want to build new worlds. And he worked at both the Seasteading Institute and Blueseed for free. What drives him?

"People like me who fall into the cracks of existing societies represent a new, emerging nation that is being formed. This new nation, just like the first people who first moved to America four hundred years ago to establish their new world, believe in no borders, no traditional concept of nationalism. I imagine myself among one of the first of these people; the truly international and global people who regard no place as their limitation. Upon these people, a new nation will be generated that starts on the ocean, and that would be the most audacious, cohesive, and entrepreneurial nation yet."

The Wave of the Future

Zhai's entrepreneurial nation would require business models to support seasteads. To compete with exiting land states, such a business would have to provide a service so superior to land-based options, it would pay for the immense risks of building a seastead. Fortunately, the reformers who most aggressively solicit the Seasteading Institute work in one of the world's largest industries, which is one of the most dysfunctional but offers the most astounding potential for hope.

Chapter 7

HEALTH

Faster, Cheaper,
Better, Fluid Care

Love Boats

What if your hospital offered an ever-changing view of the sea and coasts, round-the-clock concierge service, dancing, hot tubs, spa treatments, and gourmet food—all included for a fraction of the price of your local hospital? Undergoing surgery has never been a walk in the park, but what if it was like going on a cruise?

Many cruise ships currently offer Botox injections and other cosmetic procedures. Leaders in the industry note that most cruise ships already feature an entire deck devoted to heath care, and US Navy ships often contain full hospitals on board. It's only a short step to retrofitting navy-style surgical rooms onto existing cruise ships and increase revenue. It's predicted that in 2017 a population equivalent to Australia will board cruise ships, most of them retirees. Some of them will get sick.

And in the age of telehealth, it's not like cruise ships are in the middle of nowhere. An enterprising doctor named Dr. Mohammed Saeme, with both an MD and a PhD, designed a system called SAEMED, which links medical professionals at sea to share digital encrypted medical information in real time with their colleagues on land. When medical imaging moves fluidly around the Earth at the speed of light, the main obstacle is not the technology for telemedicine, but the rules that govern the jurisdiction in which your hospital is placed.

And not every patient is thrilled with health care rules in his or her jurisdiction, and the baby boomers are set to start an elderly boom. If you thought they were demanding as teenagers, wait until they become senior citizens. At least 10 percent of Americans remain uninsured. As health care costs rise and wait times lengthen, the industry to provide better options offshore rises with it.

According to the US Centers for Disease Control and Prevention

(CDC), nearly a million Americans go overseas for procedures every year. Patients Beyond Borders, a resource that counsels patients seeking medical travel, estimates that those numbers will grow 15 percent to 20 percent each year as baby boomers overwhelm the system.

Globally the growth is even faster. Dr. Helmut Wachowiak, a professor at the International University of Applied Sciences in Germany, estimates that the global medical tourism market is *already* growing at about 20 percent per year. Referring to the exodus of sick people as "tourism" belies the fact that many people travel for life-saving procedures because they are facing certain death in their home countries. In some countries, entire towns have been known to pitch in to send one person abroad for adequate care.

Health in the United States isn't going to get cheaper any time soon. According to the Centers for Medicare & Medicaid Services (CMS), a federal agency, "In 2012, US health care spending increased 3.7 percent to reach $2.8 trillion, or $8,915 per person," which means that it has increased by a factor of 10 since 1980. When we sought to confirm this claim two years later, CMS had released this update: "US health care spending grew 5.3 percent in 2014, reaching $3.0 trillion, or $9,523 per person." A terrifying study published in the March/April 2012 issue of the medical journal *Annals of Family Medicine* claimed that the typical American family would spend $20,000 on health care that year, and that if current trends continue, health insurance premiums will surpass the median US household income in 2033. Half the citizens in one of the richest countries in the world may have to choose between health insurance and destitution.

Today's rusty health care industries couldn't be more vulnerable to new nimble competitors. According to the Institute of Medicine of the National Academy of Sciences, the US health care system squanders $750 billion on paperwork, fraud, and waste. That's roughly 30 cents of every medical dollar. If Apple wasted 30 cents of every dollar, how fast would new competitors steal away its customers with better service? Ricardo Alonso-Zaldivar of the Associated Press tried to put this in perspective, reporting that this amount of health care waste in one year "costs more than the Pentagon budget. And it's more than enough to pay for the [US] uninsured."

Cruise lines have the competitive edge. They can hire the most talented physicians from anywhere in the world, each held to the accreditation standards of his or her home country. Many are educated in the United States or Europe. But in a global market, certification standards are breaking free of countries and going global. A private, nonprofit voluntary accreditation society called the Joint Commission International works to certify hospitals in at least sixty countries as a guarantee that a facility will live up to Western medical standards—and often surpass them.

Have you noticed that many of your doctors are from India? They appear to be outcompeting Western physicians for top positions at the most elite hospitals. Many have stopped working through the onerous process of migrating to Western nations and are cashing in on the growing market of Western medical tourists in their home country. Josef Woodman, author and founder of Patients Beyond Borders, said, "The growth of American-style hospitals around the world has grown geometrically in the last eight to ten years."

Why move Indian doctors permanently to the United States when their patients can move temporarily to India? The Medical Tourism Association claims that the cost savings for US residents traveling to India "can be up to ninety percent" and points the customer to a list of enticing 2015 price comparisons.

> Heart valve replacement: US, $170,000; India, $9,500
> Heart bypass surgery: US, $123,000; India, $7,900
> Hip replacement: US, $40,364; India, $7,200
> Breast implants: US, $6,400; India, $3,000
> Lasik procedure (both eyes): US, $4,000; India, $1,000

Ready to buy plane tickets? Your employer might. We all know health care is expensive. But how would you like to *get paid* to receive health care?

Hickory Springs Manufacturing, or HSM, a furniture manufacturer in North Carolina, offers its workers a choice: pay $3,000 out of pocket for a knee replacement in the United States or receive a bonus check of at least $2,500 to take an all-expenses-paid trip for surgery in Costa Rica. For many US companies, it works economically. A knee replacement in the United States costs $35,000. In Costa Rica, it's less than half that: presently $12,500. HSM says it has saved almost $10 million in health care costs over five years by paying more than 250 employees to take sick leave and go on vacation at the same time.

With a cost savings like that, many companies will pay their employees to travel overseas, and throw in all the amenities they would never dream of in their home country. HSM employees receive first-class tickets to a resort town, a personal chauffeur, concierge service, and a personal assistant to lead them through every step of the process from landing to leaving. They are treated by physicians who are partially trained in the United States and who serve them in state-of-the art hospitals built specifically to attract medical tourists fleeing the onerous rules in their home countries that require so much expense. Costa Rica features an established tourism infrastructure where Americans, Canadians, and most Europeans are not required to show an entrance visa for stays shorter than ninety days, during which time medical tourists may enjoy Costa Rica's famous beaches and volcanoes. For some, getting a knee replacement surgery is the most fun they have that year. Almost makes you want to be less careful on the stairs.

If you travel abroad for care, you may even get your own personal nurse. The Global Surgery Network, which helps Americans and Canadians travel abroad to save 40–60 percent on surgical, dental, and cosmetic procedures, claims that while bureaucratic restrictions in the United States provide for a nurse-to-patient ratio that is "8, 10, and sometimes 12 to 1 in the US," the nursing ratio for patients traveling abroad is usually one to one. Flying Nurses International is an international company that provides private nurses to accompany patients throughout their entire excursion.

Naturally, islands near the United States are investing prodigiously in the market for medical tourism. The Cayman Islands, Jamaica, Barbados, the Bahamas, and Saint Martin are all building advanced hospitals and magnificent "health cities" to catch the rising wave of patients traveling for superior care, shorter wait times, and cheaper service.

Peter Wei, a radiology resident at Houston's University of Texas Health Science Center, coauthor of *Learning Medicine: An Evidence-Based Guide*, asks, "Why fly across an ocean for superior health care when you can take a ferry just off shore?"

Don't Convince, Compete

In 2012 Dr. Wei addressed a room full of seastead enthusiasts in San Francisco with the following opener.

"There are just short of a million doctors in the US, and there's 1.2 million medical billers and coders."

Peter grinned to hear the groans, because he smelled an industry vulnerable to competition. He rams home his point: "For every doctor out there, there's another person whose entire job is to do all the paperwork so that the hospital can actually get paid."

We groan at such facts only because we know our hospitals are trapped in a particular jurisdiction of laws. But if we think like entrepreneurs competing to provide better, cheaper services, this sounds like an exciting potential for profits.

"Medicine needs seasteading," says Peter. "I don't need to belabor the fact that American health care is in crisis. Costs are spiraling out of control, millions lack access to health care, and, perhaps worst of all, the bureaucracy around health care is stifling the innovation we need to get our way out of this. As a medical student, and as a future physician [Pete has since become a resident] that's something I find deeply troubling. But I think medical tourism might be an answer, and this comes from the same logic that drives seasteading. We in this room believe that competition in governance can make government better. And medical tourism can do the same for medicine. By demonstrating superior practices in the full light of the marketplace, we can give people the care and treatments they need, and push American health care to do better.

"Medical tourism is a great industry for seasteads," Peter says. "It's a huge, growing market, and it makes full use of the freedoms that seasteads provide. And if we play our cards right, it might even have a hand in fixing American health care. A lot of the costs of health care in the US comes from red tape that seasteads can avoid. The system by which doctors and hospitals get paid for their services is legendarily awful. [It involves] frustrating levels of paperwork that doctors have to do on the clinical side—which, in some cases, is motivated by legal reasons as much by enhancing patient care. Everyone in health care knows about this, but doctors and administrators are trapped by the web of regulations that surrounds health care. Seasteads by their nature provide a way around these inefficiencies, while still maintaining high quality care and providing patient protection."

Free health care for all may be mandated with the best of intentions, but the best intentions can't defy economic law. When services are free, demand overwhelms supply. Countries with socialized medicine inevitably suffer from shortages. Patients wait for months for procedures their physicians deem necessary but their overworked health care system does not deem "critical." Such policies drive millions to seek help outside their borders.

"People travel from all countries for medical care," continues Peter. "We're talking about a multibillion-dollar industry, and the savings involved can be substantial. The AMA [American Medical Association] has found that a heart bypass operation that costs $130,000 in the United States may cost $18,000 in Singapore. Other procedures provide similar savings—even when you account for the cost of travel. And insurers, always looking for a good bargain, have picked up on this. Some of them, including Aetna and Blue Cross Blue Shield, are now offering plans with incentives for patients to seek this cheaper care abroad. And the market is set to grow."

As an industry, medical tourism far outstrips regular tourism. For instance, Israel scrambled to overhaul its tourism industry when a report released in April 2013 from its Health Ministry estimated that medical tourists, on average, spend nearly $5,000 per visit, compared with about $1,500 for sightseers. People aren't as motivated to travel for pleasure as they are to travel for health. But long-established countries such as Israel aren't as thrilled with this influx as new countries might be. Sasha Issenberg, author of the 2016 book *Outpatients: The Astonishing New World of Medical Tourism*, explained the Israeli backlash against foreign patients to the *Huffington Post.* "[T]hey see foreigners buying their way into a system they helped build—which is what is going on in Israel—that's the resentment."

Can borders hold back the tide? A survey by IPK International, the world's largest provider of tourism and travel data, showed that 3 percent to 4 percent of the world's population travels abroad seeking superior medical treatment with shorter wait times and lower costs, and more than half of all Europeans say they could imagine doing so in the future. Results in America are about the same. A survey published by the giant financial services firm Deloitte Consulting way back in 2009 found that 40 percent of Americans polled said they would pursue medical travel if they could save 50 percent or more on costs. Well, by 2016, they could save a lot more than 50 percent on costs.

"How do these hospitals, these medical tourism centers, manage to charge so little?" Peter Wei asks rhetorically. "Certainly part of the story is that doctors and nurses earn lower wages in Thailand and India than in the US. A little labor arbitrage—and we can certainly think about how that might play out on seasteads. But I don't think that's the whole story. Unlike in the US, medical tourism centers have to compete on cost: if you can find a way to lower your expenses, you can pass along those savings and lure in more patients. It's almost like a normal market!"

It's a sad fact that Peter's audience laughs when he says this. In normal markets, prices tend to go down while services tend to improve.

"One example is the Narayana Hrudayalaya hospital in India, which specializes in heart operations. It has used an assembly-line model to slash the cost of a bypass operation—to just two thousand dollars. That's peanuts compared with what you'd pay in America, of course. But what's even more impressive is that it's a huge reduction on what you'd pay elsewhere in India, where a [bypass] runs about five thousand dollars. So medical tourism centers aren't just relying on lower staffing costs. At least some of them are pioneering these process innovations that produce really impressive efficiencies. But because these hospitals are so scattered, the academic literature has almost nothing to report about these innovations. And a medical seastead—one that can avoid the red tape and insurance bureaucracy that plague hospitals today—can fully implement these innovations and become a formidable competitor."

Peter is not the only seasteader to use Narayana Hrudayalaya Hospital as a business model for a floating hospital. As he concluded his presentation, nearly a hundred seastead enthusiasts leaned forward in their seats, eager to hear from the much-buzzed-about cofounder of Nuehealth, who claims that his innovation would allow the rising tide of medical tourism to carry Western health care to the poorest of the poor.

Generation Y Not?

When Nishant Bagadia introduced himself to Joe, Joe held up his hand to focus on the announcement coming from the nearby auditorium.

"Hang on a second, kid. A very important figure is about to speak about medical tourism in the third world, and I need get in there to make an impression on him so I can interview him."

"Yeah, I guess I better get in there, too," Nishant said.

Joe rushed in and took his seat in the front row just as the man he wanted to impress was announced, and Nishant took the stage to speak.

Nishant is accustomed to people's Larry David moments. Only thirty, his resume implies he's older because he's run his business and academic careers simultaneously. Not many Silicon Valley entrepreneurs we interviewed are preoccupied with "the problem of subjectivity" and "the crisis of representation." Nor do they routinely refer to Karl Marx and Jean-Bernard-Léon Foucault when discussing the practical realities of bringing health care to the inland poor.

"What I'm trying to do in our start-up is to create a globally connected health care platform such that any patient anywhere can be referred to any doctor anywhere. If we connect patients, doctors, and hospitals all around the world, we can lower the barriers of health care accessibility."

While at the University of Wisconsin, Nishant double-majored in biochemistry and English, with a minor in business, and simultaneously worked in a genome research lab. Then he got in early as the third employee at a company called BrainReactions, a creative think tank that employed young college students to develop innovative ideas for Fortune 500 companies. He became such the epitome of what he calls "Generation Y at its finest," he was featured in a *Wisconsin State Journal* newspaper story that opened: "Fresh out of college and armed with a laptop, cell phone, and piña colada, Nishant Bagadia reclined on a Puerto Rican beach as he worked toward a six-figure company sales record."

But being a young hotshot didn't sit well with Nishant. Most of his extended family is in India, which he describes as "a country in dire need of a social revolution to improve the quality of life." He tries to visit once a year and says he is humbled each time.

"It's unbelievable that some people have access to care that can save their lives, while others die just because they were born in a particular place or time. I could have been born in India, which would have been great in its own way, but instead I'm a first-generation US citizen, part of an Indian diaspora which has the luxury of solid infrastructure and flexible opportunities. Why is health care access based on your political institution? Medicine has become a global business, yet health care access is a local privilege."

After BrainReactions, Nishant joined Deloitte Management Consulting, where he helped consumer goods and manufacturing companies improve their business processes and sales output. Eventually he said, "Who cares? Why am I helping major corporations sell and produce more? Isn't this the problem with our civilization—in the West? I applied to graduate school to explore the economics of our human growth, and luckily enough got into the London School of Economics to get a master's in Sociology of Science and Medicine."

In London, Nishant first studied the sociopolitical issues related to international medical travel. After his master's, he pursued a PhD in medical anthropology from the joint program at the University of California at Berkeley and the University of California at San Francisco, "studying the influence of capitalism, markets, and liberalism on the access to and limitations of health care for a variety of patients who move across borders for medical procedures."

Based on his scholarly work on medical travel, Nishant joined a team of entrepreneurs and became director of business development at Health Travel Technologies. The company is implementing a cloud technology to help patients access health care they can't receive locally.

"International health care is a very complex industry, and we need to step away from just looking at the economics of it," says Nishant. "For some of these people seeking care in developing countries, it's a community coming together to donate the money for one cardiac bypass surgery. It's an individual story wrapped up in a political and community history. It's real people and solidarities. Pakistani Muslims are traveling to India for life-saving cardiac procedures, where Hindu doctors deliver a cardiac bypass surgery for two thousand US dollars, which can be several years salary for some."

His research taught him that the desire to give and receive care is defying all boundaries. So why should medical therapies be constrained by what Nishant calls "geographic partitions in health care access"? The challenges to be overcome can be listed on one hand:

One, Western rules make health care prohibitively expensive for the poor.

Two, much of the developing world is thousands of miles from a developed nation.

Three, much of the inland poor cannot access the Internet.

Four, very few qualified doctors are within healing distance of people in Africa. For instance, the ratio of people to physicians in Kenya is at least 5,000 to 1.

Five, governments in many developing nations enforce laws that make health care access all but impossible.

If this seems like a hopeless situation, you are probably older than forty. To an entrepreneurial humanitarian of Generation Y, this isn't a problem. It's a business opportunity.

"The Henry Ford of Health Care"

One of Nishant's inspirations for the humanitarian health care business model is Devi Shetty, an Indian cardiac surgeon, philanthropist, and entrepreneur who once served as the personal physician of Mother Teresa. Declaring "Charity is not scalable. If you give something free, you will run out of money," Shetty set about founding Narayana Hrudayalaya Health City in Bangalore, India. *Narayana hrudayalaya* means "God's compassionate home" in Sanskrit, so we'll call it God's Compassionate Home Health City. Sound like a fantasy? It's the largest cardiac hospital in the world, performing the most cardiac procedures in the world. The average open-heart surgery costs less than a third of what it costs in other Indian hospitals.

Nishant described Narayana Hrudayalaya Health City as "a perfect example of how a world-class hospital can radically undercut global price of operations not by sacrificing care but by streamlining costs and eliminating waste. Dr. Shetty has created an amazing cluster of hospitals that offer cardiac procedures for one one-hundredth the cost of a procedures in the US, with success rates that are equal to or better than the United States. He is now offering health insurance to four million rural Indians for less than *twenty-five cents a month*, and he's trying to get coronary artery bypass surgeries down from $1,500 US to $850 US for these millions of patients. He might charge $7,000 to foreigners like you and me because we can afford it, and that helps subsidize his care for the destitute. That's no big deal to us when you compare it to a cost over a hundred thousand dollars for coronary artery bypass surgery in the US."

Since Dr. Shetty is making a luxury for the rich available to the poor, the *Wall Street Journal* dubbed him "the Henry Ford of Heart Surgery." Shetty's business model has expanded to fourteen hospitals across India that achieve astounding price reductions by using economies of scale—in other words, applying the cost-cutting strategies of cruise ships on land. God's Compassionate Home Health City has twenty times as many beds as the average American hospital. Devi Shetty is personally credited with performing fifteen thousand heart procedures in his career. Right now his team of forty or so cardiologists performs about twenty-four thousand *per month*. Achieving a success rate equal to the highest-rated American hospitals, Shetty demonstrated that higher volumes of patients lead to better quality of health care. Shetty calls it "the Walmart approach."

"Nobody is competing with them," says Nishant. "With a 1.4 percent mortality rate, which is one of the lowest in the world, they are obviously owning that space."

A year after Nishant cited these figures, they were obsolete. Americans are not charged $7,000 for a bypass surgery. They are charged $2,000, according to Devi Shetty. Ten million rural Indians near Narayana Hospital don't pay 25 cents a month for bypass insurance. They pay an average of 11 cents a month. And their heart bypass survival rate of 1.4 percent beats the American rate of 1.9 percent. Health care costs are dropping, and quality is improving. Sounds like Peter Wei's "normal market."

Devi Shetty's hospital franchise took spot thirty-five in *Fast Company* magazine's Top One Hundred fastest-growing companies. His streamlining approach has provoked hospitals in distant countries to compete to lower their prices.

And here comes the step to seasteading. Shetty isn't waiting for underserved patients to come find him. He reaches out to them by advancing three innovations: mobility, telemedicine, and islands.

First, mobility: Dr. Shetty has dispatched "clinics on wheels" to nearby rural hospitals to test for heart disease.

Second, telemedicine: Shetty initiated the God's Compassionate Home Health City telesurgery practice, where a remote surgeon performs on a patient hundreds of miles away, operating robot fingers with more precision than human hands. Thus Shetty's team of about forty heart surgeons extend their healing reach to at least a hundred facilities throughout India and more than fifty in Africa, now spreading into Malaysia.

Third, islands: Dr. Shetty wants to reach underprivileged populations located too far around the curve of the globe to receive a reliable telesurgery beam. Devi Shetty built a $2 billion US Compassionate Home Health City in the Cayman Islands, between Latin America and Cuba, to offer the same low-cost, high-quality services to those of modest means—including millions of uninsured Americans.

Mobility, telemedicine, islands. Nishant had to ask himself, Why not combine all three?

Fantasy Hospital Island

That's when Nishant saw the seastead solution emerging as a possible solution to radical global inequality with regard to health care access. The Cayman Islands can be thought of as a cluster of seasteads that can't move. Doctors like Devi Shetty are already building facilities in the Cayman Islands to compete with less-than-perfect Latin American health-care systems. Nishant imagined hundreds of mobile manmade Cayman Islands surrounding the world's continents, each with Dr. Shetty's business model.

"What if the doctors or clinics that you need are not halfway around the world but off the coast of your country's shoreline? And better yet, what if that destination on the sea can offer better prices, more advanced or accessible technology, and alternative treatments, with the same quality as having to go to the finest center of medical excellence?"

Mercy Ships has been executing this strategy since 1978. This fleet of Christian charity ships was founded after Donald and Keyon Stephens learned that hundreds of millions of people lack clean water, electricity, and health care, yet more than 75 percent of the world's population lives within a hundred miles of a port city. They concluded that a ship was the most efficient way to deliver a clean, safe, state-of-the art hospital to the poor. Sponsored by corporate and individual donors, Mercy Ships volunteers have provided services and materials valued at over $1 billion to ports in fifty-seven developing nations. That amounts to about 2.5 million beneficiaries.

Despite this inspiring demonstration of good will, the fleet of Mercy

Ships, on a global scale, serves as Band-Aids on a planet-sized wound. Charity, as Devi Shetty said, is not scalable. Only profits can spur the hypergrowth required to bring Western health care to a billion people.

Nishant wrote an article for *Medical Tourism* magazine called "Investigating Medical Tourism Beneath the Surface," where he cited his former company Deloitte Consulting's 2009 survey. "The findings suggest that by 2017, fifteen million innovation-seeking consumers will transfer $400 billion US (base case scenario) of health care spending from US providers to hospitals overseas."

Four hundred billion dollars? Nishant quotes the World Health Organization, which estimates that 10 million physicians practice medicine around the world. "Ninety-two percent are outside the US." Most of them are willing to work for less than the salaries of doctors in America. "What's amazing is that it could take six to ten years for some medical innovations to be available in the US that are already available internationally," says Nishant. "The approval process outside the US is not less rigorous. It just has less bureaucracy."

Health care providers in India are driving down costs, while the health care system in the United States is driving up costs. With a world full of mobile patients, this situation will not hold. The world's richest, largest generation is approaching retirement, they know how to travel, and they don't want to wait in lines. No amount of internal regulations can hold back the demand.

Devi Shetty proved that by using economies of scale, you could underprice health care providers in rich countries, yet charge enough to subsidize massive poor populations with state-of-the-art health care that was as good or better than Western health care. But if floating hospitals were going to bring health care to the poor, they needed more than ships and seasteads. They needed a massive network of information connecting every poor person in the world to every doctor in the world.

How could such a feat be achieved? For the impoverished to become empowered consumers, they needed two things: One, information. Two, the power to choose among providers competing for them.

Nishant recalled an intriguing observation when he was investigating Africa.

"I was in a small remote village in northern Senegal, and running water only came to the village once a day for thirty minutes. But people had cell phones."

As of 2014, 75 percent of the world's adult population owned a mobile phone.

As we write, three global connectivity projects are in the works. The company where Patri works, Google, is testing Project Loon, a global network of stratospheric balloons it hopes will wirelessly connect a billion remote rural people to the Internet. Mark Zuckerberg announced that Facebook has partnered with Samsung, Nokia, and four other companies to launch a project called Internet.org, to provide World Wide Web access to the billions of people still not connected to the Internet. The Media Development Investment Fund has financed the Outernet, a plan to launch private satellites into space to provide free worldwide Wi-Fi access for billions of people locked in oppressive governments.

Nishant says, "So why not give all people the ability to connect through the web to a global health care network? What if we get more patients into a worldwide network, where not only can they search for providers but then be *fully* supported to get to their provider destination and back?"

The confluence of mobile phones with mobile health care was ready to explode with possibilities. But a massive information infrastructure needed to be in place. How do you even build something like that? Nishant discovered inspiration in Kenya. It was an app: MedAfrica, the brainchild of Steve Mutinda, founder of Shimba Technology.

"MedAfrica has an app that allows Kenyans and Ugandans to receive basic health information," says Nishant, "including checking symptoms in a knowledge base of health care information. There have been hundreds of thousands downloads of this smartphone app."

MedAfrica provides basic medical information to its users in the developing world, who can check their symptoms, self-diagnose, and be counseled by remote experts about first aid procedures and drug information. Two-thirds of downloaders find MedAfrica valuable enough to continue using it on an ongoing basis. That beats most apps you have on your phone. The MedAfrica team won the Pivot15 Challenge, earning the chance to pitch its idea in Silicon Valley, where the website The Next Web listed them one of the top ten start-ups at the conference. Soon after, MedAfrica won the first prize in the company category of the worldwide 2012 Ericsson Application Awards in Stockholm, Sweden. "Jan Färjh, head of Ericsson Research and host of the awards, said MedAfrica was an excellent example of applications in a networked society," reported *Standard Digital News* in Kenya.

But information, of course, is not enough.

"Kenya has seventy-five hundred doctors and over forty million people," Nishant says. "You can do the simple math. What if a MedAfrica user gets some information and learns they need a procedure, and they can't get to one of the seventy-five hundred doctors in Kenya?"

Compounding the problem, the Kenyan government declared it illegal for doctors to advertise their services. As Mbugua Njihia, founder of Mobile Marketing Association, said, "If I can't find you, you don't exist."

To get past the limitations imposed by governments, the network needed to be bigger than any government. As Devi Shetty showed, the poor need technological innovations that defy borders. "MedAfrica needed to become MedAnywhere," says Nishant.

A Global Network of Care

Nishant joined a team of Silicon Valley entrepreneurs at Nuehealth, a tech company that allows any patient in the world to download a free, secure, cloud-based application to help him or her find medical treatments from doctors anywhere in the world. Doctors can track their patient's progress anywhere in the world. All you have to do is download an app.

"Our vision," says Nishant, "is to provide the patient with a global database of pricing and procedure costs, a database of what providers or physicians are available in a global network. No matter what, wherever you are, you will be hand held by 'virtual' patient care coordinators to get you where you need to go, and get back home again."

This application essentially breaks up the monopoly of locality, empowering millions of doctors with diverse specialties to compete to find the right patient with unique needs. According to Nishant, this means better customer service, more referrals to the best doctors, and the guaranteed best possible care available at that moment.

"Now, what about seasteads and procedures on ships?" Nishant says. "Well, you can just imagine a seastead off the shore in Africa. MedAfrica would be connected to Nuehealth, so that now when a MedAfrica patient needs a procedure done, that inquiry can come through the Nuehealth app and tap into a global network of providers brought by strategic partnerships. Now, if one of the providers in this global network is right offshore, in the ocean between Kenya and India, it makes the travel component a nonissue."

If Mercy Ships can attract, by their estimation, more than 2.5 million beneficiaries in more than seventy countries through *hearsay*, imagine what medical seasteads could accomplish if potential patients were able to contact a global network of doctors through a mobile phone. Mercy ships can only visit occasionally. Seasteads could be stationed permanently a ferry ride from port.

"In a way, Nuehealth could provide the 'Facebook plus the Amazon' of health care. First we're connecting patients and doctors to each other through collaborative social technologies, and then, like Amazon, helping to fulfill the procedure in order to get the patient to their medical destination."

Mercy Ships has provided health services valued at more than $1 billion entirely through charity. As we write, Mercy Ships just received a $20 million US donation from Bill Gross, founder of Pacific Investment Management Company (PIMCO), and his wife, Sue. Now imagine a Shetty-style floating hospital that doesn't rely on charity but makes a profit. In Devi Shetty's current business model, God's Compassionate Home Health City offers coronary bypass surgery to Westerners for $2,000 so he can offer medical insurance to millions of poor for mere cents a month. Success allows him to build more hospitals on more islands, starting with the Caymans. Now that Shetty's business model has been amply demonstrated, we need to build more islands. Instead of "clinics on wheels" riding around the back streets of India and other poor countries, we could have "ambulances by helicopter" stationed offshore. If cruise ships can stay in constant helicopter contact with hospitals on land, a poor person with a health crisis could contact an offshore hospital on his or her mobile phone, receive a real-time telediagnosis, and be helicoptered to the seastead in an emergency. Matternet, in partnership with UNICEF (United Nations Children's Fund), has already designed unmanned drones to deliver medicines to people in remote parts of Malawi. No pilot is necessary. The patient taps an app, and the small drone follows a GPS signal to the location of need.

"Through innovative technologies, through connectivity, we feel like we're getting closer to that borderless global health care network, where health systems are talking to each other and providing global customer service," says Nishant. "So one might well ask, How is it possible to make medical care on seasteads or ships a reality? Step one? You guessed it. Focus on the inaccessible, high-cost treatments for well-off locals."

Stem cells are mother cells that have the potential to become any type of cell in the body.

"Stem cell treatments are absolutely incredible. Why is this exciting for seasteading? First, it's inaccessibility in the US. The FDA [Food and Drug Administration] is still not behind it in any advanced or motivated way."

The FDA takes the position that any stem cell, once taken outside the body and cultured, is considered a drug and must be regulated as such before it can be reinjected into the same body. Yet Dr. Christopher Centeno, one of the first physicians to repair severe orthopedic tears with a patient's own stem cells, points out that in vitro fertilization requires a much more complex culturing process, and fertilized eggs are not regulated as drugs.

"Asia and some parts of Latin America are ten years ahead of the US," continues Nishant. "Why not market stem cell procedures for US patients for conditions that are rare or untreatable with typical medical options?"

The marvel of stem cell cures is not held up by technology, lack of doctors, or lack of funding. They are held back only by politics. Many suffer for decades and even die waiting for procedures to be approved in their home countries that have long been available elsewhere.

Every time a government restricts a medical procedure, it simply migrates to another jurisdiction. Why wait for stem cell surgeries to be approved in your host country when Claudia Castillo, suffering for years in Colombia with a narrow trachea, or windpipe, caused by tuberculosis, travelled to Spain in 2008 to have her stem cells harvested from her leg bone marrow? It took four days to grow a brand new trachea in the lab, and four days after it was surgically implanted, the medical team found that the new organ was indistinguishable from the rest of Castillo's body. "I was a sick woman; now I will be able to live a normal life," Castillo told the BBC. Five years later, she is still in perfect health.

Harvard Law School professor I. Glenn Cohen, the author of *The Globalization of Health Care: Legal and Ethical Issues*, says the stem cell industry could be patient regulated if patients have access to online information verified by independent third parties.

How to start out? Don't we need investors to buy a whole boat? No, says Nishant. "Don't have a whole boat dedicated to medicine. That's too expensive. But if we can lease one medical room on a boat as a clinic performing stem cell procedures—or some other unique procedure—we can start marketing it and build a buzz around the fact that offshore medical services are coming in a couple years."

What about malpractice?

"Malpractice has not come up. Most of these hospitals and doctors abroad do not have the same limitations on acknowledging that they made a mistake. In the US, you bear so many costs if you say, 'It was my fault.' Whereas one of our hospital clients in Mexico received a patient from the US who had a lap-band procedure done, which is a weight loss surgery, and came back home and got an infection. Well, we found out the infection had nothing to do with the procedure but resulted from some undisclosed medical history of the patient. We talked to the doctor, and he actually said, 'No problem, happy to take them back and help them with whatever they need.' Because they can do that."

This complex network of relationships is overseen by the Medical Tourism Association, an international nonprofit group dedicated to making medical tourism transparent and safe. Declaring, "One patient with a bad medical tourism experience has the potential to seriously hurt your hospital's image and ruin years of marketing efforts," MTA offers strict certification services to connect patients with qualified providers around the world. Backing them up is the US-based Joint Commission International (JCI). Part of the Joint Commission, it was established in 1951 as the Joint Commission on Accreditation of Hospitals (JCAH), which assesses and accredits more than twenty-one thousand health care organizations and programs in the United States. "More than 600 facilities around the world have now been awarded JCI accreditation, and that number is growing by about 20% per year," it claims.

As national health care systems get slower and more expensive, medical entrepreneurs are scrambling to build their state-of-the-art hospitals on islands. For instance, Samuel Hess, an orthopedic surgeon from the United States cofounded the American Clinic, to organize a cadre of physicians to build a state-of-the-art hospital in the Cayman Islands—until they learned one had been built already by an Indian heart surgeon named Devi Shetty. Darn that competition! So they moved to the Caribbean island of Saint Martin, where they are building a full-service clinic and premier cancer center.

As all the natural islands surrounding dysfunctional health care systems get used up, there will be increasing demand for man-made islands, starting with medical ships stationed even closer to frustrated patients. Overall, Nishant is ambitious to help seasteads become a valuable option for patients to receive access to medical procedures they cannot get locally.

We'll give the final word to Devi Shetty, who in 2112 was awarded the Padma Bhushan, the third highest civilian award in the Republic of India, for medicine/cardiology. In an interview with Priya Menon, scientific media editor at the online forum *Curetalk*, Dr. Shetty summed up the possibilities.

> *Today telemedicine is the way primary health care is delivered across the world. People are not going to hospitals for primary health care. They talk to the doctor through the mobile phones using the tele-medicine tools. We have treated over 53,000 heart patients in remote locations and saved thousands of lives.*
>
> *India will become the first country in the world to dissociate health care from the affluence. We will have a very interesting scenario ten years down the line. We may continue to have millions and millions of people living in the slums with no running water or toilets; however, when they are unwell, they will have access to high tech health care with dignity.*

But how to pay for it? In 2014 Devi Shetty followed the inexorable logic that leads to Nishant's vision for seasteading.

"The best location to build a hospital on the planet today is a ship that is parked in the US waters just outside its territory," Shetty told the *Economic Times.* "The site at the Cayman Islands is the closest approximation that fits the bill." He went on to say, "The health care models in the US are considered the ultimate and keenly studied by the entire world, but the regulatory restrictions in that country are so stifling that innovations in health care delivery are very difficult to implement."

Let's meet two people who plan to help organize a consortium of medical professionals to start a modern regulatory regime at sea.

New Blue Fluid Rules

It's been less than week since they were married, and Allison and Chris Heddon won't stop talking about seasteading. When the newlyweds sit down at a picnic table outside Clarium Capital, Peter Thiel's hedge fund company, and start talking with their infectious sense of urgency, they make you feel they have a social obligation to produce extremely smart, driven children.

Chris and Allison, cofounders of Resonance Medical, are preparing to present their medical innovation—a therapy for the hearing impaired that involves a novel brain machine interface and drug delivery technology—at the Exponential Medicine conference hosted by Singularity University, a unique academic institution founded by futurists Peter Diamandas and Roy Kurzweil dedicated to studying how the approaching intersection of several exponentially accelerating technologies will massively increase human well-being. The four-day event invites innovators from across technology to speak about how to make medicine "exponentially faster, smaller, cheaper, better." They are here to request that the Seasteading Institute accompany them onstage.

Dr. Chris Heddon served as an anesthesiologist at Presence Saint Francis Hospital in Evanston, Illinois, through August 2014, when he left to devote his full energies as CEO of Resonance Medical Technologies. Chris is the sole inventor of the ear canal bone anchor (patent pending) and coinventor of laser drug delivery technology and "transspecies library algorithm." In English: You've heard of seeing-eye dogs? Chris proposes hearing-ear dogs, facilitated by brain implants permitting a deaf human to hear what his dog hears. Chris authored three peer-reviewed articles on drug delivery for autoimmune hearing disorders, related specifically to cochlear neurotransmission.

When asked what his interests are, he reports, "disaster and humanitarian relief." He travelled to New Orleans to volunteer as a physician on St. Anna's Medical Mission mobile unit following Hurricane Katrina in 2005, and he served as a medical volunteer in Chiquimulilla, Guatemala, and surrounding villages.

Cofounder of Resonance Medical Technologies is his new wife, bioethicist Allison Hebron, who changed her name to Heddon just a few days ago. Allison is a consultant at Sg2, a health care analytics and consulting firm, where she studies emerging medical technologies, focusing on the impact that virtual health innovations have on care delivery. When asked what her interests are, she says, "Bioethics is the perfect intersection of my dual interest in medicine and philosophy." She's written for the *Journal of Medical Ethics*, specializing in issues surrounding patient consent and autonomy. In 2014 Allison was featured on *Crain's Chicago Business*'s "20 in Their 20s" list, which featured Resonance Medical.

When we asked Dr. Heddon why'd left medicine two months before, he answered pointedly.

"We have a moral obligation to be better. Medicine is in a shambles right now. It makes me sad. The fact that I became involved in the development of truly novel technology outside of my specialty played a big part in the speed at which I left medicine, but the day-to-day ethical dilemmas of my job as an anesthesiologist made it doubly easy to leave without looking back. The fact that my wife was in her training as a bioethicist while I was in training as an anesthesiologist only added factual and philosophical weight to the argument that many of the things that we do in medicine are not ethical, even if they are completely legal and even encouraged. Maybe starting over with seasteading will allow us to see our technological power with fresh eyes, so that idealistic kids can grow up to be doctors without having to accept the ethical compromises that I found myself a part of.

"If you're in an industry like medicine," Chris continues, "where I spent most of my professional life, you see that we have a bag of bricks attached to our legs. And that's all regulation. I think it's become obvious that one segment of business, namely Silicon Valley, is taking off, because they're so much more efficient, and we're left behind. There's a disparity between the speed at which information technology is improving, the speed at which medical technology is improving, and it's holding humanity back. I think it's important that we speed that process up and show people that there's a better way. Seasteading is a way to illuminate that disparity, to become the lighthouse on the hill that everybody looks to for innovative medicine and other highly regulated industries. It's very important. I think it's a moral imperative."

"Our desire is to fundamentally reframe the current medical regulatory environment," says Allison. "This goal will require us to present an alternative that is not just a little better, but dramatically better. This is going to require the assembly of a team of bioethicists, medical professionals, entrepreneurs, and regulators themselves who understand that the current regulatory paradigm is an impediment to the advancement of humanity. Once we have assembled our team of thought leaders of the future, we need a laboratory in which to cast the distinction between the broken system and the path forward. We believe that the Seasteading Institute is that laboratory."

Why seasteading?

"By taking our medical research offshore and partnering with the right individuals, we have a unique opportunity to efficiently and safely reshape the regulatory pathway. My husband and I believe in the seasteading message and feel a comradeship with those supporting the Seasteading Institute. Through collaboration, we can set an example of how medical research can be conducted in the hopefully not-so-distant future. I believe that seasteading is the first step in a new regulatory paradigm that ensures patients have access to life-saving treatments without having to wait years for the drug or medical device to travel through the US regulatory pathway. In no way does this mean that testing and assessment on a seastead would be lax or haphazard. Rather, it is easier for a smaller organization to move quickly and with agility than a larger, government-run department.

"To pursue our goal of developing and performing clinical research on seasteads," she continues, "we will need champions among the medical, scientific, and even government communities. It is vital that the FDA and other regulatory bodies do not see seasteading as a threat or enemy but rather as a group that has synergistic values and goals. We are not trying to replace them; we are hoping to support them and be an advocate for timely, effective, and much-needed change. It might be easy to place blame upon the staff at the FDA for the immense hurdles that their department creates but, ultimately, they are a group of people doing the best they can with very limited resources."

When Chris and Allison aren't criticizing the inefficiencies of the FDA, they are defending the individuals who work there. Allison and Chris insist that the FDA faces unfair insurmountable obstacles.

"Some medical professionals think they dislike the FDA," says Chris, "but they don't realize what their purpose is and the constraints that they're under. So that distrust causes them not to be open and honest with the FDA. That's why I keep on saying, you have to have this radical honesty when we do it. The only way we're going to have any chance of legitimacy with the general public is to invite the FDA onto the seastead and say, 'This is your office. We want you here. We even want your feedback. We might not agree with you, but we want your input and criticism. We want to be safe.' If people want to look at our data, and the FDA wants to come in and audit us, they are free to do so."

Allison proposes that seasteads accept the burdens that the FDA is not equipped to handle.

"Our proposed use of seasteading for medical research will be designed to supplement the FDA and shift some of the regulatory burden away from their overworked team and to a more agile regulatory option. If properly organized and with careful design, seasteading has the potential to alleviate some of the stress on regulatory agencies by taking on medical research. Today promising drugs and medical devices take years to get to the market. Unfortunately, this lengthy and slow process often keeps potentially life-saving treatments out of the hands of patients who could benefit greatly from them. Very often, clinical research is published in other countries—that are often ahead of US research by several years—touting the success and limitations of a given treatment. Yet these data do not alter the required clinical protocols here in the US. From an ethical perspective, if there is global data that a new therapy accomplishes its primary endpoints in one country, patients in all countries should have access to the treatment within a given time period and at an appropriate cost. By shifting some of this research to seasteading, I believe that medical researchers can safety expedite the clinical trial process." Clinical trials are research studies involving human volunteers to determine the safety and effectiveness of treatments.

So why do they want us to help them address a conference of elite professionals at Exponential Medicine? We're not medical experts. Chris and Allison say they want to present the seasteading option to leaders in the field, because they believe that many of the best and brightest would be attracted to a new regulatory regime.

"I think there's enough of a community," says Allison, "that you can find support from people who believe in this; enough to constitute a certification board. That builds credibility."

"If the team is not unquestionably better than what the government has put together in the FDA, then it's not worth undertaking," says Chris. "Think about how quickly things turned around when the Obama administration brought in Silicon Valley talent to fix HealthCare.gov." In 2013, when thousands of technocrats employed by 55 different contractors delivered a website that didn't work, a small crack team of developers from Silicon Valley raced into the debacle and helped the federal bureaucracy exceed its goal of 8 million insured households nationwide. "That's the kind dramatic increase in team quality and accountability that you want on a seastead. You just have to be better than the government at building teams, and if you can't build a better team than the US government, then you probably have no business on a seastead in the middle of the ocean."

But why should patients trust a seastead more than a land-based research facility?

"I'm not sure that they should—or shouldn't," says Chris. "Only excellence and a proven safety record over time merit trust. The first people who choose to be treated are going to be pioneers, and it's going to be up to them to do their own research on the team behind the seastead's research. If the team is top notch and has excellent backing, that's a good sign, but those criteria go for almost anything. I think that seasteads will have a higher burden of proof than a typical research institution, so it will be important to be extraordinarily open and welcoming to interested regulatory bodies. If you want to set yourselves up as a model for how things should be, you subject yourselves to scrutiny willingly."

What's to stop quacks?

"There's nothing stopping them now."

Fearing Fear Itself

The current regulatory regime might prevent some quacks from practicing medicine, but it provides a safe haven for many others. Chris shares harrowing stories of his experience as an anesthesiologist that include expensive, dangerous devices that cause harm when cheaper safer ones are available but disallowed and dying elderly patients who can't speak for themselves, tormented by traumatic repeat attempts to extend their lives, which their families approve but don't witness.

Allison explains that many devices implanted in patients are developed behind a shroud of secrecy. This seemed so shocking in retrospect, we followed up with her by email, asking, "You emphasize transparency on seasteads. Aren't all medical research facilities transparent?"

"Quite the opposite," she wrote back. "A study released in *JAMA Internal Medicine* in September 2014 reported the extreme lack of publicly available scientific evidence for implanted medical devices. The Safe Medical Devices Act of 1990 requires that the scientific evidence for safety and efficacy of 510(k) device submissions [a form to demonstrate that a new device is at least as safe and effective as a device already on the market] be made publicly available. However, the study authors report that of 50 newly cleared implants, scientific data was made available on only 8 of the devices . . . Clearly, the legal requirement of transparency for FDA-cleared medical devices is ineffective. With regard to our proposed medical research facilities on a seastead, we would have access to all of the safety and efficacy (and other) data produced from our medical research, and we would have the liberty to make these data and the study outcomes available to the public."

"On our seastead, I would like us to be *more* vigilant and have *more* regulation than the FDA has put in place," insists Chris. "That's why I want this radical transparency with the FDA, so they have access to the data and offer opinions. The reason I think our company is a perfect test case for a seastead is that we have potentially a very easy regulatory pathway that even the FDA wouldn't object to."

"But have all the same regulations," says Allison. "We'd develop something that was ninety-nine percent similar. We'd just be able to move faster. All the same protections would still be in place."

"I think there are some redundancies we can eliminate," says Chris. "And we'd escape politics, too. Lobbyists are lobbying for certain regulations, because they're paid by the pharmaceutical companies and large medical device companies. The politicians in their states want the people's votes. The sessions might only meet twice a year, so if you miss a session in the spring, you have to wait six more months to even be heard. That's just for reimbursement. There's just no opportunity to move fast."

"Obviously, safety and efficacy would be top priorities on a seastead research facility, just like the land-based IRBs [institutional review boards]," says Allison. (These are local bodies appointed by the FDA to authorize research.) "Simply stated, I think we can mirror the beneficial aspects of existing review structures and combine them with a lean, agile seastead venture. Many aspects of current IRBs are vital and should never be overlooked, including the informed consent process, the focus on protecting the rights and welfare of the patients, and the inclusion of review members from both the clinical and nonclinical communities. I think this is an avenue to show that we can be just as safe and effective and produce really great therapies quicker without having to go through the cumbersome FDA."

The FDA, founded in 1906, has held a monopoly over the production of regulations for more than a century, and the citizens it is charged with serving need the agency to be challenged by offshore competitors to reinvigorate its mission.

If You Can't Join 'Em, Beat 'Em

"It is our hope that seasteading will introduce several efficiencies into the review process," says Allison. "For example, the FDA has stated on the IRB webpage that many IRBs are exploring the use of electronic review submissions to the FDA rather than paper."

Until recently, the FDA required pharmaceutical companies to submit their innovations for its review by snail mail, on paper. This situation held until 2011 when the White House unveiled its plan to trim hundreds of regulations that it claimed would save $10 billion over five years. The agency reacted by announcing plans to modernize and allow electronic filing, releasing this unintentionally funny update:

"FDA is going green! Did you know that you can send investigational new drug applications (INDs), new drug applications (NDAs), abbreviated new drug applications (ANDAs), biologics license applications (BLAs), and drug master files (DMFs) to FDA/CDER [Center for Drug Evaluation and Research] electronically?"

We're supposed to gasp with gratitude at this innovation announced on June 14, 2012. So it turns out agencies can innovate in response to outside threats to their dominance. Imagine if challenges to their monopoly didn't have to come from the president of the United States but from a market of millions seeking care.

"Clearly, electronic communications are more efficient," Allison continues politely, "but this type of change unfortunately cannot happen as quickly as one would hope in a larger agency like the FDA."

"You have to make the forms shorter," adds Chris. "If you look at an FDA submission, it's ridiculous. It takes months to prepare and hundreds of thousands of dollars and lawyers and consultants in order to do it right. That's a huge barrier to entry."

Allison proposes that the sea should provide a mirror of the FDA that offers a flattering reflection of its potential. "Highlighting the inefficiencies of the current regulatory system by contrasting it with an internal seasteading system that ensures quality, safety, and efficacy may be one way to induce change at the FDA, but seasteading would have to be dramatically, not marginally, better.

"At the heart of my goal to see medical research succeed on a seastead," says Allison, "is my belief that we have an ethical responsibility to make effective treatments available to all patients in an expedited manner. Other ethical considerations that should be in a seastead charter include the focus on preserving and protecting human rights and welfare in medical research, and the importance of informed consent and patient autonomy. Developing an ethically sound seastead collaboration will require input from many stakeholders, including patients. By creating an environment based upon trust and transparent communication, I believe that we can empower patients and design a medical research community that is safe, effective, and free of unnecessary burdens and regulatory hurdles."

"Seasteading has to be the beacon on the hill," says Chris, "the lighthouse that everybody looks to. Right now people look to Silicon Valley for all the great innovations to happen, because they're very efficient about how they innovate, and they've got great leadership, and all the smartest people in the world come here because they know the reputation. That's what I want for a seastead."

"It's going to need to be a group decision when all of this becomes public knowledge," says Allison.

"I do believe seasteading is one of the most important things that I could ever do in my life," says Chris. "It may change the course of history if we're the first people to successfully do this, because then people start experimenting with new societies, and then we figure out what the best way is, and maybe you don't like the way this one is, so you go to another one. It's just like Patri said. It's a marketplace of societies."

The Secret Half of the Earth

The futuristic ocean civilization that Dr. Heddon asks us to imagine currently flourishes. Patri and Joe don't live there, but some of our colleagues have lived there for decades, and they wonder how we dream without the sound of waves. It's difficult to understand these ocean folk until you eavesdrop on a conversation between, say, Robert Ballard and Chris Muglia. Sailors, mariners, and seamen understand something about naked human interaction that most land folk do not.

It is this: 45 percent of the Earth is unclaimed by any state but provides a fertile ecosystem for emergent law. This secret voluntary society has been developing in parallel to the rise of nation-states over the last few blood-soaked centuries. It doesn't need our land-focused attention because its serves us without us needing to notice. Every second of every day, it floods us with 90 percent of the cornucopia of goods we enjoy on a day-to-day basis. Right now this secret seavilization was well into its Golden Age.

Such a claim provokes many questions among land folk. Let's answer them.

PART IV

FREEDOM

Chapter 8

FEAR

War, Waves, Pirates, Pollution, Price!

The Cruise Ship Test

Often when we introduce the seasteading movement to audiences or individuals, we are met with the same cascade of questions. Each is easy to answer if you think like a citizen of the aquatic world, especially if you ask, "Has the cruise ship industry already solved this problem?"

In 1916, thirteen years after the first airplane was launched at Kitty Hawk, North Carolina, people demanded to know how this crazy technology was going to serve humanity safely. By 1950, flying machines were common, and the answers became common sense.

In 2016, sixteen years after large aircraft landed on a floating airport in Tokyo Bay, people demanded to know how this crazy technology was going to serve humanity safely. We hope that by 2050, floating cities are common and the answers common sense.

The age of flight is fast becoming the age we float. Here are the answers to the most commonly asked questions about seasteading.

Q: *How will seasteads survive tsunamis?*

Tsunamis are harmless on the open ocean, only dangerous as they approach land. If you're one of the 2 billion people who live in a coastal city, you'd be safer on a seastead. Unlike common waves, a tsunami wave is elongated for hundreds of miles. Passengers on boats can barely detect a tsunami raise the sea level a few feet. Not until the great swell meets the upward slant of land toward shore does it begin to rise and roll and pile up to ten feet high or more. Even then, a tsunami is not a breaking wave but a surge of water that damages fixed structures via flooding. The fact that tsunamis are barely noticeable at sea and suddenly catastrophic when they contact land is part of what makes tsunamis so terrifying to helpless coastal cities.

Imagine: you're playing tennis on a seastead, a tsunami passes beneath your feet, and you don't even notice it.

Q: *What about hurricanes?*

Thousands of modern oil rigs are already built to withstand hurricanes. Small mobile seasteads should be able to speedily move away from storms thanks to the global network of weather satellites. Building town-sized platforms that can withstand hurricanes remains a naval engineering challenge, but we expect these challenges to be met with increased economic incentives to colonize the seas. Larger sea settlements will be designed—like oil rigs—to endure the worst waves and fierce winds, making them even safer than ships.

Q: *Rogue waves?*

Rogue waves are not the largest waves found on the ocean, but large and sudden compared to the wave state in the vicinity. Dr. Daniel R. Solli studies lonlinear systems, a branch of physical sciences known for predicting the properties of dynamic fluid systems, at the physics department at University of California, Los Angeles. When *Scientific American* asked him he reported, "[Rogue waves] are all short-lived, and because ships are not everywhere, the probability that a ship encounters one is relatively small." Rogue waves are so uncommon that many oceanographers thought they were mythical until the first rogue wave was measured with a digital instrument in 1995, thirty-five years after Bob Ballard claims he was hit with one. (He hasn't seen one since.)

Twenty years after the first rogue wave was confirmed scientifically, they are beginning to be understood scientifically. A 2015 paper called "Predictability of Rogue Events," published in *Physical Review Letters*, concluded that "rogue events do not necessarily appear without a warning, but are often preceded by a short phase of relative order." Oceanographer Tim Janssen devised a computer model to help identify "rogue wave hotspots" and hopefully predict rogue waves the future. His model, published in the *Journal of Physical Oceanography*, shows that coastal areas with variations in water depth can result in the sudden focusing of wave energy. Floating cities should not station near "rogue wave hotspots," such as Mavericks and Cortez Banks in California. The most advanced technology to survive rogue waves near shore in 2016 is the surfboard.

Q: *Won't seasteads pollute the oceans?*

The great threat to the ocean environment is not the sea folk. "Land-based sources—such as agricultural runoff, discharge of nutrients and pesticides, and untreated sewage including plastics—account for approximately 80% of marine pollution, globally," reports UNESCO, the United Nations Educational, Scientific, and Cultural Organization.

We land dwellers pollute the oceans because we don't see where our waste goes. Seasteaders won't be able to live in such denial. On a seastead, the ocean is your backyard. Seasteads that produce the tastiest, most contaminant-free seafood in the world will have a market incentive to restore the oceans. Aquapreneurs such as Ricardo, Neil, Lissa, Patrick, and Ballard know that the way to shut down polluters is to outcompete them for profits.

Q: *How will seasteads dispose of trash?*

The greenest form of transport is shipping. As measured by carbon emissions per ton moved, trucking emits ten times more than shipping, and flying emits a hundred times more. Seasteads will dispose of trash more efficiently than inland cities simply because it's cheaper to move trash by barge or ship than by truck. Cruise ships are already governed by international waste control protocols such as MARPOL 73/78, the International Convention for the Prevention of Pollution from Ships, as well as domestic laws like the Clean Water Act in the United States. The first to build floating cities may be DeltaSync, which is committed to environmental sustainability. Company cofounder Karina Czapiewska expects to build a floating city that recycles 100 percent of its trash.

Q: *But won't seasteads need to be self-sufficient?*

Malta isn't self-sufficient, nor are the Cayman Islands. Besides tourism, Bermuda sells little more than offshore insurance and reinsurance. Stranded alone in the middle of the hurricane belt, this island community of sixty-five thousand has maintained one of the world's highest GDPs per capita for many decades while absorbing large numbers of immigrants.

Thomas Jefferson suggested, "Peace, commerce, and honest friendship with all nations—entangling alliances with none." We recommend that seasteads become a center of excellence in some field—say, hip replacement surgeries, or as an airport hub, or as a lynchpin in the ocean trade network. The key to prosperity is not natural resources but sound legal rules and international trade. As Ben Franklin said, "No nation was ever ruined by trade."

Q: *How will seasteads get food?*

We've never lived in a city that grew its own food—yet the food in cities is superb. And when we take a cruise, the menu doesn't seem to be all seaweed and fish. Like all island economies, from Aruba to the Isle of Man, seasteads will have to produce something unique to trade for the goods of the world.

Q: *How will seasteads provide water?*

Cruise ships feature built-in desalination plants and process hundreds of thousands of gallons a day. Desalination is practiced in more than 150 countries and provides clean, fresh water for more than 300 million people around the world. Saudi Arabia produces at least half of its drinking water through desalination. The largest floating desalination plant in the world supplies the Saudi cities of Medina and Yanbu with clean water from the Red Sea, which is one of the saltiest bodies of seawater in the world. If the technology can support a significant fraction of a desert nation with 30 million inhabitants, it can support a floating nation.

Q: *How will seasteads produce energy?*

Energy is abundant on the oceans, whether you are talking about sun, wind, or wave energy. Ocean waves are a continuous source of energy that can be harvested by wave energy conversion technologies.

Winds are strong and constant on the oceans, with no topographical irregularities to break up the wind flow, which make land windmills seem so inefficient be comparison. Floating wind turbines are currently stationed on the ocean near Norway, Portugal, England, and, soon the United States and France.

The world's largest tidal energy project is underway off the coast of Scotland. A Singapore company called Atlantis Resources "broke ground" at the bottom of the sea, beginning a project to install 269 water turbines on the seabed to provide clean, sustainable power for 175,000 Scottish homes. Now that scientists have discovered that many spots on the oceans are shallow, underwater turbines can be affixed to seamounts, of which there are thousands, to power ocean communities.

But we're still thinking like landlubbers, not ocean innovators. Teresa van Dongen, a Dutch designer living in the same city as Delta-Sync, has already created lightbulbs filled with seawater and lit from within by bioluminescent bacteria harvested from an octopus. The gorgeous technology had attracted more innovators interested in what we like to call blue-green energy. Though the lamps are lantern pale compared with an electric light, the photobacterium are currently being bred by B. M. Joosse and R. M. P. Groen, two Life Science and Technology students at the Delft University of Technology who are currently working to prolong the life span of the bacterium for a possible next generation of lamps that need no fossil fuels or electricity—only seawater and life.

Eventually we expect sea residents to ask land folk, "How do cities stranded deep inside continents provide energy? They have to drill into rock? How primitive!"

Q: *Do you want to privatize the oceans?*
Though the lack of defined property rights on the ocean has certainly contributed to overfishing in a classic "Tragedy of the Commons" situation, the law of the sea forbids any group or nation from claiming an area of the high seas to be under their ownership. By law, the sea remains free.

Q: What about overfishing? Don't we need land governments to protect the oceans?

Sadly, governments don't protect the oceans; governments provide incentives to abuse the oceans. Countries grant at least $35 billion US a year in fishing subsidies, which fuels unregulated and unreported fishing, amounting to 20 percent of total marine catch. If you don't want fisherman to overfish, don't pay them to do it. Seasteads will have no tax loot to hand over to fisherman, and if seasteaders profit by fishing, they will be highly incentivized to preserve and manage fisheries. The best way to shut down the fish trawlers is to better serve their customers with the Neil Sims method: offer a tastier, healthier, and environmentally benign species of humanely raised fish that can be provided in no other way but Neil's cages.

Q: Still, how do we stop bad people from doing bad things on oceans so vast that even navies can't police them effectively?

People of genius already apply peaceful solutions to compel criminals to cooperate with international law. Scott Amos, founder of SkyTruth, discovered in 2011 that ships avoid collisions at sea with a satellite-based technology called Automatic Identification System (AIS). First he used the technology to detect oil spills on the ocean. Then, working with Google, Amos developed software to monitor the fishing practices of 150,000 vessels worldwide. Together with the non-profit Pew Charitable Trusts, they launched Project Eyes on the Seas, which uses artificial intelligence and gaming software to allow a single analyst to do the work of whole navies, and public humiliation to do the work of guns. As of 2015, if you wanted to protect your ship from collision using AIS, you had to submit to surveillance by Eyes on the Seas, which allows any fish buyer in the world to visit the online Virtual Watch Room and check whether the real-time blip representing your ship is green (low interest), yellow (flag and analyze), or red (suspicious or illegal activity). The technology for market transparency is a much cheaper, more effective, and nonviolent way to end illegal fishing than the June 2015 stunt by the governments of Indonesia and Palau, which chased down, captured, and set aflame forty-four pirate fishing vessels, belching black smoke into the sky and eliminating the livelihoods of seventy-seven poor Vietnamese. Voluntary solutions are more creative than violent ones.

Q: *Aren't seasteaders all libertarians?*

Interrogators appear to mean different things when they say "libertarian," and they are often referring to Peter Thiel. If by *libertarian* you mean working to empower individuals, seasteading is as libertarian as cofounding PayPal or investing in Facebook or building wooden ships and sailing to the New World. If you propose a fundamentally new venture that requires individual initiative, expect libertarians to show up and volunteer. Self-described libertarians rarely say, "Let's convince governments to do it," and often say, "Let me do it."

If you plan to create your own country, you are by definition a libertarian, even if you plan on state control of the means of economic production. Seasteaders plan to empower you with the technology to test your idea, which by design will empower others to join or leave you voluntarily.

Q: *How will laws be created on seasteads?*

Several attorneys and legal scholars have designed what they consider to be the best possible legal system and solicited the Seasteading Institute to instantiate their vision on a floating city. We now have a small portfolio of constitutions for twenty-first-century societies. We are not qualified to assess these legal systems, so we leave it to future seastead founders to set up their legal structures and see which attract immigrants.

Seasteading is not about imposing specific policies; it's about resetting the parameters of progress. We want to enable many groups of social entrepreneurs to create many new societies, each of which creates laws in a different way. For us to answer this question would be like asking the inventors of the transistor what computers would be used for. The point of seasteading is that we don't know the answer to this question, but if lots of people get lots of chances to test different answers to it, and any seastead resident can leave if he or she chooses, some law-creating techniques will provide radically more justice than the archaic "sausage grinder" by which politicians produce "pork barrel legislation" in government monopolies today.

Q: *But what laws will apply to the first few seasteads?*

The first seasteads will operate under the same maritime laws as existing ships, which already hold great legal autonomy. For example, Carnival Cruise Lines's ships fly flags from Panama and the Bahamas, while Royal Caribbean International cruise lines fly the flag from Liberia. Although these companies conduct major operations within US territorial waters, the United States interferes minimally with their operations. This is due in part to the fact that cruise lines bring jobs and revenue to the US economy. If America were to meddle too much, the cruise lines would move their operations elsewhere, as they have repeatedly in the past. Similarly, seasteads will trade extensively with land-based businesses. The people who profit from those relationships will encourage their government not to interfere and drive away the seastead. When people love seasteads as much as they love cruise ships, permanent voluntary societies will evolve from the temporary voluntary societies we have now. The cruise ship industry has already profitably pioneered the market niche of mobile crafts with de facto legal autonomy that compel land nations to compete to please them.

Q: *Isn't the ocean an untamed wilderness?*

Landlubbers don't hear much about UNCLOS, the United Nations Convention on the Law of the Sea. This is evidence of how well it functions. Myriad ocean industries in concert with maritime lawyers have already civilized the seas, fostering global cooperation among diverse cultures. We wish we could say that for some old land cities. The untamed wildernesses today are lawless lands, not oceans.

People do not populate a domain without developing rules, and markets cannot prosper without them. The United Nations oversees the International Maritime Organization, which regulates ships, crews, and safety. Borders are murky among moving ships and contested among jurisdictions, but the UN International Tribunal on Maritime

Law settles most border disputes. Unscrupulous shipping companies may cheat the people they hire, but the UN International Labor Organization (ILO) seeks to protect ship workers' rights, and the International Transport Workers' Federation (ITF) claims it recovers tens of millions US in unpaid wages for its members every year.

Q: *How will seasteads gain sovereignty?*

The international law of the seas is an advanced functioning framework that is ready to support the next layer of legal evolution: sovereign mobile nations. True sovereignty comes when established nations recognize a new nation. This can't happen overnight. In the early stages, seasteads will want to take advantage of existing laws and treaties between nations in order to exercise their own autonomy, and be diplomatic and friendly with their neighbors. Eventually, decades from now, when tens of thousands of people live on the ocean, and seasteads are an economic force in the world, other nations should recognize them as sovereign.

Before sovereignty, however, must come autonomy. We hope to establish this with our Floating City Project, which will float in the protected waters of a host nation willing to grant it substantial political independence. *Sovereign* means that a political entity has a seat in the United Nations, is recognized by other states, issues passports that are recognized by other nations' border controllers, and has its own stamp and Internet domain. *Autonomy*, on the other hand, we define as the degree to which a nation or group of people is free to create whatever legal system it wants without interference from the outside world.

Q: *Wouldn't it be more expensive to live on a seastead because of the cost of shipping goods manufactured elsewhere to the seastead?*

Iceland has to import most of its goods. So do Chicago and Kiev. Every developed city in the world relies on goods being shipped to it. Why not? Shipping costs are astoundingly low. For ten cents, you can get a bottle of wine shipped from New Zealand to Europe, and the wine auctioning website WineBid offers "one-cent shipping" from Europe to the continental United States if you buy six bottles or more. It's more challenging to sustain lines of supply to inland cities than to island cities. Ports make countries rich, and seasteads could be all port. Once a seastead can manage a protected harbor for cargo transfer, it will be plugged into the global trade network and distribution system. Over time, the costs of living on a seastead will decrease as the population increases.

Q: *But won't seasteads start out expensive?*

At the beginning, seasteads will be expensive, and much more likely to host hospitals for the first world than refugee camps for the third. Just like any technology, early adopters will buy the pricey early models, and over time, economies of scale will bring down the costs to make them more widely accessible.

In 1965, cruise vacations were a luxury reserved for the wealthy. They even had butlers! Now they're considerably more luxurious and can cost less per night than an average hotel in an American city. Mobile phones started out expensive—a sign of status for rich people only. In 1996 the Motorola StarTAC cost $1,000, and activists complained that the poor were exploited to build them. Today the poor are talking on them. By 2020, 90 percent of the world's population over the age of six will have access to a mobile phone. Not too long ago, laptops were only for rich people. Now we have solar-powered XO laptops distributed for free to 2.5 million poor children in Africa by the nonprofit One Laptop per Child in partnership with Fruit Roll-Ups. Whether it's soap, sneakers, cotton, clothes, or cars, most technologies follow the same trend from unique to ubiquitous.

Q: *Aren't seasteads for rich people only?*

If you were a billionaire, would you want to live on a seastead? If you were one of the bottom billion, would you want to take a blue job working a seastead algae farm? We don't need bailouts for billionaires. We need life rafts for the bottom billion. Our long-term plan is to build new city-states for the hundreds of millions of would-be emigrants around the world who are ready to give up on their failed states. After all, it's the poor who suffer the most from backward governance, not those wealthy enough to rig governments in their favor.

Immigrants in previous centuries came to the American frontier. We think immigrants in the twenty-first century will migrate to floating frontiers because seasteads won't survive without offering them better options. If seastead businesses cheat the first wave of immigrants, they lose their chance at the second wave of immigrants to seasteads that offer a square deal. Seasteads, to prosper like nineteenth-century America, must welcome immigrants by the millions, and that won't happen unless the first immigrants convince their families to join them.

For centuries, seasteading has served as an escape for the world's rejected. The Tanka people have been living in floating houses off the southeast coast of China since the seventh century, when they were pushed out to sea by war. These "gypsies of the sea" were not permitted to set foot on land until the founding of the People's Republic of China in 1949. For generations, they were born, married, and died adrift. Tankans still follow the traditional ways today, rarely coming to land. They make their livings by growing giant kelp. If seaborne refugees can survive afloat for more than a thousand years by cultivating algae farms and trading, modern seasteads can too.

Q: *But won't seasteads be ugly and bleak like oil platforms?*

Venice is an architectural masterpiece that has been known as the "City of Water" and "the Floating City," described in the *New York Times* as "undoubtedly the most beautiful city built by man." Venice emerged during a series of Hun invasions when refugees fled Roman towns to hide in wetland swamps. On 118 submerged islets, these castoffs built a civilization on stilts, discovering that canals were easier to travel than roads. Access to the sea and the easy flow of goods allowed Venice to attract commerce and immigrants. These lagoon dwellers dedicated their first church in the fifth century and emerged as a formidable aquatic city-state by the tenth.

From the ninth to the twelfth centuries, the Most Serene Republic of Venice, as it was then known, developed into a city-state *thalas-*

socracy, meaning "rule by sea," developing an undefeatable Adriatic navy, eliminating piracy along the Dalmatian Coast, and becoming the wealthiest trade center in the world, connecting Western Europe, the Islamic world, and the Byzantine Empire. Venice dominated the Mediterranean Sea for a thousand years, producing explorers like Marco Polo, composers like Antonio Vivaldi, writers like Giovanni Giacomo Casanova, architects like Andrea Palladio, painters like Giorgione. If Venetians could build a wealthy republic a thousand years ago with little but muscle power and firewood, we can build floating cities with diesel and hydraulics.

Is Venice for rich people only? Cities emerge over time. The general trend of all cities is: pioneers homestead the spot for economic or political reasons, often to trade near a body of water or to found a farm. As the community succeeds economically, immigrants move there seeking a better life, businesses blossom to serve them, and trade becomes brisk. If the city creates enough value for enough people, resources pour in, and the city grows. Cities always emerge through such baby steps, and we expect floating cities to do the same.

Q: *But what's to stop rich people from buying their own seasteads and creating island lairs of selfishness and greed?*

Just about every A-list Hollywood celebrity you can name owns a private island he or she rarely visits, while still paying for upkeep from workers who apply to work there. Billionaire Richard Branson, founder of the Virgin Group, author of *Screw It, Let's Do It. Lessons in Life and Business,* purchased and named Necker Island and Makepeace Island to try out his ideals.

Q: *Isn't the real goal to avoid taxes?*

Seasteads can't help you avoid taxes. The United States, for instance, claims the right to tax citizens with foreign earnings of more than $97,600 a year no matter where they move, unless they go through the onerous process of renouncing their citizenship and paying an exit tax which was raised 422 percent in 2014. This provoked an uproar, which preceded another 422 percent raise in 2015. American citizens can't escape taxes whether they move to a seastead or Sweden. Besides, the market for tax havens is well served by existing countries. The micro-state of Andorra is a tax haven with no military, surrounded entirely by the great nations of Europe, and it is doing quite well for itself. If you want an island tax haven, the Bahamas will do. Seasteads will prosper by trying something new, not by competing with existing island paradises.

Q: *Won't the oceans become crowded with seasteads?*

People already live on more than a hundred thousand natural islands. Forty-nine island nations and forty-three island dependencies and notable island groups already flourish—Caribbean, Indonesian, Polynesian, Macaronesian, Mediterranean, Indian, and many others—each producing a unique way of life. If volcanoes hadn't sprouted randomly in some of those spots, people would not have migrated there, and those cultures would not exist. Why should the number of islands created by random geological forces be the "optimum" number of islands that "should" exist, and why fixed in those particular spots? There's no particular reason we shouldn't add more man-made mobile islands to the tens of thousands that already flourish.

Q: *What about pirates?*

Pirate seas represent less than 2 percent of the world's oceans. If danger within Pakistan, Iran, Yemen, and Somalia doesn't make us fear land everywhere, then danger off their coasts shouldn't cause us to fear oceans everywhere. Pirates typically lurk offshore in unstable regions in the world, such as the Horn of Africa, the Gulf of Guinea, or among the 17,500 islands of Indonesia. Ocean vessels protect themselves with high-powered water propulsion, high-decibel sound propulsion, and deadly firepower as a backup. Seacurus, a marine insurance broker willing to pay kidnapping ransoms, says it can cut insurance costs by up to 75 percent if ships employ private armed guards. Roughly two-thirds of ships carry private armed security personnel, and, so far, no pirate has ever boarded a ship with a security team aboard.

Seafarers who work on unarmed container ships off the coast of Somalia face real risk. The Internationally Recommended Transit

Corridor (IRTC) is a nearly five-hundred-mile two-lane ship highway going straight across the pirated seas between Somalia and Yemen, and it is patrolled by warships from three separate counterpiracy forces: the European Union, NATO, and the multinational Combined Task Force. Just in case that's not enough, the navies of Russia, Korea, India, China, and Japan also patrol it. Rich nations profit from sea trade and protect their interests. Our advice? Don't walk in dangerous neighborhoods, and don't park your seastead in pirate waters.

Q: *But won't large countries invade seasteads?*

China has not invaded Hong Kong. Malaysia has not invaded Singapore. The United States has not invaded the Cayman Islands. Twenty-one nations don't even have armies, and thirteen of them are island nations. For instance, Mauritius has not had an army since it gained independence from England in 1968. It's gotten quite rich since. Why don't the mighty nations of the world attack this defenseless island? Venezuela, ranked as one of the most corrupt countries in the world, with repeat military coups and drug trafficking, has not invaded the island nation Trinidad and Tobago, which is one of the wealthiest nations in the Caribbean, and it's only 6.8 miles offshore.

Conquerors have incentives. Mounting a military attack is a costly enterprise. The aggressor must believe he will acquire something from the violence that will pay back his cost of invasion. Large countries go to war to control resources inside nations. They don't generally go to war with island nations. When island nations maintain mutually profitable alliances with other countries, large nations are not provoked to invade. Neither China nor Al Qaeda is interested in Fiji.

Even when seasteads are young and vulnerable, countries probably won't invade them for the same reason they don't invade ships. If nations permit "innocent passage" of ships through their territorial waters, they should permit "innocent floating" outside their territorial waters.

Q: *But how rebellious can seasteads be in the face of military empires?*

The Cayman Islands, with no standing army, adopts a spiteful stance toward US and EU regulatory policies, getting rich in small part by welcoming financial mavericks and medical outlaws from other nations. Imagine an island nation that imposes *no tax whatsoever* on personal income, corporate income, capital gains, dividends, interest, withholding, payroll, social security, inheritance, and property—and maintains the eighteenth highest per capita income in the world. Talk about a slap in the face to everything land-based politicians represent! When President Obama formally criticized the Cayman Islands as a tax shelter in 2009, the Cayman Islands Financial Services Association, *the very next day*, submitted an open letter reminding the president of their value to the US financial system. The Cayman Islands returned to business, and the US government remained quiet.

That's how a defenseless dependency with 57,000 people stood up to a military empire with 320 million people. Whether you are Luxembourg or Liechtenstein, small, defenseless nations protect themselves by providing value to mighty nations next door. When you start your seastead, think like a cleaner fish in a world of sharks.

Q: *What if seasteads go rogue and attack peaceful nations?*

At least thirty-four countries have been created between 1990 and 2008, and nobody says they shouldn't exist because they might start wars. There's nothing uniquely warlike about floating nations. In fact, they have less incentive, and virtually no ability, to amass militaries and mount invasions, which is why so many island nations today remain serenely defenseless. Aquapreneurs need to build a profitable business, attract immigrants, and maintain mutually beneficial legal agreements with host nations. Malaysia is not worried that Singapore will attack. History suggests that massive militaries are a continent-based problem, not an island problem.

Q: *What if seasteads exploit the poor?*

The poor are already being exploited by their dysfunctional governments. Offering an impoverished worker a better option is humane as long as the worker volunteers for it. Today's poor pioneers travel to a new place first, and only if they report back that life is better do more of their friends and relatives seek a living there. That's how the cruise ship industry has grown. If life on a seastead is worse than their home countries, word will get out, and people will stop moving there. If life is better, and they choose it freely, then we have empowered the poor, not exploited them.

Q: *Didn't you see that movie* **Waterworld?** *Didn't you ever play that video game BioShock?*

Fiction is meant to entertain, not describe reality. In 1969, as the cruise ship industry was picking up steam, Paul Gallico published *The Poseidon Adventure*, featuring a ninety-nine-foot wave that capsizes a cruise ship, and the disaster movie in 1972 became one of the six most successful movies of all time as of 1974. It had little predictive value. In previous centuries, European fabulists published popular fantastical stories about the early Americas that were as wild as *Waterworld*, as romantic as *The Love Boat*, and as violent as *BioShock*, and they have all been forgotten, because reality always turns out much more interesting. A half century ago, as spacesteaders worked toward spaceflight, we're sure detractors asked, "Haven't you ever seen *The War of the Worlds*?"

Q: *But what about a nightmare disaster scenario? Seasteaggedon?*

Let's imagine the worst-case scenario possible. Seasteads build walls around themselves, trapping their residents inside to confiscate their possessions. Seasteads declare war on one another, killing and bombing their helpless populations, and then turning their weapons inward and murdering millions of their own citizens. Nuclear reactors dump toxic waste into the environment near poor populations, causing genetic diseases that last for generations. Seastead cults intentionally starve millions to death. Seastead democracies enact medical experiments on ethnic minorities. With implicit government approval, children are used as slaves in deadly factories, tied to the machines they work. Sex trafficking becomes ubiquitous, and drug trafficking becomes the number one industry of numerous polities. The most evil tyrants imaginable torture their citizens for fun and threaten civilized society with weapons of megadeath.

We just described what actually happened in the previous century among land-based nations. These are not the institutions we should petition to protect us against the possibility that seasteads might repeat their performance. Seasteads will not outcompete land-based nations in murder and mayhem. That niche is pretty much dominated by governments on continents.

There's so much peace and prosperity in the world. Pepsi doesn't go to war with Coke. When our neighbors engage in a disagreement over the fence, they don't start shooting. Patri and Joe have disagreed about what should be included or excluded from this book, and, so far, neither of us has been stabbed. Where do we get the idea that people are more eager for violence than for a civil society? We get it by consulting the behavior of old terrestrial governments that control millions and prevent them from pursuing new options. Rogue nations are land nations. Small island nations are often vacation nations. The civilized world worries about Libya, not Malta, its prosperous island neighbor.

Q: *But aren't seasteaders proposing a hopeless bluetopia?*

Let's imagine the most starry-eyed seastead scenario. Soon after a continental nation murders and starves a few million of its own citizens and impoverishes many more, it benevolently declares that an offshore seastead may flourish as an independent political and economic zone. Within one year, the fresh experiment receives as much direct foreign investment as the great nation from which it was granted autonomy. Within two years, well over a half million people move there, most of them poor people from the continental nation. Within six years, the new polity's industrial output increases 1,256-fold, creating job opportunities that draw poor people from all over the world. Within twenty years, the population increases more than twenty-three times to 7 million, while the population of temporary workers increases 1,640-fold. In twenty-five years, 12 percent of the population is involved with starting a new business. Over thirty years, the population grows from 30,000 to 10 million, igniting property values to ascend by 18,000 percent. Flourishing in the shadow of a murderous tyranny that could crush it at any time, the political experiment produces a humanitarian singularity that shows no signs of pausing in its ascent.

We just described what actually happened in the coastal village of Shenzhen, China, after it was declared a special economic zone (SEZ) in 1979. And every time it needed to expand to absorb the stampede of eager immigrants, Shenzhen leaders had to ask the great nation of China for more territory, to which China repeatedly said yes. Today Shenzhen manufactures 90 percent of computer keyboards, 90 percent of computer mice, and 70 percent of computer screens sold globally. Migrant workers account for some 90 percent of Shenzhen's population. Per capita GDP is the highest among mainland Chinese cities. If so much prosperity can be accomplished in thirty years, how much could be accomplished on a fluid medium, where the floating city is free to expand as people choose to move there or dissolve as people leave?

Q: *Isn't it reckless to empower people to start their own nation? Shouldn't we empower today's nations to regulate and control the new island nations?*

Civilization is not threatened by the numerous island cultures that exist currently. Civilization is threatened by nation-states that rose to military dominance during the bloody twentieth century. Asking empires to protect civilization against the threat of island nations is a misplacement of priorities. A glance at two-thirds of the world's surface will tell you that most human interaction on Earth is a placid network of fluid commerce and cooperation. It is primarily through the abundance of this ocean economy that the divided and conquered continents are appeased. Our aquapreneur friends who work on the frontier of law to build algae farms and hospital ships are not afraid of Barbados or Bora-Bora. They are afraid of the mighty nations that control continents and crush by confiscation. Citizens of existing nations must endure wars they can't refuse to fund, hurricanes they can't dodge, earthquakes and tornadoes they can't predict, and politicians whose schemes they can't refuse to participate in. The dynamic nation that Patri and Joe reside in already orders drone strikes on wedding parties, spies on innocent people who aren't even citizens, initiates more than a hundred SWAT team raids every day against nonviolent citizens, imprisons one out of every hundred adults, and runs up debts that today's toddlers have to pay back with their future labor. These are the sorts of intractably worsening problems that emerge from a century of no market competition among governments. We think new floating nations of the twenty-first century can do better, in part because floating cities won't be founded by conquerors but creators. "I can't understand why people are frightened of new ideas," said John Cage, the composer. "I'm frightened of the old ones."

What worries anyone about seasteading should worry them about oversight. Both empower people. State politics is about enforcing our vision of society on others. Seasteading is about empowering others to create their visions of societies.

Q: *What will seasteads look like?*

We can't know. Asking what floating ocean nations will look like is akin to European monarchists asking Benjamin Franklin, "What will Manhattan Island look like?" Those of us who live in governments founded in the eighteenth century can't imagine the wondrously diverse nations that will emerge from peaceful market competition among twenty-first-century seasteads. We're still in the first decade of the seasteading movement. We can't predict our future on the Blue Frontier. For guidance, we can only look at past frontiers.

Chapter 9

HISTORY

Rights Flow from Frontiers

A Market of Governance Is an
Engine of Moral Progress

Most of human prehistory was barbaric. Humans shared roughly the same human nature for at least 40,000–35,000 years since the sudden cultural flourishing, maybe 120,000 years since the first evidence of trade was found, and possibly as long as 196,000 years since Cro-Magnon sported a skull just like ours. For as long as human nature existed, people cared about family and friends, traded with strangers, mourned their lost loved ones, and argued about tribal politics. But they couldn't find a way to permanently cease tribal warfare. The principles of game theory, which is the study of mathematical models of conflict and cooperation between rational decision makers, made lasting trust among strangers impossible. The market dynamics for political evolution couldn't take root.

Suddenly, out of the long night of barbarism, a candle of humanism flared. Civil society emerged in ancient Greece, a jagged coastline of peninsulas and islands jeweled with more than a thousand independent city-states, each with its own constitution. In the fifth century BC, Greece was not a country but a culture. All Greeks shared a common language. This made it relatively easy for people to choose where to live, and it was not uncommon for individuals to move to neighboring city-states or for whole populations to abandon a city if events became intolerable. Small states would sometimes voluntarily merge with larger ones, and dissatisfied groups would set off to found new cities. The result was that lots of political ideas were tried out, good ones were retained and copied, and particularly harmful ones were abandoned, or they destroyed the polity while neighbors watched and learned. Aristotle studied the varieties of polities and categorized them as monarchies, aristocracies, and democracies. Not until the unprecedented marvels of robust civil society emerged did Plato and Aristotle place a negative connotation on the old, respected means of governing: *tyranny.*

The social, economic, cultural, and political dynamism spurred an economic boom for the entire region as economic specialization and interregional trade exploded. Those who trade, trade in ideas—especially in how to get along peaceably and profitably. This dynamic produced many remarkable innovations in governance—not only democracy but also republicanism, strong interstate federations to protect against conquest, robust divisions of power, and standardized units of money and measure. Market regulations emerged and were enforced, as well as sophisticated mechanisms for dispute resolution. With the mightiest empires poised within striking distance, ancient Athens produced governance innovations that would be preserved and studied lovingly through all the ages hence and eventually permeate global civilization.

It wasn't the people. Humans have always been marvelous. It was the physical medium in which humans interacted that provided for fluid variation and selection in the creation of and choice among polities. Joseph Camilleri and Jim Falk write in *Worlds in Transition: Evolving Governance Across a Stressed Planet* that "Greece was divided into many small self-governing communities, a pattern largely dictated by Greek geography: every island, valley, and plain is cut off from its neighbours by the sea or mountain ranges."

Gregory F. Rehmke, coauthor of *The Complete Idiot's Guide to Global Economics*, elucidated this view in his essay "Property Rights and Law Among the Ancient Greeks":

> *Central to the rapid progress of Greek civilization was its very lack of a political center. No great king ruled the Greeks. Instead, dozens and later hundreds of independent poleis, or city-states, developed in concert but with full political independence. They flourished, both in Greece and in its colonies around the Mediterranean and Black Seas, from 800 to 300 BC.*
>
> *Each city-state became a testing ground for small innovations in laws, economic policies, and political organization ... City-states*

whose laws and customs encouraged innovation and wealth creation passed on news of these practices through trade, and exported their laws and institutions by establishing colonies (which competed with the colonies of other Greek cities).

With conquest and control so difficult, and mobility among people, ideas, and goods so easy, market competition outstripped military competition.

The city of Corinth, for example, became the early commercial leader of the Greek world by developing its harbor and port facilities to take advantage of its prime location. By the early fifth century BC, however, Athens had supplanted Corinth as the commercial center of the Greek world. When its policies made it less competitive with Athens, Corinth, which had no political power over other Greek cities, was unable to hold onto its commercial power.

In his 2015 book, *The Rise and Fall of Classical Greece*, scholar Josiah Ober links the unparalleled economic growth in ancient Greece to the decentralization of power that compelled polities to compete to create fair rules, low taxes, and innovative attractions. He writes, "[A] world in which there is no centralized political organization, no empire running things, is perfectly capable of self-organizing into a condition of high growth."

What Ober calls "a marketlike ecology of states" was astoundingly resilient from roughly 600 BC to the Roman conquests in 146 BC. Summing up his book for *PBS NewsHour*, Ober writes, "In an inversion of the experience of Europe from 1500 to 1900 or China from circa 700 to 200 BCE, where systems of small states fell to the centralizing logics of state-building and empire, there were many more independent states in the Greek ecology at the height of the classical efflorescence than there had been several hundred years previously." Ober credits the ability of artisans to switch among poleis. "Experts in various arts and crafts migrated to new homes and established new centers of specialized production."

The wonders of ancient Greece emerged from hundreds of seasteads that couldn't move. Greek citizens, though, could move. It's vital to recognize that Athens *emerged*; it was not designed. Athens could not have developed its polity without learning from the past governance experiments of earlier Greek city-states. Free people have been benefiting from their legacy ever since. We shudder to imagine our world if this ecosystem of governments competing to attract citizens had never existed.

Tragically, the parameters for a market of competitive governance—variation by innovators and selection by consumers—came together much more rarely over the succeeding millennia, and only in small pockets, until the Italian Renaissance. The retreat of the monopolistic Holy Roman Empire from the Italian peninsula left a land without an overarching government. This land happened to be surrounded by three seas sprinkled with 450 islands, crisscrossed by three major rivers richly veined with tributaries, and cragged with mountains and valleys peppered with politically independent city-states. Roughly two millennia after the Golden Age of Greece, the dynamics for a decentralized market of governance were in place. Armies of monarchs couldn't get across the Alps in one piece, leaving the Italian peninsula a natural experiment in polycentric governance with easy access to water.

It was a terrible time to be conqueror, but a great time to be a trader. Entrepreneurs hopped in their boats and got to business along waterways and seaports, supporting a merchant and banking class who patronized the arts, whereupon status-hungry city-states spurred the Renaissance between the tenth and fifteenth centuries. When they weren't fighting, these sovereign cities engaged in ceaseless economic and artistic competition, jealously gobbling up talent from among the most highly mobile people in the world at that time, amid a widespread increase in literacy, numeracy, and an unprecedented near tripling of per capita income in northern Italy from the eleventh century to the fifteenth century. The competition ignited a firestorm of commerce, cathedrals, capitalism, and communes—not to mention flowing fountains of public freshwater in cities like Siena—seducing farmers to immigrate to cities en masse and making Italy the most urbanized region in the world at that time, with an estimated 20 percent of Italians living in cities. Exports overseas exceeded imports by far, free-trade zones sprouted in Tuscany, and entrepreneurs who served became wealthier than nobility who ruled, and scientists flourished.

North of the Alps was rigid European feudalism: rural villages governed by lords and monarchs vested with absolute power to confiscate peasant surplus and stunt emerging commerce. South of the Alps was the dynamic aquatic peninsula: sovereign republics run by magnates who built cities of wonder employing the magic of commerce to produce staggering surpluses.

Only in the land without a king did business innovations outstrip military innovations, and the most aquatic city became one of the wealthiest. By 1192, the elected chief magistrate of Venice known as the doge could do little without approval by an elected parliament known as the Great Council. Here we see a microcosm of Renaissance Italy itself: Venice was rich, urban, and intensely aquatic, a center for commerce with no center of political power. This was the birthplace of modern business practices. By the early fourteenth century, Venetians had developed equity and mortgage instruments, bankruptcy laws, double-entry accounting, the first business schools, and risk management through limited liability joint stock companies that allowed poorer merchants to gain access to international trade, fostering a great deal of income mobility. A grandson of a slave established a dynasty of ruling elites, and a pirate became Pope. Little of this involved saintly behavior. Wealthy families engaged in conspiracies, bribes, and assassinations just as royal families did, but with no ultimate summit in the pyramid of state power, commerce was often more profitable than conquest. Tourists still visit to gawk not at the might but the majesty created in this period. Every region at all times has been rich with da Vincis, Galileos, Gutenbergs, Michelangelos, Shakespeares, Keplers, Newtons, and Voltaires, but the social dynamics that encourage innovation and patronage must be in place. These appear to emerge from geographical features that for a time discourage centralized control and encourage decentralized creation and choice.

The next great stride for variation and selection among governments would require a New World. On the American frontier, the market of societies competing for residents accelerated in the proliferation of states, territories, and laws, driving what would emerge as a global transformation in consciousness. To understand how the myriad rules that created the most prosperous people on Earth emerged, you have forget everything you learned in government schools, which teach children that wise government leaders bestowed universal voting rights from on high because they were such a nice bunch of Caucasians who enjoyed ceding power to their lessers. The real story is that women, blacks, and the poor earned voting rights by provoking a bidding war among polities on the American frontier.

"Shesteading"

At our third Seasteading Conference in San Francisco in 2012, after we finished congratulating one another for our vision and forethought, we passed around the microphone to share elaborations upon our previous thoughts. This is a common ritual in Silicon Valley, where we inspire one another with ambitious conjectures before the cascade of catastrophes reveals the tiny number of ideas that turn out to prosper in merciless reality. Libertarian feminist Brit Benjamin took the mic and asked how many seasteaders would like to maintain the gender balance of the conference on our actual seasteads. Ten seconds of dumbstruck silence passed as a room full of naval engineers, economists, agronomists, maritime lawyers, and marine biologists realized a key element of their seastead fantasy was missing.

This was not the first time men strode confidently onto the frontier only to notice belatedly that no women had followed them. In early America, the solution involved no saintly political leaders, only competition in the market of marriage. Patri and Brad Taylor, a postdoctoral fellow at the Australian National University School of Politics and International Relations, researched and wrote a paper tracing this curious story, leading Brit Benjamin to coin the word *shesteading*.

Once the American colonies enacted the zany idea from ancient

Athens that important matters of state should be decided not by royal decree but by popular vote, the question arose: Who, exactly, should be granted this privilege? Certainly not children. Not "negroes, mulattoes, and Indians." Not poor whites or "paupers." Not illiterates. Not people who can't afford to pay taxes. Not the landless. And certainly not women! Extending voting rights to these groups was advocated only by misfits with strange ideologies.

Basically, everybody was excluded except periwigged property owners, the class who wrote the laws in established states. This arrangement is hunky-dory when you're the man who already owns settled land with captive citizens. When a state court judge proposed that the property requirement for voting be removed, former firebrand John Adams argued against it, claiming that institutional experimentation was not worth the risk. The former risk-taking radical was already acting like a bureaucrat now that he had a vested interest to protect. Pennsylvania and Rhode Island shared his caution, retaining tax qualifications for voting into the twentieth century. Remember this next time somebody tells you governments are eager to adjust.

On the frontier, however, things were dynamic. In an effort to attract mobile workers, the new western territories abolished economic qualifications for voting. Suffrage was apparently a big lure for these migrants, who sent letters to their families back east to effuse about their voting rights. As a result, western states generally saw higher voter turnout than eastern states. As the competition for citizens on the frontier became feverish, the circle of seductive rights was extended. One by one, the fringe states granted voting rights to formerly disenfranchised groups: "paupers," those without property, illiterates, blacks, and all other adult persons—except for the half of humanity that happened to be penisless. It's all *men* who are created equal, after all.

As the newly empowered migrants arrived in the deep territories to seek their fortunes, men found themselves in a conundrum. By 1870, there were six men for every woman in Wyoming. All across the Great Plains of the western frontier, a grassroots wave of high-mindedness swept the ranks of celibate men. One correspondent urged his fellow bachelors to support a community property law in California, in which property acquired during the marriage is owned jointly by both spouses, on the basis that it would attract "women of fortune" and was thus "the very best provision to get us wives."

When radicals in the old states proposed female suffrage, politicians defended tradition, expressing fear that an empowered fairer sex might ruin the flawless world that male politics had forged. What if they started voting for feminine values? The new nation might lose its edge. The suffragettes who battled without success in the old states gained their first foothold in the newly formed fringe states. Beginning with Kentucky in 1838, women were permitted to vote—but only if they had certain qualifications, and only on womanly issues such as education and wet nursing and whatever else it was that women did; men were not exactly sure. This was not enough to satisfy the suffragettes, so other territories competed to coax the fairer sex to their communities.

In 1869 the newly organized Territory of Wyoming—the place with the six to one gender ratio—was the first polity in America to offer complete, unqualified voting rights to women. In fact, men were so motivated that they passed this act in their very first legislative session, whereupon frontier feminists finally came a-courtin'. This caused a firestorm of sudden male enlightenment, as fourteen other states followed suit.

Of the thirty states that entered the union before 1850, two offered women the right to vote. Of the eighteen continental states that joined the union after 1850, thirteen offered women the right to vote. In other words, new-frontier polities were far more likely to adopt the radical innovation of women's suffrage than eastern and midwestern states. More than a half century after the first of these formerly unthinkable frontier experiments was founded, the Nineteenth Amendment was enacted nationwide in 1920 by saintly federal politicians, who instructed their government schools to give them all the credit.

In ancient Greece, Aristophanes wrote a play called *Lysistrata*, which many historians think is based on a real Athenian feminist. The premise? The women of Athens, Sparta, and other city-states are sick and tired of their men fighting wars, so they boycott sex until the men agree to declare peace, whereupon the battle of the armies ends and the battle of the sexes begins. The nearly 2,500-year-old play reads like a modern situation comedy. Though civilizations can be crushed, the best strategies for moral progress in human motivations can be preserved across time.

The humanist innovations of the United States were not bestowed by a famous group of patriarchs Americans call "forefathers" in some primal instinct for ancestor worship. Witness grumbly Adams not wanting the landless to vote, licentious Jefferson making babies with his slave, and warrior Washington riding in at the head of an army to crush the whisky tax rebellion eleven years after he won the tea tax rebellion. The radical rights enactments of the United States, which inspired nations all over the world, evolved from the efforts of obscure social entrepreneurs in competing jurisdictions innovating to attract citizens by treating them like customers. Nobody designed the genius of the United States in the nineteenth century. It emerged from the unique medium of a frontier country, in which new polities were being formed regularly and competed vigorously to attract residents.

Break Up the Log Jam

As we study the reality of political evolution, we discover that moral progress does not spring from the brows of visionary politicians who decide to be morally superior and enforce justice upon their misbehaving societies. Moral progress emerges from millions of individuals competing for novel ways to profit by pleasing one another. Without islands of experimentation on the western frontier, each eager to attract the oppressed, landless, poor, and pretty, elections in the United States might still be determined by wealthy white property owners.

Human rights come from the fringe on the frontier, and so does technological innovation. In fact, every nation follows a business cycle of sorts. They begin as innovators and then become stagnant monopolies protecting themselves against innovation. Technological inertia is enforced by entrenched industries that manipulate the political system to suppress new breakthroughs that threaten their turf and revenue stream. The current winners prefer stability, while innovation is destabilizing—hence the word *disruptive*. But consumers crave novelty. The rise and fall of technological innovation within countries is so persistent it's dubbed "Cardwell's Law," after the British historian Donald Cardwell. Mike Gibson, apostate philosophy scholar, vice president for grants at the Thiel Foundation, and cofounder of the 1517 Fund, which invests in companies led by young founders "with a contrarian edge" explained on Patri's blog, *Let a Thousand Nations Bloom*:

"Cardwell's Law says that no nation remains technologically innovative for long. It is a truth rarely acknowledged that with great stability comes hard mental and political cholesterol. Vested interests, wanting to hold fast to their dominant position, will erect all sorts of impediments to stifle would-be challengers. Innovation flags. Stagnation ensues. Life is worse for all."

Cardwell's Law held for each European country during the industrial revolution, but technological innovation continued for the continent as a whole. How? There were many polities with relatively similar cultures, which made it easier for people to switch countries. Rulers could stifle new ideas among their own people, but they couldn't control immigration and emigration, nor the overall dynamism of the continent. As one nation became stagnant, the torch of technological leadership was passed to another, thus allowing sustained technological progress in Europe overall. European rulers basically played a hopeless game of Whack-A-Mole, stamping out threatening technological breakthroughs in one jurisdiction only to find them popping up in another.

Consider Christopher Columbus. His quest across the ocean wasn't nearly as arduous as his quest for royal sponsorship, which is a story of repeated failure. Rejected twice in Portugal, he went to Venice and Genoa, which both rejected him. So he sent his brother to England, which also royally rejected him. So off he went to visit the royalty of Spain, who bounced him around bureaucracies for months—and then rejected him. Columbus resolved to submit his wackadoodle proposal to young King Charles VIII of France, whereupon Luis de Santángel, a baptized Jew and finance minister to Queen Isabella's husband/cousin, King Ferdinand II stepped in with some private advice for the queen.

In a sudden about-face, Isabella defied her experts and arranged for Columbus to receive the finances. Why? As Will Durant noted in *The Reformation: The Story of Civilization*, volume 6, "perhaps they wished to keep an option on his project lest by some chance it should bestow a continent on a rival king." Competition really has a way of driving risky ventures.

Compare this to China, where the centralization of power over the wide plains caused innovation to come to a halt around 1600, despite an extraordinarily imaginative culture in earlier periods that produced a bonanza of breakthrough technologies, including printing, paper money, porcelain, tea, restaurants, gunpowder, the compass, and pasta. If the Italian merchant Marco Polo's tales are true, he arrived in China in 1271 to find a futuristic wonder world far surpassing what he had known in Europe. Polo described with astonishment the size of the cities, the complexity of commercial activity, the elegance of the ships, and the impossibly numerous canals. How could the most technologically dynamic culture in the world fall into abrupt regression?

In his book *Guns, Germs, and Steel*, Jared Diamond proposes that innovation in China was stifled by the lack of competitive governance. China is mostly an expansive flatland of fertile river plains. Once a great ruler was able to control it, technological innovations could be prevented from threatening the status quo. There was no frontier or enclave to which scholars, inventors, and dissidents could flee with their novel notions. In contrast, Europe's geography of zigzagging mountains, seas, islands, peninsulas, and jagged coasts created a governance ecosystem of smaller polities in perpetual competition for talent and status. China produced a culture of obedience, Europe produced a culture of rebellion, and America produced a culture of radical self-reliance. The theme of history repeats: monopolies enforce the status quo; frontiers provoke progress.

A Chinese explorer with a nutty notion could not bounce from king to king to queen. If the emperor said no, that was final. Thus uncountable Linus Paulings, Thomas Edisons, Rosalind Franklins, and Christopher Columbuses were suppressed in China. A Christian missionary in Ming China wrote, "Any man of genius is paralyzed immediately by the thought that his efforts will bring him punishment rather than rewards." The Ming dynasty fortified the Great Wall to keep out foreigners, created a new capital known as "the Forbidden City" to keep out its own people, and ordered that the most advanced fleet of ships in the world be burned, enforcing a self-serving siege mentality that cemented Chinese stagnation.

By 1961, tens of millions had starved to death. How did China reverse this trend and become an economic powerhouse? Nobel laureate Ronald Coase and Ning Wang, in their essay "How China Became Capitalist," suggest that once the monopoly held by central planners was broken, the solution arose from a vast market of competitive governance:

"When China's 32 provinces, 282 municipalities, 2,862 counties, 19,522 towns, and 14,677 villages threw themselves into an open competition for investment and for good ideas of developing the local economy, China became a gigantic laboratory where many different economic experiments were tried simultaneously. Knowledge of all kinds was created, discovered, and diffused fast. Through the growth of knowledge, the enormous scale of Chinese industrialization made its rapid speed possible."

Jonathan Rauch's wonderful book *Government's End: Why Washington Stopped Working* traces how Cardwell's Law works in America. If you still think voting for the right party or politician could enact meaningful reform, give it a read.

Mesopotamia, ancient Egypt, and the Roman Empire have become classic examples of civilizations founded on rapid technological advancement and then foundering for centuries in technological stagnation. But once we can shuffle around our buildings, the sea becomes a permanent frontier for pilgrims on a thousand floating Plymouth Rocks.

Ten Thousand Ben Franklins

Washington, DC, displays monuments to Ben Franklin, Thomas Jefferson, and George Washington. If these three met in the nation's capital today, what could they do? Argue about revolutionary ideas, advocate eloquently for some change in policy, work through the paralyzed political system, and probably get their periwigs all apuff with frustration. Their intellectual breakthroughs could never break through.

Sure, Franklin was a genius. But he was also in the right place at the right time. Only a few hundred million people existed on the planet at that time, and very few found themselves in a position to forge a government for a New World. Today we live among 7 billion people, and a much higher percentage of misfit thinkers are poised to found their New Worlds. They just need a platform. The best societies that flourish in 2050 will not subscribe to today's ideologies. Some of those 7 billion people are going to evolve new social systems we've never even thought of, based on technologies that don't exist yet.

When we argue about politics, we are like primitive meteorologists arguing over which steps in the dance will bring the rain. Whatever we discover about how to flourish peaceably in the laboratory of the oceans, it will defy our most passionate opinions now.

Chapter 10

FLOW STATES

How to Double Global Wealth

Radical Liquidity

Reach out your hand and touch whatever item is within arm's reach. Chances are strong that some element of it was delivered from across the planet by ship. If it weren't for this fluid mobility of goods, most of what we own would be much more expensive, which means we wouldn't be able to own it. Trade carried by sea has quadrupled since 1970. Over that same period, global GDP per person has increased by at least as much.

When contemplating why the United States is so prosperous, consider that the National Ocean Policy Coalition, a private company that develops national ocean policy, reports, "One of every 6 jobs in the U.S. is marine-related . . . Over 50% of the U.S. population lives within 50 miles of the coast . . . The coastal states together produce a GDP that is bigger than that of any single country in the world, except the U.S." Eight of the top 10 richest countries in the world are coastal states. In modern civilization, wealth relies on water.

Hundreds of wars have been fought to gain access to the liquid nourishment of nations. Economist Paul Collier, in his book *The Bottom Billion: Why the Poorest Countries Are Failing and What Can Be Done About It*, argues that most of the poorest billion reside in landlocked countries. As measured by the United Nations Human Development Index (HDI), not a single landlocked country outside Europe is successful, and nine of the twelve countries with the lowest HDI scores are landlocked. Whether we are talking about goods, people, or information, wealth emerges from fluidity and flow.

Patri's dad, economist, physicist, and legal scholar David Friedman, tossed out a famously whimsical proposal on the benefits of mobility:

Consider our world as it would be if the cost of moving from one country to another were zero. Everyone lives in a housetrailer and speaks the same language. One day, the president of France announces that because of troubles with neighboring countries, new military taxes are being levied and conscription will begin shortly. The next morning the president of France finds himself ruling a peaceful but empty landscape, the population having been reduced to himself, three generals, and twenty-seven war correspondents.

Political economists have been dreaming about an economic solution to political gridlock for decades. If only governance providers had to compete to keep mobile citizens as if they were customers! Then citizens would hold the two key powers you need to keep innovation robust: the power of the customer to exit, and the power of new providers to enter.

Well, the incalculable economic power of mobility recently got calculated, and it makes the wild-eyed optimists like David Friedman seem like pessimists by comparison.

We know from studying the proliferation of special economic zones (SEZs) that when states step back from micromanaging people's behavior, unpredictable network effects emerge that swiftly accomplish humanitarian goals. The ever-increasing density of the voluntary transaction network creates more conditions for creative connections that the best intentions of bureaucratic designers never predicted. People are smarter than their politics.

Yet engage in politics they will. The Left works to protect free speech, displaying an intrinsic understanding that the free flow of ideas fosters a healthy competition that gives rise to a wealth of insights. The Right works to protect free markets, displaying an intrinsic understanding that the free flow of goods fosters a healthy competition that gives rise to a wealth of delights. These are the left and right sides of the universal principle of peaceful competition and free choice that drives human fulfillment. What if this universal principle of free flow in speech and goods were applied to people?

Michael Clemens works for the Washington think tank Center for

Global Development, and he sought to answer this question. In 2011 he published a paper titled "Economics and Emigration: Trillion-Dollar Bills on the Sidewalk?," wherein he looked at four groups of researchers who "built models of the world economy to estimate the gains from eliminating various barriers to trade, capital flows, and migration."

How much power for prosperity is hidden in the principle of mobility? Most economists agree that eliminating barriers to the free trade goods would greatly increase total global wealth. If only nations allowed goods to flow freely, without restrictions imposed by political borders, humanity as a whole would prosper. By looking at the figures from four independent studies on the matter, Clemens discovered that the principle of flow applies more to people than to products. Summing up the conclusions, the distinguished Clemens wrote in plain English:

"[T]he few estimates we have should make economists' jaws hit their desks. When it comes to policies that restrict emigration, there appear to be trillion-dollar bills on the sidewalk."

According to those four independent studies, eliminating barriers to emigration would increase global GDP *ten* to *a hundred times* as much as eliminating barriers to trade. In fact, a conservative reading of the gains in networked efficiency suggests that if less than 5 percent of the populations from poor regions were welcomed to new nations, it would equal the effect of 100 percent of all goods flowing across all borders.

"All this suggests," wrote Clemens, "that the gains from reducing emigration barriers are likely to be enormous, measured in the tens of trillions of dollars."

Clemens concedes that each of the studies he looked at relies on assumptions, and those assumptions vary among the four studies, yet each estimate independently shows that open borders could boost global GDP in the 50 percent to 150 percent range. This would virtually eliminate all poverty on the planet. If these estimates are correct, this means the greatest evil preventing human flourishing is our superstition that people belong to governments they didn't choose.

Let Love Flow

Economist Bryan Caplan asks the average middle-class American to imagine visiting Haiti on a humanitarian mission. After a half month of good works, the American attempts to return to America, where a customs official informs him that he can never enter the United States again. The American demands an explanation. The official refuses to give one.

"But—but—but—," the American stammers, "Haiti is hell! Infants are eight times more likely to die! I'll only make one-fortieth of the money! On average, I'll die sixteen years earlier! Almost half the people are illiterate! You can't make me stay here!"

The border enforcer says, "Too bad. Have a nice life in Haiti."

Almost anyone would say this is unjust. But what's the moral difference between a person born in one country and another?

It's one thing to see a suffering child on Facebook and offer to donate. It's quite another when that child is your niece or nephew. Remittances are transfers of money from a foreign worker to his or her home country. Worldwide, recent immigrants from poor countries send more money back to their homes than the richest governments in the world do. The World Bank reports that in 2012, remittances topped $530 billion US, or more than a half trillion, which more than triples the aid budgets of all the governments in the world combined. As the largest flow of migrant workers in history has crossed borders to live and work abroad, many to SEZs, the amount of remittance money has tripled in one decade. Moisés Naím, senior associate in the International Economics Program at the Carnegie Endowment for International Peace, calls this phenomenon of the last decade "the Mobility Revolution."

This flow of wealth to poor countries comes from poor people in rich countries. This is a comparatively small number of lucky migrants who are able to leave their families and find work in current states. Imagine if the bottom billion were offered better opportunities in blue-green nations competing to attract them.

Bryan Caplan continues this theme in an *EconLog* blog entry called "Sitting on an Ocean of Talent":

> *Now consider: economists already know how to extract many trillions of dollars of additional value from the global economy. How? Open borders. Under the status quo, most of the world's workers are stuck in unproductive backwaters. Under free migration, labor would relocate to more productive regions, massively increasing total production. Standard cost-benefit analysis predicts that global GDP would roughly double. In a deep sense, we are sitting on an ocean of talent—most of which tragically goes to waste year after year.*

According to a Gallup poll released in 2009, 700 million poor and oppressed people want to leave their countries forever and find freedom and prosperity for their children. That's more than twice the population of the United States. It's equivalent to the entire population of Europe minus Poland. This is not counting the people who are afraid to make such claims. This is not counting the people who want to leave, make their fortunes, and return.

These people have no place to go because immigration laws stop them. Today land-based nations serve as gated communities, shutting out those yearning to unleash their dreams upon the world. Existing countries don't want to absorb them. Seasteads will require them to survive economically. When we think about the potential in seasteading, we contemplate the Gallup poll map and think about all those souls longing to create a better set of governance rules.

From Grief to Gratitude

To escape the relentless innovation and eccentricity of the San Francisco Bay Area, the cutting edge of the continent, people trying to finish their books often seek sanctuary in Mendocino.

A walk through the old graveyard of Mendocino, California, is an exercise in gratitude. In the oldest section, the buried died between 1880 and 1910. Many of them died a few years after they were born. Many are buried next to spouses they outlived by thirty to fifty years, among children who died before they did. In plot after plot, you see headstones in pairs, surrounded by smaller headstones of the children and teenagers they lost. Often you see young mothers and babies who died the day the baby was born. Many gravestones announce that the family founders were born in Sweden, Ireland, Mexico, and other far-flung coastal nations. These were the lucky few who had access to the sea.

A century later, Mendocino is a tourist spot where the affluent descendants of immigrants visit to enjoy the surf breaking against its famous coast while they soak in private hot tubs. For the people buried in the old graveyard, Mendocino was not a sanctuary from stress. It was a town of mariners who came here to fish those rough seas, hew out a hard living for their families, and die in such numbers the survivors must have labored through their lives in a perpetual state of grief.

What drove those people to travel so many thousands of miles by boat, railway, and horse, to build their homes in such a harsh, lonely place they knew only through hearsay, knowing they'd likely witness many die on the journey? The nations they left must have been very difficult indeed. The desperate from the Old World fled to the giant life raft of the Americas with a wild futurist fantasy that they could find a better life for their children. When they requested that the busy stone mason carve "sleep my little darling" into their children's gravestones, they must have shifted their hopes another generation ahead, to their grandchildren.

During the same period, Patri's great-grandparents—Milton Friedman's parents—arrived to the New World from Hungary after Jews in neighboring regions experienced pogroms, and before the Holocaust nearly eliminated the Jewish population in their hometown of Beregszasz. Around that time, Joe's great-grandparents arrived from Ireland after their families survived two famines. Joe's great-grandmother had sixteen children, and four didn't make it to age five. Starving must be a difficult way to die, and a difficult thing to survive. Patri and Joe are living lives of stupendous futuristic prosperity beyond what those immigrants were capable of dreaming. Yet the immigrants dreamed nonetheless, embraced incredible risk to pursue those dreams, and often died still dreaming of prosperity for their descendants. We wish we could go back and tell them how marvelously successful they would be.

In Mendocino, a glass of good wine costs a week's wages for a billion people who have not followed the New World into pleasure and affluence. Many live today with the kinds of famines and slaughters our great-grandparents escaped. A 2009 Gallup poll found that 16 percent of the world's adults are ready to leave their dysfunctional governments permanently and find a place that will welcome them with work. Any takers?

The ghost of Milton Friedman inhabits this book. If you take away any message from this book, it is this:

Seasteading is about emigrant rights.

People should be allowed to opt out of governments they didn't choose. Seastead pioneers don't need you to vote for them. They only need you to not petition your politicians to stop them.

Going off the Deep End

Milton's parents, Jeno and Sarah, were young entrepreneurs who believed they could cast off the protections and prescriptions of the Austro-Hungarian government and find a better life in grand experiment of America. Milton's life was enhanced enormously by the New World's newfangled governance rules, yet he tirelessly taught that good intentions expressed through government laws often cause more problems than they solve. His son, David, studied the evolution of legal systems and explained why static governments (rulers) don't need to exist at all, because governance itself (rules) evolves naturally through peaceful human interactions. Patri studied the evolution of industries and announced that every element of governance would progress quickly on a fluid medium like the ocean. From Jeno to Milton to David to Patri, every generation of Friedmans has said the same thing: "Son, you've gone off the deep end."

It's what Milt's grandparents must have said to Jeno and Sarah when the young couple announced, "We don't know what's going to emerge from this, but we are going to try our luck in the New World." The first words out of their mouths must have been some translation of, "Why rock the boat?"

Patri is a parent and knows it's natural for parents to fear the unknown. But he is also an investor and entrepreneur in Silicon Valley, where unpredictable waves of change launch innovators to heights, and cast them often into bankruptcy. Wave upon wave of startling new ideas relentlessly wash away any foothold in stability. In this fluid, dynamic, unregulated tech market, you learn the hard way that fearing change isn't a fallacy. Change is scary. The fallacy is equating stability with safety. Not changing is far scarier.

To paraphrase Shakespeare, there are more ideas in the oceans and earth than are dreamt of in our arguments. Over the horizon, new solutions are being generated at increasing speed, and we need to create a forum where they can be tested. The mounting emergencies of sea level rise, peak oil, peak water, peak phosphorus, peak soil, health care costs, poverty, war, and government gridlock aren't going away while we cling to the status quo. Governments forged in previous centuries are the institutionalization of the status quo. For the sake of the brilliant children being born right now, we must embrace our ignorance, relinquish our desire to control others, and allow innovators to take the plunge. By no other means are solutions found.

APPENDIX

The 1958 Geneva Convention on the High Seas

Article 1

The term "high seas" means all parts of the sea that are not included in the territorial sea or in the internal waters of a State.

Article 2

The high seas being open to all nations, no State may validly purport to subject any part of them to its sovereignty. Freedom of the high seas is exercised under the conditions laid down by these articles and by the other rules of international law. It comprises, inter alia, both for coastal and non-coastal States:

(1) Freedom of navigation;

(2) Freedom of fishing;

(3) Freedom to lay submarine cables and pipelines;

(4) Freedom to fly over the high seas.

"Because international law promulgated by the United Nations [which codifies the major principles of international relations] addresses only state actors and TSI [The Seasteading Institute] is a nonstate actor, this Note argues that international law does not prohibit the seastead communities from merely existing in international waters before they pursue their ambitions for international recognition ... Considering historical practice and what guidance

international law does provide, this Note concludes that the United States will recognize seasteads as envisioned by TSI [The Seasteading Institute] . . ."

—Fateh, Ryan H. "Note. Is seasteading the high seas a legal possibility? Filling the gaps in international sovereignty law and the law of the seas." 46 Vanderbilt University. *Journal of Transnational Law.* 899–931 (2013).

NOTES

Chapter 1. HOME: This Isn't Planet Earth

5 *52 percent of the world population will be exposed to severe water scarcity by 2050*: "Finding the Blue Path to a Sustainable Economy" (white paper, Veolia Water/International Food Policy Research Institute [IFRPI], June 24, 2011), www.wateronline.com/doc/finding-the-blue-path-for-a-sustainable-0001. See also Veolia Water/International Food Policy Research Institute (IFRPI), "Greater Efficiency in Water Management Will Reduce Risk for Half of the Global Economy," news release, March 21, 2011, www.veolianorthamerica.com/en/media/media/greater-efficiency-water-management-will-reduce-risk-half-global-economy; Veolia Water/International Food Policy Research Institute (IFRPI) *Sustaining Growth via Water Productivity: 2030/2050 Scenarios* (2011), http://growingblue.com/wp-content/uploads/2011/05/IFPRI_VEOLIA_STUDY_2011.pdf.

6 *by 2050 we will need to increase the land space devoted to farmland 22 million square kilometers*: Rutger de Graaf, *Adaptive Urban Development: A Symbiosis Between Cities on Land and Water in the 21st Century* (Netherlands: Rotterdam University Press, 2012), 40, www.hogeschoolrotterdam.nl/contentassets/451ed426db5a402fa6c53d2d32a3cd92/adaptive-urban-development---de-graaf.pdf. See also *How to Feed the World in 2050*, on the website of the Food and Agriculture Organization of the United Nations, accessed March 7, 2012, www.fao.org/fileadmin/templates/wsfs/docs/expert_paper/How_to_Feed_the_World_in_2050.pdf; "2050: A Third More Mouths to Feed: Food Production Will Have to Increase by 70%," on the website of the Food and Agriculture Organization of the United Nations, last modified September 23, 2009, www.fao.org/news/story/en/item/35571.

6 *"peak oil"*: Ian Chapman, "The End of Peak Oil? Why This Topic Is Still Relevant Despite Recent Denials," *Energy Policy* 64 (January 2014): 93–101. See also Nuno Luis Madureira, *Key Concepts in Energy* (London: Springer International, 2014), 125–26; Richard G. Miller and Steven R. Sorrell, "The Future of Oil Supply," *Philosophical Transactions of the Royal Society A: Mathematical, Physical and Engineering Sciences* 372, no. 2006 (January 13, 2014),

http://rsta.royalsocietypublishing.org/content/372/2006/20130179. See also Steve Sorrell et al., "Oil Futures: A Comparison of Global Supply Forecasts," *Energy Policy* 38, no. 9 (September 2010): 4990–5003.

6 *the world will run out of wild-caught seafood in 2048*: Juliet Eilperin, "World's Fish Supply Running Out, Researchers Warn," *Washington Post*, November 3, 2006, www.washingtonpost.com/wp-dyn/content/article/2006/11/02/AR2006110200913.html. See also Boris Worm et al., "Impacts of Biodiversity Loss on Ocean Ecosystem Services," *Science* 314, no. 5800 (November 3, 2006): 787–90, www.sciencemag.org/content/314/5800/787.abstract.

6 *"peak phosphorus,"or the point at which*: Ingrid Steen, "Phosphorus Availability in the 21st Century: Management of a Non-Renewable Resource," *Phosphorus & Potassium* 217 (1998): 25–31. See also Patrick Déry and Bart Anderson, "Peak Phosphorus," Energy Bulletin, August 13, 2007, www.greb.ca/GREB/Publications_files/Peakphosphorus.pdf; Dana Cordell, Stuart White, and Tom Lindström, "Peak Phosphorus: The Crunch Time for Humanity?," *Sustainability Review* (April 4, 2011): https://thesustainabilityreview.org/peak-phosphorus-the-crunch-time-for-humanity; D. Cordell, "The Story of Phosphorus: 8 Reasons Why We Need to Rethink the Management of Phosphorus Resources in the Global Food System," on the website of Sustainable Phosphorus Futures, last modified January 6, 2011, http://phosphorusfutures.net/why-phosphorus; David A. Vaccari, "Phosphorus Famine: The Threat to Our Food Supply," *Scientific American.* June 3, 2009, www.scientificamerican.com/article/phosphorus-a-looming-crisis/. Chelsae Rose Johansen, "Solving 'The Gravest Natural Resource Shortage You've Never Heard Of: Applying Transnational New Governance to the Phosphate Industry," *Vanderbilt Journal of Transnational Law* 46 (2013): 933–68.

6 *Eighty percent of the world's expanding megacities . . . More than 1 million people move to cities . . . by 2050, about half of the human population will live within 100 kilometers of a coast*: Rutger de Graaf, "Blue Revolution" (inaugural lecture, Rotterdam, November 6, 2012 Netherland, Rotterdam University of Applied Sciences), https://www.youtube.com/watch?v=T7FqjpG-sI4.

7 *balderdash*: Vaclav Smil, "Jeremy Grantham, Starving for Facts," The *American*, December 5, 2012, www.aei.org/publication/jeremy-grantham-starving-for-facts.

7 *human creativity*: Julian Simon, *The Ultimate Resource* (Princeton, NJ: Princeton University Press), 1981.

8 *a machinery of freedom to choose*: Patri Friedman, "Dynamic Geography: A Blueprint for Efficient Government," accessed from the website of the Seasteading Institute, n.d., http://seasteading.org/seastead.org/new_pages

/dynamic_geography.html. See also B. Taylor, "Governing Seasteads: An Outline of the Options," 2010, Seasteading Institute, www.seasteading .org/files/research/governance/Taylor_2010_GoverningSeasteads.pdf; P. Friedman and B. Taylor, "Seasteading and Institutional Innovation" (paper presented at the Association of Private Enterprise Education Conference, Nassau, 2011).

9 *twenty-seven Japanese baseball stadiums*: http://picturesdotnews.com/tag/re newable-energy "Kyocera Floats Mega Solar Power Plant in Japan" March 9, 2014. Accessed July 13, 2016.

11 *Some cruise ships are two-thirds the size of the Empire State Building*: Empire State Building volume = 37M ft 3. Also, roof is 381m, spire is 443.2m. Royal Caribbean's *Oasis* and *Allure of the Seas* are 362m and 22.5M ft 3.

12 *If the cruise ship industry were a country*: Global Cruise Passengers Carried, 1990–2014, https://people.hofstra.edu/geotrans/eng/ch7en/appl7en/global _cruise_passengers.html. See also https://people.hofstra.edu/geotrans /eng/ch7en/appl7en/ch7a4en.html. Dr. Jean-Paul Rodrigue and Theo Notteboom "Chapter 7: The Cruise Industry" *The Geography of Transport Systems.* "While in the 1990s, cruise ships rarely exceeded 2,000 passengers, by 2010 ships of 6,000 passengers were being deployed"; http://www .cruisemarketwatch.com/growth/ and analysis, https://people.hofstra.eduD /geotrans/eng/ch7en/appl7en/ch7a4en.html. "The global growth rate of the cruise industry has been enduring and stable, at around 7% per year in spite of economic cycles of growth and recession. For instance, the financial crisis of 2008–2009 has not impacted the demand for cruises." See Cruise Industry Overview—2015: "The industry estimates 23 million to cruise globally in 2015. The cruise industry is the fastest-growing category in the leisure travel market," n.d. www.f-cca.com/downloads/2015-Cruise-Indus try-Overview-and-Statistics.pdf. Cruise ship industry statistics September 3, 2015, American Association of Port Authorities, Florida-Caribbean Cruise Association. Accessed July 13, 2016 www.statisticbrain.com/cruise-ship-in dustry-statistics.

12 *Prelude floating liquefied natural gas facility*: December 3, 2013 Shell press release. Accessed July 13, 2016. www.shell.com/global/aboutshell/media /news-and-media-releases/2013/shell-floats-hull-for-worlds-largest-float ing-facility.html.

13 *United Nations Convention on the Law of the Sea (UNCLOS)*: Part V— Exclusive Economic Zone (II). (n.d.). United Nations Convention on the Law of the Sea, 489-510. *Online version*: PREAMBLE TO THE UNITED NATIONS CONVENTION ON THE LAW OF THE SEA. (n.d.), accessed February 17, 2016, www.un.org/depts/los/convention_agreements /texts/unclos/part5.htm.

13 *45 percent of the planet's surface that is unclaimed by countries*: Global
Ocean Commission, (n.d.). "Governing the High Seas," accessed February 17, 2016, www.globaloceancommission.org/the-global-ocean/the
-global-governance-gap. See also infographics at: http://theterramarproj
ect.org/#&panel1-1. The Pew Charitable Trusts The Global Ocean Commission (2013) www.pewtrusts.org/en/research-and-analysis/collections
/2013/02/the-global-ocean-commission.

13 *legal jurisdictions on the sea overlap and are contested*: Irini Papanicolopulu,
"Enforcement Action in Contested Waters: Legal and Policy Issues" (paper
presented at the sixth IHO-IAG ABLOS Conference *Contentious Issues in
UNCLOS—Surely Not?* Monaco, October 25–27, 2010), 4, www.iho.int
/mtg_docs/com_wg/ABLOS/ABLOS_Conf6/S7P2-P.pdf. See also: www
.gmat.unsw.edu.au/ablos/ABLOS10Folder/S7P2-P.pdf.

14 *"floating territory doctrine" . . . "nationality principle"*: E. J. Molenaar, *Coastal
State Jurisdiction over Vessel-Source Pollution*, The Hague: Kluwer Law International (1998), 83–102. See also O. Shane Balloun (2012). "The True
Obstacle to the Autonomy of Seasteads: American law Enforcement Jurisdiction over Homesteads on the High Seas."

14 *A crazy idea became common sense*: V. Freed, "Royal Caribbean Asks 'Why
Not?' Starts Own Floating Nation at Sea," *Why Not Herald* 1, no. 1 (2012).
www.creative.rccl.com/nation_of_why_not/images/WNH_Individual
_Pages.pdf. University of San Francisco Maritime Law Journal (June 19,
2012) Vol. 24, No. 409, 2012.

15 *no other nation on Earth*: "RCCL Aims to Double EPS by 2017," Reuters,
July 24, 2014, www.reuters.com/article/royal-carib-crus-strategy-idUSL6
N0PZ5HL20140724.

15 *incorporated in Liberia*: Liberian-flag fleet reaches 3,500 - gCaptain. (2011),
accessed February 17, 2016, http://gcaptain.com/liberian-flag-fleet-reaches
-3500/. See also Liberian International Ship and Corporate Registry
(LISCR). (n.d.), accessed February 17, 2016, www.directmeliberia.com/gov
ernment/148-liberian-international-ship-and-corporate-registry-liscr.html;
"Liberian-Flag Fleet Doubles in 10 years," Issue 32, March 2011 *Flagship*
Liberian Registry www.liscr.com/liscr/Portals/o/FlagshipMarch2011hand
out.pdf.

16 *Lee Wachtstetter has lived on the ocean*: Evan Bleier, "Florida Widow Has
Lived on a Cruise Ship for *Seven Years*: Eighty-Six-Year-Old Sold Her Home
After Husband's Death And Moved Into Stateroom at a Cost of $164,000
a Year," *Daily Mail* (UK), last modified January 22, 2015, www.dailymail
.co.uk/news/article-2918175/86-year-old-Florida-widow-Lee-Wachtstetter
-living-Crystal-Serenity-luxury-cruise-ship-nearly-seven-year s.html.

16 *crewmember retention rates as high as 80% for cruise lines*: Cruise Forward

Fact Sheet, accessed February 17, 2016, n.d. www.cruiseforward.org/docs
/default-source/default-document-Cruise Lines International Association
(CLIA) library/full-crew-toolkit.pdf?sfvrsn=0. See also John Hutchinson,
"CLIA Responds Vigorously to Salacious Author Who Wrote Tell-All Book,"
Daily Mail (UK), last modified, February 26, 2015, www.dailymail.co.uk
/travel/travel_news/article-2969989/100-hour-working-weeks-sex-deck
-REALLY-think-passengers-Confessions-cruise-ship-worker.html. "Staff
development and retention are also of great importance, as a motivated
crew is essential to ensure the continued success of cruising which sees an
employee retention rate of around 80 per cent . . . Cruise lines operate in
full accordance with International Labour Organisation (ILO) recommen-
dations for minimum wages for seafarers . . . In addition to their salary, crew
are provided with a number of benefits free of charge including room and
board and cruise-line sponsored medical care."

17 *the UN's . . . success at negotiating national self-determination is the great unsung
triumph of the institution*: The United Nations and Decolonization—History,
accessed February 17, 2016, www.un.org/en/decolonization/history.shtml.
"When the United Nations was established in 1945, 750 million people—
almost a third of the world's population—lived in territories that were
non-self-governing, dependent on colonial powers. Today fewer than 2 million people live in such territories."

18 *"The port business is all about real estate"*: S. Wampler, "Plan Floated to Ship
Cargo Inspection Offshore," Lawrence Livermore National Laboratory
News, July 2, 2010, www.llnl.gov/news/plan-floated-ship-cargo-inspection
-offshore. See also "On June 8, three of the nation's top 10 business schools—
Northwestern University's Kellogg School of Business, UC Berkeley's Haas
School of Business and Dartmouth's Tuck School of Business—presented
economic analyses of the offshore port concept . . ."

18 *"The world's population is going to continue to grow"*: William Reidy on economic viability of large floating structures at the Seasteading Conference
2012, www.youtube.com/watch?v=O0qZVejDcdo. See also Hank Glauser,
"The Portunus Concept," *Maritime Reporter*, September 2014, 52–55, www
.pacmar.com/story/2013/04/01/features/commerce-security-from-off
shore-port-design/146.html?m=true. See also summary at Morissa, "Understanding the Portunus Project," October 23, 2014, *World Wide Metric
Blog*, October 23, 2014, http://blog.worldwidemetric.com/problem-solving
/understanding-the-portunus-project.

18 *Portunus Project*: Floating port technologies could revolutionize container
commerce." Lawrence Livermore National Laboratory (March 25, 2014),
www.slideshore.net/ipo-admin/portunus-webinar-floating-port-technolo
gies-could-revolutionize-container-commerce.

19 *"I've seen flying fish"*: Kathi Gilbreath quotes from video at: Brian O'Keefe, "Chevron Goes to Extremes in the Gulf of Mexico," *Fortune,* June 9, 2014, http://fortune.com/2014/06/09/chevron-goes-to-extremes-in-the-gulf-of-mexico.

19 *2004 tsunami struck Thailand, deep-sea scuba divers reported*: "American Diver Underwater During Catastrophe," CNN.com, December 29, 2004, www.cnn.com/2004/US/12/28/tsunami.diver.

20 *Maersk . . . yearly revenue nearly equivalent to that of Microsoft*: Maersk press release, February 27, 2012. Microsoft 2011 revenues: www.microsoft.com/en-us/news/press/2011/jul11/07-21fy11q4earningspr.aspx. See also, for comparison, R. George, *Ninety Percent of Everything: Inside Shipping, the Invisible Industry That Puts Clothes on Your Back, Gas in Your Car, and Food on Your Plate* (New York: Metropolitan Books/Henry Holt, 2013), 7.

20 *The island's unbeatable economic strategy*: Size comparisons: www.maerskfleet.com/#compare-it/Emma_Maersk. Hull alone the size of Chrysler Building: www.passportdiary.com/cruise/ventura-vs-independence-of-the-seas-does-bigger-mean-better, compared to Burj Al Arab and Roman Colosseum: http://twicsy.com/i/45AfUi.

20 *almost halfway around the Earth*: Facts and Figures—Maersk Line shipping containers worldwide. (n.d.), accessed February 17, 2016, https://classic.maerskline.com/link/?page=brochure.

20 *the largest company of which there are hundreds*: http://en.wikipedia.org/wiki/List_of_freight_ship_companies.

20 *More than 17 million shipping containers*: www.billiebox.co.uk/facts-about-shipping-containers.

21 *"It is much more a gateway to freedom"*: C. F. Schuetze, "Living Above and Below the Water's Surface in Amsterdam," *New York Times,* April 23, 2015, www.nytimes.com/2015/04/24/greathomesanddestinations/living-above-and-below-the-waters-surface-in-amsterdam.html?_r=0.

21 In 2015 more than a million arrived in Europe by sea: "Migrant Crisis: Migration to Europe Explained in Graphics," on the webpage of BBC News, January 28, 2016, www.bbc.com/news/world-europe-34131911.

22 *"city apps"*: www.waterstudio.nl/archive/859. See also, https://www.floatingcityapps.com/blog.

22 *"Just as you can download apps,"*: B. Meinhold, "Inhabitat Interview: Water Architect Koen Olthuis on How to Embrace Rising Sea Levels," August 28, 2014, http://inhabitat.com/inhabitat-interview-water-architect-koen-olthuis-on-how-to-embrace-rising-sea-levels.

22 *Korail Wet Slum in Dhaka, Bangladesh*: www.unesco-ihe.org/sites/default/files/floating_city_apps.pdf.

23 *"seadromes"*: Bill Bryson, *One Summer: America, 1927* (New York: Knopf Doubleday, 2013).

24 *Buckminster Fuller revealed his detailed vision of Triton City*: http://cup2013 .wordpress.com/tag/triton-city/.

24 *There are three types of floating cities*: Buckminster Fuller, *Critical Path* (New York: St. Martin's Press), 332–33.

25 *The Maldives, a nation of 1,300 or so islands, may soon be submerged: Maldives Most At-Risk Economy in South Asia from Climate Change—Report*, August 19, 2014, www.adb.org/news/maldives-most-risk-economy-south-asia -climate-change-report.

25 *"This master plan for the Maldives"*: http://www.waterstudio.nl/vision.

25 *"architects of the climate change generation"*: K. Olthuis and D. Keuning, *Float!: Building on Water to Combat Urban Congestion and Climate Change* (Amsterdam: Frame, 2010).

26 *"This is incredibly frustrating," eighteen-year-old Max told his audience at TechCrnch Disrupt*: "Shipstr Makes Shipping Brokers Obsolete | Disrupt SF 2014," accessed February 17, 2016, http://techcrunch.com/video/shipstr -makes-shipping-brokers-obsolete/518410655.

27 *"former Harvard University president Larry Summers"*: Gregory Ferenstein, "Thiel Fellows Program Is 'Most Misdirected Piece Of Philanthropy,' Says Larry Summers," TechCrunch, October 10, 2013, http://techcrunch.com /2013/10/10/thiel-fellows-program-is-most-misdirected-piece-of-philan thropy-says-larry-summers.

27 *by the summer of 2015, companies started by Thiel Fellows had an aggregate value exceeding $1 billion*: thielfellowship.org. Well above $1.1 billion, according to personal communications with Jim O'Neill, cofounder of the Thiel Fellowship, and confirmed by personal communication with Michael Gibson, former VP for grants for the Thiel Foundation.

28 *"revolutionary for the developing world"*: Eric M. Jackson. *The PayPal Wars: Battles With eBay, the Media, the Mafia, and the Rest of Planet Earth* (Kindle Locations 321–27), Kindle Edition.

28 *Palantir Technologies*: H. Kutchler and R. Waters, "Fundraising Values Palantir at $20B," CNBC *Financial Times*. June 24, 2015, www.cnbc.com/2015 /06/24/fundraising-values-palantir-at-20b.html.

29 *"Among students of business, PayPal may be known less for its own success than for the subsequent achievements of the people Thiel helped attract to build it."* R. Parloff, "Peter Thiel Disagrees with You," *Fortune*, September 4, 2014, http://fortune.com/2014/09/04/peter-thiels-contrarian-strategy.

30 *start-ups are the way to discover solutions*: S. G. Winter, "Schumpeterian Competition in Alternative Technological Regimes," *Journal of Economic Behavior*

and Organization 5, nos. 3/4 (1984): 287–320. From abstract: "the 'historical' shape of industry evolution, particularly on the relative importance of entrants and established firms as sources of innovation."

31 *"displace no existing ecosystems"*: Marshall T. Savage, *The Millennial Project: Colonizing the Galaxy in Eight Easy Steps* (Boston: Little, Brown, 1992/1994).

38 *Since 1990, at least thirty-four countries have been created*: M. Rosenberg, "New Countries Created Since 1990," December 16, 2014, http://geography .about.com/cs/countries/a/newcountries.htm.

38 *Defining politics as "interfering with other people's"*: Peter Thiel, "The Education of a Libertarian," on the website of the Cato Institute, April 13, 2009, www.cato-unbound.org/2009/04/13/peter-thiel/education-libertarian.

Chapter 2. HOUSES: Cities That Clean the Seas

Unless noted otherwise, all quotes in this chapter from Rutger de Graaf and Karina Czapiewska were taken from interviews with the author.

42 *"the first steps in living on the ocean will be coastal expansion of existing cities"*: Inaugural lecture "Blue Revolution" professor Rutger de Graaf, www.you tube.com/watch?v=T7FqjpG-sI4. See also B. Roeffen et al., "Reducing Global Land Scarcity with Floating Urban Development and Food Production," Rotterdam University of Applied Sciences, Heijplaatstraat 23, Rotterdam, the Netherlands, www.deltasync.nl/deltasync/fileadmin/template/ main/projectimg/paper_land_scarcity.pdf.

43 *"[sixty thousand] floating houseboats in Amsterdam"*: J. Fehrenbacher, "Inhabitat Interview: Koen Olthuis of WaterStudio.nl Talks About Design for a Water World," February 7, 2016, http://inhabitat.com/interview-koen-olth ius-of-waterstudionl.

43 *"This is reality in the Netherlands," says Remko van Buren*: FLOAT (Flexible Land On Aquatic Territory), September 23, 2013, www.archfondas.lt/en /discussion/post/float-flexible-land-on-aquatic-territory.

45 *"Water is a very good solar collector"* "Floating Cities: Environmental Atlas of Europe," European Environmental Agency interview Rutger de Graaf, www .youtube.com/watch?v=nFcxaymOpes.

46 *buoyant foam slab encased in solid concrete*: Interview with Koen Olthuis on Discovery Channel, www.youtube.com/watch?v=61Wi5NcvOTw.

46 *At least fifteen of the world's twenty megacities grow on a coast or river plain*: Interview with Rutger de Graaf on Discovery Channel, www.youtube.com /watch?v=61Wi5NcvOTw.

46 *in 2050 the world will lack 22 million square kilometers of arable land*: de Graaf, *Adaptive Urban Development*, www.hogeschoolrotterdam.nl/contentassets /451ed426db5a402fa6c53d2d32a3cd92/adaptive-urban-development ---de-graaf.pdf. See also Global Footprint Network (2012) World Footprint. Do we fit on the planet?, www.footprintnetwork.org/en/index.php/GFN /page/world_footprint. "Moderate UN scenarios suggest that if current population and consumption trends continue, by the 2030s, we will need the equivalent of two Earths to support us."

49 *According to DeltaSync's plan*: K.M. Czapiewska, B. Roeffen, and R.E. de Graaf, "Cyclicity, A New Direction to Protect Deltas and Preserve Marine Ecosystems," in I. Krueger et al. (ed.), *Delta Alliance Young Professionals Award, Innovative Solutions for Delta Challenges Worldwide, Delta Alliance Report number 3*, Delta Alliance International, Wageningen-Delft, the Netherlands (2012): 157–175).

50 *if humans cultivate less than two-tenths of 1 percent of the ocean*: R.E. de Graaf, F. H. M. van de Ven, and N.C. van de Giesen, "Alternative Water Management Options to Reduce Vulnerability for Climate Change in the Netherlands," *Natural Hazards* (2007), www.springerlink.com/con tent/0921-030X. See also R.E. de Graaf, F. H. M. van de Ven, and N.C. van de Giesen, "The Closed City as a Strategy to Reduce Vulnerability of Urban Areas for Climate Change," *Water Science and Technology* 56, no. 4 (2007): 165–73, www.iwaponline.com/wst/toc.htm.

51 *"When rigs are left standing, the fish biomass is ten times greater"*: S. Kolian, "The Benefits of Leaving Oil and Gas Rigs Intact to Serve as Artificial Reefs," *Exploration & Production* 9, no. 2 (January 2011): 62, www.ecorigs.org/re centDocuments/O&G%20Journal%20Article.pdf.

52 *Algae could allow us to put it back*: Pascal Schlagermann et al., "Composition of Algal Oil and Its Potential as Biofuel," *Journal of Combustion* 2012 (January 2012): 1–14, www.hindawi.com/journals/jc/2012/285185.

53 *"a non-monetary, symbiotic economic model"*: de Graaf, *Adaptive Urban Development*, 49, www.hogeschoolrotterdam.nl/contentassets/451ed426db5a 402fa6c53d2d32a3cd92/adaptive-urban-development---de-graaf.pdf.

58 *Karina Czapiewska led the team*: DeltaSyncBV, Final Report *Seasteading Implementation Plan*, January 2013, www.seasteading.org/floating-city-proj ect/#anchor.

Chapter 3. FOOD: Feed the World with Greenhouse Gas

All quotes in this chapter from Ricardo Radulovich were taken from interviews with the author.

65 *devoured 90 percent of the large fish stock*: "Big-Fish Stocks Fall 90 Percent Since 1950, Study Says," National Geographic News, May 15, 2003, http://news.nationalgeographic.com/news/2003/05/0515_030515_fishdecline.html.

65 *5.3 billion scheduled to experience water shortages by 2025*: Water One World Solutions, accessed March 21, 2016, www.wateroneworldsolutions.org/index.php?option=com_content. "It is estimated that 5.3 billion people, two-thirds of the world's population, will suffer from water shortages by 2025." See also "What Makes Clean Water So Important?," accessed March 21, 2016, http://blueplanetnetwork.org/water.

67 *The twenty-five poorest countries spend 20 percent of their GDP on water*: Dean Kamen, quoted in *Abundance: The Future Is Better Than You Think* (New York: Free Press, 2012), 86. Also in *Forbes*: www.forbes.com/sites/brian caulfield/2012/01/26/abundance-why-the-future-will-be-much-better-than-you-think.

67 *More than a billion people do not have access to safe drinking water*, and *Six thousand children die every day for lack of clean water to drink*, and *African and Asian women walk an average of six kilometers each day to provide water*: accessed March 21, 2016, http://econopure.com/drinking-water.

67 *120 gallons of water to produce one egg*: accessed www.amwater.com/learning-center/water-101/what-is-water-used-for.html.

68 *by 2020, 135 million people will die for lack of safe drinking water*: Peter H. Gleick, *Dirty Water: Estimated Deaths from Water-Related Diseases 2000–2020*, (Pacific Institute Research Report, August 15, 2002), www.pacinst.org/wp-content/uploads/sites/21/2013/02/water_related_deaths_report3.pdf.

68 *By 2025, two-thirds of the world's population—the equivalent of all humans alive in 1990, which was 5.3 billion people—will suffer from water shortages*: Scarcity, Decade, Water for Life, 2015, UN-Water, United Nations, MDG, water, sanitation, financing, gender, IWRM, Human right, transboundary, cities, quality, food security, accessed March 21, 2016, www.un.org/waterforlifede cade/scarcity.shtml. See also United Nations "Water For Life" 2005–2015, www.un.org/waterforlifedecade.

68 *Worldwide, 70 percent of all available freshwater is used to irrigate agriculture*: International Fund for Agricultural Development (IFAD), a specialized agency of the United Nations: www.ifad.org/english/water/key.htm. OECD

agrees: www.oecd.org/environment/wateruseinagriculture.htm. Water One World Solutions: www.wateroneworldsolutions.org/index.php?option=com _content&view=category&layout=blog&id=38&Itemid=59.

68 *Roughly a third of all land is used for agriculture*: J. Owen, "Farming Claims Almost Half Earth's Land, New Maps Show," National Geographic News, December 9, 2005, http://news.nationalgeographic.com/news/2005/12 /1209_051209_crops_map.html. "40 percent of the Earth's land is now given over to agriculture." World Bank says about 38 percent: http:// data.worldbank.org/indicator/AG.LND.AGRI.ZS/countries/1W?display =graph. Food and Agriculture Organization of the United Nations (FAO) says 36 percent: "At present some 11 percent (1.5 billion ha) of the globe's land surface (13.4 billion ha) is used in crop production (arable land and land under permanent crops). This area represents slightly over a third (36 percent) of the land estimated to be to some degree suitable for crop production," www.fao.org/docrep/005/y4252e/y4252e06.htm.

68 *1,374 square miles of land turned to desert each year*: "World's Land Turning to Desert at Alarming Speed," *USA Today*, June 15, 2004, http://usatoday30 .usatoday.com/weather/news/2004-06-15-global-drying_x.htm.

69 *global food production doubled*: Food and Agriculture Organization of the United Nations, "FAOSTAT," accessed January 23, 2012, http://faostat.fao .org. "As fast as population has risen—from just over 3 billion in 1960 to around 7 billion in 2010—food production has outpaced it."

69 *Green Revolution*: William Gaud, Agency for International Development Department of State, "The Green Revolution: Accomplishments and Apprehensions," last modified March 8, 1968, www.agbioworld.org/biotech-info /topics/borlaug/borlaug-green.html.

69 *increased farmers' earnings 90 percent*: World Bank, *World Development Report 2000/2001: Attacking Poverty* (New York: Oxford University Press, 2001), https://openknowledge.worldbank.org/handle/10986/11856.

69 *All 7 billion of us, standing shoulder to shoulder, would fit inside the city of Los Angeles*: http://news.nationalgeographic.com/news/2011/10/111031-pop ulation-7-billion-earth-world-unseven. Suppose we gave everyone a comfortable house and yard? Assume an average four-person family. At New York City's density, the world's population in 2011 could fit inside Texas, leaving the rest of the world vacant, http://persquaremile.com/2011/01/18/if-the -worlds-population-lived-in-one-city.

69 *Carbon Pollution*: N. Gilbert, "One-Third of our Greenhouse Gas Emissions Come from Agriculture," *Nature* (October 31, 2012), www.nature.com /news/one-third-of-our-greenhouse-gas-emissions-come-from-agriculture -1.11708.

69 *Coastal Pollution*: Joel Archenbach, "A 'Dead Zone' in the Gulf of Mexico,"

Washington Post, July 31, 2008. See also J. Quirk, *Call to the Rescue: The Story of the Marine Mammal Center* (San Francisco: Chronicle Books, 2009), 46–63.

69 *Food Limits*: B. S. Karnowski, AP Worldstream, "General Mills Sets Ambitious Goal for Greenhouse Gas Cuts," August 30, 2015, www.highbeam.com /doc/1A1-8b168cfb9a76476f87438c206284c909.html?refid= easy_hf.

69 *Poverty*: Food Crisis—The World Bank. (updated 2013, October 7), http:// www.worldbank.org/foodcrisis/bankinitiatives.htm.

69 *Health Crisis*: Michael Pollan, *The Omnivore's Dilemma: A Natural History of Four Meals* (Large Print Press), 108.

69 *Running Out of Room*: FAO Water Unit | Water News: The State of Land and Water Resources (2015), accessed February 22, 2016, www.fao.org/nr /water/news/solaw_launch.html.

76 *global atmospheric concentrations of CO_2 are roughly 35 percent higher than they were before the industrial revolution*: National Oceanic and Atmospheric Administration (NOAA) National Centers for Environmental Information: http://www.ncdc.noaa.gov/monitoring-references/faq/, global temperature data: http://www.cru.uea.ac.uk/cru/data/temperature, NASA Surface Temperature Analysis: http://data.giss.nasa.gov/gistemp, Intergovernmental Panel on Climate Change: https://www.ipcc.ch/publi cations_and_data/ar4/wg1/en/faq-2-1.html.

76 *Since the industrial revolution, ocean acidity has increased 30 percent*: NOAA's PMEL Carbon Program: http://www.pmel.noaa.gov/co2/story/What +is+Ocean+Acidification%3F and http://www.pmel.noaa.gov/co2/story /Ocean+Acidification. Since the industrial revolution, ocean acidity has increased 30 percent after holding steady for about 21 million years, www .ocean-acidification.net/About.html.

76 *"each square kilometer (about 0.4 square miles) will sequester 40 tons of carbon"*: R. Radulovich, "Maricultura en Costa Rica," *Ambientico* 179 (2008): 7–14.

76 *"Algae can double [their] mass in anywhere from twenty-four to forty-eight hours"*: M. Espinoza, "Algae Farming Technology Yields Renewable Fuel, Uses Waste as Fertilizer," CFAES. *The Ohio State University College of Food, Agricultural, and Environmental Sciences*, January 9, 2013, http://cfaes.osu .edu/news/articles/algae-farming-technology-yields-renewable-fuel-uses -waste-fertilizer.

77 *"The next Green Revolution should be blue"*: R. Radulovich et al., "Farming of Seaweeds," chap. 3 in *Seaweed Sustainability*, 1st ed., *Food and Non Food Applications*, ed. B. K. Tiwari and D.J. Troy (Neth.: Elsevier, 2015), 27–59.

77 *"Each ton of seaweed harvested frees one million liters of freshwater from agriculture"*: R. Radulovich et al., "Tropical Seaweeds for Human Food, Their Cultivation and Biodiversity Enrichment," *Aquaculture* 436 (2015):

40–46. See also R. Radulovich et al., "Aquatic Agriculture: Floating Crops on Lakes," *World Agriculture Society* 46, no. 1 (2015): 62–67, www.was .org/articles/aquatic-agriculture-cultivating-floating-crops-on-lakes.aspx #.VetLxJWFOM8.

79 *rickets*: J. Pettifor, "Nutritional Rickets: Deficiency of Vitamin D, Calcium or Both?," *American Journal of Clinical Nutrition* 80, supp. (2004): 1725S–9S, www.ncbi.nlm.nih.gov/pmc/articles/PMC2528709/#b16-pch12185. "Because vitamin D is most commonly found in fortified milk products, egg yolk, or oily fish, it is the most likely vitamin to be deficient in vegetarian and macrobiotic diets, but not in lacto-ovo-vegetarian diets." See also J. T. Dwyer et al., "Risk of Nutritional Rickets Among Vegetarian Children," *American Journal of Diseases of Children* 133, no. 2 (February 1979): 134–40, www .ncbi.nlm.nih.gov/pubmed/420181.

79 *Spiralina*: www.energybits.com/about-algae/about-spirulina.html.

81 *Norman Borlaug*: "Iowans Who Fed the World: Norman Borlaug: Geneticist." AgBioWorld, last modified October 26, 2002, www.agbioworld.org /biotech-info/topics/borlaug/iowans.html.

82 *David Pimentel . . . will scare the dirt out of you*: D. Pimentel, "Soil Erosion: A Food and Environmental Threat," *Environment, Development and Sustainability* 8, no. 1 (2006): 119–37.

82 *"Around the world, soil is being swept and washed away 10 to 40 times faster than it is being replenished"*: S. S. Lang, " 'Slow, Insidious' Soil Erosion Threatens Human Health and Welfare as Well as the Environment, Cornell Study Asserts," *Cornell Chronicle*, March 20, 2006, www.news.cornell.edu /stories/2006/03/slow-insidious-soil-erosion-threatens-human-health-and -welfare.

82 *destruction of marine mammal habitats*: J. Quirk, *Call to the Rescue: The Story of the Marine Mammal Center* (San Francisco: Chronicle Books, 2009).

83 *David Pimentel himself hints at a solution*: D. Pimentel and M. Burgess, "Soil Erosion Threatens Food Production," *Agriculture* 3, no. 3 (2013): 443–63, www.vetiver.org/USA_pimentel_agriculture-03-00443.pdf.

83 *What if we . . . farmed the seas?* See also J. Forster and R. Radulovich. Seaweeds for Food Security. *Seaweed Sustainability: Food and Non Food Applications*. Neth., Elsevier, 2014. Holland. See also R. Radulovich, "Foods from Aquaculture," in *Handbook of Sustainable Food, Beverages and Gastronomy*, ed. P. Sloan and W. Legrand (Bonn, Ger.: Routledge, 2014. See also Ricardo Radulovich, "Foods from Aquaculture," in *The Routledge Handbook of Sustainable Food and Gastronomy*, ed. Philip Sloan, Willy Legrand, and Clare Hindley (Abingdon, UK: Routledge, 2015), www.researchgate.net /publication/281494435_Foods_from_aquaculture_varied_and_growing _2015. See also R. S. Radulovich, S. Umanzor, and R. Cabrera, *Algas Tropi-*

cales: Cultivo y Uso como Alimento (San José: University of Costa Rica Press, 2013), 42, www.researchgate.net/publication/272168650_Algas_Trop icales_Cultivo_y_Uso_como_Alimento_2013_Tropical_Seaweeds_Cul tivation_and_Use_as_Food. See also R. Radulovich, "Autotrophic Lake Aquaculture for Sustainable and Water-Free Food Production," SARNISSA, *African Aquaculture Digest* 44, no. 33 (2012). Samissa Digest. See also R. Radulovich, Massive water savings from producing food at sea. *Water Policy Journal*, 13:547–554. See also R. Radulovich, "Marine Agriculture: Land Plants Cropped Floating at Sea," *World Aquaculture* 41, no. 4 (2010): 36–39.

84 *Thierry Chopin*: S. Simpson, "Taming the Blue Frontier—Conservation," *Conservation* April 22, 2009, http://conservationmagazine.org/2009/04 /taming-the-blue-frontier. See also Chopin et al., "Freshwater IMTA— Developing Integrated Multi-Trophic Aquaculture Systems for Commercial Salmon Hatcheries," *Hatchery International* 17, no. 1: January/February 2016: 31, www2.unb.ca/chopinlab/articles/files/Chopin%20et%20al%20 2016%20Hatchery%20International%20FIMTA%20HR.pdf. Also personal interview.

84 *"This idea has been tested successfully"*: R. Radulovich, "Take Biofuels off the Land and Grow Them at Sea," SciDev.Net, June 6, 2008, www.scidev.net /global/farming/opinion/take-biofuel-crops-off-the-land-and-grow-them -at-s.html.

84 *a franchise for poor coastal fisherman to initiate their own enterprises*: W. N. R. Garcia, "Open-Source Seafarming: A Blue Revolution in Costa Rica?," *Radical Social Entrepreneurs* March 7, 2013, www.radicalsocialen treps.org/2013/03/open-source-seafarming-a-blue-revolution-in-costa -rica.

86 *"Everybody says the peasant farmer in these countries is resistant to change. That's not true."* Norman Borlaug quoted from interview: www.livinghistoryfarm .org/farminginthe50s/movies/borlaug_crops_16.html.

86 *subsistence fishermen and fisherwomen*: N. Nurhayati, "Seaweed Farmers in Nusa Lembongan Pushed Aside by Tourism Development," *Jakarta Post*, December 11, 2011, www.thejakartapost.com/news/2011/12/07/seaweed -farmers-nusa-lembongan-pushed-aside-tourism-development.html.

86 *five hundred adult shrimp* per cubic meter: R. Radulovich, "Caged Pro duction Experiments Conducted with Shrimp in Costa Rica," *Global Aquaculture Advocate* 13, no. 4 (2010): 82–83, www.researchgate.net/pub lication/277008512_Shrimp_production_in_cages_in_Costa_Rica.

88 *a farm of sea vegetables totaling 180,000 square kilometers . . . could provide enough protein for the entire world population*: R. Klies, "Growing Seaweed

Can Solve Acidification," December 23, 2010, phys.org, http://phys.org /news/2010-12-seaweed-acidification.html. "[B]iologist Ronald Osinga . . . and his colleagues calculated that a 'marine garden' of 180,000 square kilometers could provide enough protein for the entire world population." See also M. Y. Roleda and C. L. Hurd, "Seaweed Responses to Ocean Acidification. Ecological Studies," *Seaweed Biology* (2012): 407–31. See also T. Flannery, "Seaweed Could Save the World's Oceans from Becoming Too Acidic. *Quarts,* November 4, 2015, http://qz.com/534553/seaweed-could -save-the-worlds-oceans-from-becoming-too-acidic.

88 *Here's the way the natural carbon cycle stays in balance:* J. DeCicco, "Can We Rebalance the Carbon Cycle While Still Using Fossil Fuels?," *World Economic Forum,* April 29, 2015, www.weforum.org/agenda/2015/04/can-we -rebalance-the-carbon-cycle-while-still-using-fossil-fuels.

88 *volcanoes:* Robin Wylie, "Long Invisible, Research Shows Volcanic CO2 Levels Are Staggering (Op-Ed)," Live Science, October 15, 2013, www.live science.com/40451-volcanic-co2-levels-are-staggering.html.

89 *World population is expected to level off:* R. Kunzig, "A World with 11 Billion People?," *National Geographic,* September 19, 2014, http://news.national geographic.com/news/2014/09/140918-population-global-united-nations -2100-boom-africa.

91 *"A two-hundred-fifty-square-foot island can remove about ten pounds of phosphorus":* Kelly Waters, "Watershed Management Project," *Wayne (PA) Independent,* October 16, 2012, www.wayneindependent.com/article/20121012 /NEWS/121019927. See also F. Lubenow, "Westtown Lake: Floating Wetlands Islands," Floating Wetlands Solutions (2012). http://floatingwet landsolutions.com/pdfs/Lubnow%20LakeLine%20article.pdf.

92 *In 1962, Borlaug and his colleague:* J. Skorup, "Norman Borlaug: An American Hero," Mackinac Center for Public Policy, last modified December 15, 2009, www.mackinac.org/11516.

95 *Between 1970 and 2009, aquaculture production grew at an annual average rate of 8.4 percent:* OECD Green Growth Studies, (April 21, 2015) *Green Growth in Fisheries and Aquaculture.* OECD Publishing, 15. See also S. J. Hall et al. "Blue Frontiers: Managing the Environmental Costs of Aquaculture," *The WorldFish Center,* Penang, Malaysia, 2011.. *ii,* 2, and 8_www.conservation .org/publications/documents/BlueFrontiers_aquaculture_report.pdf.

98 *environmentally friendly ocean vegetable that tastes like bacon:* Barb Randall, "Superfood Sea Vegetable Soon to Be All the Rage," *Lake Oswego (OR) Review,* September 11, 2014, www.pamplinmedia.com/lor/54-my-community /233124-96843-superfood-sea-vegetable-soon-to-be-all-the-rage.

99 *"My job is to make [my customers] understand":* Iron Chef Vitaly Paley quote:

J. Jitchotvisut, "This Seaweed Tastes Like Bacon, Is Twice as Nutritious as Kale," First We Feast, last modified July 16, 2015, http://firstwefeast.com /eat/this-seaweed-tastes-like-bacon-is-twice-as-nutritious-as-kale.

99 *"We think it's the most productive protein source on earth," said Chuck Tombs*: B. E. Palermo, "Finally, Bacon-Flavored Health Food Has Arrived," Live Science, July 16, 2015, www.livescience.com/51588-bacon-flavored-seaweed -dulse.html.

Chapter 4. FISH: Farms That Swim with Fish

Unless noted otherwise, all Neil Sims quotes are taken from personal interviews by the author.

103 *Sims and Greenberg share the same heartbreak*: Paul Greenberg, *Four Fish: The Future of the Last Wild Food* (New York: Penguin Press, 2010).

104 *at least 90 percent of large fish such as marlin, tuna, and swordfish have vanished*: Ransom A. Myers, "Boris Worm," *Nature* 423 (May 15, 2001): 280–83.

104 *"In the US, ninety-one percent of seafood is imported"*: "Basic Questions About Aquaculture," NOAA Fisheries, accessed April 17, 2016, www.nmfs.noaa .gov/aquaculture/faqs/faq_aq_101.html.

104 *In 2009 the UN's Third Global Biodiversity Outlook reported that 80 percent of fisheries are exploited or overexploited*: Stephen Leahy, "Tight Controls Could Save Global Fisheries," Inter Press Service, July 31, 2009, www.ipsnews.net /news.asp?idnews=47912.

104 *Three years later . . . the estimate had risen to 87 percent*: R. Fujita, "FAO Reports 87% of the World's Fisheries Are Overexploited or Fully Exploited," July 12, 2012, http://blogs.edf.org/edfish/2012/07/11/fao-reports-87-of -the-worlds-fisheries-are-overexploited-or-fully-exploited. See also Food and Agriculture Organization of the United Nations, "Fisheries at the Limit?," accessed March 7, 2012, www.fao.org/docrep/u8480e/U8480E0f.htm.

108 *absorption of man-made CO_2 in the North Atlantic doubled in the last decade*: R. Woosley et al., "Rapid Anthropogenic Changes in CO_2 and pH in the Atlantic Ocean: 2003–2014," *Global Biogeochemical Cycles* 30 (2016): doi:10.1002/2015GB005248. See also, C. L. Sabine et. al., "The Oceanic Sink for Anthropogenic CO2," *Science* 305 (July 16, 2004): 367–71 Copenhagen Diagnosis, 36. See also "Amount of Carbon Dioxide Absorbed by the Upper Layer of the Oceans Is Increasing by About 2 Billion Tons Per Year," http://climate.nasa.gov/evidence.

108 *Corals and mollusks require a certain pH level in the surrounding water*: Justin

Ries et al., "Marine Calcifiers Exhibit Mixed Responses to CO_2-Induced Ocean Acidification," *Geological Society of America* (July 21, 2009). See also A. Ridgwell and D. N. Schmidt, "Past Constraints on the Vulnerability of Marine Calcifiers to Massive Carbon Dioxide Release," *Nature Geoscience* 3, no. 3 (2010): 196–200. See also Carl Zimmer, "An Ominous Warning on the Effects of Ocean Acidification," Yale Environment 360, last modified February 15, 2010, http://e360.yale.edu/feature/an_ominous_warning_on_the effects_of_ocean_acidification/2241.

111 *In 1980 10 percent of the world's seafood came from fish farms*: "A Milestone for U.S. Aquaculture: 35th Anniversary of the National Aquaculture Act," September 21, 2015, www.fisheries.noaa.gov/aquaculture/homepage_sto ries/18_35th_anniversary.html.

111 *To supply this growing demand*: "Fisheries at the Limit?," on the website of the Food and Agriculture Organization of the United Nations," accessed March 7, 2012, www.fao.org/docrep/u8480e/U8480E0f.htm. See also Food and Agriculture Organization of the United Nations, *The State of World Fisheries and Aquaculture* (Rome: 2010).

111 *anchovies*: American, "Peruvian Anchovy Case," accessed March 7, 2012. "Coping with These Irregular Cycles and the Problem of Over Harvesting Threaten the Peruvian Anchovy Industry," http://www1.american.edu /TED/anchovy.htm.

114 *"Aquaculture is the fastest-growing food production sector in the world"*: Sarah Simpson, "The Blue Food Revolution," *Scientific American* 304 (2011): 54–61, www.scientificamerican.com/article/the-blue-food-revolution.

116 *TwoXSea invented an entirely plant-based fish pellet*: "Fish Farm of the Future Goes Vegetarian to Save Seafood," Bloomberg News, February 23, 2015, www.bloomberg.com/news/videos/2015-02-23/fish-farm-of-the-future -goes-vegetarian-to-save-seafood.

116 *The first to swear by the creamy texture and health benefits*: Alan Wong's Hawaii. (2004) *Food & Wine*, www.foodandwine.com/articles/alan-wongs-ha waii. "Actually, they're not hamachi, they're Kona Kampachi, which Wong finds even more exciting. As he explains, reef fish, like the wilder siblings of these farm-raised kampachi, are normally risky to eat because of ciguatera poisoning. Kona Blue Water Farms' kampachi, he says, is good news for chefs." See also "Kona Kampachi Sashimi Tiradito at Amasia," *Honolulu*, *accessed* February 22, 2016, www.honolulumagazine.com/Honolulu-Mag azine/August-2013/Hawaii-2014-All-Island-Restaurant-Guide/Kona-kam pachi-sashimi-tiradito-at-Amasia. "Wong's version—with 100 percent local ingredients—is a winner: the Kona kampachi is satisfyingly fatty."

117 *Diesel is the greatest source of greenhouse gases for the fishing industry*: Rob-

ert W. R. Parker and Peter H. Tyedmers, "Fuel Consumption of Global Fishing Fleets: Current Understanding and Knowledge Gaps," *Fish and Fisheries* 16, no. 4 (December 2015): 686–96, http://onlinelibrary.wiley.com/doi/10.1111/faf.12087/abstract.

120 *(NOAA) conducted an environmental assessment (EA) of the Velella Project*: National Oceanic and Atmospheric Administration National Marine Fisheries Service Environmental Assessment (March 17, 2011), www.fpir.noaa.gov/Library/SFD/NMFS%20PIRO%20Special%20Permit%20Kona%20Blue%20Draft%20Environmental%20Assessment%20(March%202011).pdf.

120 *pass the NOAA test with flying colors*: United States Department of Commerce National Oceanic Atmospheric Administration, "Finding of No Significant Impact" with Velella Concept" (July 6, 2011) www.fpir.noaa.gov/SFD/pdfs/EA%20&%20FONSI%20Kona%20Blue%20(2011-07-06).pdf.

121 *"The success of the Velella Research Project"*: "Milestone for Kampachi Farms," SeafoodSource.com, March 1, 2012, www.seafoodsource.com/news/aquaculture/14260-milestone-for-kampachi-farms.

126 *"Aquaculture has expanded about 14-fold since 1980"*: Joel K. Bourne Jr., "How to Farm a Better Fish," *National Geographic*, 2014, www.nationalgeographic.com/foodfeatures/aquaculture.

127 *"In the US, the regulatory framework is highly restrictive"*: Neil Sims, quoted in Neil Ramsden, "Kampachi Farms: Fighting for Aquaculture," Undercurrent News, November 8, 2012, www.undercurrentnews.com/2012/11/08/seafood-entrepreneurs.

127 *"Aquaculture is a modern industry that requires a modern legislative framework"*: Miranda Pryor, quoted in Brandon Anstey, "Cutting Red Tape," *Beacon* (Gander, Newfoundland), May 30, 2014, www.ganderbeacon.ca/news/local/2014-05-30/article-3744507/cutting-red-tape/1.

Unless noted otherwise, all quotes from Lissa Morgenthaler-Jones are taken from personal interviews by the author.

131 *"four new Saudi Arabias."* Transcript of interview with Fatih Birol: A. Forbes, "We need to find four new Saudi Arabias." World Energy Future, accessed March 21, 2016, http://europeanenergyreview.com/site/pagina.php?id=793. Repeated in April 25, 2011, *Manila Bulletin*: www.worldenergyoutlook.org/pressmedia/quotes/58/index.html.

131 *relentless realism*: Rutgers University, "Could Pond Scum Undo Pollution, Fight Global Warming and Alleviate World Hunger?," ScienceDaily, July 11, 2008, www.sciencedaily.com/releases/2008/07/080708111144.htm.

132 *Algae Becomes Oilgae*: Jason C. Quinn et al., "Geographical Assessment of Microalgae Biofuels Potential Incorporating Resource Availability," *BioEnergy Research* 6, no. 2 (June 2013): 591–600. See also Scott C. James et al.,

"Simulating pH Effects in an Algal-Growth Hydrodynamics Model," *Journal of Phycology* 49, no. 3 (June 2013): 608–15. See also P. M. Slegers et al., "Scenario Evaluation of Open Pond Microalgae Production," *Algal Research* (June 2013). See also Pascal Schlagermann et al., "Composition of Algal Oil and Its Potential as Biofuel," *Journal of Combustion* 2012 (January 2012): 1–14. See also C. Jason et al., "Current Large-Scale US Biofuel Potential from Microalgae Cultivated in Photobioreactors," *BioEnergy Research* (November 2011). See also Jason Quinn, Lenneke de Winter, and Thomas Bradley, "Microalgae Bulk Growth Model with Application to Industrial Scale Cystems," *Bioresource Technology* 102, no. 8 (April 2011): 5083–92. See also Mark S. Wigmosta et al., National Microalgae Biofuel Production Potential and Resource Demand," *Water Resources Research* 47, no. 3 (March 2011).

134 *"dead zone"*: Gulf of Mexico dead zone 2012 and 2013: www.nola.com/en vironment/index.ssf/2013/07/above_average_low_oxygen_dead.html, Dead zone 2015: www.noaanews.noaa.gov/stories2015/080415-gulf-of -mexico-dead-zone-above-average.html.

134 *"Most people believe that algae will give you more biomass per area in time than anything else"*: Dave Jones, interview by Nora McDevitt, "Future of Biofuels Points to Algae," Connected Social Media, March 15, 2007, http://con nectedsocialmedia.com/731/future-of-biofuels-points-to-algae.

135 *99 percent of biofuels produced and consumed worldwide in 2011 were made from food cops*: "The Hidden Costs of Turning Food into Fuel," .accessed March 21, 2016, http://video.nationalgeographic.com/video/magazine /food-by-the-numbers/140915-ngm-food-fuel-ngfood?source=searchvideo.

135 *By 2016 Solazyme had renamed itself TerraVia and signed a supply agreement with Unilever*: TerraVia "TerraVia (Solazyme) and Unilever Sign Multi-Year Supply Agreement for $200 Million-Plus of Sustainable High Performance Algae Oils," news release, March 14, 2016, http://investors.solazyme.com /releasedetail.cfm?releaseid=960548.

136 *"We could replace up to seventeen percent of the oil we import"*: Remarks by the President on Energy, White House Office of the Press Secretary, February 23, 2012, www.whitehouse.gov/the-press-office/2012/02/23/remarks -president-energy.

136 *"It is not just about natural security"*: Rear Admiral Philip Cullom, quoted on Navy.mil Home Page, "Navy Sailing Toward a Great Green Fleet," October 22, 2010, www.navy.mil/submit/display.asp?story_id=56757.

136 *Researchers at the U.S. Naval Research Laboratory . . . demonstrated . . . ability to draw carbon dioxide and hydrogen from seawater and turn it into forms of gasoline*: B. Lendon, "Navy's Future: Electric guns, Lasers, Water as Fuel," CNN.com, April 10, 2014, www.cnn.com/2014/04/10/tech/innovation /navy-new-technology.

136 *a hundred times more oil*: U.S. Department of Energy (DOE), "Algae May Be Able to Produce 100 Times More Oil Per Acre Than Soybeans," http://www1.eere.energy.gov/bioenergy/pdfs/algalbiofuels.pdf.

136 *soybeans can produce only sixty to seventy gallons of biofuel*: B. Wingfield and J. Snyder, "Obama Promotes Pond Scum as Renewable Fuel Source," Bloomberg Business, February 23, 2012, www.bloomberg.com/news/articles/2012-02-24/obama-promotes-pond-scum-as-renewable-fuel-source.

137 *"not just to reduce emissions of carbon dioxide but to recycle their emissions"*: M. Paris, "NRC Teams Up on CO_2-Eating Algae Farm," CBC News, May 10, 2013, www.cbc.ca/m/touch/politics/story/1.1337984.

138 *what scoops into the deep ocean floor and mixes it with the surface ocean?*: R. H. Thurstan, S. Brockington, and C. M. Roberts, "The Effects of 118 Years of Industrial Fishing on UK Bottom Trawl Fisheries, *Nature Communications* (May 4, 2010): www.nature.com/ncomms/journal/v1/n2/full/ncomms1013.html. "This implies an extraordinary decline in the availability of bottom-living fish and a profound reorganization of seabed ecosystems since the nineteenth century industrialization of fishing."

Chapter 5. FUEL: The Ocean Is a Solar Panel

Unless noted otherwise, all quotes from Lissa Morgenthaler-Jones, Patrick Takahashi, Robert Ballard, Chris Muglia, Rutger de Graaf, and Masaki Takeuchi are taken from personal interviews by the author.

144 *where humanity's hope lies*: Patrick Takahashi's OTEC advocacy: http://bluerevolutionhawaii.blogspot.com/2011/04/pacific-international-ocean-station.html.

145 *Incredibly, nearly half of all wild seafood is harvested from 1/10th of 1 percent of the ocean*: J. Ryther, II. "Photosynthesis and Fish Production in the Sea," *Science* 166, no. 3901 (1969): 72–76. See also A. E. Gill, "Atmosphere-Ocean Dynamics," International Geophysics Series, Vol. 30. Academic, San Diego, 1982. 403: "Upwelling regions, totaling no more than one-tenth of 1 percent of the ocean surface (an area roughly the size of California) produce about half the word's fish supply." See also M. Weber and J. Gradwohl, *The Wealth of Oceans* (New York: W. W. Norton, 1995), 62: "Although upwellings account for one-tenth of one percent of the sea surface, half of the world's fish catch occurs in these areas." See also Paul Arthur Berkman, *Science into Policy: Global Lessons from Antarctica*, vol. 1 (San Diego, 2002), 148–49. See also Tim Stephens, "From Wind to Whales: Understanding an Ecosystem,"

UC Santa Cruz Review (Summer 2002), http://review.ucsc.edu/summer-02 /wind2whales.html. "There are only a few major coastal upwelling regions worldwide. While they make up about one-tenth of a percent of the ocean's surface area, 95 percent of the global marine biomass is produced in these regions. Not surprisingly, upwelling regions support many of the world's most important fisheries."

146 *each atom of iron added to the water would foster enough plankton growth to draw between ten thousand and a hundred thousand atoms of carbon out of the atmosphere*: Q. Schiermeier, "Iron Seeding Creates Fleeting Carbon Sink in Southern Ocean," *Nature* 428, no. 6985 (2004): 788, www.nature.com /nature/journal/v428/n6985/full/428788b.html.

146 *"When the nutrient-rich water from the depths reaches the sunlit waters of the surface"*: Savage, *Millennial Project*, 40.

146 *"We have three hundred times the amount of energy in the tropical ocean than the world currently consumes"*: Bob Nicholson on OTEC International at the Seasteading Conference 2012, https://vimeo.com/44255125.

146 *Lockheed Martin*: OTEC: North American Clean Energy. "OTEC: The time Is Now," accessed February 24, 2016, www.lockheedmartin.com/us/100 years/stories/otec.html.

148 *Lockheed Martin has partnered with the Hong Kong-based Reignwood Group to build an OTEC plant off the coast of China*: Lockheed Martin, "Lockheed Martin and Reignwood Group to Develop Ocean Thermal Energy Conversion Power Plant," press release, April 16, 2013, www.lockheedmartin .com/us/news/press-releases/2013/april/lockheed-martin-and-reignwood -group-to-develop-ocean-thermal-ene.html. See also D. Quick, "World's Largest OTEC Power Plant Planned for China," Gizmag, April 18, 2013, www.gizmag.com/otec-plant-lockheed-martin-reignwood-china/27164. See also "Lockheed Set to Go Green," Zacks Equity Research, February 12, 2014, www.zacks.com/stock/news/122933/lockheed-set-to-go-green.

149 *"each commercial OTEC Plant would create 3,500 to 4,000 direct jobs"*: ibid.

150 *"OTEC power generation in deep-ocean waters"*: Leighton K. Chong and Patrick K. Takahashi, "The Blue Revolution: Oceans as the Ultimate Sustainable Resource" (paper presented by Leighton Chong at the Eco-Balance Conference, Tokyo, 2010), http://bluerevolutionhawaii.blogspot.com/2011 /01/blue-revolution-oceans-as-ultimate.html.

151 *"Mini-OTEC"*: M. Meyer, D. Cooper, and R. Varley. "Are We There Yet? A Developer's Roadmap to OTEC Commercialization," *Hawaii National Marine Renewable Energy Center OTEC References*, Lockheed Martin Missions Systems and Sensors, Manassas, VA. (2011) See also www.otecnews.org /portal/otec-articles/ocean-thermal-energy-conversion-otec-by-l-a-vega-ph-d.

153 *"OTEC and seastead are just the perfect combination"*: Bob Nicholson on OTEC International at the Seasteading Conference 2012, https://vimeo.com/44255125.

154 *"Water will be the next oil"*: Mike Straub, "Q&A with Dr. Ted Johnson," www.theonproject.org/2011/qa-with-dr-ted-johnson.

155 *"the cost of OTEC energy is comparable to fossil fuel"*: Jess Phillips, "Dr. Ted Johnson Interview—April 2015," on the website of OTE Corporation, June 23, 2015, http://otecorporation.com/2015/06/23/dr-ted-johnson-interview-april-2015.

160 *at least seventy-eight places on our seabed*: Yasuhiro Kato et al., "Deep-Sea Mud in the Pacific Ocean as a Potential Resource for Rare-Earth Elements," *Nature Geoscience* 4, no. 8 (August 2011): 535–39, www.nature.com/ngeo/journal/v4/n8/full/ngeo1185.html.

160 *"Just one square kilometre (0.4 square mile) of deposits,"* Yasuhiro Kato, quoted in El Tan and Yuko Inoue, Reuters, "Huge Rare Earth Deposits Found in Pacific—Japan Experts," July 4, 2011, www.reuters.com/article/idINIndia-58061720110704.

161 *"It destroys the bridge"*: *Alien Deep with Bob Ballard*, National Geographic documentary, www.youtube.com/watch?v=lO4ZTBHReXw.

170 *In New York City, architect Adam Kushner partnered with Italian architect Enrico Dini*: B. Peregoy and A. Kushner, "The U.S. Is Getting Its First 3-D-Printed House," *Architectural Digest*, May 31, 2015, www.architecturaldigest.com/story/3-d-printed-house-adam-kushner.

170 *"The organic nature of Aquarius"*: Savage, *Millennial Project*.

172 *Seascrapers*: M. Chino, "Underwater Skyscraper Is a Self-Sufficient City at Sea," Inhabitat, February 15, 2011, http://inhabitat.com/underwater-skyscraper-is-a-self-sufficient-city-at-sea.

172 eVolo *magazine's 2010 Skyscraper Competition*: "Water-Scraper: Underwater Architecture," *eVolo*, March 8, 2010, www.evolo.us/competition/water-scraper-underwater-architecture.

173 *When the company was founded by Kisuke Shimizu in 1804 . . . yet again, unfathomable*: www.shimz.co.jp/english/about/history.html.

174 *"The carbon dioxide, wastewater, and garbage from the urban area become nutrients for the plant factory below."* GREEN FLOAT—a Floating City in the Sky, November 2, 2010, www.diginfo.tv/v/10-0196-r-en.php.

175 *"At the equator, temperatures are constant, and typhoons aren't a problem."*: Masaki Takeuchi, quoted in, K. Nagamura, "The Edified and TEDified in Japan," *Japan Times*, May 31, 2011, www.japantimes.co.jp/life/2011/05/31/lifestyle/the-edified-and-tedified-in-japan. Unless noted otherwise noted, all quotes from Masaki Takeuchi were taken from interviews with the author.

176 *As Yoichi Miyamoto, president of Shimizu Corporation, wrote in the Shimizu* 2012 Social Responsibility Report: www.shimz.co.jp/english/theme/dream /greenfloat.html.

Chapter 6. WEALTH: The Miracle of Start-up Societies

185 *$34,000 US after taxes*: Branko Milanovic, *The Haves and the Have-Nots: A Brief and Idiosyncratic History of Global Inequality* (New York: Basic Books, 2011).

186 *"Next to this mysterious black hole"*: Barbara Demick, *Nothing to Envy: Ordinary Lives in North Korea* (New York: Spiegel & Grau, 2009), 3–5.

187 *"Between 1946 and the beginning of the Korean War"*: Ralph Hassig and Kongdan Oh, *The Hidden People of North Korea: Everyday Life in the Hermit Kingdom* (Lanham, MD: Rowman & Littlefield, 2009), 161.

187 *average South Korean earns eighteen times as much . . . lives an average of ten years longer*: S. Rogers, A. Sedghi, and M. McCormick, "South v. North Korea: How Do the Two Countries Compare? Visualised," *Datablog* (blog), *Guardian* (UK), April 8, 2013, www.theguardian.com/world/datablog /2013/apr/08/south-korea-v-north-korea-compared.

187 *"low-skilled worker ten to twenty times higher"*: Arnold Kling and Nick Schulz, *Invisible Wealth: The Hidden Story of How Markets Work* (New York: Encounter Books, 2011), 136.

188 *"Poor countries are poor . . . because they lack effective political institutions"*: Francis Fukuyama, *The Origins of Political Order: From Prehuman Times to the French Revolution* (New York: Farrar, Straus and Giroux, 2011), 14. See also Dani Rodrik, Arvind Subramanian, and Francesco Trebbi, "Institutions Rule: The Primacy of Institutions over Geography and Integration in Economic Development," *Journal of Economic Growth* 9, no. 2 (June 2004): 131–65, www.sss.ias.edu/files/pdfs/Rodrik/Research/institutions-rule.pdf. Comparing effect on national income between trade, geography, "the quality of institutions 'trumps' everything else."

188 *1981 half the developing world's population . . . living on less than $1.25 a day . . . by 2012, less than a fifth were that poor.* Summed up: F. Zakaria, "Global Poverty Is Falling, So What's the Problem?," Global Public Square, May 1, 2013, http://globalpublicsquare.blogs.cnn.com/2013/05/01/global -poverty-is-falling-so-whats-the-problem. See also "Poverty: Not Always with Us," *Economist*, June 1, 2013. www.economist.com/news/briefing /21578643-world-has-astonishing-chance-take-billion-people-out-extreme -poverty-2030-not.

189 *poverty rate in East Asia descended to 1.7 percent*: Mark J. Perry, "New Study Shows Significant Drop in World Poverty," *Carpe Diem* (blog), Novem-

ber 1, 2009, http://mjperry.blogspot.com/2009/11/new-study-shows-sig
nificant-drop-in.html#sthash.DQ4eX0JM.dpuf. Summing up work by
Maxim I. Pinkovskiy and Xavier Sala-i-Martin, "Parametric Estimations of
the World Distribution of Income" (working paper 15433, National Bureau
of Economic Research, Cambridge, MA, 2009), http://economics.mit.edu
/files/7265.

189 *In 1960 Hong Kong's 3 million inhabitants were less than 0.5 percent*: 3.13 mm
in Hong Kong 1961 to 658 mm in China in the same year.

190 *During the 130 years between 1870 and 2000, US GDP per person grew ten
times*: G. M. Angeletos, "Introduction and Growth Facts," Lecture Notes,
Intermediate Macroeconomics. MIT Open Courseware, 2006, http://ocw
.mit.edu/courses/economics/14-06-intermediate-macroeconomic-theory
-spring-2004/lecture-notes/14_06lec_nts_chl.pdf. "US per-capita GDP
grew by a factor ≈ 10 from 1870 to 2000: In 1995 prices, it was $3300 in
1870 and $32500 in 2000."

190 *During the thirty-six years from 1961 through 1996, Hong Kong's GDP per
person grew eighty-seven times*: Rikkie Yeung, *Moving Millions: The Commercial Success and Political Controversies of Hong Kong's Railways* (Hong
Kong: Hong Kong University Press, 2008). Hong Kong's total GDP grew
180 times. See also Peter Wallace Preston and Jürgen Haacke, *Contemporary
China: The Dynamics of Change at the Start of the New Millennium* (Abingdon, UK: Routledge, 2003), 80–107.

190 *"In short, from 1960 to 1996, Hong Kong's per capita income"*: Milton Friedman, "The Real Lesson of Hong Kong," *National Review*, December 31,
1997, www.hoover.org/research/hong-kong-experiment.

191 *China's conversion . . . had humanitarian effects*: "Towards the End of Poverty;
the World's Next Great Leap Forward," *Economist*, June 1, 2013, www.econ
omist.com/news/leaders/21578665-nearly-1-billion-people-have-been
-taken-out-extreme-poverty-20-years-world-should-aim.

191 *"China now exports in a single day more than it exported during the entire year of
1978"*: Robyn Meredith, *The Elephant and the Dragon: The Rise of India and
China and What It Means for All of Us* (New York: W. W. Norton, 2007), 16.

192 *the fresh sound of exuberance arriving with Beatles music*: Leslie Woodhead,
(2009-11-08). How the Beatles Rocked the Kremlin (Television production). New York, NY: WNET.org accessed November 13, 2009. See also Michael Walsh, "The Beatles Ignited a Cultural Revolution in the Soviet Youth
That Helped Overthrow the USSR: Former Spy," *Daily News*, June 1, 2013,
www.nydailynews.com/news/world/beatles-beat-communism-spy-article
-1.1360024.

192 *"the Celtic Tiger" had surpassed the per capita wealth of the United Kingdom*:
Benjamin Powell, "Economic Freedom and Growth: The Case of the Celtic

Tiger," *Cato Journal* 22, no. 3 (2003): 431–48, http://mercatus.org/up
loadedFiles/Mercatus/Publications/Tiger.pdf.

192 *Hong Kong has one of the highest GDPs per person*: "Nominal GDP List of
Countries. Data for the Year 2010," *World Economic Outlook Database*, September 2011, International Monetary Fund.

192 *one of the highest life expectancies*: "Life Expectancy Around the World," Live
Science, 1 August 1, 2012, www.livescience.com/22005-highest-and-lowest
-life-expectancy-at-birth-infographic.html.

192 *one of the lowest murder rates*: www.mapsofworld.com/world-top-ten/coun
tries-with-lowest-murder-rates.html.

192 *most skyscrapers of any city in the world*: www.emporis.com/statistics/most
-skyscraper-cities-worldwide.

193 *The government's Housing Authority provides homes for 30 percent*: Public
Rental Housing Application | Hong Kong Housing Authority and Housing
Department, accessed February 26, 2016, www.housingauthority.gov.hk/en
/public-housing.

193 *about half of Hong Kongers live in some form of subsidized housing*: In 2006
census, 48.8 percent lived in rental or subsidized public housing: Census and
Statistics Department, Government of the Hong Kong Special Administrative Region. See also Bernie Lo, "Is Hong Kong's Subsidized Housing Fair?,"
on the website of CNBC, May 31, 2012, www.cnbc.com/id/47640064.

193 *By 2007, the bottom 60 percent of earners paid no income tax*: M. Littlewood,
(2007) The Hong Kong Tax System. *Prosoperitas*. http://archive.freedom
andprosperity.org/Papers/hongkong/hongkong.pdf. "The wealthy pay
most of the tax in Hong Kong. The bottom 60 percent pay no income tax,
while the richest 100,000 taxpayers (the top 8 percent) pay 57 percent of the
total tax burden."

193 *Malaysian parliament voted 126 to 0 to expel Singapore*: "Singapore and Leadership," on the website of the Asian Century Institute, July 20, 2014, www
.asiancenturyinstitute.com/development/389-singapore-and-leadership.

193 *When it was left to run itself in 1965, Singapore was a tiny British naval base
and trading outpost with a per capita GDP of $516*: Locknie Hsu, "Inward FDI
in Singapore and Its Policy Context," Vale Columbia Center on Sustainable
International Investment FDI Profiles project, May 31, 2012, http://ccsi.co
lumbia.edu/files/2014/03/Singapore_IFDI_-_FINAL_-_31_May_2012
.pdf. "The modern economic history of Singapore begins around the period
of the country's independence in in 1965. The per capita GDP of Singapore
at that time was US $516; in 2010 it was US $43,867, a remarkable 85-fold
increase in only 45 years."

193 *Over that time, Singapore has grown at more than triple the rate of the nation
from which it broke away*: Shamim Adam, "Singapore Seen Overtaking Ma-

laysia 45 Years After Lee's Tears," *Bloomberg News*, November 11, 2010, www
.bloomberg.com/news/2010-11-10/singapore-seen-overtaking-malaysia
-45-years-after-split-left-lee-in-tears.html. The World Bank shows even more
astonishing statistics: 974 million in 1964 to 274 billion in 2012—more than
a 282-fold growth in forty-eight years.

194 *In 1965, 70 percent of Singaporean households lived in dangerously overcrowded conditions, half its population was illiterate, and a third of its people
squatted in slums*: World Development Report 2009, World Bank, http://
web.worldbank.org/WBSITE/EXTERNAL/EXTDEC/EXTRESEARCH
/EXTWDRS/0,,contentMDK:23080401~pagePK:478093~piPK:477627
~theSitePK:477624,00.html.

194 *Seventeen percent of all Singaporean households possess at least $1 million US
in disposable wealth*: Shibani Mahtani, "Singapore No. 1 for Millionaires—
Again," Southeast Asia (blog), *Wall Street Journal*, June 1, 2012, http://blogs
.wsj.com/searealtime/2012/06/01/singapore-no-1-for-millionaires-again.

194 *2016 Index of Economic Freedom ranked Singapore as the second freest economy
in the world, with Hong Kong the first.* Heritage Foundation (Washington,
DC), and Wall Street Journal (Firm). (1995). The index of economic freedom. Washington, DC: Heritage Foundation. www.heritage.org/index

194 *Global Competitiveness Index 2015–2016 ranked Singapore as the second
most competitive country in world. Global Competitiveness Report 2015–2016,*
"Competitiveness Rankings," *xv*, www3.weforum.org/docs/gcr/2015–2016
/Global_Competitiveness_Report_2015–2016.pdf. See also Ichiro
Sugimoto, *Economic Growth of Singapore in the Twentieth Century* (2011).
See also K. Y. Lee, *From Third World to First: The Singapore Story, 1965–2000*
(New York: HarperCollins, 2000).

195 *GDP per capita in Taiwan was $154*: T. Kuo and R. H. Myers, *Taiwan's Eco-
nomic Transformation: Leadership, Property Rights and Institutional Change
1949–1965* (London: Routledge, 2012), 120. See also C. Tan, *Routledge
Handbook of the Chinese Diaspora* (London: Routledge, 2013), 135, www
.igef.cuhk.edu.hk/igef_media/working-paper/IGEF/igef_working_paper
_no13_eng.pdf. "Between 1952 and 2011, Taiwan real GDP per capita grew
22.6 times, from US $890 to US $20,110, at an average annual compound
rate of 5.2% . . . In 2011 Taiwan real GDP per capita was almost four times
the Mainland real GDP per capita."

195 *Today it boasts GDP per capita levels similar to Germany*: D. Runde, "Taiwan
Is a Model of Freedom and Prosperity," *Forbes*, May 26, 2015, www.forbes
.com/sites/danielrunde/2015/05/26/taiwan-development-model-free
dom-prosperity/#1ed03d0351ab. "Today, Taiwan has a human development index score that is comparable to France's and GDP per capita levels
similar to Germany."

196 *"What is unprecedented is not poverty"*: Big Think Interview with John Mackey, accessed February 26, 2016, http://bigthink.com/videos/big-think -interview-with-john-mackey.

197 *"dedicated to liberating the entrepreneurial spirit for good."* Michael Strong, *Be the Solution: How Entrepreneurs and Conscious Capitalists Can Solve All the World's Problems* (Hoboken, NJ: Wiley, 2009).

197 *lacking even a traffic light*: Yue-man Yeung, Joanna Lee, and Gordon Kee, "China's Special Economic Zones at 30," *Eurasian Geography and Economics* 50, no. 2 (2009): 222–40, www.espre.cn/111/manage/ziliao/china%26 _039.pdf.

197 *In fifteen years, property values in Shenzhen soared 8,000 percent*: Michael Strong and Mark Frazier, "Creating an Effective Alliance Around Women's Empowerment Free Zones," www.flowidealism.org/Downloads /WEFZ%20Coalition.pdf.

197 *When looked at over thirty years, land values in Shenzhen increased 18,000 percent*: Michael Strong, "Free Cities: How Countries Worldwide Are Unleashing New Economic Prosperity," City A.M., January 27, 2012, www.cityam .com/article/free-cities-how-countries-worldwide-are-unleashing-new-eco nomic-prosperity.

197 *one year after it was designated an SEZ, Shenzhen accounted for 50.6 percent of all foreign direct investment in China*: D. Wall, "China's Economic Reform and Opening-Up Process: The Role of the Special Economic Zones," *Development Policy Review* 11, no. 3 (1993): 243–60. See also Yeung, Lee, and Kee, "China's Special Economic Zones at 30," 222–40.

197 *Shenzhen's industrial output increased 1,256-fold*: M. Cracian, "Shenzhen Speed," *New Perspectives Quarterly* 17, no. 4 (Fall 2000), www.digitalnpq .org/archive/2000_fall/shenzhen.html. "As indicated by the 1,256-fold in-crease in Shenzhen's industrial output between 1979 and 1995, the sudden influx of capital investment was beyond imagination."

198 *When the SEZ was founded*: Mee Kam Ng and W. S. Tang, "The Role of Planning in the Development of Shenzhen, People's Republic Of China: Rhetoric and Realities," *Eurasian Geography and Economics* 45, no. 3 (2004): 190–211, http://scripts.mit.edu/~11.306/wiki/images/archive /20080108222452!NgTang_2004.pdf. "From 1980 to 2001, Shenzhen's population increased fourteenfold, its GDP by 724 times, fixed capital in-vestment 488 times, gross output value of industry 3,014 times, and imports and exports 3,918 times."

198 *"Throughout the developing world"*: Strong, *Be the Solution*.

199 *"This is the new frontier of poverty alleviation"*: "The Most Progressive Move-ment on the Planet," *Huffington Post*, July 15, 2009, www.huffingtonpost .com/michael-strong/the-most-progressive-move_b_234649.html.

199 *"would like to move permanently to another country"*: N. Esipova and J. Ray, "700 Million Worldwide Desire to Migrate Permanently," Gallup, November 2, 2009, www.gallup.com/poll/124028/700-million-worldwide-desire -migrate-permanently.aspx.

200 *James Meade, later a Nobel Prize recipient in economics, predicted in 1961 that Mauritius was doomed*: Meade expressed his doubts in a book first published in 1961 that has since been reissued: James E. Meade, *Economic and Social Structure of Mauritius* (New York: Routledge, 2011).

200 *the island nation's GDP per person grew tenfold . . . financial intermediation"*: Ali Zafar, "Mauritius: An Economic Success Story" (draft), World Bank Group, Africa Success Stories Project, January 2011, http://siteresources. worldbank.org/AFRICAEXT/Resources/Mauritius_success.pdf.

200 *per capita income is one of the highest in all Africa*: Mauritius: Economy. *Global Edge.* Accessed February 27, 2016, http://globaledge.msu.edu/countries /mauritius/economy.

201 *the diverse population of Mauritians behaved like a smart start-up*: Ali Zafar, *Yes Africa Can: Success Stories from a Dynamic Continent*, ed. Punam Chuhan-Pole and Manka Angwafo (Washington DC: World Bank, 2011), 91–106, http://siteresources.worldbank.org/AFRICAEXT/Resources/25 8643-1271798012256/YAC_Consolidated_Web.pdf. See also World Bank chapter 5 published separately: http://siteresources.worldbank.org/AF RICAEXT/Resources/258643-1271798012256/Mauritius-success.pdf.

201 *Between 1970 and 2010*: M. Blin and B. Ouattara, "Foreign Direct Investment and Economic Growth in Mauritius: Evidence from Bounds Test Cointegration," School of Oriental and African Studies-University of London (Blin) and the University of Manchester (Ouattara), 2004, www.socialsciences .manchester.ac.uk/medialibrary/economics/discussionpapers/EDP-0418 .pdf.

201 *87 percent of Mauritians owned their own homes*: Joseph E. Stiglitz, "The Mauritius Miracle," Project Syndicate, October 23, 2011, www.project-syndicate .org/commentary/the-mauritius-miracle.

202 *By the late 1980s, it was 3 percent*: P. Rampadaratg, "Competitiveness Strategies for Small States—Case of Mauritius," 2013, www.um.edu.mt/_data/as sets/pdf_file/0004/188293/MAURITIUS.pdf. "[U]nemployment dropped to 3% by end of 1980s."

202 *Almost all of this increase in employment (87 percent)*: M. McQueen, "ACP Export Diversification: The Case of Mauritius," Overseas Development Institute, August 1990, 29, www.odi.org/sites/odi.org.uk/files/odi-assets /publications-opinion-files/6921.pdf. "[T]he EPZ has provided 87% of the additional employment in the economy over the period 1982–88 and

enabled unemployment to fall from around 20% to 5%, while female participation rates have increased from 28% in 1983 to 42% in 1988."

202 *and local entrepreneurship (90 percent)*: M. Vandemoortele and K. Bird,
"Progress in Economic Conditions in Mauritius: Success Against the Odds"
(London: Overseas Development Institute, 2011), 10, www.development
progress.org/sites/developmentprogress.org/files/mauritius_report_-_mas
ter_0.pdf. "The Gini coefficient fell from 45.7 in 1980 to 38.9 in 2006." pf 14.
"Around 90% of entrepreneurs in the EPZ and the manufacturing sector were
Mauritian nationals."

202 *savor these glorious numbers*: J. A. Frankel, "Mauritius: African Success Story"
(working paper 15533. National Bureau of Economic Research, Cambridge,
MA, 2010), www.nber.org/papers/w16569. See also E. Dommen and
B. Dommen, *Mauritius an Island of Success: a Retrospective Study 1960–1993*
(Wellington, UK): Oxford: Pacific Press, 1999). James Currey. See also
P. Hein, "Structural Transformation in an Island Country: The Mauritius
Export Processing Zone," *Unctad Review* 1, no. 2 (1989): 41–57. See also
Stephen King, "The Southern Silk Road," HSBC Global Research, June
2011. See also World Bank, African Development Bank, and Mauritius
Board of Investment 2009. "Investment Climate Assessment: Mauritius
2009." World Bank, Washington, DC, http://siteresources.worldbank.org
/MAURITIUSEXTN/Resources/ica-mauritius-0110.pdf.

203 *At the same time that the nation experienced stellar growth, its income inequality, as measured by the Gini coefficient, fell from 45.7 in 1980 to 38.9 in 2006*:
Vandemoortele and Bird, "Progress in Economic Conditions in Mauritius," 10.

203 *"The sugarcane fields, the mountains in the backdrop"*: Satish Chand, *Pacific
Could Learn From Prosperous Mauritius, Pacific Islands Report*, October 19,
2010, http://archives.pireport.org/archive/2010/October/10-20-ft.htm.

204 *As we were writing this*: "Paradise Gained: How Tiny Mauritius Became
Africa's Most Competitive Economy," *International Business Times*, September 4, 2013, www.ibtimes.com/paradise-gained-how-tiny-mauritius-became
-africas-most-competitive-economy-1402694. "The island nation of Mauritius has claimed Africa's top spot in the annual *Global Competitiveness Report
for 2013–14*, which was released Wednesday by the World Economic Forum,
or WEF."

204 *Much debate has been stirred about the "Mauritius miracle."*: Arvind Subramanian, "The Mauritian Success Story and Its Lessons" (research paper
2009/36, United Nations University, World Institute for Development
Economic Research, 2009), http://ideas.repec.org/p/unu/wpaper/rp2009
-36.html. "Mauritius success may be due to 'idiosyncratic factors' unique

to Mauritians." See also Arvind Subramanian and Roy Devesh, "Who Can Explain the Mauritian Miracle: Meade, Romer, Sachs, or Rodrik?" (working paper 01/116, International Monetary Fund, Washington, DC, 2001), www .imf.org/external/pubs/cat/longres.cfm?sk=15215.0.

205 *trade union membership is up above 65 percent*: Trade Union Density. OECD. Stat. accessed February 29, 2016, http://stats.oecd.org/Index.aspx?DataSet Code=UN_DEN.

205 *In broad outline, the Nordic nations' method goes like this*: J. A. McWinney, "The Nordic Model: Pros and Cons," Investopedia, June 25, 2013, www .investopedia.com/articles/investing/100714/nordic-model-pros-and-cons .asp.

206 *Swedish author and scientist*: Nima Sanandaji, "Scandinavian Unexception-alism: Culture, Markets, and the Failure of Third-Way Socialism," Institute of Economic Affairs, June 23, 2015, www.iea.org.uk/sites/default/files /publications/files/Sanandajinima-interactive.pdf. From p. *xvi*: "It is very clear that many of the desirable features of Scandinavian societies, such as low income inequality, low levels of poverty, and high levels of economic growth, predated the development of the welfare state."

207 *So which system works the best for overall human welfare?*: Shahid Yusuf and Kaoru Nabeshima, *Some Small Countries Do It Better: Rapid Growth and Its Causes in Singapore, Finland, and Ireland* (Washington DC: World Bank, 2012).

208 *"Many of life's failures"*: quoted in Deborah Headstrom-Page, *From Telegraph to Light Bulb with Thomas Edison* (Nashville: R&H, 2007), 22.

Unless noted otherwise, all quotes from Baoguang Zhai were taken from interviews with the author.

215 *Xiaogang Village produced more grain than it had in the previous five years combined*: D. Kestenbau and J. Goldstein, "The Secret Document That Transformed China," on the website of National Public Radio, January 20, 2012, www.npr.org/sections/money/2012/01/20/145360447/the-secret -document-that-transformed-china.

215 *per capita income rose twentyfold*: Wang Ke, "Xiaogang Village, Birthplace of Rural Reform, Moves On," China.org.cn, December 15, 2008, www.china .org.cn/china/features/content_16955209.htm.

Chapter 7. HEALTH: Faster, Cheaper, Better, Fluid Care

221 *in 2017 a population equivalent to Australia will board cruise ships*: Cruise Market Watch. Growth. accessed March 3, 2016, www.cruisemarketwatch .com/growth.

221 *At least 10 percent of Americans remain uninsured*: Key Facts About the Uninsured Population, October 5, 2015, http://kff.org/uninsured/fact-sheet /key-facts-about-the-uninsured-population.

222 *global medical tourism market is* already *growing at about 20 percent per year*: M. Sheahan and A. Korener, Reuters, "Medical Tourism Offers Travel Firms Untapped Growth," March 7, 2013, www.reuters.com/article/us-medical -tourism-idUSBRE9260C220130307.

222 *entire towns have been known to pitch in to send one person abroad for adequate caretowns*: Personal communication, Nishant Bagadia.

222 *According to the Centers for Medicare & Medicaid Services (CMS)*: www .cms.gov/research-statistics-data-and-systems/statistics-trends-and-reports /nationalhealthexpenddata/nationalhealthaccountshistorical.html. See also the Milliman Medical Index (MMI), which calculated that employee-sponsored health care costs for an American family of four rose 5.4% in 2014 to a total of $23,215: Health care costs for a typical American family >$23,000 in 2014. (2014). *PharmacoEconomics & Outcomes News* 704, no. 1, 9-9, http://link.springer.com/article/10.1007/s40274-014-1296-y/fulltext .html.

222 *health insurance premiums will surpass the median US household income in 2033*: R. A. Young and J. E. Devoe, "Who Will Have Health Insurance in the Future? An Updated Projection," *Annals of Family Medicine* 10, no. 2 (2012): 156–62, www.annfammed.org/content/10/2/156.abstract.

222 *US health care system squanders $750 billion*: Annie Lowrey, "Study of U.S. Health Care System Finds Both Waste and Opportunity to Improve," *New York Times*, September 11, 2012, www.nytimes.com/2012/09/12/health /policy/waste-and-promise-seen-in-us-health-care-system.html?_r=0.

223 *"costs more than the Pentagon budget"*: Ricardo Alonso-Zaldivar, Associated Press, "Report: U.S. Healthcare System Wastes $750B a Year," September 7, 2012, http://bigstory.ap.org/article/report-us-health-care-system-wastes -750b-year.

223 *"The growth of American-style hospitals around the world"*: E. Jim, "Can Medical Tourism Save Us from Obamacare?" Reason TV, January 29, 2013, http://reason.com/reasontv/2013/01/29/free-trade-health-care.

223 *enticing 2015 price comparisons*: Compare Cost | Health Tourism, Health

Care, Medical Travel | MedicalTourism.com. (2015). accessed March 4, 2016, www.medicaltourism.com/Forms/price-comparison.

224 *Hickory Springs Manufacturing, or HSM, a furniture manufacturer in North Carolina, offers its workers a choice*: B. Pitts and N. Battiste, "As More Americans Have Surgeries Overseas, US Companies Consider 'Medical Tourism' a Health Care Option," on the website of ABC News, September 30, 2013, http://abcnews.go.com/Health/americans-surgeries-overseas-us-compa nies-medical-tourism-health/story?id=20423011.

224 *nursing ratio for patients traveling abroad is usually one-to-one*: Colglobal Medical Tourism, accessed March 4, 2016, www.cg.yourdeliverysite.com.

Unless noted otherwise, all quotes from Peter Wei come from the transcript of his speech to the Seasteading Conference 2012 and from personal communication with the author.

226 *Israel scrambled to overhaul its tourism industry*: H. Goldmeier, "Your Business: Medical Tourism—Growth Industry or a Burden?," *Jerusalem Post*, September 1, 2013, www.jpost.com/Business/Business-Features/Your -Business-Medical-tourism-growth-industry-or-a-burden-324988.

227 *"[T]hey see foreigners buying their way into a system they helped build"*: Nick Robins-Early, "Why People Are Traveling Around the World to See a Doctor," *Huffington Post*, last modified February 17, 2016, www.huffingtonpost .com/entry/medical-tourism-sasha-issenberg-book_us_56c3509ee4b0c 3c55052aa5d?zsuzyqfr. See also Sasha Issenberg, *Outpatients: The Astonishing New World of Medical Tourism* (New York: Columbia Global Reports, 2016).

227 *3 percent to 4 percent of the world's population travels abroad seeking superior medical treatment*: Maria Sheahan and Andreas Kröner, Reuters, "Medical Tourism Offers Travel Firms Untapped Growth," March 7, 2013, www.reu ters.com/article/medical-tourism-idUSL5N0B5BY320130307.

227 *A survey published*: Deloitte Center for Health Solutions. "Medical Tourism: Update and Implications." Deloitte, 2009. "Over 40 percent said they would travel outside their immediate area for care if their physician recommended it or for a 50 percent cost savings." See also A. Saenz, "Demand for Stem Cells Growing Fast, Many Turn to Medical Tourism," Singularity HUB, February 28, 2010, http://singularityhub.com/2010/02/28/demand-for-stem-cells -growing-fast-many-turning-to-the-allure-of-medical-tourism.

Unless otherwise noted, all quotes from Nishant Bagadia come from transcript of speech to Seasteading Conference 2012 and personal interviews with author.

229 *"Fresh out of college and armed with a laptop, cell phone, and piña colada"*: E. Williams-Masson, "Something Old, Something New: Getting Baby

Boomers, Generation Xers and Millennials to Work as One Team," *Wisconsin State Journal*, December 1, 2007, http://host.madison.com/business/b2b /something-old-something-new-getting-baby-boomers-generation-xers -and/article_61beb4a4-f624-51df-9de9-1ca4ee2d8a67.html.

230 *ratio of people to physicians in Kenya is at least 5,000 to 1*: Physicians (per 1,000 people), World Bank, accessed March 5, 2016, http://data.worldbank .org/indicator/SH.MED.PHYS.ZS.

231 *"Charity is not scalable"*: "ET Awards 2012: Devi Prasad Shetty Is Entre-preneur of the Year, *Economic Times*, September 19, 2012, http://articles .economictimes.indiatimes.com/2012-09-19/news/33952757_1_hospital -chain-narayana-hrudayalaya-cardiac-surgery".

231 *Dr. Shetty is making a luxury for the rich available to the poor*: G. Anand, "The Henry Ford of Heart Surgery," *Wall Street Journal*, November 25, 2009, www .wsj.com/news/articles/SB125875892887958111. See also Devi Shetty presentation: http://www.nuffieldtrust.org.uk/sites/files/nuffield/dr_devi _shetty_heart_surgery_290212.pdf.

232 *11 cents a month*: Fred De Sam Lazaro, "Doctor Slashes the Cost of Surger-ies for India's Poor," on the website of *PBS NewsHour*, September 16, 2015, www.pbs.org/newshour/updates/india-doctor.

233 *services and materials valued at over $1 billion*: https://mercyships.s3.amazon aws.com/wp-content/uploads/2014/07/MSUS_AR-2013-lr.pdf.

233 *2.5 million beneficiaries*: www.mercyships.org/wp-content/uploads/2015/10 /MS_FS2015_10_17_US_Letter_MS.pdf.

234 *"The findings suggest that by 2017, fifteen million innovation-seeking consumers will transfer $400 billion US"*: Nishant Bagadia, "Investigating Medical Tour ism Beneath the Surface," *Medical Tourism*, April 1, 2009, www.medicaltour ismmag.com/article/investigating-medical.html.

235 *75 percent of the world's adult population owned a mobile phone*: www.cia.gov /library/publications/the-world-factbook/fields/2151.html.

239 *"I was a sick woman; now I will be able to live a normal life," Castillo told the BBC*: Michelle Roberts, "Windpipe Transplant Breakthrough," BBC, No-vember 19, 2008, http://news.bbc.co.uk/2/hi/health/7735696.stm.

240 *"More than 600 facilities around the world have now been awarded JCI ac-creditation"*: Joint Commission, June 30, 2015, www.jointcommission.org /facts_about_joint_commission_international.

241 *"telemedicine is the way primary health care is delivered across the world"*: Priya Menon, Dr. Devi Prasad Shetty on Vaccine for Heart Attack and Future of Telemedicine—Interview Part Two, *Curetalk*, April 3, 2012, http://trialx .com/curetalk/2012/04/dr-devi-prasad-shetty-on-vaccine-for-heart-attack -and-future-of-telemedicine-interview-part-two.

241 *"The best location to build a hospital on the planet today is a ship that is parked in*

the US waters just outside its territory": S. Das, "Devi Shetty Opens Low-Cost Healthcare Venture in Cayman Islands Outside US Regulatory Reach," *Economic Times*, February 24, 2014, http://articles.economictimes.indiatimes .com/2014-02-24/news/47635802_1_devi-shetty-narayana-health-indian -doctors.

249 *"FDA is going green!"*: www.fda.gov/downloads/Drugs/DevelopmentAp provalProcess/SmallBusinessAssistance/UCM309640.pdf.

Chapter 8. FEAR: War, Waves, Pirates, Pollution, Price!

258 *"[Rogue waves] are all short lived . . . probability that a ship encounters one is relatively small"*: L. Peeples, "The Real Sea Monsters: On the Hunt for Rogue Waves," *Scientific American*, September 12, 2009, www.scientificamerican .com/article/rogue-waves-ocean-energy-forecasting.

258 *the first rogue wave was measured with a digital instrument in 1995*: www.ifre mer.fr/web-com/stw2004/rogue/pres/Session_3.2/Haver_Draupner.pdf.

258 *beginning to be understood scientifically*: Simon Birkholz et al., "Predictability of Rogue Wave Events," *Physics Review Letters* 114, no. 21 (May 2015): 213901, http://journals.aps.org/prl/abstract/10.1103/PhysRevLett.114.21 3901.

258 *"rogue wave hotspots"*: T. T. Janssen and T. H. C. Herbers, "Nonlinear Wave Statistics in a Focal Zone," *Journal of Physical Oceanography* 39 (2009): 1948–64.

259 *pollute?* "Facts and Figures on Marine Pollution," United Nations Educational, Scientific and Cultural Organization (UNESCO), accessed March 7, 2016, www.unesco.org/new/en/natural-sciences/ioc-oceans/priority-areas /rio-20-ocean/blueprint-for-the-future-we-want/marine-pollution/facts -and-figures-on-marine-pollution.

259 *The greenest form of transport is shipping. As measured by carbon emissions per ton moved*: R. George, *Ninety Percent of Everything*: 91.

260 *Desalinization*: "Timelines—Desalination Technology," Desware: Encyclopedia of Desalination and Water Resources, accessed February 21, 2012, www.desware.net/Timelines-Desalination-Technology.aspx. See also "Case History: Tapping the Oceans," *Economist*, June 5, 2008, www.economist .com/node/11484059. See also Menachem Elimelech and William A. Phillip, "The Future of Seawater Desalination: Energy, Technology, and the Environment," *Science* 333. no. 6043 (August 5, 2011): 712, http://science .sciencemag.org/content/333/6043/712.

260 *Energy?*: Dennis Elliot et al., "Assessment of Offshore Wind Energy Potential in the United States," on the website of the National Renewable Energy Lab-

oratory, accessed February 24, 2012, www.nrel.gov/docs/fy11osti/51332
.pdf. "The United States has enormous gross energy potential from the offshore wind resource."

261 *water turbines on the seabed*: "UK Leads Marine Energy Revolution as World's Largest Tidal Stream Project Agrees Investment to Begin Construction in Scotland," on the website of MeyGen, accessed March 8, 2016, www.meygen .com/2014/08/uk-leads-marine-energy-revolution-as-worlds-largest-tidal -stream-project-agrees-investment-to-begin-construction-in-scotland.

261 *light bulbs filled with seawater and lit from within*: Liz Stinson, "A Lamp Whose Light Comes from Bioluminescent Bacteria," *Wired*, January 13, 2015, www .wired.com/2015/01/lamp-whose-light-comes-bioluminescent-bacteria.

261 *Though the lack of defined property rights on the ocean has certainly contributed to overfishing in a classic "Tragedy of the Commons" situation*: "In Deep Water," *Economist*, February 22, 2014, www.economist.com/news /international/21596990-humans-are-damaging-high-seas-now-oceans -are-doing-harm-back-deep-water. See also "A Rising Tide: Scientists Find Proof That Privatising Fishing Stocks Can Avert a Disaster," *Economist*, September 18, 2008, www.economist.com/node/12253181. See also Daniel K. Benjamin, "Fisheries Are Classic Example of the Tragedy of the Commons," *PERC Reports* 19, no. 1 (March 2001): https://web.archive .org/web/20050219192447/http://perc.org/publications/percreports /march2001/tangents.php.

262 *Countries grant at least $35 billion US a year in fishing subsidies*: U. R. Sumalia et al., "Global Fisheries Subsidies," European Parliament, Policy Department, October 2013, www.europarl.europa.eu/RegData/etudes/note/join /2013/513978/IPOL-PECH_NT(2013)513978_EN.pdf.

265 *"the International Transport Workers' Federation (ITF) claims it recovers tens of millions US in unpaid wages"*: International Transport Workers' Federation, "ITF Reveals MLC Experiences to International Shipping Conference," press release, September 9, 2015, www.itfglobal.org/en/news-events/press -releases/2015/september/itf-reveals-mlc-experiences-to-international -shipping-conference.

266 *"By 2020, 90 percent of the world's population over the age of six will have access to a mobile phone."*: Ben Woods, "By 2020, 90% of World's Population Aged over 6 Will Have a Mobile Phone: Report," The Next Web, accessed April 21, 2016, http://thenextweb.com/insider/2014/11/18/2020-90-worlds-popu lation-aged-6-will-mobile-phone-report/#gref.

268 *taxes?*: R. W. Wood, "U.S. Raises Fee to Expatriate by 422% a Second Time," *Forbes*. September 18, 2015, www.forbes.com/sites/robertwood/2015/09 /18/second-422-hike-in-fee-to-exit-u-s-in-12-months/#6253fa9f339d.

269 *Pirate seas represent less than 2 percent of the world's oceans*: World's oceans

cover 139.7 million square miles. Pirates prowl about 2.5 million square miles of ocean, which is about 1.8 percent.

269 *Internationally Recommended Transit Corridor (IRTC)*: www.intertanko.com /upload/IRTC%20%20GT%20Explanation%20-%20March%202009%20 %282%29.pdf. See also Vestergaard Madsen et al., *The State of Maritime Piracy 2013* (Broomfield, CO: Oceans Beyond Piracy, May 2014), http:// oceansbeyondpiracy.org/sites/default/files/attachments/SoP2013-Digital _0.pdf.

270 *Rich nations profit from sea trade and protect their interests*: Personal correspondence with R. P. Newman, Department of Defense certified antiterrorism officer (level II) (highest level possible); and Department of the Navy certified master training specialist (highest US Navy instructor certification).

274 *a hundred SWAT raids on nonviolent citizens per day*: R. Balko, *Rise of the Warrior Cop: The Militarization of America's Police Forces* (New York: Public Affairs, 2013).

Chapter 9. HISTORY: Rights Flow from Frontiers

279 *human prehistory was barbaric*: L. H. Keeley, *War Before Civilization* (New York: Oxford University Press, 1996).

279 *120,000 years since the first evidence of trade*: Hillary Mayell, "When Did 'Modern' Behavior Emerge in Humans?," National Geographic News, February 20, 2003, http://news.nationalgeographic.com/news/2003/02/0220 _030220_humanorigins2_2.html.

279 *196,000 years since Cro-Magnon sported a skull just like ours*: M. Day, "Fossil Reanalysis Pushes Back Origin of Homo Sapiens," *Scientific American*, February 17, 2005 www.scientificamerican.com/article/fossil-reanalysis-pushes. Homo sapiens skull dated 196,000 to 190,000 years.

279 *The principles of game theory, which is the study of mathematical models of conflict*: Cristina Bicchieri, John Duffy, and Gil Tolle, "Trust Among Strangers" *Philosophy of Science* 71, no. 3 (July 2004): 1–34, www.socsci .uci.edu/~duffy/papers/trustamongstrangers.pdf. See also Robert Axelrod, *The Evolution of Cooperation* (New York: Basic Books, 1984). See also R. Wright, *NonZero: The Logic of Human Destiny* (New York: Pantheon Books, 2000).

279 *Aristotle studied the varieties of polities*: Aristotle, *Politics*, B. Jowett, trans., in *The Complete Works of Aristotle*, vol. 2, ed. Jonathon Barnes (Princeton, NJ: Princeton University Press, 1984). See also S. Lewis, "Tyranny." *Encyclopedia Britannica*, September 23, 2014, www.britannica.com/topic/tyranny.

280 *"Greece was divided into many small self-governing communities"*: Joseph

Camilleri and Jim Falk, *Worlds in Transition: Evolving Governance Across a Stressed Planet* (Cheltenham, UK: Edward Elgar, 2009). For more on small self-governing communities dictated by Greek geography, see also Raphael Sealey, *A History of the Greek City States, Ca. 700–338 B.C.* (Oakland: University of California Press, 1976), 10–11.

280 *"Central to the rapid progress of Greek civilization was its very lack of a political center."*: Gregory F. Rehmke, "Property Rights and Law Among the Ancient Greeks: The success of Western Civilization Owes Much to the Greeks," on the website of the Foundation for the Economic Education, February 1, 1997, http://fee.org/articles/property-rights-and-law-among-the-ancient -greeks.

281 *"[A] world in which there is no centralized political organization . . . is perfectly capable of self-organizing into a condition of high growth"*: Josiah Ober, *The Rise and Fall of Classical Greece* (Princeton, NJ: Princeton University Press, 2015.

281 *Summing up his book for PBS:* "What Explains the Glory That Was Greece? Actually, Sound Economic Policy," on the website of PBS NewsHour, July 14, 2015, www.pbs.org/newshour/making-sense/explains-glory-greece-actu ally-sound-economic-policy.

282 *the dynamics for a decentralized market of governance were in place:* "Geography of the Renaissance: Understanding the Renaissance Through the Five Themes of Geography," accessed February 11, 2016, http://www.st.cr .k12.ia.us/Renaissance/geography.htm. See also Brian Milne, *The History and Theory of Children's Citizenship in Contemporary Societies* (New York: Springer, 2013), 64–65.

282 *tripling of per capita income in northern Italy:* Keith Devlin, *The Man of Numbers: Fibonacci's Arithmetic Revolution* (London: Walker, 2011). 113–14.

283 *Exports overseas exceeded imports by far, free-trade zones in Tuscany:* Marcia Christoff-Kurapovna: "The Case for the City-State: Ancient Greece and Renaissance Italy Provide a Model for Economic Dynamism That Modern-Day Europe Could Use," *Wall Street Journal*, July 12, 2012, www.wsj.com /articles/SB10001424052702303919504577522641691745740.

283 *birthplace of modern business practices:* Diego Puga and Daniel Trefler, "International Trade and Institutional Change: Medieval Venice's Response to Globalization," *Quarterly Journal of Economics* 129, no. 2 (2014): 753–821, http://diegopuga.org/papers/Puga_Trefler_QJE_2014.pdf. for a good sum-up of the paper, see also: http://www.businessinsider.com/the-eco nomic-history-of-venice-2012-8.

283 *A grandson of a slave:* Zaccaria Staganzo, *The Pirate Pope: Baldassarre Cossa.*

285 John Adams to James Sullivan, 26 May 1776; from Charles Francis Adams, ed., *The Works of John Adams, Second President of the United States* (Boston: Little, Brown, 1854).

285 *Pennsylvania and Rhode Island . . . retaining tax qualifications for voting into the twentieth century*: Stanely L. Engerman and Kenneth L. Sokoloff, "The Evolution of Suffrage Institutions in the New World," *Journal of Economic History* 65 (2005): 16, http://economics.yale.edu/sites/default/files/files /Workshops-Seminars/Economic-History/sokoloff-050406.pdf.

285 *On the frontier, however, things were dynamic*: P. Friedman and B. Taylor, "Barriers to Entry and Institutional Evolution" (paper presented at the Association of Private Enterprise Education Conference, Nassau, 2011), www.academia .edu/2748488/Barriers_to_Entry_and_Institutional_Evolution. See also P. Friedman and B. Taylor, "Entry Barriers and Innovation in the Market for Governance" (2011), www.academia.edu/959477/Entry_Barriers_and _Innovation_in_the_Market_for_Governance. See also J. L. Walker, "The Diffusion of Innovations Among the American States," *American Political Science Review* 63, no. 3 (1969): 880–99. See also K. H. Porter, *A History of Suffrage in the United States* (Chicago: University of Chicago Press, 1918). See also G. Riley, *The Female Frontier: A Comparative View of Women on the Prairie and the Plains* (Lawrence: University Press of Kansas, 1988). See also C. Williamson, *American Suffrage from Property to Democracy, 1760–1860* (Princeton, NJ: Princeton University Press, 1960).

287 *Technological inertia is enforced by entrenched industries*: J. Mokyr, "Innovation and Its Enemies: The Economic and Political Roots of Technological Inertia," in *A Not So Dismal Science*, ed. Mancur Olson and Satu Kähkönen (Oxford, UK: Oxford University Press, 2000), 61–91, http://faculty.wcas .northwestern.edu/~jmokyr/Delhi.pdf. See also J. Mokyr, "Invention and Rebellion: Why Do Innovations Occur at All? An Evolutionary Approach," in *The Role of Minorities and Elites in Economic Growth*, ed. Elise Brezis and Peter Temin (Amsterdam: Elsevier, 1999), 179–203, http://faculty.wcas .northwestern.edu/~jmokyr/bar-ilan.pdf.

288 *"Cardwell's Law says that no nation remains technologically innovative for long."*: M. Gibson, "From Poverty to Prosperity: An ATN Book Review," *Let a Thousand Nations Bloom* (blog), December 8, 2009, http://athousandna tions.com/2009/12/08/from-poverty-to-prosperity-an-atn-book-review.

288 *Cardwell's Law held for each European country during the industrial revolution, but technological innovation continued for the continent as a whole and Europe*: J. Mokyr, "Creative Forces," *Reason*, May 1993, http://reason.com /archives/1993/05/01/creative-forces.

288 *Consider Christopher Columbus. His quest across the ocean wasn't nearly as arduous as his quest for royal sponsorship*: Will Durant and Ariel Durant, *The Reformation: The Story of Civilization*, vol. 6 (New York: Simon & Schuster, 1957). See also www.onehundredbestbooks.com/note12.htm.

289 *innovation in China was stifled by the lack of competitive governance*: Jared M.

Diamond, *Guns, Germs, and Steel: The Fates of Human Societies* (New York: Norton, 1999). See also "The Story Of . . . The Shapes of the Continents," on the website of PBS, accessed October 6, 2016, www.pbs.org/guns germssteel/variables/continents.html. See also P. Turchin, "Why Europe Is Not China," September 29, 2012, https://evolution-institute.org/blog /why-europe-is-not-china.

289 "Any man of genius is paralyzed": D. S. Landes, The Wealth and Poverty of Nations: Why Some Are So Rich and Some So Poor (New York: W. W. Norton, 1998), 342.

290 *"When China's 32 provinces, 282 municipalities"*: Ronald Coase and Ning Wang, "Policy Report: How China Became Capitalist," on the website of the Cato Institute, February 15, 2013, www.cato.org/policy-report/januaryfeb ruary-2013/how-china-became-capitalist.

Chapter 10. FLOW STATES: How to Double Global Wealth

295 *Trade carried by sea has quadrupled since 1970*: International Maritime Orga- nization, International Shipping, Carrier of World Trade, background paper, 2005.

295 *global GDP per person has increased by at least as much*: Gross domestic product (GDP); World; 1970–2014. (n.d.), accessed April 23, 2016, www .kushnirs.org/macroeconomics_/en/world__gdp.html.

295 *"One of every 6 jobs in the U.S. is marine-related"*: "Oceans Impact the Econ- omy," on the website of the National Ocean Policy Coalition, accessed October 6, 2016, http://oceanpolicy.com/about-our-oceans/oceans-impact -the-economy. See also J. Kildow and A. McIlgorm, "The Importance of Estimating the Contribution of the Oceans to National Economies," *Marine Policy* 34, no. 3 (2010): 367–74. See also Map of ocean-related GDP in USA: www.wateraccessus.com/econ/econfig6_19.pdf.

295 *most of the poorest billion reside in landlocked countries*: Paul Collier, *The Bottom Billion: Why the Poorest Countries Are Failing and What Can Be Done About It* (New York: Oxford University Press, 2007).

295 *nine of the twelve countries with the lowest HDI scores are landlocked*: M. L. Faye et al., "The Challenges Facing Landlocked Developing Countries," *Journal of Human Development* 5, no. 1 (2004): 31–68, 31–32. "Nine of the twelve countries with the lowest Human Development Index scores are landlocked, thirteen landlocked countries are classified as 'low human development,' and not one of the non-European landlocked countries is classified as 'high human development.'" www.unmillenniumproject.org/documents /JHD051P003TP.pdf. Sixteen of the top twenty richest countries in the

world are coastal states except Switzerland, Luxembourg, Austria—and San Marino is a ten-minute drive from the Adriatic Sea.

295 *wealth emerges from fluidity and flow*: J. Hagen, "Trade Routes for Landlocked Countries," *UN Chronicle* 40, no. 4 (2003): 13.

296 *"Consider our world as it would be if the cost of moving from one country to another were zero"*: David Friedman, *The Machinery of Freedom: Guide to a Radical Capitalism* (New York: Harper & Row, 1973), 123.

297 *"estimate the gains from eliminating various barriers to trade, capital flows, and migration"*: Michael A. Clemens, "Economics and Emigration: Trillion-Dollar Bills on the Sidewalk?," *Journal of Economic Perspectives* 25, no. 3 (Summer 2011): 83–106, http://pubs.aeaweb.org/doi/pdfplus/10.1257/jep.25.3.83.

298 *"the average middleclass American to imagine visiting Haiti on a humanitarian mission"*: Bryan Caplan, "Why Should We Restrict Immigration?," *Cato Journal* 32, no. 1 (2012): 5–24, http://econfaculty.gmu.edu/bcaplan/pdfs/why immigration.pdf.

298 *Life in Haiti compared to US, as of 2016*: A. Linter, "If It Were My Home: Haiti Compared to U.S.," Royal Oak Interactive (2016), www.ifitweremyhome.com/compare/US/HT. *Literacy rate in Haiti as of 2015*: https://haitipart ners.org/about-us/haiti-statistics, using CIA Factbook Data.

298 *in 2012, remittances topped $530 billion US . . . tripled in one decade*: C. Provost, "Migrants' Billions Put Aid in the Shade," *Guardian* (UK), January 30, 2013, www.theguardian.com/global-development/2013/jan/30/migrants-bilions-overshadow-aid.

298 *"the Mobility Revolution"*: Moisés Naim, *The End of Power: From Board-rooms to Battlefields and Churches to States, Why Being In Charge Isn't What It Used to Be* (New York: Basic Books, 2013), 72. Also good sum-up here: Arnold Kling, "Naim's End of Power," on the website of the Library of Economics and Power, June 3, 2013, www.econlib.org/library/Columns/y2013/KlingNaim.html.

299 *"Now consider: economists already know how to extract many trillions of dollars of additional value from the global economy"*: Bryan Caplan, "Sitting on an Ocean of Talent," *EconLog* (blog), January 7, 2014, http://econlog.econlib.org/archives/2014/01/sitting_on_an_o.html.

299 *According to a Gallup poll released in 2009*: N. Esipova and J. Ray, "700 Million Worldwide Desire to Migrate Permanently," on the website of Gallup, November 2, 2009, www.gallup.com/poll/124028/700-Million-Worldwide-Desire-Migrate-Permanently.aspx.

301 *16 percent of the world's adults are ready to leave their dysfunctional governments permanently*: ibid.

NOTES

Appendix

303 Geneva Convention on the High Seas, *1958* (U.N.T.S. 450, no. 6465, 82103). http://sedac.ciesin.columbia.edu/entri/texts/high.seas.1958.html.

303 Ryan H. Fateh, "Note Is Seasteading the High Seas a Legal Possibility? Filling the Gaps in International Sovereignty Law and the Law of the Seas," *Vanderbilt Journal of Transnational Law* 46, no. 899 (May 29, 2013): 899–931, https://wp0.its.vanderbilt.edu/wp-content/uploads/sites/78/Fateh-FINAL-1.pdf.

THANK YOU

Our story was enhanced greatly by extensive editing, feedback, and guidance from Bob Bender, Jim Levine, Michael Chorost, Randolph Hencken, Paul Aljets, Eelco Hoogendoorn, John Frederic Kosanke, Anupama Jain, Tim Potter, Max Borders, Matt Regusci, Tamim Ansary, John Bechtol, Erika Mailman, Julian le Roux, Heather Johnson, Josiah Tullis, Amanda Winther, Balaji S. Srinivasan, John Smart, Adam Dick, PJ Manney, Eric Gruendemann, Blake Witham, Kevin Grigorenko, Frank Karsten, Allison Basel, and R. P. Newman, ATO (II), MTS.

Special thanks to Brad Taylor, Daniel Holt, and Charlie Deist for research and writing.

Extra special thanks to lead editor Diana Bond, for volunteer editing, research, and guidance far beyond the call of duty.

Thanks to Mike Joyce and O. Shane Balloun for legal research.

INDEX

Page numbers in *italics* refer to illustrations.

ABC Arkenbouw (coastal factory), 21
Abyss, The (movie), 124
abyssal plain, 124
acid rain, 82
Adams, John, 285
*Adaptive Urban Development: A
    Symbiosis Between Cities on
    Land and Water in the 21st
    Century* (de Graaf), 49, 53, 55
Aetna, 226
Africa, 230, 235–36
    see also specific countries
Agency for International
    Development, US, 68
agriculture:
    vs. aquaculture, 50
    effect upon soil depletion of, 52
    irrigation for, 68
    reliance of coastal cities on, 47
    as source of pollution, 69; *see also*
        runoff
Agriculture Department, US, 116
algae:
    for biofuel, 49, 84, 94, 129–34,
        135, 136
    and biomass, 73, 89, 91, 134, 136
    blooms of, 69, 134
    and CO_2, 52, 75–76, 78, 84, 90–91

to decrease ocean acidity, 56
farming, 79–81, 112–13, 134, 158
in genetic engineering, 122
as oldest photosynthesizer, 73
in symbiosis, 49, 122–23
on trophic ladder, 111
see also aquaculture; Project Oasis;
    seaweed
aquaculture:
    vs. agriculture, 50
    and biodiversity, 77–78
    and Blue Revolution, 126–27
    definition of, 109
    efficiency of, 47–48, 49
    environmental impacts of, 104,
        128
    expansion of, 126
    and floating cities, 50, 53
    future of, 110–11
    methods, 49, 95–96, 114, 117–19
    mortality rates, 119–20
    profitability of, 85, 95, 139
    to reduce world hunger, 74, 85–87,
        107, 150
    and regulations, 127
    Velella Mariculture Research
        Project, 118–21
    see also kampachi; seaweed

INDEX

AquaDock, 45
aquaindustry, 41
aquainnovation, 41
aquanauts, 38
AquaPods, 119
aquapreneurs, 56–57, 65–66, 74,
    85–86, 138–39, 259, 271
    see also specific aquapreneurs
Aquaterra Conferences, 41
Aristophanes, 286
Aristotle, 279–80
Armstrong, Edward Robert, 23
Armstrong, Neil, 38
Army Corps of Engineers, 52
Associated Press, 69, 222
asteroids, 160
astronauts, 79, 162
Atala, Anthony, 167–68
Athens, 281, 282, 285, 286
Atlantis Resources, 261
Aurora Borealis, 26
Automatic Identification System
    (AIS), 262
Autopia Ampere (seacrete island),
    178

B_{12}, 79
Bagadia, Nishant, 228–41
Bahamas, 148, 199, 225, 264, 269
Bahamas Electricity Corporation, 155
Bajau Laut (nomadic people), 166
Ballard, Robert, 120, 121, 161–71,
    173, 258
Bangladesh, 22
Barclays Bank, 194
Barrows, Rick, 116
Bayhill Therapeutics, 130
"Benefits of Leaving Oil and Gas
    Rigs Intact to Serve as Artificial
    Reefs, The" (Kolian), 51
Ben & Jerry's ice cream, 135

Benjamin, Brit, 284
*Be the Solution: How Entrepreneurs
    and Conscious Capitalists Can
    Solve All the World's Problems*
    (Mackey & Strong), 197
Big Think (Internet Forum), 196
Bill & Melinda Gates Foundation, 72
biodiversity, 76–78, 87–90, 123
bioeconomy, 75–78
bioengineering, 84, 129–31
bioethics, 242–43
biofuel:
    from algae, 49, 84, 94, 129–34,
        135, 136
    for floating cities, 50
    floating production of, 43
    photosynthesis for, 83
    from soybeans, 136
    storage, 52
biogenerators, 94
biomass:
    algae as, 73, 89, 91, 134, 136
    to alleviate hunger, 80, 89
    as change in ecosystem, 123
    degradation of, 132
    for fuel, 89, 94
    impact of rigs on fish, 51
    photosynthesis for, 83
biomimicry, 50–51
bioremediation, 84
Biorock Inc., 179
BioShock (video game), 272
Birol, Fatih, 131
Bismarck (battleship), 161
black smokers, 161
Blanket Fort Island (spinoff from
    Ephemerisle), 35–37
blogs, 8–9, 22, 29, 288, 299
    see also specific blogs
Blue Cross Blue Shield, 226
blue economy, 53, 78, 85, 137, 148

Blue Ocean Mariculture, 116, 121
Blue-on-Blue Initiative, 123
Blue Planet Network, 67
Blue Revolution, 7, 53–54, 56, 126–27
"Blue Revolution, The: Oceans as Ultimate Sustainable Resource" (Takahashi & Chong), 145, 149
Blue Revolution Hawaii, 151–52
Bluerise, 54, 148
Blueseed, 216
Borlaug, Norman, 68, 81, 86, 92–93
Bottom Billion, The: Why the Poorest Countries Are Failing and What Can Be Done About It (Collier), 295
BrainReactions, 229
Branson, Richard, 268
Brazil, 135
Breakout Labs, 29
Breyers, 135
Brown, Neal A., 18
Brylcreem, 135
Bunge (agribusiness company), 135
Burgess, Michael, 83
Burj Al Arab (hotel), 20
Burj Khalifa (skyscraper), 177

Cage, John, 275
Cameron, James, 124
Camilleri, Joseph, 280
Canada, 25, 127, 136, 137
Caplan, Bryan, 298, 299
carbon cycle, 76, 88, 90–91, 122
carbon dioxide (CO_2):
    and algae, 52, 75–76, 78, 84, 90–91
    and Keeling Curve, 123
    and ocean acidification, 49, 108
    as pollution, 69

as product of photosynthesis, 73
    reducing, 45, 146
carbonic acid, 76, 108–9
carbon sequestration, 120, 163
Cardwell, Donald, 288
Cardwell's Law, 288, 290
Carnegie Endowment for International Peace, 298
Carnival Cruise Line, 264
carrageenan, 80, 86
Casanova, Giovanni Giacomo, 268
Castillo, Claudia, 239
Causes, 28
Cayman Islands, 155, 233, 238, 241, 270–71
Cayman Islands Financial Services Association, 271
Celebrity Eclipse, 11–12
Cell Genesys, 130
Centeno, Christopher, 238
Center for Global Development, 296–97
Centers for Disease Control and Prevention (CDC), 221–22
Centers for Medicare & Medicaid Services (CMS), 222
Chand, Satish, 203–4
Chevron Corporation, 19
Chief of Naval Operations Energy and Environmental Readiness Division, 136
China:
    and Hong Kong, 189–92
    isolation of, 289–90
    seaweed production in, 90
    special economic zones, 190, 197–98
    Tanka people, 267
    3-D printing in, 168
    see also Shenzhen; Xiaogang Village

Chong, Leighton K., 145, 149
Chopin, Thierry, 84, 110
Churchill, Winston, 37
ciguatera, 112, 113
Citadel, 45
cities:
  as parasites, 47–48
  see also floating cities
city apps, 22–23
city-states, 57, 59
  see also Singapore
Clarium Capital Management, 29, 241
Clean Water Act, 259
Clemens, Michael, 296–97
climate change, 46, 65, 69, 156
closed-loop continuous harvest
  system, 137
CNN Tech, 136
Coase, Ronald, 290
Cohen, I. Glenn, 239
Cold War, 180
Coleridge, Samuel Taylor, 72
Collier, Paul, 295
Columbus, Christopher, 289–90
Committee to Protect Journalists, 29
Communism, 186, 191, 208
*Complete Idiot's Guide to Global
  Economics, The* (Rehmke),
  280–81
Conscious Capitalists and Capitalism,
  196–97
Conservation International, 127, 128
contiguous zone, 13
Cook Islands, 104
corals and coral reefs, 49, 51, 108,
  170, 179
Corinth, 281
Coriolis force, 159
corn, 134
  in fish pellets, 116
  low in lysine, 78

as pollutant, 93
slow growth of, 76
subject to blight, 80
subsidies for, 70, 93
Costa Rica:
  aquaculture in, 71, 80, 85, 86, 93
  medical tourism in, 224
Crain's Chicago Business, 243
Critical Path (Fuller), 24
Cruise Lines International
  Association (CLIA), 16
cruise ships:
  desalination on, 260
  employment on, 16–17, 271–72
  as floating cities, 11–17
  as health care providers, 221–23
  laws governing, 13–15, 264
  profitability of, 12
  and waste disposal, 259
  see also specific ships
Crystal Serenity (cruise ship), 16
Cullom, Philip, 136
Cultivated Seaweeds for Food Project,
  72, 80–81
Curetalk (online forum), 241
cyanobacteria, 73
cyclicity, 122
Czapiewska, Karina:
  on Blue Revolution, 53–56
  on cities, 45, 46–49, 48–49, 259
  on seasteading, 50, 57–58

Dai-Ichi National Bank, 173
Daily Mail, 16
Darwin, Charles, 137
dead zones, 69, 74, 83–84, 134, 139
Deep Ecology, 123
Deep Space Industries, 160
Defense Appropriations
  Subcommittee, 151
deforestation, 76

de Graaf, Rutger:
  on Blue Revolution, 53–56
  on cities as parasites, 47–50
  on floating cities, 42–57
  on flood control, 41
  on peak phosphate, 51–52
  on snap-on modules, 43
Deist, Charlie, 123
Delft, 42
Deloitte Management Consulting,
  227, 229
DeltaSync:
  on aquaculture, 47–48, 49, 126
  on cyclicity, 122
  designs and constructs Floating
    Pavilion, 44–45
  mission of, 42, 180, 259
  partners with Waterstudio, 45–46
  seastead feasibility project, 57–59
Demick, Barbara, 186
democracy, 8, 37, 208
  see also government and
    governance
Deng Xiaoping, 190, 215
desalination, 260
Diamandis, Peter, 65, 242
Diamond, Jared, 125, 289
diesel fuel, 117, 137, 268
DigInfo (online video news site), 174
dikes, 41, 46
Dini, Enrico, 170
Discovery Channel, 46
diving industry, 51
DNA, 52
Dominican Republic, 187
Dove soap, 135
drifter cages, 117–19
drones, 238
Drucker, Peter, 78
Duarte, Carlos M., 115
Durant, Will, 289

Dura Vermeer, 45
Dutch, see Netherlands
Dutch Docklands, 25, 26
"Dynamic Geography" (essay), 9

ear canal bone anchor, 242
eBay, 28
EconLog (blog), 299
"Economics and Emigration: Trillion-
  Dollar Bills on the Sidewalk?"
  297
Economic Times, 241
Economist, 55
EcoRigs, 51
Edison, Thomas, 208
Einstein, Albert, 19, 176
electricity:
  generated by OTEC, 147, 151,
    155–56
  for Green Float, 179
  for seasteads, 23, 45, 153, 173
  using windmills to supplement, 94
energy:
  alternatives, 129–31, 136
  for seasteads, 17, 45, 48, 94, 146;
    see also fossil fuels; ocean
    thermal energy conversion
    (OTEC); photosynthesis
Energy Department, US, 132, 136
Environment, Development and
  Sustainability (journal), 82
environmental assessments (EA), 120
Environmental Defense Fund, 127
environmental degradation, 70
environmentalists, 10, 30–31, 69, 92,
  115, 158, 165–66
Ephemerisle, 34–37
Ericsson Application Awards, 236
Ericsson Research, 236
European Environment Agency, 45
European Union, 45

Evernote, 131
E/V Nautilus (ship), 162
eVolo (magazine), 172
evolution, 32–33
Exclusive Economic Zone (EEZ), 13
Exponential Medicine conference, 242
export processing zones (EPZs), 201
Eyes on the Seas, 262

Facebook, 28, 235
Falk, Jim, 280
Färjh, Jan, 236
Fast Company (magazine), 232
Fatey, Ryan H., 304
feedstock, 136
Fertile Crescent, 124
fertilizer, 6, 49, 77, 81, 108, 145, 154
1517 Fund, 288
Fiji, 203–4
Finding Nemo (movie), 113
Fischer-Tropsch reactor, 153
fish:
    as biofuel, 132–34
    biomass from rigs, 51
    overfishing, 6, 103–6, 145, 261–62
    poop, 110, 120, 144, 163
    predator, 111
    as source of omega-3 fatty acids, 75
    on trophic ladder, 111
    vegetarian carnivorous, 113–15
    see also aquaculture; *specific fish*
Fisher, Fred, 164
Fisheries Act, 127
Fleet (supply chain company), 27
flexible land on aquatic territory
    (FLOAT), 46
Flipper (movie and tv show), 165
Float at Marina Bay, 9
*Float! Building on Water to Combat
    Urban Congestion and Climate
    Change* (Olthuis), 46

Float Incorporated, 18
floating cities:
    cruise ships as, 11–17
    and environmentalism, 30–31
    food and energy needs, 49–52,
        153
    oil rigs as, 18–19
    potential for, 143–44, 146, 170
    as sovereign nations, 177
    types of, 24
    see also Green Float project;
        seascrapers
Floating City Project, the 11, 57, 59,
    265
floating farms, *see* aquaculture;
    seaweed
floating instrument platforms (FLIP),
    164–65, 167, 170
Floating Pavilion, 44
floating territory doctrine, 14
Flower Gardens Fish Sanctuary, 51
Flying Nurses International, 224
food, 6, 69–70, 260
    see also aquaculture; seaweed
Food and Drug Administration
    (FDA), 238, 244–49
Fortune, 28
Fortune 500, 229
fossil fuels:
    annual use of, 52
    compared to OTEC energy, 148,
        151, 154, 155
    diesel, 117
    floating cities to replace, 144
    and ocean acidification, 137
    product of ancient photosynthesis,
        74
    replacement of with biofuels,
        129–32
    see also electricity; energy
Foucault, Jean-Bernard-Léon, 228

Four Fish: The Future of the Last Wild Food (Greenberg), 103, 121
Franklin, Ben, 260, 275, 290–91
Freedom Lights Our World (FLOW movement), 197
Free to Choose (M. and Rose Friedman), 7, 207
Friedman, David, 7, 8, 296–97, 301
Friedman, Milton, 7, 8, 190, 205, 207, 300, 301
Friedman, Rose, 7, 207
Friendster, 28
Fruit Roll-Ups, 266
Fukushima disaster, 175
Fukuyama, Francis, 188
Fuller, Richard Buckminster, 24–25, 48, 59, 84

Gallico, Paul, 272
Gallup World Poll, 199, 299, 301
game theory, 279
gas emissions, 136
Gates, Bill, 158
General Mills, 69
Geneva Convention on the High Seas, 303–4
Ghetto at the Center of the World: Chungking Mansions (Mathews), 192
Gibson, Mike, 288
Gilbreath, Kathi, 19
Gini coefficient, 203
Giorgione, 268
Gladwell, Malcolm, 213
Gleick, Peter, 68
Global Competitiveness Reports (World Economic Forum), 194, 204
Global Gender Gap Report, The (World Economic Forum), 206

Global Hunger Index, 85
Globalization of Health Care, The: Legal and Ethical Issues (Cohen), 239
Global Partnership for the Oceans, 128
Global Surgery Network, 224
global warming, 123, 146
God's Compassionate Home Health City, 231–33, 237
golden ratio, 115–16
Goldstein, Adam, 15
Google, 7, 29, 235, 262
government and governance:
    city-states, 279–83
    on cruise ships, 13–15, 264
    democracy, 8, 37, 208
    differences in, 186–88
    Friedmans on, 56, 301
    GDP of, 33
    as information technology, 29
    lack of protection for oceans, 262
    law as code, 29
    for seasteads, 8–9, 263–65
Government's End: Why Washington Stopped Working (Rauch), 290
GPS, 119
Gramlich, Wayne, 29, 56
gravity, 171–72, 178
Great Antarctic Convergence, 150
Great Depression, 23
Great East Japan Earthquake, 176
"Greatest Country on Earth, The: What the United States Can Learn from the Tiny Island Nation of Mauritius" (Stiglitz), 204
Great Leap Forward, 214
Greenberg, Paul, 103–4, 121
Green Float project, 174–79

greenhouse gas emissions:
  not produced by OTEC, 148, 158
  reduction of, 42, 69, 74–75, 91,
    158
  sources of, 69, 83, 117, 158
Green Revolution, 68, 69, 77, 81, 86
Greenstar (proposed floating hotel),
  25
Groen, R. M. P., 261
Gross, Bill, 237
Gross, Sue, 237
gross domestic product (GDP), 12,
    193, 200–201, 206
  calculating, 195–96
  of Chinese provinces, 209, 274
  global, 33, 295, 297, 299
  of Mauritius, 195–96
  and water bankruptcy, 67
Growing Blue, 5
growth cycle, see carbon cycle
Gulf of Mexico, 51, 158, 166
Guns, Germs, and Steel: The Fates of
    Human Societies (Diamond),
    125, 289

Haber, Fritz, 77
Haiti, 187
Hardin, Garrett, 106
Hard Minerals Act, 159–60
Hassig, Ralph, 187
Hawaii, 113, 114, 117, 151–52, 154,
    155
HealthCare.gov, 246
Health Travel Technologies, 230
hearing impaired, 242
Heddon, Allison Hebron, 242,
    243–50
Heddon, Chris, 241–50
Heinlein, Robert, 143
Hellmann's, 135
Hess, Samuel, 240

Hickory Springs Manufacturing
    (HSM), 224
Hidden People of North Korea, The:
    Everyday Life in the Hermit
    Kingdom (Hassig & Oh), 187
high seas, 303–4
Hilbertz, Wolf, 178
Hispaniola, 187
$^{h}O_2$-Scraper, 172
Holland, see Netherlands
Hong Kong, 166, 187–93, 194, 203
Hospitalist Company, 131
hotels, 20, 25, 26, 46, 173
houseboats, 34, 42
Housing and Urban Development
    Department, US, 24
"How China Became Capitalist"
    (Coase and Wang), 290
Huffington Post, 199, 227
hukou (Chinese discriminatory
    practice), 209
human genome, 122
Human Rights Foundation, 29
hunger, 65, 85, 98, 135
  see also aquaculture; seaweed
hunter-gatherers, 107
hurricanes, 158–59, 258
  Hurricane Katrina, 166, 242

Illinois Soybean Association, 127
immigration and immigrants, 266–67,
    268, 298, 299, 300
India:
  and food supply, 68, 69, 81
  foreign investment in, 203
  medical care in, 223, 227, 230–32,
    234, 241
  soil depletion in, 82
  solar power plants in, 9
Indiegogo (crowdfunding website),
    57

Indonesia, 86, 90, 269
Inhabitat (blog), 22
Inner Space Science Center, 170
Inouye, Daniel, 151
institutional review boards (IRBs), 248
Integrated Marine Agronomy and Geo-Engineering (IMAGEn), 123
International Convention for the Prevention of Pollution from Ships, 259
International Copper Association, 127
International Energy Agency (IEA), 131
International Laboratory for Global Change, 115
Internationally Recommended Transit Corridor (IRTC), 269–70
International Maritime Organization, 264
International Space Station, 151, 169
International Transport Workers' Federation (ITF), 265
International Union for the Conservation of Nature, 127
International Water Week, 41
Internet, 78, 196, 230
Internet.org, 235
investors, 23, 26, 93, 95–96, 152, 153, 192, 197, 216
Invisible Wealth: The Hidden Story of How Markets Work (Kling & Schulz), 187
in vitro fertilization, 238
IPK International, 227
iron, 78, 98, 146
Iron Chef America, 98

islands and island nations:
    and algae biomass, 91
    floating, 9, 52
    for medical treatment, 10
    regulating, 13
    and seasteads, 269– 270
Israel, 226–27
Issenberg, Sasha, 227

JAMA Internal Medicine, 247
Janssen, Tim, 258
Japan, 9, 90, 155, 173–75, 186
Japan Aerospace Exploration Agency (JAXA), 179
Japan Times, 175
JASON Project, 162
Jefferson, Thomas, 260, 287, 290
Johnson, Lyndon B., 24
Johnson, Ted, 154–56
Joint Commission International (JCI), 223, 240
Joint Commission on Accreditation of Hospitals (JCAH), 240
Jones, Dave, 129–32, 134–35, 137, 139
Joosse, B. M., 261
Journal of Medical Ethics, 243
Journal of Physical Oceanography, 258
Journal of Transnational Law, 304

kampachi, 112–13, 115–16
    kahala, 112
    Kona, 116
Kampachi Farms, 113–14, 121, 126, 127
Kasista (company), 21
Kato, Yasuhiro, 160
Keeling Curve, 123
kelp, 73, 77, 267
Kennedy, John F., 180

Kenya, 230, 235, 236
Kepler Energy & Space Engineering, 160
Kling, Arnold, 187
Kolian, Steve, 51
Kona Blue Water Farms, 103, 121
Krystall (proposed floating hotel), 26
Kulovaara, Harri, 15
Kurzweil, Roy, 242
Kushner, Adam, 170

Lane, Phil, 76
Lang, Susan S., 82
laptops, 266
Learning Medicine: An Evidence-Based Guide (Wei), 225
Lending Club, 131
Let a Thousand Nations Bloom (blog), 9, 288
Liberia, 15, 264
Libertarians, 30, 263
Lindbergh, Charles, 23
LinkedIn, 28, 29
Lipton, 135
LiveFuels, 129, 133, 134, 135
livestock production, 158
lobsters, 94, 108
Lock, Max, 25–27
Lockheed Martin, 118, 127, 146–47, 148, 149, 151, 154
Lonsdale, Jeff, 29
Lord of the Rings (Tolkien), 124
Los Angelopes (LA bicycle gang), 35
Louisville Slugger baseball bat, 164
Love Boat, The (tv show), 272
Loveridge, Russell, 169–70
Lubnow, Fred, 91
lysine, 78
Lysistrata (Aristophanes), 286

Machine Intelligence Research Institute (MIRI), 29
Machinery of Freedom, The (D. Friedman), 7
Mackey, John, 196, 197
macroalgae, 74, 77, 109, 122
Maersk Lines, 20
magnesium, 174, 178
Maher, Bill, 129
mahimahi, 108, 109, 125
Makepeace Island, 268
Malawi, 238
Maldives, 25
malnutrition, 80
    see also hunger
malpractice, 239
Mandelbrot set, 177
Mao Tse-tung, 209, 214
Marco Polo, 268
Marianas Trench, 124
mariculture, 109
marine colonies, 31–32
marine sport fishing, 51
Maritime Alliance, 18
market competition, 32
MARPOL 73/78 (waste control protocol), 259
Mars (food company), 70
Mars (planet), 23, 162, 169
Martinique, 149
Marx, Karl, 228
Mascarenhas Archipelago, 200
Mathews, Gordon, 192
Matsunaga, Spark, 151
Matternet, 238
Mauritius, 200–205, 270
"Mauritius: An Economic Success Story" (Zafar), 203
Ma Yihe, 168
Meade, James, 200
MedAfrica, 235–36, 237

Media Development Investment
 Fund, 235
Medical Tourism (magazine), 234
Medical Tourism Association (MTA),
 223, 240
medicine:
 medical tourism, 222–28, 234
 and seasteading, 225–28, 232–34,
 237–50
Meditation Platform, 35
megacities, 6, 47
Menon, Priya, 241
Mercy Ships, 233, 237
Meredith, Robyn, 191
Mexico, 20, 92, 96, 103, 127
microalgae, 79–80, 139
Microchip, 131
microcountries, 31
microfarms, 85
Milanovic, Branko, 185
milkfish, 108, 112
*Millennial Project, The: Colonizing
 the Galaxy in Eight Easy Steps*
 (Savage), 30, 146, 170
Ministry of Marine Resources, Cook
 Islands, 104
miscanthus giganteus, 134
Mississippi River, 134
Miyamoto, Yoichi, 176
Mizunami Underground Research
 Laboratory, 177–78
Mobile Marketing Association, 236
mobile phones, 235, 266
mobility, xv, 21, 283, 295–96, 297
Mobility Revolution, 298
modules, 18, 43, 46
moi, 108, 112
molecular genetics, 68
mollusks, 93, 108
Montesquieu, 214
Montessori schools, 197

moon landing, 180
Morgenthaler, David Turner, 129
Morgenthaler-Jones, Lissa, 56,
 129–41
Morgenthaler Ventures, 129
mortality rates:
 of children, 67–68, 298
 of fish farms, 119–20
Motorola StarTAC (mobile phone),
 266
Muglia, Chris, 167–71, 179
mullet, 108, 112
Murphy New World Biotechnology
 Fund, 129
Musk, Elon, 169, 170
mussels, 84, 93
Mutinda, Steve, 235

Naím, Moisés, 298
Naipaul, V. S., 200
Narayana Hrudayalaya Health City,
 231–32
Narayana Hrudayalaya Hospital,
 227–28
National Academy of Sciences,
 Institute of Medicine, 222
National Aeronautics and Space
 Administration (NASA), 43,
 79, 162, 169, 179, 186
National Centre of Competence in
 Research (NCCR) Digital
 Fabrication, 169
National Geographic (magazine), 126,
 135
National Geographic (tv channel), 161
nationality principle, 14
National Marine Sanctuary
 Foundation, 166
National Oceanic and Atmospheric
 Administration (NOAA), 120,
 127

National Ocean Policy Coalition, 295

National Science Foundation, 108, 118, 127

Nature, 69

Nature Conservancy, 127

Nature Geoscience, 160

Nautilus Minerals, 160

Naval Research Laboratory, US, 136

Navy Bureau of Ships, US, 24

Navy Bureau of Yards and Docks, US, 24

Necker Island, 268

Nestlé, 70

Netherlands, 20, 21, 22, 41–47, 50, 172

Newfoundland Aquaculture Industry Association (NAIA), 127

New York Times, 21, 115

NexTag, 131

Next City (magazine), 22

Nextel, 131

Next Web, 236

Nicholson, Bob, 146, 152–54

Nile River, 146

nitrogen, 69, 74, 75, 77, 83, 144–45, 156

Njihia, Mbungua, 236

Nokia, 235

Northern Hemisphere, 159

North Korea, 90, 186–88

Norway, 26, 205, 206, 261

Nothing to Envy: Ordinary Lives in North Korea (Demick), 186

Noxzema, 135

Nuehealth, 236

Nusa Lembongan, 86

Obama, Barack, 136, 271

Ober, Josiah, 281

obesity, 70

Ocean Conservancy, 128

Ocean Energy Council, 154–55

Ocean Energy Pioneer Award, 155

Ocean Farm Technologies, 119, 127

oceans:
  acidification of, 108–9, 133, 137
  as bioeconomy, 76
  contribution to economy, 17–20
  repopulating with fish, 110
  as solar collector, 144–49
  see also aquaculture

Ocean Stewards Institute, 109–10

ocean thermal energy conversion (OTEC), 54, 146–56

octopus, 261

offshore military forts, 37

Oh, Kongdan, 187

oil, *see* algae; biofuel; oil rigs; peak oil; seaweed

oil rigs, 18–19, 23, 51, 130, 258

Okinawa, 155

Olthuis, Koen, 21, 22, 25, 26, 46, 172

omega-3 fatty acids, 75, 133

Omnivore's Dilemma, The: A Natural History of Four Meals (Pollan), 70

One Laptop per Child, 266

1 percent graph, *185*

OPEC, 129, 132

Ord, Toby, *185*

Origins of Political Order, The: From Prehuman Times to the French Revolution (Fukuyama), 188

Osinga, Ronald, 88

OTEC International, 146, 152–54, 160

Outernet, 235

Outliers: The Story of Success (Gladwell), 213

Outpatients: The Astonishing New World of Medical Tourism (Issenberg), 227
oxygen, 69, 75
  see also photosynthesis
oysters, 93, 94, 108, 110

Pacific Institute, 68
Pacific International Center for High Technology Research, 143
Pacific International Ocean Station, 151
Pacific Investment Management Company (PIMCO), 237
Padma Bhushan (award), 240
Paideia schools, 197
Pakistan, 68, 86, 92
Palantir Technologies, 28, 29
Paley, Vitaly, 98
Palladio, Andrea, 268
Palmerston Atoll, 105
Panama, 85, 93
parasites, 47–48, 112, 113, 117, 119, 120
parrot fish, 105
Patients Beyond Borders, 222, 223
Pauley, Phil, 173
PayPal, 28, 29, 169
PBS NewsHour, 281
peak oil, 6, 65, 145
Pennsylvania, 52, 91
PeopleMatter, 131
Perception, 130
Perry, Mark J., 189
pests and pesticides, 70
Pew Charitable Trusts, 262
Philippines, 90
pH level, 108
phosphorus, 6, 52, 69, 90–91, 144
  peak phosphorus, 6, 51, 302

photosynthesis, 73–74, 83, 97, 109, 122, 145
Physical Review Letters, 258
phytoplankton, 73, 150
Pimentel, David, 82, 83
pirates and piracy, 269–70
Pivot15 Challenge, 236
Planetary Resources, 160
Planetary Sustainability Collaboratory, 79
plankton, 76, 156–57
plant factory (vertical garden of vegetables), 174
plate tectonics, 161
Pollan, Michael, 70
pollution, 69, 74, 82, 84, 259
  see also carbon dioxide; runoff
Pond Biofuels, 136–37
pond scum, 91, 133, 135–36
Portunus (Roman god), 18
Portunus Project, 18
Poseidon Adventure, The, 272
poverty, 69, 70, 189, 198–99, 202
  see also aquaculture
Powell, Ken, 69
power purchase agreements (PPA), 156
Practice Fusion, 28, 131
"Predictability of Rogue Events," 258
Prelude (floating natural gas facility), 12, 147
Princeton Hydro, 91
Project Eyes on the Seas, 262
Project Loon, 235
Project OASIS (Ocean Aquaculture for Seastead Integrated Solutions), 123, 212
Pryor, Miranda, 127
Public-Domain Architects, 44

Radulovich, Ricardo, 71–72, 75,
  76–78
  aquaculture, 87–88, 90, 95–96,
    110
  as aquapreneur, 56, 66–68, 80–81,
    85–86
  on blue revolution, 126–27
  on photosynthesis, 73–74, 83–85
  on regulations, 91–92
  at Seasteading Conference, 93–97,
    109
  on subsidies, 93
rainforests, 53
Ramsden, Neil, 127
rare earth minerals, 159–60
Rauch, Jonathan, 290
Reagan, Ronald, 151
Redfield, Alfred C., 144
Redfield ratio, 144, 156
Red Sea, 260
refugees, 22–23
regulations:
  health care, 225–26, 230, 239, 241,
    243–47
  restrictions in aquaculture, 127
  and seasteading, 55, 247–50
  and special interests, 91–92
  US and EU, 45, 165, 270–71
regulatory capture, 91
Rehmke, Gregory F., 280–81
Reidy, William, 18
Reignwood Group, 148
remittances, 298
Resonance Medical Technologies,
  242
Réunion, 149
Revenge of Cuba (spinoff from
  Ephemerisle), 36
Ribozyme Pharmaceuticals, 131
rice, 78
rickets, 79

Rime of the Ancient Mariner, The
  (Coleridge), 72
Rise and Fall of Classical Greece, The
  (Ober), 281
robots, 160, 169, 171, 232
rogue waves, 161, 258–59
Roman Colosseum, 20
Rotterdam, see Netherlands
Royal Caribbean International,
  14–15, 264
Rudnick, Phillip, 164
Rule of Law Index, 201
runoff, 69, 74, 83, 90, 126, 134,
  259

Saeme, Mohammed, 221
SAEMED, 221
Sagan, Carl, 72
Saint Martin (island), 240
St. Marys Cement, 137
salmon farms, 84, 110
Samsung, 235
Sanandaji, Nima, 206
sardines, 94, 134
Sarkum, Sarly Adre Bin, 172
Sarver, Dale, 110, 116
sashimi, 74, 111, 112, 120
Saudi Arabia, 260
Savage, Marshall T., 30–31, 146,
  170
Scandinavia, 205–7
Schulz, Nick, 187
SciDev.Net (website), 84
Science, 6
Scientific American, 6, 114, 258
Screw It, Let's Do It. Lessons in Life and
  Business (Branson), 268
seacrete (seament), 178, 179
sea cucumbers, 84
Seacurus (marine insurance broker),
  269

seadromes, 23
SeafoodSource.com, 121
Sea Gardens Project, 72, 95
seament (seacrete), 178, 179
seascrapers, 171–73
sea snail (trochus), 106–7
SeaStation, 110–11
Seasteading Conferences, 29–30, 38, 93, 109, 138, 146, 284
"SeaSteading—Homesteading on the High Seas" (Gramlich), 29
Seasteading Implementation Plan, 58
Seasteading Institute:
  aquapreneurs contact, 65
  and business plans, 167
  collaboration with Exponential Medicine, 244–46
  and Ephemerisle community, 34, 37
  founding and mission of, 10, 29, 31–32, 38
  and Geneva Convention on the High Seas, 303–4
  offers internship to Zhai, 212
  proposals for seament breakwaters, 179
Sea Tree (floating natural habitat), 22, 172
sea trellis, 87–88, 90
seawater, 23, 51, 109, 122, 136, 149, 153, 178, 260, 261
seaweed:
  bioengineering, 83–85, 91
  farming, 74–78, 85–90, 93–95
  flour, 81
  like electricity, 81
  macroalgae, 74, 77, 79–80, 109, 122, 139
  number of species, 78
  uses for, 122
  weight of oil in, 84

Seaweed Sustainability: Food and Non-Food Applications (Radulovich), 89
Senate, US, 159
SENS Research Foundation, 29
Sg2 (health care consulting firm), 242
Shakespeare, William, 283, 302
Shell Oil, 12, 147
Shenzhen, 190, 197–98, 273–74
shesteading, 284–87
Shetty, Devi, 231–36
Shimba Technology, 235
Shimizu, Kisuke, 173, 174
Shimizu Corporation, 9, 173–78
shipping containers, 18, 20–22
Shipstr (online supply chain logistics service), 26–27
shrimp farms, 86, 94
Sierra Club, 110
Silicon Valley, 152, 243, 246, 250, 302
Simon, Julian, 7
Simpson, Sarah, 114
Sims, Neil Anthony:
  and aquaculture, 110–15, 117–19, 121–23, 126–29, 163
  on the golden ratio, 115–16
  on ocean acidity, 56, 108–10
  on overfishing, 103–7
  on predatory fish, 111–12
  on selective breeding, 124–26
  and Velella Mariculture Research Project, 119–21
Singapore, 9, 193–95, 226
Singularity University, 65, 242
Siri, 131
"Sitting on an Ocean of Talent" (blog), 299
skin flukes, 120
Skyscraper Competition, 172
skyscrapers, 171–74, 192–93
SkyTruth, 262

slums, 22–23, 194, 241
Smil, Vaclav, 6
Social Institutions and Gender Index
    (SIGI), 202
Social Responsibility Report (Shimizu
    Corp.), 176
Socratic schools, 197
"Soil Erosion: A Food and
    Environmental Threat"
    (Pimentel), 82
"Soil Erosion Threatens Food
    Production," (Pimental and
    Burgess), 83
solar power, 9, 94, 144–49, 174, 179
Solazyme, 135
Solli, Daniel R., 258
Somalia, 269–70
Sony Walkman, 151
Southern Hemisphere, 159
South Korea, 9, 90, 186–88
soybeans, 114, 116, 127, 136, 163
Space Exploration Technologies
    Corporation (Space X), 28, 29,
    169
spacesteading, 79
special economic megazones
    (SEMZ), 191
special economic zones (SEZs),
    190–93, 196, 197–98, 296
Spiess, Fred, 164
Spirit of St. Louis (airplane), 23
spirulina, 78–79
Standard Digital News, 236
St. Anna's Medical Mission, 242
Star Trek (tv show), 169
start-ups, 28, 30, 36, 37, 140, 148,
    216, 228–29, 236
    see also specific start-ups
stem cell treatment, 238–39
Stephens, Donald, 233
Stephens, Keyon, 233

Stiglitz, Joseph E., 204
Story of Civilization, The (Durant),
    289
strategic incrementalism, 59
Straub, Mike, 154
Strong, Michael, 188, 197, 198–99
Sub-Biosphere 2, 173
subsidies, 93
Summers, Larry, 27
Summer Youth Olympics, 9
Sun Microsystems, 29
surveys, 11, 50, 57–59
sushi, 116
Swaminathan, Monkombu
    Sambasivan, 68
swordfish, 104, 157
symbiosis, 49
Synopsys, 131

Tahiti, 149
Tahiti Field (oil production platform),
    19
Taiwan, 157, 195
Takahashi, Patrick Kenji, 54
    on closing growth cycle, 122, 143,
        158
    on floating cities, 143, 144
    on hurricanes, 158–59
    influence on Blue Revolution, 56,
        126–27, 143
    introduces Hard Minerals Act,
        159–60
    on oceans as solar collectors,
        144–49
    on OTEC, 149–52, 156, 158
    on whale sharks, 157–58, 159
Takeuchi, Massaki, 174, 176, 179
Tanka people, 267
Tao Ju, 168
taxes, 260–61
Taylor, Brad, 284

TechCrunch Disrupt (conference), 26
TEDMED (medical conference), 167
telemedicine, 221, 232, 241
teosinte, 81
TerraVia (formerly Solazyme), 135
territorial waters, 11, 13, 264, 270
Tesla Motors, 29, 169
Tetanus (spinoff from Ephemerisle), 35
Thailand, 19, 90, 176, 227
thalassocracy, 267
"thalassophilanthropy," 23
thalassotherapy, 23
Thiel, Peter, 27–29, 38, 57, 169, 212–13, 216, 241, 263
Thiel Fellowship, 27
Thiel Foundation, 29, 57, 58, 288
3-D printing, 167–71
Time, 121
Titan (spinoff from Ephemerisle), 34–35, 36
Titanic (movie), 124
Titanic (ship), 65, 120, 161
Tocqueville, Alexis de, 214
tofu, 114
tofu shark, 157
Tokyo Bay, 9, 175
Tokyo Bay Aqua-Line, 173
topsoil, 82
Touchstone Research Laboratory, 76
"Tragedy of the Commons, The" (Hardin), 106
Transcend Biomedical, 131
Triton City (floating city), 24
trochus (sea snail), 107
trophic steps, 111, 122, 133, 157, 163
Tsukiji Hotel, 173
tsunamis, 257–58
Tufts Energy Competition, 213
tuna, 104, 111, 157

20 Under 20 community, 216
TwoXSea, 116
typhoons, 12, 172, 173

Ultimate Resource The (Simon), 7
Umihotaru (artificial island), 173
Undercurrent News, 127
Unilever, 70, 135
United Nations:
    Convention on the Law of the Sea (UNCLOS), 13, 264
    Food and Agriculture Organization, 49, 70, 104, 158
    Human Development Index (HDI), 201, 295
    International Labor Organization (ILO), 265
    and international law, 303
    International Tribunal on Maritime Law, 264–65
    political entities in, 265
    sovereignty for seasteaders, 17, 177
    Third Global Biodiversity Outlook, 104
    UNESCO (United Nations Educational, Scientific, and Cultural Organization), 259
    UNICEF (United Nations Children's Fund), 238
    on water use, 67, 68
    World Environment Day, 132
Uptightan (spinoff from Ephemerisle), 34–37
urchins, 84
United States, health care costs in, 221–25, 226
US Compassionate Home Health City, 233
US Oosterschelde Barrier, 41
US Steel, 137

van Buren, Remko, 43–44
van de Camp, Paul, 25, 26
van Dongen, Teresa, 261
van Helmont, Jean-Bapiste, 73
Velella (hydrozoan), 118
Velella Mariculture Research Project,
    115, 118–21, 149
Venice, 267–68, 283
Venter, Craig, 122
VeriFone, 131
video cameras, 23
Virage, 130
Virgin Group, 268
Virtual Watch Room, 262
Vivaldi, Antonio, 268

Wachowiak, Helmut, 222
Wachtstetter, Lee, 16–17
Wall Street Journal, 231
Wang, Ning, 290
War of the Worlds, The (movie), 272
wars, 132, 166, 267, 270
Washington, George, 287, 290
wastewater treatment plants, 43
water, 5, 65, 67–68, 260
water bankruptcy, 67
Waterstudio, 9, 21, 25, 44, 45–46,
    172
Waterworld (movie), 272
wave energy converters, 18
websites, 10, 57, 84, 121, 177, 235,
    246, 248, 265
    see also specific websites
Wei, Peter, 225–28
Weinger, Paul, 59
Welthungerhilfe (World Hunger Aid),
    85
whale sharks, 157–58, 159
wheat, 68, 78–79, 80, 81, 92, 139
Wheat Revolution, 92

Willauer, Heather, 136
Williams, John, 136
wind turbines, 18, 261
WineBid, 265
WinSun, 168
Wisconsin State Journal, 229
Wolff, James, 170
Wolf Hilbertz process, 178–79
Wong, Alan, 116
Woodman, Josef, 223
World Bank, 70, 72, 128, 185, 188,
    191, 201, 203, 298
World Development Report
    2000/2001: Attacking Poverty,
    69
World Economic Forum, 204, 206
World Health Organization, 234
World Hunger Aid (Welthungerhilfe),
    85
Worlds in Transition: Evolving
    Governance Across a Stressed
    Planet (Camilleri & Falk), 280
World Wildlife Fund, 127
Wright, Orville, 38

Xiaogang Village, 214–15
XPRIZE Foundation, 65
Xu Xiaoping, 216

Yammer, 28, 29
Yelp, 28, 29
YouTube, 29, 212

Zafar, Ali, 203
Zanzibar, 85, 89, 155
Zhai, Baoguang, 122, 209–16
ZhenFund, 216
Zocdoc, 28
Zuckerberg, Mark, 212, 235
Zynga, 28